A DOCUMENTARY HISTORY OF EDUCATION IN THE SOUTH BEFORE 1860

A Documentary History of Education in the South Before 1860

Edited by

EDGAR W. KNIGHT

IN FIVE VOLUMES

Volume III

THE RISE OF THE STATE UNIVERSITY

Chapel Hill

THE UNIVERSITY OF NORTH CAROLINA PRESS

Manufactured in the United States of America
VAN REES PRESS, NEW YORK

CONSULTANTS

Charles F. Arrowood
Stuart G. Noble
Dorothy Orr
Nita K. Pyburn
James B. Sellers

PREFACE

Volume I of this series, *European Inheritances*, contains much material on the College of William and Mary, the only college established in the South before the American Revolution. Volume II, *Toward Educational Independence*, contains documents that reveal interest in higher education in the latter part of the eighteenth century, including the bill of 1770 in South Carolina and the charters of colleges at Winnsboro, Ninety-Six, and Charleston in that state and materials on the charter of Queen's College in North Carolina. The Crown disallowed that charter but the institution operated for a time without royal approval.[1] These unsuccessful efforts nevertheless were significant of a growing interest in higher educational facilities independent of Europe.

As the Revolutionary period approached, the position of institutions which had been established under denominational control during the colonial period seemed to have become less and less secure. The people of this country were becoming more varied in their denominational affiliations and in religious matters were less homogeneous than formerly. The increased diversity of religious belief and denominational affiliation was one of the main causes of the separation of Church and State, without which neither complete religious freedom nor freedom of educational enterprise could be enjoyed.

In Virginia, the Carolinas, Georgia, and Maryland and in a few counties in New York the Anglican Church had been by law established and its ministers paid as other officers of the state. These had to receive ordination in England. Teachers in those colonies were required to hold appropriate certification of that church through the permission of the Bishop of London or other ecclesiastical authority in England or his representative in America. With the separation of the Church and State and the movement for religious liberty these difficulties for teachers were in part removed.

Increasing distrust of the collegiate establishments of the colonial period gradually developed in the belief that these colleges were not fully meeting the public need for higher educational opportunity.

1. On his southern tour in 1791 George Washington referred to Charlotte as "a trifling place.... There is a School (called a College) in it at which, at times there has been 50 or 60 boys."

Each of these colleges had been and for a long time remained the representative of a faction or a sect within the colony or the commonwealth in which it was located and did not represent the people as a whole. A slowly growing spirit of democracy tended to increase this feeling of distrust. Two ways appeared in which higher educational institutions might serve the public welfare: state governments might exercise the right of visitation and coerce the colleges to change their charters so as to make them more useful to society in general; or the states could ignore the colleges already established and set up new institutions more sensitive to public responsibility. One of these possible ways was tried but failed, culminating in the famous Dartmouth College Case. Although the movement for state universities did not generally develop until after that significant decision, it had acquired considerable momentum in the South where the University of Georgia (1785), the University of North Carolina (1789), the University of Tennessee (beginning with Blount College in 1794), the University of South Carolina (1801), the University of New Orleans (1805), and, in the year of the Dartmouth decision, the University of Virginia were chartered. The University of Alabama was chartered in 1820, the University of Mississippi in 1844, and the University of Texas in 1858. The University of Texas, of Arkansas, and of Florida did not begin operations until after the period covered by this study.

Before the Dartmouth College decision there were more or less energetic efforts to make some of the colonial colleges more responsive to government. Among these were the College of New Jersey, Yale, King's College in New York, the College of Philadelphia, and Liberty Hall Academy, a Presbyterian institution in Virginia which later developed into Washington and Lee University.[2] Efforts had been made also to transform the College of William and Mary into an institution to crown the state system of education planned by Jefferson in 1779. But these efforts were not successful chiefly because of the fixed ecclesiastical character of the College of William and Mary.

The documents that follow deal with state universities established in the South before 1860. Documents on private and denominational effort in secondary and higher education in the South before 1860 appear in Volume IV of this series.

2. See James M. Hutcheson, "Virginia's 'Dartmouth College Case,'" *Virginia Magazine of History and Biography*, LI (July, 1943); Edgar W. Knight, "North Carolina's 'Dartmouth College Case,'" *Journal of Higher Education*, XIX (March, 1948); E. E. Brown, *Origin of the American State University* (Berkeley: University of California Press, 1903).

The compiler and editor is especially indebted to the consultants whose names appear on the copyright page. In addition he is indebted to many other people: the Staff of the University of North Carolina Library, and especially Miss Georgia Faison and Mrs. Louise Partrick Newton, Reference Librarians; the late Professors R. D. W. Connor and A. R. Newsome and Professors Fletcher M. Green, J. G. deR. Hamilton, and Hugh T. Lefler of the University of North Carolina; Librarian Emeritus Earl G. Swem of the College of William and Mary; John M. Jennings, Librarian of the Virginia Historical Society; Robert H. Land, Librarian of the College of William and Mary; William J. Van Schreeven, Dr. Wilmer L. Hall, and other members of the staff of the Virginia State Library; Dr. Ed. McCuistion of the State Department of Education in Arkansas; Dr. A. F. Kuhlman of the Joint University Libraries, Nashville; Professor Emeritus I. L. Kandel of Columbia University; Professor S. J. Folmsbee of the University of Tennessee; Professor R. L. Meriwether and members of the staff of the South Carolinians Library, University of South Carolina; A. S. Salley, State Historian of South Carolina; Professor J. H. Easterby, South Carolina Historical Society; Mary A. Sparkman, Secretary of the Historical Commission of Charleston; H. O. Strohecker, Principal of the Charleston High School, South Carolina; Mrs. J. E. Hays, State Historian, and members of the staff of the Department of Archives and History of Georgia; Clarence S. Brigham, Director of the American Antiquarian Society; Dr. St. George L. Sioussat and members of the staff of the Division of Manuscripts, the Library of Congress; Stephen T. Riley of the Massachusetts Historical Society; and many others.

The compiler and editor has been most fortunate also in the research fellows: George A. Beebe, Selby Coffman, Carolyn A. Daniel, Ellen Diggs Bodman, Clifton L. Hall, Robert S. Lambert, Margaret E. Lerche, and Roberta McKenzie Hamilton. In addition graduate students who have been most helpful include J. C. Colley, George W. Patrick, Thomas L. Patrick, William R. Risher, C. M. Clarke, Katherine McGeachy, Olena S. Bunn, H. B. Story, R. H. Hamilton, James W. Hill, John Littleton, Helen Macon, William F. Burton, Jr., Mary Lois Staton, and Isaac Copeland, to all of whom I am most grateful. Thanks are due also to Mrs. Mabel T. Hill, Mrs. Dorothy Lyon, and Mrs. Sibyl Goerch Powe for assistance with the classification and arrangement of the documents and with most competent help in typing and editing.

Special thanks go to the General Education Board, whose grants-in-aid helped to make this study possible and to Mr. C. T. Council of Durham, North Carolina, for generously providing some research fellowships.

Edgar W. Knight

The University of North Carolina
April, 1952.

CONTENTS

VOLUME III

THE RISE OF THE STATE UNIVERSITY

I

CHARTERING OF UNIVERSITIES BEFORE 1800

1. President John Witherspoon of Princeton certifies to the attendance and proficiency at that institution of William R. Davie, "father of the University of North Carolina," 1776

I here testify that the Bearer William R. Davie studied in this College for two years preceeding this Date behaving himself regularly & applying to his Studies with Success, that he was examined & admitted to the Bachelors Degree of which an authentick Instrument will be delivered to him at the first Meeting of the Board of Trustees, he is in the meantime recommended to all Lovers of Religion & Learning as deserving of Encouragement. The above is written & Signed at Princeton Oct. 20th, 1776, by

John Witherspoon.

—William L. Saunders, (ed.) *The Colonial Records of North Carolina*, X, 870.

2. A bill to establish a university in North Carolina and to provide for its support by an income tax, 1784

A Bill for establishing a University in this State to be distinguished by the title of the President and Trustees of the North Carolina University.

Whereas it is provided in the forty-first article of the constitution of this State "That a school or schools shall be established by the Legislature for the convenient instruction of youth with such salaries to the masters, paid by the Public, as may enable them to instruct at low prices; and that all useful learning shall be encouraged and promoted in one or more universities."

Be it enacted by the General Assembly of the State of North Carolina and it is hereby enacted by the Authority of the same— That he and they are hereby declared to be a body corporate and politic, to be known and distinguished by the title of   and by that name and title shall have perpetual succession and a common seal and that they the said   and trustees and their successors by name aforesaid or a Majority of them shall be able and Capable in law to take demand recover and possess all monies goods and Chattels that shall be given them for the use of the said University.

And the same apply according to the will of the donors and by gift purchase or devise to take, have, receive, possess, enjoy and retain to them and their successors for ever any lands, rents, tenements, and Hereditaments of what kind nature or quality soever, the same may be in special trust and confidence that the same or the profits thereof shall be applied to and for the uses and purposes of establishing and endowing the said University ——————, ——————, ——————, —————— building or purchasing suitable and convenient houses for the same providing a philosophical apparatus and Public Library and supporting and paying Salaries to the president professors and other officers

And such number of professors and tutors thereof as shall be necessary to instruct the students and they shall be able to pay out of the public funds that shall be in their hands.

And be it further enacted by the Authority aforesaid that the said President and Trustees —————— —————— and their successors or a majority of them by the name aforesaid shall be able and capable in Law to bargain sell grant demise alien or dispose of and convey and assure to the purchasers any such lands, rents, tenements or Hereditaments aforesaid when the condition of the grant to them or the will of the devisor does not forbid the same and further that the said President ——————, and Trustees, ——————, ——————, and their successors forever or a Majority, ——————, ——————, of them shall be able and capable in law by the name aforesaid to sue and implead be sued

and impleaded answer and be answered in any court of record whatsoever

And be it further enacted by the Authority aforesaid That the said Trustees or any

be and they are hereby impowered authorized and required to convene at on the day of and then and there and at all other times forever hereafter when the said and their successors or a of them shall be convened and met together in the said they shall have full power and lawful authority to elect and constitute one or more professors or tutors and also to make and ordain such Laws rules and ordinances not repugnant to the laws of this State for the well ordering and governing the students their morals studies and Academical exercises as to them shall seem expedient and necessary

Be it further enacted by the Authority aforesaid that the said President ——————, —————— and Trustees ——————, ——————, before they enter upon the execution of the trust reposed in them by this act shall take the oath appointed for public officers and also the following oath. I, A.B. do swear that will duly and faithfully to the best of skill and ability execute and discharge the several

trusts powers and authorities wherewith I am invested by an act of the General Assembly intituled an act for

and that I will endeavour that all monies, goods and chattels and the profits of lands belonging to this corporation shall be duly applied to the use of the North Carolina University for the advancement of learning and as near as may be agreeable to the will of the doner

, So help me God,

And be it further enacted by the authority aforesaid that the President ——————, ——————, and Trustees or an of them shall annually ——————, in the month of elect and Commissionate some person to be treasurer for the said University —————— during the term of one year which treasurer shall enter into bond with sufficient security to the President and Trustees ———————————— in the sum of conditioned for the faithful discharge of his office and the trust and the trust reposed in him and that all Monies and Chattels belonging to the said corporation that shall be in his hands at the expiration of his office shall then be immediately paid and delivered into the hands of the succeeding Treasurer and every Treasurer shall receive all monies Donations, Gifts, bequests and Charities whatsoever that may belong or accrue to the said University —————— during his office and at the expiration thereof shall Account with the President and Trustees for the same and the same pay and deliver over to the succeeding Treasurer

And whereas it is necessary to make provisions for the appointment of succeeding President ——————, ——————, and Trustees ——————, ——————, in order to keep up a Perpetual Succession. Be it therefore enacted by the authority aforesaid that on the death refusal to act or Qualify resignation or removal out of the State of the said President ________, or any of the Trustees ________, ________, for the time being it shall be lawful for the remaining Trustees—any them and they are hereby authorized and required to convene and meet together in the said University ________, ________ and there elect and appoint another President ________ or one or more Trustees ________, as the case may be in the room and stead of such President, Trustee or Trustees ________ dead, refusing to Qualify, resigned, or removed out of the State which President Trustee or Trustees ________, ________, ________ so elected and appointed shall be vested with the same Trusts powers and authorities as any other President ________ and or Trustees are invested by virtue of this Act.

And be it further enacted by the authority aforesaid that the said President & Trustees ________ and their successors or of them at their meeting on and at any other meeting called for that purpose after due notice given at least of the signifying the occasion of such meeting shall have full power and authority to hear any complaint against the President or any professor or Tutor or and (any) other officer for misbehaviour or neglect, to suspend or wholly remove him or them from office and appoint others to fill the same office or offices respectively and any Person ________ so removed from office shall from thenceforth cease to be a member of the corporation and the Person so appointed in his room and stead shall be vested with all the authorities and privileges with which His Predecessor by this Act appointed is invested.

And be it further enacted by the authority aforesaid that the said President ________ and Professors ________ shall have full powers and authorities to grant and confer the degrees Doctor Master & Batchelor of Arts ________, ________, ________ and they are hereby empowered and required to grant Diploma's certifying the same to such Students or others as shall possess a sufficient degree of literary merit.

Be it further enacted by the Authority aforesaid that his Excellency and Governor for the time being with the council of State shall and may at any time visit and examine the Accounts, funds endowments of the said colledge and report to the General Assembly whatever may be necessary for the encouragement and well being thereof

And be it further Enacted by the authority aforesaid, that the said Trustees may be enabled to carry this act into effect the following Tax shall be levied annually for the support & endowment thereof, that is to say a poll Tax on each Importing Merchant of
on each inland Trader of
on each Pedler or itenerant Trader of
on each Lawyer of
on each Phisician of
on each Clerk of a Court of
on each and every Sheriff of
with two and half per cent on all annual Salaries
the above Tax shall be collected
accounted for as directed by an act intitled an act for
and the above monies when so collected shall be subject to the draughts of the Treasurer of the said University only, which order or draught shall be countersigned by the president of the University. –*Legislative Papers*, 120, House of Commons, 1784. This bill was not enacted into law.

3. Charter of the University of Georgia, 1785: An act for the more full and complete establishment of a public seat of learning in this state

As it is the distinguishing happiness of free governments, that civil order should be the result of choice, and not necessity, and the common wishes of the people become the laws of the land, their public prosperity, and even existence, very much depends upon suitably forming the minds and morals of their citizens. Where the minds of the people in general are viciously disposed and unprincipled, and their conduct disorderly, a free government will be attended with greater confusions, and with evils more horrid than the wild uncultivated state of nature: It can only be happy where the public principles and opinions are properly directed, and their manners regulated. This is an influence beyond the sketch of laws and punishments, and can be claimed only by religion and education. It should therefore be among the first objects of those who wish well to the national prosperity, to encourage and support the principles of religion and morality, and early to place the youth under the forming hand of society, that by instruction they may be moulded to the love of virtue and good order. Sending them abroad to other countries for their education will not answer these purposes, is too humiliating an acknowledgment of the ignorance or inferiority of our own, and will always be the cause of so great foreign attachments, that upon principles of policy it is not admissible.

This country, in the times of our common danger and distress, found such security in the principles and abilities which wise regulations had before established in the minds of our countrymen, that our present happiness, joined to pleasing prospects, should conspire to make us feel ourselves under the strongest obligation to form the youth, the rising hope of our land, to render the like glorious and essential services to our country.

And whereas, for the great purpose of internal education, divers allotments of land have, at different times, been made, particularly by the legislature at their sessions in July, one thousand seven hundred and eighty-three; and February, one thousand seven hundred and eighty-four, all of which may be comprehended and made the basis of one general and complete establishment: THEREFORE *the representatives of the freemen of the State of Georgia, in General assembly met, this twenty-seventh day of January, in the year of our Lord one thousand seven hundred and eighty-five, enact, ordain, and declare, and by these presents it is* ENACTED, ORDAINED, AND DECLARED.

1st. The general superintendance and regulation of the literature of this State, and in particular of the public seat of learning, shall be committed and intrusted to the governor and council, the speaker of the house of assembly, and the chief justice of the State, for the time being, who shall, *ex officio,* compose one board, denominated the *Board of Visitors,* hereby vested with all the powers of visitation, to see that the intent of this institution is carried into effect, and John Houstoun, James Nathan Brownson, John Habersham, Abiel Holmes, Jenkin Davies, Hugh Lawson, William Glascock, and Benjamin Taliaferro, esquires, who shall compose another board, denominated the *Board of Trustees.* These two boards united, or a majority of each of them, shall compose the SENATUS ACADEMICUS of the University of Georgia.

2d. All statues, laws, and ordinances, for the government of the university shall be made and enacted by the two boards united, or a majority of each of them, subject always to be laid before the general assembly, as often as required, and to be repealed or disallowed, as the general assembly shall think proper.

3d. Property vested in the university, shall never be sold without the joint concurrence of the two boards, and by act of the legislature; but the leasing, farming, and managing of the property of the university for its constant support, shall be the business of the board of trustees. For this purpose they are hereby constituted a body corporate and politic, by the name of *Trustees of the University of Georgia*, by which they shall have perpetual succession, and shall and may be a person in law, capable to plead, and be impleaded, defend, and be defended, answer, and be answered unto, also to have, take, possess, acquire, purchase, or otherwise receive lands, tenements, hereditaments, goods, chattels, or other estates, and the same to lease, use, manage or improve, for the good and benefit of said university, and all property given or granted to or by the government of this State for the advancement of learning in general, is hereby vested in such trustees in trust as herein described.

4th. As the appointment of a person to be the president and head of the university is one of the first and most important concerns, on which its respect and usefulness greatly depend, the board of trustees shall first examine and nominate, but the appointment of the president shall be by the two boards jointly, who shall also have the power of removing him from office for misdemeanor, unfaithfulness, or incapacity.

5th. There shall be a stated annual meeting of the *Senatus Academicus* at the university, or at any other place or time to be appointed by themselves, at which the governor of the State, or in his absence, the president of the council shall preside; their records to be kept by the secretary of the university.

6th. As the affairs and business of the university may make more frequent meetings of the trustees necessary, the president and two of the members are empowered to appoint a meeting of the board, notice always to be given to the rest, or letters left at the usual places of their abode at least fourteen days before the said meeting, seven of the trustees thus convened shall be a legal meeting: In case of the death, absence or incapacity of the president, the senior trustee shall preside; the majority of the members present shall be considered a vote of the whole, and where the members are divided, the president shall have a casting vote.

Provided always, That nothing done at these special meetings, shall have any force or efficacy after the rising of the then next annual meeting of the trustees.

7th. The trustees shall have the power of filling up all vacancies of their own board, and appointing professors, tutors, secretary, treasurers, steward, or any other officers which they may think necessary, and the same to discontinue or remove, as they may think fit; but not without seven of their number, at least, concurring in such act.

8th. The trustees shall prescribe the course of public studies, appoint the salaries of the different officers, form and use a public seal, adjust and determine the expences, and adopt such regulations, not otherwise provided for, which the good of the university may render necessary.

9th. All officers appointed to the instruction and government of the university, shall be of the christian religion; and within three months after they enter upon the execution of their trust, shall publicly take the oath of allegiance and fidelity, and the oaths of office prescribed in the statutes of the university; the president before the governor or president of council, and all other officers before the president of the university.

10th. The president, professors, tutors, students, and all officers and servants of the university whose office require their constant attendance, shall be, and they are hereby excused from military duty, and from all other such like duties and services; and all lands and other property of the university is hereby exempted from taxation.

11th. The trustees shall not exclude any person of any religious denomination whatsoever, from free and equal liberty and advantages of education, or from any of the liberties, privileges, and immunities of the university in his education, on account of his or their speculative sentiments in religion, or being of a different religious profession.

12th. The president of the university, with consent of the trustees, shall have power to give and confer all such honors, degrees and licenses as are usually conferred in colleges or universities, and shall always preside at the meeting of the trustees, and at all the public exercises of the university.

13th. The *Senatus Academicus* at their stated annual meetings shall consult and advise, not only upon the affairs of the university, but also to remedy the defects, and advance the interest of literature through the State in general. For this purpose it shall be the business of the members, previous to their meeting, to obtain an acquaintance with the State, and regulations of the schools and places of education in their respective counties, that they may be thus possessed of the whole, and have it lie before them for mutual assistance and deliberation. Upon this information they shall recommend what kind of schools and academies shall be instituted, agreeable to the constitution, in the several parts of the State, and prescribe what branches of instruction shall be taught and inculcated in each: They shall also examine and recommend the instructors to be employed in them, or appoint persons for that purpose. The president of the university, as often as the duties of his station will permit, and some of the members, at least once in a year, shall visit them, and examine into their order and performances.

14th. All public schools, instituted or to be supported by funds or public monies in this State, shall be considered as parts of members of the university, and shall be under the foregoing directions and regulations.

15th. Whatsoever public measures are necessary to be adopted for accomplishing these great and important designs, the trustees shall, from time to time, represent and lay before the general assembly.

16th. All laws and ordinances heretofore passed in any wise contrary to the true intent and meaning of the premises, are hereby repealed, and declared to be null and void.

17th. In full testimony and confirmation of this charter, ordinance and constitution, and all the articles therein contained, *The representatives of the freemen of the State of Georgia in general assembly, hereby order*, That this act shall be signed by the honorable Joseph Habersham, Esquire, speaker of the house of assembly, and sealed with the public seal of this State, and the same, or the enrollment thereof in the records of this State, shall be good and effectual in law, to have and to hold the powers, privileges, and immunities, and all and singular the premises herein given, or which are meant, mentioned, or intended to be hereby given to the said *Board of Visitors*, and *Trustees*, and to their successors in office for ever.

JOSEPH HABERSHAM, *Speaker*.

Savannah, January 27, 1785

—Robert and Georgia Watkins, *A Digest of the Laws of the State of Georgia*, pp. 299-302.

4. Charter of the University of North Carolina, 1789: An Act to Establish a University in this State

Whereas, in all well regulated governments it is the indispensable duty of every Legislature to consult the happiness of a rising generation, and endeavour to fit them for an honourable discharge of the social duties of life, by paying the strictest attention to their education: And whereas, an university supported by permanent funds and well endowed, would have the most direct tendency to answer the above purpose:

I. Be it therefore enacted by the General Assembly of the State of North Carolina, and it is hereby enacted by the authority of the same, That Samuel Johnston, James Iredell, Charles Johnson, Hugh Williamson, Stephen Cabarrus, Richard Dobbs Spaight, William Blount, Benjamin Williams, John Sitgreaves, Frederick Harget, Robert W. Snead, Archibald Maclaine, Honourable Samuel Ashe, Robert Dixon, Benjamin Smith, Honourable Samuel Spencer, John Hay, James Hogg, Henry William Harrington, William Barry Grove, Reverend Samuel M'Corkle, Adlai Osborne, John Stokes, John Hamilton, Joseph Graham, Honourable John Williams, Thomas Person, Alfred Moore, Alexander Mebane, Joel Lane, Willie Jones, Benjamin Hawkins, John Haywood, Senior, John Macon, William Richardson Davie, Joseph Dixon, William Lenoir, Joseph M'Dowall, James Holland, and William Porter, Esquires, shall be and they are hereby declared to be a body politic and corporate, to be known and distinguished by the name of The Trustees of the University of North Carolina; and by that name shall have perpetual succession and a common seal; and that they the Trustees and their successors by the name aforesaid, or a majority of them, shall be able and capable in law to take, demand, receive and possess all monies, goods and chattels that shall be given them for the use of the said university, and the same apply according to the will of the donors, and by gift, purchase or devise to take, have, receive, possess, enjoy and retain to them and their successors forever, any lands, rents, tenements and hereditaments, of what kind, nature or quality soever the same may be, in special trust and confidence that the same or the profits thereof shall be applied to and for the use and purpose of establishing and endowing the said university.

II. And be it enacted by the authority aforesaid, That the said Trustees and their successors, or a majority of them, by the name aforesaid, shall be able and capable in law to bargain, sell, grant, demise, alien or dispose of, and convey and assure to the purchasers, any such lands, rents, tenements and hereditaments aforesaid, when the condition of the grant to them, or the will of the devisor, does not forbid it. And further that they the said Trustees and their successors forever, or a majority of them, shall be able and capable in law by the name aforesaid, to sue and implead, be sued and impleaded, answer and be answered, in all courts of record whatsoever; and they shall have power to open and receive subscriptions; and in general they shall and may do all such things as are usually done by bodies corporate and politic, or such as may be necessary for the promotion of learning and virtue.

III. And be it further enacted by the authority aforesaid, That the said Trustees, in order to carry the present act into effect, shall meet at Fayetteville on the third Monday in the session of the next General Assembly, at which time they shall choose a President and Secretary; and shall then fix the time of their next annual meeting; and at every annual meeting of the Trustees, the members present, with the President and Treasurer, shall be a quorum to do any business, or a majority of the members, without either of those officers, shall be a quorum; but at their first meeting as above directed there shall be at least fifteen of the above Trustees present in order to proceed to business; and the Trustees at their annual meeting may appoint special meetings within the year; or in case unforseen accidents shall render a meeting necessary, the Secretary, by order of the President and any two of the Trustees signified to him in writing, shall by particular notice to each Trustee, as well as by an advertisement in the State Gazette, convene the Trustees at the time proposed by the President; and the members thus convened shall be a quorum to do any business except the appointment of a President or professors in the University, or the disposal or appropriation of monies; but in case of the death or resignation of the President or any professor, the Trustees thus convened may supply the place until the next annual meeting of the Board of Trustees and no longer; and the meeting at which the seat of the said University shall be fixed, shall be advertised in the Gazette of this state at least six months, and notice in manner aforesaid to each of the Trustees of the object of the said meeting.

IV. And be it further enacted by the authority aforesaid, That the Trustees shall elect and commissionate some person to be Treasurer for the said university during the term of two years; which Treasurer shall enter into bond with sufficient securities to the Governor for the time being, in the sum of five thousand pounds, conditioned for the faithful discharge of his office and the trust reposed in him; and that all monies and chattels belonging to the said corporation that shall be in his hands at the expiration of his office shall then be immediately paid and delivered into the hands of the succeeding Treasurer: And every Treasurer shall receive all monies, donations, gifts, bequests and charities whatsoever that may belong or accrue to the said university during his office, and at the expiration thereof shall account with the Trustees for the same, and the same pay and deliver over to the succeeding Treasurer; and on his neglect or refusal to pay and deliver as aforesaid, the same method of recovery may be had against him, as is or may be provided for the recovery of monies from Sheriffs or other persons chargeable with public monies: And the Treasurer of the University shall cause annually to be published in the State Gazette, for the satisfaction of the subscribers and benefactors, a list of all monies and other things by him received for the said University, either by subscription, legacy, donation or otherwise, under the penalty of one hundred pounds, to be recovered at the suit of the Attorney General, in the name of the Governor for the time being, in any court of record having cognizance thereof; and the monies arising from such penalties shall be appropriated to the use of the said University.

V. Be it further enacted by the authority aforesaid, That all monies received by the Treasurer of the said University, shall be annually paid by him to the Treasurer of the state, who is hereby authorized and ordered to give a receipt to the said Treasurer of the University in behalf of the said Trustees, for all such sums by him received; and the said Treasurer shall pay annually unto the Treasurer of the said University, six per cent. interest on all such sums received by him in the manner aforesaid; which amount of interest paid by the State Treasurer as aforesaid, shall be allowed to him in the settlement of his accounts: And the said Trustees shall on no event or pretence whatsoever, appropriate or make use of the principal of the monies by them received on subscription, but such principal shall be and remain as a permanent fund for the use and support of the said University forever.

VI. And be it further enacted by the authority aforesaid, That on the death, refusal to act, resignation or removal out of the state, of any of the Trustees for the time being, it shall be lawful for the remaining Trustees, or any fifteen of them, and they are hereby authorized and required to elect and appoint one or more Trustees in the place of such Trustee or Trustees dead, refusing to act, resigned or removed; which Trustee or Trustees so appointed shall be vested with the same powers, trust and authorities as the Trustees are by virtue of this act. Provided nevertheless, That the Trustee or Trustees so appointed, shall reside in the superior court district where the person or persons reside in whose room he or they shall be so elected.

VII. And be it further enacted by the authority aforesaid, That when the Trustees shall deem the funds of the said University adequate to the purchase of a necessary quantity of land and erecting the proper buildings, they shall direct a meeting of the said Trustees for the purpose of fixing on and purchasing a healthy and convenient situation, which shall not be situated within five miles of the permanent seat of government, or any of the places of holding the courts of law or equity; which meeting shall be advertised at least six months in some gazette in this state, and at such superior courts as may happen within that time.

VIII. Be it further enacted by the authority aforesaid, That the Trustees shall have the power of appointing a President of the University, and such professors and tutors as to them shall appear necessary and proper, whom they may remove for misbehaviour, inability or neglect of duty; and they shall have the power to make all such laws and regulations for the government of the University and preservation of order and good morals therein, as are usually made in such seminaries, and as to them may appear necessary; provided the same are not contrary to the unalienable liberty of a citizen, or to the laws of the state. And the faculty of the University, that is to say, the President and professors, by and with the consent of the Trustees, shall have the power of conferring all such degrees or marks of literary distinction, as are usually conferred in colleges or universities.

IX. And be it further enacted by the authority aforesaid, That every person who within the term of five years shall subscribe ten pounds towards this University, to be paid within five years at five equal annual payments, shall be entitled to have one student educated at the University free from any expence of tuition.

X. And be it further enacted, That the public hall of the library and four of the colleges shall be called severally by the names of one or another of the six persons who shall within four years contribute the largest sums towards the funds of this University, in which shall be fairly entered the names and places of residence of every benefactor to this seminary, in order that posterity may be informed to whom they are indebted for the measure of learning and good morals that may prevail in the state.—Walter Clark (ed.), *The State Records of North Carolina*, XXV, 21-24. William R. Davie, known as "the father of the University of North Carolina," was author of the bill on which the above charter was enacted.

5. An Act for the support of the University of North Carolina, 1789

Whereas the General Assembly by their act, entitled "An Act to establish a university in this state," passed on the eleventh day of December instant, have declared that a university shall be established and erected in this state, which shall be called and known by the name of the University of North-Carolina: And whereas adequate funds will be found to be the means which will most effectually ensure to the state the advantages to be hoped and expected from such an institution:

I. *Be it therefore enacted by the General Assembly of the state of North-Carolina, and it is hereby enacted by the authority of the same*, That a gift of all monies due and owing to the public of North-Carolina, either for arrearages under the former or present government, up to the first day of January, one thousand seven hundred and eighty-three inclusive, (monies or certificates due for confiscated property purchased excepted) shall be and is hereby declared to be fully and absolutely made, for the purpose of erecting the necessary buildings, employing professors and tutors, and carrying into complete effect the act before recited: And the Treasurer is hereby directed and required to commence suits, and to prosecute all persons owing as above mentioned, and the monies recovered in consequence thereof to pay into the hands of the Trustees named in said act, or their successors, to be applied to the purposes aforesaid. *Provided*, That nothing herein contained shall be construed to prevent the Treasurer or Comptroller from settling with and collecting from the executors of Robert Lanier, deceased, late Treasurer of Salisbury district, such sums in cash or certificates as may on a final settlement of his accounts be found to be due to the public; nor shall it extend to prevent their collecting from the Sheriffs of that district, their arrearages of taxes which became due under the present government, and which ought to have been paid into the office of the said Lanier as Treasurer aforesaid; *provided* they make such collection within the space of two years, after which time the arrearages of that district also shall be considered as being included in this gift.

II. *And be it enacted*, That all the property that has heretofore or shall hereafter escheat to the state, shall be and hereby is vested in the said Trustees, for the use and benefit of the said university.

III. *And be it further enacted by the authority aforesaid*, That the lands and other property belonging to the university aforesaid, shall be, and the same is hereby exempt from all kind of public taxation. –*Laws of North Carolina*, 1789, Chapter XXI, 16.

6. William R. Davie to Governor Martin of North Carolina on behalf of the University of that State, 1790

Halifax, Novr 1st, 1790

Dear Sir,

...You will I am certain give the University every assistance in your power, as a man who knows the importance of education in a country just forming its manners and its Government.

I will thank you to inform me of the fate of the principal objects of the Legislature, and believe me,

With great respect,

Your most obedient
William R. Davie

–*Governor's Papers*, State Series, XVIII. Alexander Martin, Vol. I, 1790-1791.

7. A bill to prohibit trustees of the University of North Carolina from holding seats in the General Assembly of the State, 1790

A Bill to prevent the Trustees of the University of North Carolina from holding a Seat in the General Assembly or to be Elibigle thereto.

Whereas it is Impolitic and Dangerous to the priviledges of the Citizens to Suffer the said Trustees to have a Seat in the Same.

Be it enacted by the General Assembly of the State of North Carolina and it is hereby enacted by the Authority of the same–that from and after the passing of this Act it shall not be Lawfull for any of the Trustees of the University of North Carolina to hold a Seat in the General Assembly and if any person or persons shall be elected a Member to Represent any County in this State Contrary to the true intent and Meaning of this Act Such Election is hereby declared to be illegal and Voyd.–*Legislative Papers*, 97, House of Commons, 1790. Twenty-one of the forty members of the Board of Trustees named in the charter of 1789 were at that time members of the General Assembly. At the first regular meeting of the trustees at Fayetteville November 15 to 27, 1790, six vacancies were to be filled, two caused by death, two by resignation, and two by removal from that state; and of the six persons elected to those vacancies, four held membership in the General Assembly. The bill above was "read the first time and rejected." The question of "double" office holding has often come up in connection with the trustees of the University of North Carolina but many members still hold seats in the General Assembly.

8. Notice of special meeting of the trustees of the University of North Carolina, 1790

The Trustees of the University of North-Carolina, are hereby notified and reminded, that pursuant to a resolution of their body, entered into at Fayetteville, in the month of November last, the next meeting of the Board is to be held at Hillsborough, on the third Monday in July next; when it is hoped every member will attend. The object of this meeting, being to fix on the place at which the University shall be held, and to take measures for erecting the necessary buildings thereon.—*North Carolina Gazette* (Newbern), June 4, July 2, and July 16, 1791.

9. The trustees of the University of North Carolina accept the legislative grants for its support, 1790

Mr. Haywood proposed the following address, to be presented to the Genl. Assembly.

To the Honorable, the General Assembly of the State of North Carolina,

Gentlemen

The Trustees of the University of North Carolina, impressed with a high sense of that liberality & patronage towards the said institution, manifested by the General Assembly in their act entituled "An act for raising a fund for erecting the buildings and for the support of the University of North Carolina"—do for themselves and their successors, hereby gratefully accept the grants and every part thereof made by the act aforesaid; and beg leave to assure the honorable the General Assembly, they will endeavor so to apply and manage them, as effectually to answer the ends for which they were made.

On motion it was ordered that the same should be presented to the

Genl. Assembly.—Minutes of the Board of Trustees, The Library of the University of North Carolina.

10. The Trustees of the University of North Carolina memorialize the Legislature for compensation for lands, 1791

To the Honorable the General Assembly of the State of North Carolina now siting

The Memorial of the trustees of the University of North Carolina

Your Memorialists beg leave to represent to your Honorable body that Benjamin Smith Esquire of the County of Brunswick, did by a Deed of gift bearing date the date of 1789 give and make over unto the board of Trustees for the use and benefit of the University several pieces of land containing in the whole twenty thousand acres that the said Lands were by the Commissioner of the United States at the Treaty of Hopewell ceded to the Indians by which means your memorialists are deprived of the benefit that might have resulted from the said donation whereupon your memorialists request that your honorable body would cause the Certificates that were paid to the public for the said lands or the value thereof in the current money of the State to be paid to them or make them such other compensation in lieu of the said lands as in your wisdom shall seem Just.

Done in the board of Trustees of the University of the State of North Carolina Convened at Newbern the 23rd of Decemr. A d 1791.

Alex: Martin P.

—*Legislative Papers*, House of Commons, 1791-1792.

11. A committee of the Trustees invite proposals from gentlemen "who wish to teach" in the University of North Carolina, 1792

To the Public

The Subscribers having been appointed a committee of the Board of Trustees of the University of North-Carolina, for the purpose of receiving proposals from such gentlemen, as may intend to undertake the instruction of youth in that institution, take the opportunity of making known to the public their wish that such gentlemen should signify their inclination to the subscribers.

The objects to which it is contemplated by the Board to turn the attention of the students, on the first establishment, are—The study of Languages, particularly the English—History, ancient and modern—the Belles lettres—Logic and Moral Philosophy—the knowledge of the mathematics, and Natural Philosophy—Agriculture and Botany, with the principles of architecture.

Gentlemen conversant in these branches of Science and Literature, and who can be well recommended, will receive very handsome encouragement by the Board. The exercises of the institution will commence as early as possible after the completion of the buildings of the University which are to be contracted for immediately.

Samuel Ashe
A. Moore
John Hoyl
David Stone
Sam. M'Corkle

—*North Carolina Journal* (Halifax), December 26, 1792.

12. An account of the laying of the cornerstone of the first building erected at the University of North Carolina, 1793

On the 12th inst. the Commissioners appointed by the Board of Trustees of the University of this state, met at Chappel-Hill for the purpose of laying the corner-stone of the present building,[1] and disposing of the lots in the village. A large number of the brethren of the Masonic order from Hillsborough, Chatham, Granville and Warren, attended to assist at the ceremony of placing the corner-stone; and the procession for this purpose moved from Mr. Patterson's at 12 o'clock, in the following order: The Masonic Brethren in their usual order of procession, the Commissioners, the Trustees not Commissioners, the Hon. Judge Macay and other public officers, then followed the gentlemen of the vicinity. On approaching the south end of the building, the Masons opened to the right and left, and the Commissioners, &c. passed through and took their place. The Masonic procession then moved on round the foundation of the building, and halted with their usual ceremonies opposite to the southeast corner, where WILLIAM RICHARDSON DAVIE, Grand-Master of the fraternity, &c. in this state, assisted by two Masters of lodges and four other officers, laid the corner-stone, enclosing a plate to commemorate the transaction.

1. Old East, the first building erected on a state university campus.

The Rev. Dr. M'Corkle then addressed the Trustees and spectators in an excellent discourse suited to the occasion; of which the following is an extract—Observing on the natural and necessary connexion between learning and religion, and the importance of religion to the promotion of national happiness and national undertakings, he said, "It is our duty to acknowledge that sacred scriptural truth, 'Except the Lord do build the house, they labour in vain who build it; except the Lord watcheth the city, the watchmen walketh but in vain.' For my own part, I feel myself penetrated with a sense of these truths, and this I feel not only as a minister of religion, but also as a citizen of the state, as a member of civil as well as religious society. These unaffected feelings of my heart give me leave to express with that plainness and honesty which becomes a preacher of the gospel, and a minister of Jesus Christ."

Stating the advancement of learning and science as one great means of ensuring the happiness of mankind, the Doctor observed, "Happiness is the center to which all the duties of man and people tend. It is the center to which states as well as individuals are universally and powerfully attracted. To diffuse the greatest possible degree of happiness in a given territory, is the aim of good government and religion. Now the happiness of a nation depends upon national wealth and national glory, and cannot be gained without them. They in like manner demand liberty and good laws. Liberty and laws call for general knowledge in the people, and extensive knowledge in the ministers of the state, and these in fine demand public places of education. That happiness is the object of all, I believe will be denied by none. Nations and men are seeking for it. How can any nation be happy without national wealth? How can that nation or man be happy that is not procuring and securing the necessary conveniences and accommodations of life? ease without indolence, and plenty without luxury or want. How can glory or wealth be procured or preserved without liberty and laws? They must check luxury, encourage industry, and protect wealth. They must secure me the glory of my actions, and save from a bow-string or bastille—and how are these objects to be gained without general knowledge. Knowledge is wealth,—it is glory —whether among philosophers, ministers of state or religion, or among the great mass of the people. Britons glory in the name of a Newton, and have honoured him with a place among the sepulcres of their kings. Americans glory in the name of a Franklin, and every nation boasts her great men who has them. Savages cannot have, rather *cannot educate* them, though many a Newton has been born and buried amongst them. 'Knowledge is liberty and law. When the clouds of ignorance are dispelled by the radiance of knowledge, power trembles, but the authority of the laws remains inviolable.' And how this knowledge, productive of so many advantages to mankind, can be acquired without public places of education, I know not."

In viewing the rise and progress of this important institution, he concluded with these observations—"The seat of the University was next sought for, and the public eye selected Chappel-Hill—a lovely situation—in the center of the state—at a convenient distance from the capital—in a healthy and fertile neighbourhood. May this hill be for religion as the antient hill of Zion; and for literature and the muses, may it surpass the antient Parnassus!—We this day enjoy the pleasure of seeing the corner-stone of the University, its foundations, its materials, and the architects of the building; and we hope ere long to see its stately walls and spire ascending to their summit—ere long we hope to see it adorned with an elegant village, accomodated with all the necessaries and conveniences of civilized society."

This discourse was followed by a short but animated prayer, closed with the united AMEN of an immense concourse of people.

The Commissioners then proceeded to sell the lots in the village, and we have the pleasure to assure the public, that although there were but twenty-nine lots, they sold for upwards of one thousand five-hundred pounds, which shews the high idea the public entertain of this agreeable and healthful situation.—*Ibid.*, Oct. 30, 1793.

13. Charter of Blount College, Tennessee, 1794

AN ACT for the Establishment of Blount College, in the vicinity of Knoxville.

WHEREAS, The legislature of this Territory are disposed to promote the happiness of the people at large, and especially of the rising generation, by instituting seminaries of education, where youth may be habituated to an amiable, moral and virtuous conduct, and accurately instructed in the various branches of useful science, and in the principles of the ancient and modern languages:

SECTION 1. *Be it enacted by the Governor, Legislative Council and House of Representatives of the Territory of the United States of America south of the river Ohio*, That the Reverend Samuel Carrick, President, and His Excellency William Blount, the Honorable Daniel Smith, Secretary of the Territory, the Honorable David Campbell, the Honorable Joseph Anderson, General John Sevier, Colonel James White, Colonel Alexander Kelly, Colonel William Cocke, Willie Blount, Joseph Hamilton, Archibald Roane, Francis A. Ramsey, Charles M'Clung, George Roulstone, George M'Nutt, John Adair, and Robert Houston, Esquires, shall be and they are hereby declared to be a body politic and corporate, by the name of the President and Trustees of Blount College, in the vicinity of Knoxville, and shall have perpetual succession and a common seal; and that they and their successors, or the President, and any four or more of them, by the name aforesaid, shall have and they are hereby invested with all legal powers and capacities to buy, receive, possess, hold, alien, and dispose of any property for the use and benefit of the College; and may sue and be sued, commence and prosecute any legal process or processes, and have the same instituted against them in any court of record in this Territory, in the most ample manner.

SEC. 2. *And be it enacted*, That the President of the College, with any four or more of the Trustees who may be present, shall be a Board of Trustees adequate to the transaction of business; and in the absence of the President, any five or more of the Trustees being met upon their own adjournment, shall choose a Vice-President, who shall act during the absence of the President; and that the President and each of the Trustees, before their entrance upon the actual execution of their office, or their being known as such in law, shall appear before some Justice of the Peace for the county of Knox, and shall take an oath faithfully to execute their respective offices, which shall be entered on the records of the College; and that the President, or any of the Trustees, shall have a right at any time to resign his office, by signifying such resignation in writing to the Board of Trustees; and that the Board of Trustees shall have power to remove from office the President or any of the Trustees, when they may think proper, and fill up any vacancies which may happen in the Board, thro' the death, resignation, or removal of members, by electing others in their room.

SEC. 3. *And be it enacted*, That the Board of Trustees shall have full power to appoint a secretary, treasurer, professors, tutors, and all necessary officers for conducting the civil and literary concerns of the College, and to displace and supersede them at pleasure. They shall have power to meet upon their own adjournment, or upon a citation from the President or Vice-President; to examine the proficiency of the students; to confer the literary degrees of Bachelor and Master of Arts; to fix the seat of the College, and to erect the necessary buildings in the vicinity of Knoxville; to make all laws and regulations which they shall judge necessary for the good government of the College, and for promoting morality and virtue amongst the students, provided they be consistent with the laws of the United States: and they shall take affectual care that students of all denominations may and shall be admitted to the equal advantages of a liberal education, and to the emoluments and honors of the College, and that they shall receive a like fair, generous and equal treatment during their residence therein.

SEC. 4. *And be it enacted,* That the President, Vice-President, Professors, Tutors and Students of said College shall be exempted from all military duty, during their continuance as members of the college, except in a general invasion of the Territory.

WILLIAM BLOUNT, Governor.
GRIFFITH RUTHERFORD, P. L. C.
DAVID WILSON, S. H. R.

—*Acts Passed at the First Session of the General Assembly of the Territory of the United States of America, South of the River Ohio,* 89-91, Edward Scott, *Laws of Tennessee,* I, 504.

14. William R. Davie's plan of education for the University of North Carolina, 1795

Mr. Davie—offered to the Board, a plan of Education for the University which was read and referred to a committee of five, to wit. Mr. J. Williams. Mr. Hogg. Mr. Haywood. Mr. Davie and Mr. Osborne.... (December 1, 1795).

The Committee appointed to prepare and digest a plan of Education for the University. Reported the following; which was received and concurred with, to wit.

The Students of the Institution to be divided into a Preparatory School, and the Professorships of the University.

Plan of the Preparatory School.

The English Language to be taught Gramatically on the plan of Webster's & South's Grammars.

Writing in a neat and correct manner.

Arithmetic, the four first rules with the Rule of Three.

English Additional exercises.

Reading and pronouncing select passages from the present English Authors.

Copying in a fair and correct manner select English Essays.

When they can read English with fluency and write fairly legibly, Students shall begin to learn the Latin language on the following plan, to Wit. Ruddiman's Rudiments, Cordery, Erasmus, Eutropius, Cornelius, Nepos, with translations; Caesar's Commentaries & Salust without translations; but when the Parent or Guardian of the Student shall choose it the whole of these Authors shall be read with translations–Kennett's Roman Antiquities to be studied at the same time. When they can render Eutropius into correct English & explain the Government and connection of the words; then the Students shall commence the Study of the French Language on the following plan, to Wit,–Grammar, Telamachus, Cyrus, Gil-blas. If the Student is to be taught the Greek Language he will read, The Greek Grammar–the Gospels in Greek.

The rudiments of Geography on the plan of Guthrie.

After the Student commences the Study of the French Language, the Study of the French & Latin Language shall be associated, and the time so appropriated to each, that the course in both may be finished nearly at the same time.

When the Greek Language is Studied without the French the Student will commence it at the time prescribed for the French.

When the Latin, Greek, and French are all directed to be studied, the Study of Greek shall then commence so that the Student may be able to Read the Gospels in Greek and Translate them correctly when he finishes his course in the Preparatory School.

The English exercises shall be regularly continued, this Language being always considered as a primary object and the other Languages but Auxiliaries.

Any of the Languages (the English excepted) may be omitted if the Parent or Guardian of the Student shall so direct.

The Plan of Education under the Professorships of the University.

First–The President

Rhetoric & Belles lettres.

Rhetoric on the plan of Sheridan.

Belles Lettres, on the plan of Blair & Rollin Professorships.

Professorships.

First–Professor of Moral and political Philosophy and History.

Moral and political Philosophy by the Study of the following Authors.

Paley's Moral & Political Philosophy.
Montesquieu's Spirit of Laws.

Civil Government & political Constitutions.

Adams' Defence & De Lolme.
The Constitutions of the United States.
The Modern Constitution of Europe.

The Law of Nations.

Vattell's Law of Nations.
Burlamaquis principles of Natural and political law.

History.

Priestley's Lectures on History and General policy.
Millots Ancient and Modern History.
Hume's History of England with Smollets continuation.
Chronology on the most approved plan.

Second–Professor of Natural philosophy, Astronomy and Geography

Natural philosophy under the following heads–

General properties of Matter

Laws of Motion
Mechanical powers
Hydrostatics
Hydraulics
Pneumatics
Optics
Electricity
Magnetism

Geography
The Use of the Globes
The Geometrical, political & Commercial relations of the different Nations of the Earth
Astronomy on the plan of Furgerson

Third–Professor of Mathematics.

Arithmetic in a Scientific manner
Algebra, and the application of Algebra to Geometry
Euclid's Elements
Trigonometry and the application of Trigonometry to the Mensuration of heights and distances, of Surfaces & Solids, and Surveying and Navigation
Conic Section
The Doctrine of the Sphere & Sylinder

The projection of the Sphere
Spherical Trigonometry
The doctrine of fluxions
The doctrine of chances & Annuities

Fourth—Professor of Chymistry & the Philosophy of Medicine, Agriculture and the Mechanic Arts.
Chymistry upon the most approved plan.

Fifth—Professor of Languages.

The English language
Elegant Extracts in prose and verse
Scott's Collection

Latin Language
Virgil—Cicero's Orations—Horaces Epistles including his Art of poetry.
Greek Language, Lucian. Xenophon.

Thus far shall be the regular course of Study,—The remainder may be taught if requested.

The Professor of Languages to attend when required, the Reading of Cicero de officiis, and Horace & Livy in the Latin language, Longinus on the Sublime and the Orations of Demosthenes & Homer's Iliad in Greek.

The Rudiments of Languages are still to be attended to; the different forms and the figure of Speech will be noticed by the Professor, and Comments made on the Sentiments and beauties of the Authors.—parallel Sentences quoted—particular idioms observed; and all allusions to distant Customs and manners explained.

The Students under the 5th Professorship shall deliver twice a Week, to the Professor of Languages an English translation from some of the Latin or Greek Classics, in which, after expressing the sence of the Author, the Spirit and eligance of the translation are principally to be regarded.

The Students of the other Classes shall every Saturday deliver to the President an English composition on a subject of their own chusing, and he shall correct the Errors in Orthography, Grammar, Style or Sentiment, and make the necessary Observations thereon when he returns the Composition to the Writer.

A Student who shall pass an approved examination upon the Exercises of the Preparatory School shall be admitted upon the general establishment of the University.

Any Candidate shall be admitted into the University to attend the Classes of Rhetoric and Belles-lettres or as a Student under any of the three first Professorships who shall pass an approved examination upon the English language, the four first rules of Arithmetic, and the Rule of Three.

Any person may also be admitted as a Student under the fifth Professorship who can pass an approved examination on the English language and render Caesars Commentaries & Salust into English & explain the Government & connection of the words.

No specific Qualifications are required for a Student under the fourth Professorship alone.

The Preparatory School shall be considered as a branch of the Institution, and in all respects under the direction and regulation of the Trustees.

That the present Students who are not qualified to be entered on the General Establishment of the University, shall be Arranged to the Preparatory School & placed under the direction of the Tutors appointed to that part of the Institution.

That the Studies and exercises of these Students be so arranged after the next vacation as to remedy the defects of their past education, & come as nearly and as early as possible to the plan prescribed by the Board.

Resolved that the said plan of Education be referred back to the same Committee to draw an Ordinance to carry the same into effect. —Minutes of the Board of Trustees, Library of the University of North Carolina.

15. Academic laws and regulations of the University of North Carolina, 1795

Duty of President Professors &c.

1. That the President or in his absence the next in office superintend all the studies & particularly those of the senior class, & that every other teacher attend diligently on his respective Class.

2. That the President or other officers perform morning & evening prayer & examine the Students each Sunday evening on the questions previously given them on the general principles of Morality & religion.

3. That untill a professor shall be appointed for the purpose, the

president or next officer shall deliver a lecture once in the week on the principles of Agriculture, Botany, Mineralogy or Commerce.

4. That the officers of the University collectively be called the faculty & that they have power to make temporary regulations in the recess of the board & to inflict any punishment herein after mentioned.

5. That the President or next officer report annually or oftener if called upon to the trustees, the state of the University, diligence of the teachers, conduct of the Students & steward, & the necessity of makeing & repealing laws.

6. That no President or other officer be removed from his place without a fair hearing before the Authority from which he derived his appointment.

Duty of the Students

Of the Classes, Examinations &c.

1. That there be four literary Classes to be entered on annually & distinguished by the appelation of first, second, third & fourth.

2. That none be admitted into the first literary class as students, untill they shall have passed a competent examination by the faculty on Caesars Commentaries, Salust, Ovid, & Virgil or Other latin Boks equivalent & the Greek Grammar:

3. That the exercise of this Class be the Study of English Grammar, Roman antiquities & such parts of the roman historians, orators, & poets as may seem necessary to the Officers of the University; together with the study of the Greek Testament. It is to be understood that in case the studies allotted to the classes for this or the two following years shall be more than they can perform, then part of the same shall be taken up on the following year; But in case the class shall have performed the assigned duties before the end of the year then they shall anticipate part of the duties of the following year.

4. That none be admitted into the second or any other class untill they shall have passed a Competent examination on the exercise of the preceding Class.

5. That the exercise of the second class be Arithmetic, Bookkeeping, Geography including the use of the Globe, Grecian, Antiquities and Greek Classics.

6. That the exercise of the third class be the Mathematicks, Geometry, Surveying, Navigation, Algebra, Natural Philosophy & astronomy.

7. That the exercise of the fourth class be Logic, Moral Philosophy, principles of civil Government, Chronology, history antient & Modern,

the Bell lettre, & the revisal of what ever may appear necessary to the officers of the University.

8. That they only choose to study the sciences & the english Language be either formed into a class called the Scientific class, or else arranged with some of the literary classes when they shall be studying the science.

9. That they who shall enter the third or fourth classes not haveing been students in former classes shall pay a certain sum for the use of the University. That is to say for admission into the third class at or after the middle stage of its progress the sum of eight dollars, for entrance into the fourth class at any stage from the beginning to the middle period the sum of twelve & a half dollars & from the Middle period to the end the sum of fifteen dollars.

10. That in addition to the annual examinations, there shall be three quarterly examinations.

Time of Study, Vacations, &c.

11. That the students shall decently attend prayers every morning & evening. That morning prayer shall be at sunrise.

12. That from prayers to breakfast be study hours breakfast to be at Eight Oclock.

13. That One hour be allowed for Breakfast & amusement after which shall follow three hours of study & recitation, i.e. untill 12 Oclock.

14. That study hours commence again at two o'clock, & continue untill prayers at five Oclock, after which shall be a vacation untill 8 Oclock when the students shall retire to their respective lodgings & not leave them, without consent of their teacher untill prayers next morning.

15. That each class have a monitor, to be appointed by the teacher who shall note down those absent without leave, & the disorderly & the Vitious.

16. That all the students speak read or exhibit composition on saturday, A.M. & the same day P.M. be allowed them for amusement.

Duties moral & religious.

17. That all the students attend divine service on the sabbath, & Evening examination on the general principles of religion & morality, that they reverence the sabbath use no profane language nor speak

disrespectfully of religion, or any religious denomination of people. That they be not allowed to keep any ardent spirits in their Rooms nor associate with evil company, that they shall not play at any game of hazard or any other kind of game, nor make bets they shall treat their teachers with respect & also each other, according to the honour due to each class.

Pecuniary Duties.

18. That the Students in each room pay eight dollars per year, to be paid half yearly in advance to the professors or president having the care of the University, for room rent, repair accidental damages & for wilful damage pay fourfold. If the author of the damage cannot be ascertained, the damage shall be asses'd on the whole number of students in the University

19. The students in general shall observe the rules of decency & cleanliness.

20. No student shall be admitted to the honour of a degree untill he shall have settled all his pecuniary accounts at the University.

21. Each student shall prepare a book into which he shall enter these laws.

Of Trials & Punishments.

22. The Student charged shall have timely notice & testamony taken on the most solemn assurance, shall by the faculty or trustees be deemed Valid, without calling on a magistrate to administer an oath in legal form.

23. The punishments & grades of punishments shall be

1. admonition by any officer of the University 2. admonition by the faculty 3. admonition before the whole University, 4. Admonition before the trustees, 5. suspension. 6. Total & final expulsion.

24. No pecuniary mulcts shall be inflicted for non attendance on prayers or recitation, but besides admonition the officer of the University may transmit an abstract of the monitors bill as often as he choses, with a statement of the students negligence to his Guardian.

25. That the monitors bill be called for publickly every monday evening & every transgressor of these laws be brought to an account.

26. That these laws be publickly read once every year before the whole University or oftener if judged necessary & that one officer of the University deliver to the students an address on the necessity &

advantage of observing the laws; or that a student from the classes in rotation be appointed for that purpose.

27. That the sum of one Shilling per week be imposed on those Students who do not live at Commons, which shall be paid to the steward.

A True Coppy.

—Pettigrew Papers, the Southern Historical Collection, University of North Carolina.

16. The Trustees of the University of North Carolina Provide for the Examinations of the Students, 1795

December, 1795.

Resolved, That a committee of one member of the Board from each district in the state, shall attend the annual and semi-annual examinations of the students of the University; that this duty shall be performed by the members in rotation, agreeably to an alphabetical list of the names of the members of each district; and that it shall be the duty of the secretary regularly to notify the members whose duty it may be to perform that service.

That it shall be the duty of those committees respectively to make report to the next annual meeting of the Board of Trustees, of the progress of the students and the state of the institution; which report shall be signed by all the members of the committee who shall attend such examination.

SAMUEL ASHE. President.

The members of the Board of Trustees, whose duty it will be to attend the examination in July next, conformably to the foregoing resolution, are as follow:

For the district of Halifax, W. R. Davie,
Edenton, John Skinner,
Newbern, Frederick Harget,
Wilmington, William Hill,
Morgan, Joseph Dickson,
Salisbury, Alexander Martin,
Hillsborough, William Hinton,
Fayetteville, John Hay.

—*The North Carolina Journal*, June 6, 1796.

17. Liberty Hall Academy in Virginia is converted into a college, 1796

Whereas it has been communicated to this general assembly, that George Washington, President of the United States, has appropriated the shares which were directed to be subscribed, in his name, in the James River Canal Company, with the tolls and profits which shall accrue therefrom, to the use of Liberty Hall Academy, in the county of Rockbridge: And whereas the benevolent design of that most excellent citizen, will be better promoted by enlarging the nature of the said institution:

Section I. *BE it enacted*, That the academy, now stiled Liberty Hall Academy, shall be erected into a college, which shall be called and known by the name of the College of Washington, in Virginia.

Sec. II. IN this college there shall be four schools. viz:—One of Languages; one of Mathematics; one of Natural Philosophy and Astronomy, and one of Logic, Moral Philosophy and Belles Lettres; in each of which schools there shall be a professor, and as many tutors as shall, from time to time, be found necessary.

Sec. III. ONE of the professors shall be appointed president; and the said president and professors shall be a body corporate, by the name of "The President and Professors of the College of Washington in Virginia," and by that name shall have perpetual succession and a common seal.– By the name aforesaid, they shall be able and capable, in law, to have, purchase, receive, possess, enjoy and retain, to them and their successors forever, any lands, tenements, rents, goods or chattels, of what kind soever, which shall be given to them, or purchased by them for the use of the said college, and the same to sell, grant, demise, alien, or dispose of, in such manner as to them may appear most for the advantage of the said college: *Provided*, That the said president and professors shall not be capable of receiving endowments, whose annual nett profits shall exceed ten thousand dollars; and by the same name to sue and implead, be sued and impleaded, answer and be answered, in all courts of law and equity: and to grant degrees under their common seal.

Sec. IV. THE president and professors, or a majority of them, shall have the power of appointing a treasurer, tutors, and other subordinate officers, for the said college; of removing them when they see fit, and of prescribing rules and regulations for their conduct, in their respective offices. To the president and professors shall also appertain, the power of determining on, and adopting the proper system of education, for the different schools, and of framing and carrying into effect, rules and ordinances for the good order and government of the students and scholars of the said college.

Sec. V. AND for the purpose of appointing the president and professors of the said college, and perpetuating their succession, and for the more general government of the said college, the following persons are constituted a board of visitors: viz: The Governor of the commonwealth for the time being, Andrew Moore, James M'Dowell, Andrew Reed, John Caruthers, of Rockbridge, Archibald Stewart, Alexander St. Clair, John Coalter, of Augusta, John White, of Bath, John Stewart, William H. Cavendish, of Greenbrier, James Breckenridge, Robert Harvie, Henry Bowyer, Thomas Madison, William Willson, James Risque, of Botetourt, Christopher Clark, of Bedford, Nicholas Cabell and William Cabell, junior, of Amherst, who, or a majority of them, shall have the power of appointing the president and professors of the said college, of removing or suspending the same for good cause shewn, and of supplying vacancies in the said body; but no professor shall be admissible into his office, without first taking the oath of fidelity to the commonwealth.

Sec. VI. THE said visitors shall annually choose a Rector, who shall preside in their meetings, and whose duty it shall be to convene them as often as it shall appear necessary.

Sec. VII. THE said visitors, or a majority of them, shall fix the salaries of the president and professors, and the fees of tuition in the different schools, and shall have the power of making and establishing statutes and ordinances for the general government of the said college. They shall also have the power of inspecting and examining the accounts of the said college, and of enquiring into the management of its estate, and no real property belonging to it shall be sold without their consent. On the death, resignation, or refusal to act, of the rector or any of the visitors, it shall be lawful for the remaining visitors, or a majority of them, to supply such vacancies; and the rector and visitors, so elected, shall have the same powers and authority as those particularly named in this act. *Provided always,* That nine at least of the said visitors, shall reside within forty miles of the college, and that no person shall be capable of being elected, or of holding the office of a visitor, whose place of residence, is, or shall be more than sixty miles from the said college. And any visitor removing to a greater distance than sixty miles (except the governor of the commonwealth) from the college, after his election to the said office, and thereby leaving a less number than nine visitors within the said distance, shall, by such removal, vacate his office of visitor.

Sec. VIII. NOTHING in this act contained shall be constructed to give to the president and professors, or to the rector and visitors of the said college, the power of making any bye-law, rule, ordinance, statute, or regulation whatever, contrary to the constitution or laws of this commonwealth.

Sec. IX. THE rectors and visitors, before they enter upon the execution of the trust reposed in them by this act, shall severally take the following oath or affirmation, to be administered by a justice of the peace of the county of Rockbridge, and certified by him, to the said rector and visitors, to be recorded in their minutes, that is to say;

I, A.B. do swear (or affirm) that I will, to the best of my skill and judgment, faithfully and truly discharge the duties required of me, by an act, intituled, "*An act for erecting Liberty Hall Academy into a College,*" without favor, affection or partiality. So help me God.

Sec. X. *AND be it further enacted*, That until the president and professors shall be appointed for the said college of Washington, the property which has been appropriated to the use of Liberty Hall Academy, and the property which shall be appropriated to the use of the said college, shall be in the visitors thereof, and their successors, who shall have every power necessary for the management of the same, except the power of selling; and on the appointment of a president and professors, all the property aforesaid, real and personal, shall be transferred to, and vested in, the said president and professors.

Sec. XI. THIS *act shall* commence and be in force, from and after the passing thereof.—*Acts Passed at the General Assembly of the Commonwealth of Virginia*, 1796, pp. 26-28. Liberty Hall Academy had grown out of Augusta Academy, founded in 1749 in Rockbridge County. It had received charter by the State of Virginia in 1782 as Liberty Hall Academy.

18. Virginia's "Dartmouth College Case," 1796-1797

The Board having before them the late Act of the Legislature of Virginia erecting Liberty Hall into a College after maturely considering its contents unanimously declared it as their opinion that the same is an unjustifiable infringement of the Rights of the Corporation of Liberty Hall and an instance of Tyrannical imposition in the Legislature.

And moreover that it does not repeal the Act incorporating Liberty Hall Academy.

Therefore the Board resolved to persevere as they have hitherto in executing the powers invested in them.

On motion the Board appointed Doctor Campbell, Mr. Samuel Brown and Mr. S. Houston or any two of them a Comtee to draw up the reasons in full why this Board objects to the late Act erecting Liberty Hall into a College and why they resolve to persevere in executing the powers invested in them by the Act incorporating Liberty Hall. And to make Report at our next meeting.

The Comtee appointed at our last meeting to report in full at this the reasons why the Board objects to the Law erecting Liberty Hall Academy into a College and why they resolve to persevere in executing the powers invested in them by the Act incorporating them a Body Politic. Being asked if they were ready to report instead of reporting signified that the former Minute respecting the law objecting to needed first to be obliterated.

Whereupon after some deliberation the Board agreed that it should not be obliterated as a step out of due order. The Board therefore Resolved that it should stand but that it would have been more proper to have been expressed in the terms following:

We conceive said Act to be a singular instance of infringement on the rights of an incorporated body which had not by any act of theirs violated their tenure or gave cause for the abolition of their Charter.

Whereupon they gave it unanimously as their opinion, as follows:

1. A Corporation being an artificial person and the property belonging to this Corporation being held as private property cannot be at the disposal of the representatives of the people.

2. Because the Law is not only unjust in its nature but dangerous in its tendency: the same principle if admitted in one case may be extended to every such corporation throughout the State. Their charters may be violated and their estates in whatever way acquired may be wantonly sported with just as caprice or folly may dictate.

3. Because the business of education must be interrupted at this place for a considerable time and greatly impeading for the future. If the Corporation is dissolved the property being given by individuals would revert to the original Donors and in future the liberal will be discouraged from contributing to similar Institutions.

4. Because the Debts due to and from this Corporation cannot be legally recovered after its dissolution and as several such debts do exist it would be an act of injustice in the Corporation to suffer such a dissolution to take place.

5. Because the property of Liberty Hall having been committed to us in trust. We consider ourselves responsible for the use of the same and culpable if we suffer it tamely to be taken from us.

6. Because we are well assured that the late interference of our Legislature with regard to L. Hall is in a very great degree contrary to the wishes of those good citizens who for the promotion of virtue and literature gave largely of their estates to this Academy.

The Board having adopted the above as reasons for opposing the late Act erecting L. H. into a College.

Adjourned agreeably to order.—Minutes of the Trustees of Liberty Hall Academy, Rockbridge County, Virginia, January 31 and February 7, 1797. Given in James Morrison Hutcheson, "Virginia's 'Dartmouth College Case,'" *Virginia Magazine of History and Biography*, LI (April, 1943).

19. The act to convert Liberty Hall Academy into a college is repealed, 1797

Be *it enacted*, That the act passed at the last session of Assembly, intituled, *An act for erecting Liberty-Hall academy into a college*, shall be, and the same is hereby repealed.

Sec. II. AND *be it further enacted*, That the act passed in the year one thousand seven hundred and eighty-two, intituled, *An act for incorporating the rector and trustees of Liberty-Hall academy*, or so much thereof, as may have been repealed by the first recited act, shall be, and the same is hereby revived, and shall remain in as full force to all intents and purposes, as if the said first recited act had never been made. *Provided nevertheless*, That the said academy shall hereafter be called and known by the name of Washington.

Sec. III. THIS act shall commence and be in force from and after the passing thereof.—*Acts Passed at the General Assembly of the Commonwealth of Virginia*, 1797, p. 26.

20. The Senatus Academicus of Georgia makes rules for its government, 1799

Rule 1. Every Member shall attend and take his seat punctually at the hour to which the board stands adjourned.

2. Any Member intending to speak, shall rise and address the President, and when two members shall rise at the same time, the President shall determine, which shall speak first, and the other shall be in order to speak next, if he chooses.
3. Members shall not enter into private conversation, or read, whilst any other member is speaking.—Minutes of the Senatus Academicus of the University of Georgia, Vol. I, 1799-1803, p. 2. Verified typescript copy in the Southern Historical Collection, The University of Georgia.

21. The Senatus Academicus undertakes to locate a site for the University of Georgia, 1799-1800

Took up the resolution proposed by Mr. Early, to wit, the expediency of fixing upon a temporary seat only, of the University. After some debate, Mr. Early withdrew the same.

A Motion was made by Mr. Walker and seconded by Mr. Clay that this board adopt the following resolution, to wit, "Resolved, That it is not expedient at this time to fix on any site for the University either temporary or permanent." And the question being put thereon, the same was negatived.

A Motion was made by Judge Mitchell, seconded by Mr. Speaker, that the following resolution be adopted, "Resolved that this board do now proceed to determine on a place for the temporary seat of the University."

On Motion of Mr. Walker the further consideration of this resolution was postponed, until tomorrow evening.

The board then adjourned until tomorrow at four o'Clock P.M.

Saturday 30th November 1799.

The board met pursuant to adjournment.

The resolution proposed by Judge Mitchell that this board do now proceed to determine on a place for the temporary site of the University be at the present Academy of Columbia County.

A Motion was made by Judge Mitchell that Columbia be stricken out, and Hancock inserted.

A Motion was made by Mr. Speaker, that Hancock be stricken out, and Wilkes inserted.

A Motion was made by his Excellency the President, that Hancock be stricken out and Greene inserted.

A Motion was made by Mr. Lawson, that Greene be stricken out and Jefferson inserted.

And the question being put on inserting Jefferson the same was negatived.

And the question being put on Greene the same was negatived.

And the question being put on inserting Wilkes, the same was negatived.

And the question being put on Hancock the board was equally divided, so the question was lost.

A Motion was made by Mr. Clay, seconded by Mr. Jones, that the board adopt the following resolution, viz. "Resolved that it is the sense of this board, that the President is not entitled to a vote, unless there should be an equal number of votes, upon a question."

Upon motion of Mr. Speaker resolved that this board do now adjourn until Monday next at four O'Clock P.M. and the same was accordingly adjourned.

Monday 2nd December 1799.

The Board met pursuant to adjournment.

A Motion made by Mr. Speaker, seconded by Mr. Jones, that the following resolution, be substituted in lieu of the one proposed by Mr. Clay, to wit Resolved that the President shall have a vote in all questions before this board, and when by adding his vote to the Minority, it shall make the votes equal, then it shall be considered the question is undetermined. And the question being put thereon the same was agreed to.

A Motion was made by Mr. Early, that this board adopt the following resolution, to wit, Resolved, that the Academy in the County of (blank) be the temporary seat of the University.

And the question being put thereon, the same was agreed to.

A Motion was made by Mr. Jones that the blank be filled up with Columbia, and the question being put thereon the same was negatived.

A Motion was made by Mr. Early, that it be filled up with Wilkes. And the question being put thereon the same was negatived.

A Motion was made by Judge Mitchell that it be filled up with Hancock. And the question being put thereon, the same was negatived.

The Motion was made by Mr. Early that it be filled up with Greene. And the question being put thereon the same was negatived.

The Motion was made by Mr. Speaker, that it be filled up with Franklin. And the question being put thereon, the same was negatived.

A Motion was made by Judge Mitchell that the further consideration of filling up the blank be postponed, until the next meeting of the board. And the question being put thereon, the same was agreed to.

Upon Motion of Judge Carnes, Resolved that this board do now adjourn, until the third Monday in June next, and the same was accordingly adjourned until that period.

At a meeting of the Senatus Academicus of the State of Georgia in the executive Chamber in the State House at Louisville on Monday the 24th November 1800.

Read the Minutes of the former Meeting of this Board.

The Board then adjourned until tomorrow evening at four o'clock, to meet in the Executive Chamber.

The Board met pursuant to adjournment.

The Board then adjourned until tomorrow evening at half past four o'clock.

The Board met pursuant to adjournment.

A Motion was made by Mr. Walton seconded by Mr. Jones, that the blank left in the report for inserting the place where the building for a wing of the University shall be erected, be filled up with Columbia.

A Motion was made by Mr. Smith seconded by Mr. Walker that it be filled up with Greene.

A Motion was made by Mr. Clay seconded by Judge Carnes that it be filled up with Franklin.

A Motion was made by Judge Mitchell seconded by Mr. Jackson, that it be filled up with Hancock.

A Motion was made by Mr. Speaker, seconded by Mr. Clay, that it be filled up with Jackson.

Resolved, that the filling up the said blank be postponed till tomorrow evening.

The Board adjourned till tomorrow half past four o'clock P.M.

Thursday 27th November 1800.

The Board met pursuant to adjournment.

Board resumed the consideration of the report of the Committee, and took up the resolution with the several amendments proposed thereto, for filling up the blank left in said report, for inserting the place where the wing of a building of a University should be erected, and on the question to fill up the said blank with the word *Jackson*, the same was negatived.

The question was then put to fill up the same with *Hancock*, which was disagreed to.

The question was then put to fill up the same with *Franklin*, which was also disagreed to, And the question was then put to fill up the same with *Greene*, which was agreed to.

Your Committee recommend that a building be erected in the County of *Greene*, to serve as a wing to the University, and that a Committee consisting of five be appointed by this board, who, or a majority of them are authorized to receive sealed proposals and contract for the building a wing of the University sufficient for the accommodation of One hundred students, of such dimensions, and on such plan as in their judgment will best promote the good of the institution.

That a person be appointed to instruct the Youth in the said institution, and to commence the duties thereof, as the presiding professor, with a Salary of One thousand five hundred dollars per Annum, as soon as he shall notify his acceptance thereof to the president of this board, and for that appointment they recommend professor Meigs of Yale College.—*Ibid.*, 4-16.

22. THE SENATUS ACADEMICUS REPORTS A PLAN OF EDUCATION FOR THE UNIVERSITY OF GEORGIA, 1800

Your Committee with deference report the following plan of education to be taught in six years, subject to the revision and alteration of the Professor to be appointed as above with the consent of the board of trustees.

In the first and second years Latin and Greek shall be taught, and English read occasionally at the discretion of the Tutor.

In the third year, Latin, Greek and Kennet's Antiquities; English grammar, Arithmetic, and Geography; two or more of the pupils should deliver pieces committed to memory each day in rotation.

In the fourth year, Greek and Latin occasionally, English grammar to be reviewed weekly, Arithmetic to be continued; Euclid's elements or some other treatise on Geometry, at the option of the Tutor. And the students in this year should once in each week be required to write a letter or some piece of simple composition for the inspection of the Tutor and pieces should be pronounced as in the last year.

In the fifth year Latin and Greek authors and English grammar to be occasionally reviewed; Trigonometry, Surveying and other practical branches of the Mathematics, with Algebra should be taught; composition and public speaking should be attended to as in the last year.

In the sixth year natural and moral philosophy, and the Belles Lettres should be taught, and compositions written weekly as in the preceding years. If either of the tutors should be acquainted with the French language, that may be taught in addition to, or instead of, the Latin and Greek, as Parents and Guardians may choose.

Your committee report that the following apparatus and books be purchased for the use of the institution, to wit,

A pair of globes of about twenty inches diameter supposed to be worth about	$130.00
Mathematical instruments including such as are usually used in surveying	$170.00

School Books.

Rudimen's Rudiments	12	Copies	
Cordery	12	do	
Aesops fables	12	do	
Corneilius Nepos	12	do	
Caesar's Commentaries	12	do	Del. Ed.
Ovid's Metamorphoses	12	do	
Virgil	12	do	
Horace	12	do	
Caesar's Orations	12	do	
Terence	6	do	
Wittendal's Greek Grammar	6	do	
Greek Testament	6	do	
Lucian	4	do	
Xenophon	4	do	
Guthrie's Geography	12	do	Cary's Ed.
Cary's Atlas	2	do	
Ainsworth's Dictionary			large edit.
do do	4	do	small
Johnson's Dictionary			folio
Young Man's best Companion	4	do	
Sheridan's Art of Speaking	4	do	
Do's Pronouncing grammar	2	do	

Lowth's english grammar	6	do
Euclid's Elements	2	do
Petour's Navigation	2	Copies
Robinson's do	1	do
Marten's Natural Philosophy	2	do
Enfield's ...... do	2	do
Blair's Lectures	4	do
Rollin's Belles lettres		do
Hutchinson's Moral Philosophy		
Paley's ...... do		

Books for the use of the Students at intervals when not engaged in the Academical Studies, to wit, Rollin's Ancient History; Vertot's Rome; Ferguson's Roman History; Gibbon's decline and fall of the Roman Empire; Antient and Modern Europe; Gordon's Tacitus; Livy in english; Gillies' history of Greece; Anacharses's travels; Humes history of England with the continuations; Robinson's Works including his history of Charles the fifth, of Scotland, of America, and his India; Doctor Adam Smith's Works; Watson's history of the low Countries; History of France by ; De Ritz Memoirs; Sully's Memoirs; Voltaires Age of Louis the 14th & 15th in english; Do Charles the 12th do; Abbe Raynal's history of the East and West Indies in english; Ferguson's history of Civil society; Montesquieu's spirit of Laws; Vattel's law of Nations; Blackstone's Commentaries; De Lolme on the Constitution of England; Civil Law; Pope's, Swift's, Addison's, Temple's, and Locke's Works; Bolingbroke's Political works; Moore's travels; Blair's Atterbury's Seed's, Didderidge's Jorbin's and Witherspoon's sermons; Tiltotson's Works entire; Newton on the Prophecies; Letters of John Newton; Scougal's life of God in the Soul of Man; Dignity of Human Nature; Paley's evidences; Burnett's discources; Milton's paradise lost and regained; Pope's Iliad and Odyssey; Young's night thoughts; Gay's, Parnell's and Grey's poems; Dryden's works; including his Virgil; Quintilian in English; Longinus on the Sublime, in english; Demosthenes's Orations in english, and the American edition of the Encyclopedia.

Your Committee gave notice in one of the public Newspapers of Savannah, one of Augusta, and one of Louisville, that they would receive lists of subscriptions for Money, to be advanced in aid of the establishment of this institution.—*Ibid*, 16-19.

23. Thomas Jefferson to Joseph Priestly on the University of Virginia, 1800

We have in that state a college (Wm. & Mary) just well enough endowed to draw out the miserable existence to which a miserable constitution has doomed it. It is moreover eccentric in it's position, exposed to bilious diseases as all the lower country is, & therefore abandoned by the public care, as that part of the country itself is in a considerable degree by it's inhabitants. We wish to establish in the upper & healthier country, & more centrally for the state, an University on a plan so broad & liberal & *modern*, as to be worth patronizing with the public support, and be a temptation to the youth of other states to come and drink of the cup of knowledge & fraternize with us. The first step is to obtain a good plan; that is, a judicious selection of the sciences, & a practicable grouping of some of them together, & ramifying of others, so as to adapt the professorships to our uses & our means. In an institution meant chiefly for use, some branches of science, formerly esteemed, may be now omitted; so may others now valued in Europe, but useless to us for ages to come. As an example of the former, the oriental learning, and of the latter, almost the whole of the institution proposed to Congress by the Secretary of War's report of the 5th inst. Now there is no one to whom this subject is so familiar as yourself. There is no one in the world who, equally with yourself, unites this full possession of the subject with such a knowledge of the state of our existence, as enables you to fit the garment to him who is to *pay* for it & to *wear* it. To you therefore we address our solicitations, and to lessen to you as much as possible the ambiguities of our object, I will venture even to sketch the sciences which seem useful & practicable for us, as they occur to me while holding my pen. Botany, Chemistry, Zoology, Anatomy, Surgery, Medicine, Nat. Philosophy, Agriculture, Mathematics, Astronomy, Geology, Geography, Politics, Commerce, History, Ethics, Law, Arts, Fine arts. This list is imperfect because I make it hastily, and because I am unequal to the subject. It is evident that some of these articles are too much for one professor & must therefore be ramified; others may be ascribed in groups to a single professor. This is the difficult part of the work, & requires a head perfectly knowing the extent of each branch, & the limits within which it may be circumscribed, so as to bring the whole within the powers of the fewest professors possible, & consequently within the degree of expence practicable for us. We should propose that the professors follow no other calling, so that their whole time may be given to their academical functions; and we should propose to draw from Europe the first characters in science, by considerable temptations, which would not need to be repeated after the first set should have prepared fit successors & given reputation to the institution. From some splendid characters I have received offers most perfectly reasonable & practicable.—Paul Leicester Ford (ed.), *The Writings of Thomas Jefferson*, VII, 407-9.

24. The Legislature of North Carolina repeals the law on escheats for the support of the University, 1800

I. *Be it enacted by the General Assembly of the state of North-Carolina, and it is hereby enacted by the authority of the same,* That from and after the passing of this act, all acts or clauses of acts, which have heretofore granted power to the Trustees of the University of North-Carolina to seize and possess any escheated or confiscated property, real or personal, shall be, and the same is hereby repealed and made void.

II. *And be it further enacted,* That all escheated or confiscated property which the said Trustees, their Agents or Attornies, have not legally sold, by virtue of the said Laws, shall from hence revert to the State, and henceforth be considered as the property of the same, as though such laws had never been passed.—Iredell, *The Public Acts of the General Assembly of North Carolina*, II, 150.

II

1801–1810

1. Charter of South Carolina College, 1801

WHEREAS, the proper education of youth contributes greatly to the prosperity of society, and ought always to be an object of legislative attention; and whereas, the establishment of a college in a central part of the State, where all its youth may be educated, will highly promote the instruction, the good order and the harmony of the whole community:

I. *Be it therefore enacted*, by the honorable the Senate and the House of Representatives, now met and sitting in General Assembly, and by the authority of the same, That his Excellency the Governor, his Honor the Lieutenant Governor, the honorable the President of the Senate, and the Speaker of the House of Representatives, the honorable the Associate Judges of the Court of Equity, shall be, ex-officio, together with General Charles C. Pinckney, H. W. Desaussure, Thomas Taylor, the Reverend D. E. Dunlap, the Reverend Mr. John Brown of Lancaster, Wade Hampton, John Chesnut, James B. Richardson, Dr. Isaac Alexander, Henry Dana Ward, the Rev. Samuel W. Yongue, William Falconer, and Bartlee Smyth, be trustees, to continue in office for the term of four years from the passing of this Act, and at the expiration of the said four years, and every four years thereafter, the legislature to nominate thirteen trustees to succeed the said thirteen persons above named, one body politic and corporate in deed and in law, by the name of "The Trustees of the South Carolina College;" and that by the said name they and their successors shall and may have perpetual succession, and be able and capable in law to have, receive, and enjoy, to them and their successors, lands, tenements and hereditaments, of any kind or value, in fee, or for life or years, and personal property of any kind whatsoever, and also all sums of money of any amount whatsoever, which may be granted or bequeathed to them for the purpose of building, erecting, endowing and supporting the said college in the town of Columbia.

II. And be it enacted by the authority aforesaid, That there shall be a stated meeting of the said trustees on the first Wednesday in December in each year, during the session of the Legislature; and that the president of the said college, and four of the said trustees, shall have full power to call occasional meetings of the board whenever it shall appear to them necessary; and that at all stated meetings the president of the board of trustees aforesaid and ten of the trustees shall be the number to constitute a quorum, and to fill up, by ballot, any vacancies that may occur in the said trustees, except those who are hereby declared to be trustees ex-officio; and the president and six of the other trustees shall be the number to constitute an occasional meeting; and the said trustees, or a quorum of them, being regularly convened, shall be capable of doing or transacting all the business and concerns of the said college; but more particularly of electing all the customary and necessary officers of the said institution, of fixing their several salaries, of removing any of them for neglect or misconduct in office, of prescribing the course of studies to be pursued by the students; and, in general, of framing and enacting all such ordinances and by-laws as shall appear to them necessary for the good government of the said college: Provided the same be not repugnant to the laws of this State nor of the United States.

III. *And be it enacted* by the authority aforesaid, That the head of the said college shall be styled "The President," and the masters thereof shall be styled "The Professors;" but professors, while they remain such, shall never be capable of holding the office of trustee; and the president and professors or a majority of them, shall be styled "The Faculty of the College;" which faculty shall have the power of enforcing the ordinances and by-laws adopted by the trustees for the government of the pupils, by rewarding or censuring them, and finally, by suspending such of them as, after repeated admonitions, shall continue disobedient or refractory, until a determination of a quorum of trustees can be had; but that it shall be only in the power of a quorum of trustees, at their stated meeting, to expel any student of the said college.

IV. *And be it enacted* by the authority aforesaid, That the trustees of the said college shall and may have a common seal for the business themselves and their successors, with liberty to change or alter the same, from time to time, as they shall think proper; and that, by their aforesaid name, they and their successors shall and may be able to implead and be impleaded, answer and be answered unto, defend and be defended, in all courts of law within this State: and to grant, bargain, sell or assign, any lands, tenements, hereditaments, goods or chattels; and to act and do all things whatsoever, for the benefit of the said college, in as ample a manner as any person or body politic or corporate can or may by law.

V. *And be it enacted* by the authority aforesaid, That the trustees of the said college are hereby authorized and empowered to draw out of the treasury of this State the sum of fifty thousand dollars, to be appropriated to the purpose of erecting a building of brick or stone, and covered with tile or slate, suitable to the accommodation of the students of the said college, and suitable for fully carrying on the education of the said students, and for the erection of such other buildings as may be necessary for the use of said college; and that the comptroller be authorized and empowered, upon application of the said trustees, to pay over to said trustees the sum of six thousand dollars, yearly and every year, to be appropriated to the purpose of paying the salaries of the faculty of the said college, and for the further support of the same; and that the trustees of the said college shall be accountable for the proper appropriation of the said monies, to the comptroller, who shall report thereon annually to the legislature.

VI. *And be it enacted* by the authority aforesaid, That, this Act shall be deemed a public Act, and as such shall be judicially taken notice of, without special pleading, in all the courts of law or equity within this State.

VII. *And be it further enacted* by the authority aforesaid, That the said trustees, with the concurrence of the commissioners of Columbia, shall be empowered to make choice of any square or squares, yet unsold, in the town of Columbia, for the purpose of erecting said college, and the buildings attached thereto, having strict reference to every advantage and convenience necessary for such institution.—Cooper, *Statutes at Large of South Carolina*, V, 403-5.

2. The Trustees of the University of Georgia adopt a course of study, 1801

Resolved, That the established course of study, and Books of Instruction in the University be as follows, to wit,

1st Freshman's Class.

Virgil, Cicero's Orations, Greek Testament, Clarke's introduction to making latin, Arithmetic and Book keeping interspersed with frequent essays in Elocution, both before their respective classes in the presence of their Tutor, and before the University collected.

2d. Sophomore Class.

Continuation of languages, with two or three of the first books of Homer's Iliad, Horace, Algebra, Geometry, Mensuration of Superficies and Solids, Conic Sections, Plane and Spherical Trigonometry, with their application to Navigation and Surveying, and the ascertaining of heights and distances.–Geography, particularly the astronomical part, with a frequent and thorough use of the Terrestrial Globe.–Frequent essays in composition and public speaking, and reading should be considered as particularly useful during the year. English Grammar.

3d. Junior Class.

Astronomy, with the application of its Principles to the determination of Geographic longitudes and latitudes by observations of solar eclipses, by the eclipses of Jupiter's satellites, and by the Lunar observation.–The use of the celestial Globe, Natural Philosophy, to be taught in all possible cases by experiment. Chemistry with actual experiments demonstrative of its principles. The out-line of the Linnean System of Botany. Cicero de Oratore should be perfectly read this year, together with occasional attention to the Greek language. Logic, Priestly's Lectures of History. Forensic disputations in presence of the Tutors. Once or twice a week composition and essays on Elocution.

4th. Senior Class.

Rhetoric, Moral Philosophy, Laws of Nature and Nations, The constitution of the United States, and of the individual States. Forensic disputations and composition.

Books

1st. Freshman's Class.

Ruddiman's Latin Grammar; Westminster Greek Grammar; Ainsworths Latin Dictionary; Schrevolius's Greek Lexicon; Virgil Delphini, Clarke's introduction to making Latin; Pikes Arithmetic; Cicero Delphini.

2d. Sophomore Class.

Homer's Iliad; Ward's Mathematics; Hammond's Algebra; Horatius Delphini; Bonnycastle's Mensuration; Simpson's Conic Sections; Atkinson's Navigation; Gibson's Surveying; Morse's Geography; English Grammar by Doctor Lowth.

3d. Junior Class.

Ferguson's Astronomy; Ewings Practical Astronomy; Enfield's Natural Philosophy; Priestly's Lectures on History; Duncan's Logic; Cicero de Oratore.

4th. Senior Class.

Blair's Rhetorical Lectures; Paley's moral Philosophy; Vattel's law of Nature and Nations.

Resolved, That the following Books and Instruments be purchased by the President for the Use of the University, viz.

Adams's Lectures Octo.	5 vol.	Bonnycastle's Algebra	1-12 vo.
Gregory's Oeconomy of Nature	3.	Bonnycastle's Mensuration	1.
Cavello on Electricity	3.	Zimmerman on National pride	1- 8 vo.
Priestly on Air	3.	Vince's Hydrostatic's	1- ”
Chaptal's Chemistry	3.	Howard's Geometry	1- ”
Goldsmith's animated Nature	4.	Vince on Fluxions	1- ”
Fourcroy's Chemistry	5.	Simpson's Euclid	1- ”
Ainsworth's Latin Dictionary	1.	Simpson's Conic Sections	1- ”
Schrevolius's Lexicon	1.	Boyer's French Dictionary	1- ”
Fergusons Lectures	1.	Ewings Practical Astronomy	1- ”
Darwin's Zoonomia	2.	Wood's Mechanic's	1- ”
Darwins Phytologia	1.	Burretti's Italian Dictionary	1- 4
Darwins Botanie	1.	Vince's practical astronomy	1
Paley's Moral Philosophy	1.	Emerson's mechanic's	1
Blair's Lectures on Rhetoric	2.	a mercurial Thermometer.	
Vattel's Law of Nations	1.	a Barometer.	

–Minutes of the Board of Trustees of the University of Georgia, 1794-1817, Vol. I, 38-39. Original in the General Library, the University of Georgia. Photocopy in the Southern Historical Commission, the University of North Carolina.

3. A COMMITTEE OF THE TRUSTEES FIXES THE SITE FOR SOUTH CAROLINA COLLEGE, MAY 24, 1802

That in fixing upon a proper site whereon to erect the college at Columbia, they have met with considerable difficulty. The law establishing said college empowers to make choice of any square or squares of land yet unsold, for the purpose of erecting thereon the necessary buildings. Under this restriction your committee could not please themselves fully and at the same time comply with the law.... Amongst the unsold squares in the town of Columbia, there is not at present any two or more squares nearly contiguous which would be eligible sites for said college. Your committee anxious, however, to have so valuable an institution located and speedily organized, would be unanimous in favor of erecting said college on a public square, known by the name of Moultrie Square in the plan of the town of Columbia, was it not that said square lay too near a mill pond, now erecting by Mr. Purvis on Rocky Branch, just above where the road leading from Columbia to Granby crosses the same.... From this consideration your committee beg leave rather to report a square of land to the eastward of the State House as being the most eligible site whereon to erect the South Carolina College.—Edwin L. Green, *A History of the University of South Carolina*, pp. 15, 16.

4. A COMMITTEE OF TRUSTEES OF SOUTH CAROLINA COLLEGE REPORT ON PLANS FOR THE PHYSICAL PLANT, MAY 26, 1802

That after attentively considering the several plans rendered in to the trustees they were of opinion that no one is sufficiently perfect in the internal arrangements to be entitled to an exclusive adoption. They have therefore from a view of the whole, from considering the letter of Mr. Asa Messer, and their own knowledge of the subject, thought proper to recommend to the board certain principles on which in their opinion an appropriate plan should be predicated:

1st. The building should be calculated to accommodate one hundred students and three professors, allowing two students to each room generally, and three of the youngest to a few, and one room to each professor; this will require about forty-eight rooms.

2d. That as the health and comfort of the students is a primary consideration, each room should be twenty-four feet long and sixteen broad and open to the north and south. These dimensions will admit of two windows in each front and a partition at eight feet distance from the north side, which will be a sitting room of eighteen (sixteen) feet square and a smaller room of sixteen feet by eight feet, which may, if thought necessary, be sub-divided into two studies of eight feet square.

3d. That to preserve order and discipline every six rooms should form a separate division of the building; that is, the building should be three stories high and a staircase run up between every other two rooms; the doors all opening on the front of the building into an entry six feet wide leading to the staircase, and common to every two rooms. Separating the house after this manner by partition walls run up through the roof will also be a great protection from fire.

4th. It will be necessary to have a chapel or hall forty feet by fifty feet, two lecturing rooms, a library and a few spare rooms that may be converted to very excellent purposes.

If the above ideas be approved of, it will be necessary to have a building of the following plan and dimensions:

A center building fifty feet square, which will give you on the first story a half fifty by forty and leave a vestibule of ten feet for the staircase; in the second story a lecturing room, and library, and an entry.

The first story of the center building we recommend to be twenty-eight feet high; the second story fifteen feet high; the roof flat or nearly so, with a balustrade for an observatory; and covered with sheathing paper, etc.

5th. We recommend that from the center building there should extend two wings, one eastwardly, the other westwardly, each one hundred and sixty feet in length. These according to the above plan will furnish forty-eight rooms.

That the foundation of the whole building should be raised four feet from the ground, leaving cellars in the foundation of six feet in height.

That the first story of the wings be eleven feet high; the second be ten feet high; and the third be nine feet high.

And that at some future day when the funds of the college will admit of it, a balustrade shall be carried around the roof, for which purpose it should be made as flat as possible, consistently with security from leaking; and to be covered with slate or tile.

According to the above plan the width of the wings must be twenty-seven feet; and the length and narrowness of the building can be very handsomely relieved by means of pediments judiciously placed.

6th. With regard to the thickness of the walls, your committee are of opinion that it will be sufficient to make the foundation two and one-half bricks; the outer wall of the first story, two bricks; all the other walls, one and one-half bricks.

7th. Your committee cannot dismiss the subject without warmly acknowledging their obligation to the artists who have favored them with plans, particularly those gentlemen whose names are herein alphabetically written, viz: Bolter, Clark, Mills, McGrath and Nicholson, and Smith. The designs which they have furnished afford handsome specimens of American talent; and if in justice they feel themselves obliged to recommend Mr. Mills and Mr. Clark to the particular attention of the board on account of the taste, ingenuity, and variety of their designs, it is not without a sincere and hearty wish that they had premiums to bestow upon every one of the others above named.

As the front ornaments of the building are not material to the internal arrangements, your committee beg leave to submit the adoption of a front to the taste of the board.—Green, *op. cit.*, 17-19.

5. Report on examination at the University of North Carolina, 1802

The Freshmen in the University, were examined in Virgil, Latin Introduction, and Greek Testament; the Sophomores, in Cicero, Geography, Arithmetic & English Grammar; the Juniors, in Erving's Synopsis, Algebra, and Ferguson's Astronomy; the Seniors, in Adams on the American and De Lolme on the English Constitution.

An address from the Committee to the young Gentlemen pointed out the defects they had observed in their performances, and the irregularities which had occurred in their conduct, in a manner so paternal, affectionate and reluctant, and mixed with such unreserved praise where it was due, as must have made a salutary impressions upon their minds.—*Connecticut Journal* (New Haven), August 5, 1802. Given in Vera M. Butler, Education as Revealed by New England Newspapers Prior to 1850 (Doctoral Dissertation, Temple University, 1935), p. 43.

6. Laws of the Senatus Academicus for the government of the University of Georgia, 1803

I. The Government of the College at Athens shall be vested in the President, Professors and Tutors, legally elected, qualified, and introduced into Office.[1]

II. The President shall have power to direct in all matters relating to the College;– to govern the undergraduate Students and the resident Graduates, and to punish all Crimes and offences committed by them against the laws of the College; unless in cases, in which the concurrence of the Professors and Tutors is made necessary by Law.

III. The Professors and Tutors, severally, shall have power to govern the undergraduate Students, and to punish them for any crime, where the penalty by law does not exceed fifty cents.

IV. Every judgment of expulsion, dismission for fault and rustication for any term longer than nine Months, shall be by the President, Professors and Tutors, and the same shall be in writing, and published in such manner as the President shall direct.

V. Any Student charged with a crime punishable by expulsion, dismission, or rustication, shall, at least three days before his trial be furnished with a copy in writing of the charge or charges against him. And copies of all judgments of expulsion, dismission, or rustication, on application to the President, shall be given to all persons concerned. And if any Student shall apprehend himself aggrieved by any such judgment, he shall have liberty at any time within thirty days after the same shall have been given, of applying to the President by a petition, in writing, and on such petition the President shall, within a convenient time, order a new trial to be had, and provided, on such

1. Few features of higher education in this country are so conspicuous as its imitative nature. This characteristic finds abundant illustration in collegiate rules and especially in regulations governing the conduct of students. Among the first actions of boards of trustees of new colleges was the appointment of committees to find out about the rules and regulations of old institutions. Many of these ran to a fixed pattern and most of them reflected during the period before 1860 the climate of Calvinism and extreme pietism in which most of the institutions generally found themselves and of which they were themselves integral parts. The rules and regulations of an educational institution reflect its philosophy of education as well as its views on human conduct. Scores of materials on this subject have been collected and now are in the Southern Historical Collection of the University of North Carolina.

When Jefferson drew up "the rules for the University of Virginia he is supposed to have been considerably influenced by the rules then in force at Harvard. He possessed copies not only of these but of the contemporary rules of South Carolina College." (See Roy J. Honeywell, *The Educational Work of Thomas Jefferson*, [Cambridge: Harvard University Press, 1931], pp. 279-80.) A comparison of these rules below shows close similarity on several matters.

new trial, the former judgment shall be confirmed, such student still apprehending himself aggrieved, or in case he shall be a minor, his parent, or Guardian, shall have the liberty of bringing a petition to the board of Trustees for relief; which petition he shall lodge with the President, within thirty days after the said new trial: and the President shall lay the said petition before the board of Trustees at their next meeting.

VI. Annually at the Public Commencement shall be appointed a committee (which shall consist of not less than three members of the Board of Trustees) to be called the Prudential Committee; which shall be authorized and required, to order such repairs of the College and other College Buildings and appurtenances, as they shall judge necessary—to Audit the accounts of the Treasurer and the Steward—to make an annual Statement and report of the expenditures of the College, and state of the Treasury, and of the revenue and funds of the College—to examine and adjust all accounts which any person or persons may have with the College, and shall lay before them; and where balances shall be found due to any such person or persons, to give orders on the treasurer for the payment of them, to institute or cause to be instituted in the name of the Board of Trustees suits for the recovery and preservation of the College property and interest, whenever it shall be necessary—and to do and manage all other matters and things, whereunto they are or shall be further authorized or required, by law, or by any special resolve of the Board of Trustees.

VII. In case of the death of the President, it shall be the duty of the Prudential Committee to meet immediately at the College; and to make such regulations, and give such orders and directions as they shall judge necessary; which the Professors, Tutors and Students, shall observe untill there shall be a meeting of the Senatus Academicus, which meeting the Committee shall call, as soon as may be convenient.

Chapter II.

Of admission into the College; of the distinction of the Classes; of resident Graduates; and of the manners of the Students.

I. Candidates for admission into the College shall be examined by the President, or under his direction, by one or more of the Professors, or Tutors; and no one shall be admitted, unless he shall be found able to read, translate, and parse Cicero, Virgil, and the Greek Testament, and to write true latin in prose; and shall also have learned the rules of vulgar arithmetic; and shall produce satisfactory evidence of a blameless life and conversation; nor untill some sufficient person shall have given to the President and Board of Trustees a bond for the payment of his quarter bills to be approved by the Prudential Committee from time to time, so long as he shall continue a member of the College.

II. Every candidate, at his admission, shall receive a Copy of the laws of the College, which being signed by the President, shall be the evidence of his admission: and being admitted he shall be obliged to pay all College dues (except for victualling) when he shall be absent as well as present, so long as he shall continue a member of the College.

III. Every candidate for admission to an advanced standing shall be examined by the President and one or more of the Professors, or, Tutors, or, under the direction of the President, by two or more of the Professors and Tutors: And no such candidate shall be admitted to, such standing in the College, unless he shall be found fully qualified in all branches of learning proper for the same; nor until he shall have first paid to the Treasurer, a sum equal to the whole of the Tuition money, which shall have been paid by others of the Class, into which he is admitted. And when any Scholar after a dismission from the College shall be readmitted, he shall first pay to the Treasurer, a sum equal to the whole of the tuition Money, which he should have paid had he not been dismissed. Any scholar, however, who comes recommended from any other College may be admitted without any pecuniary consideration, to the standing for which he shall be found qualified on an examination, as before directed for the admission of Candidates to an advanced standing.

IV. Masters and Bachelors of Arts, who shall signify to the President their purpose of residing at the College or in Athens with a view of pursuing literature, under his directions, and under the government of the College, and give a sufficient bond to the Board of Trustees for the payment of their quarter bills, shall be considered as resident Graduates and students of the College.

V. Every Student, whether a Graduate or undergraduate, shall be subject to the laws and government of the College and shew in speech and behaviour, all proper respect and obedience to the President, Professors and Tutors of the College.

VI. The undergraduate students shall be divided into four distinct Classes, the first year they shall be called Freshmen; the Second Sophomores; the third Junior-Sophisters; and the fourth Senior-Sophisters: And in order to preserve a due subordination among the Students, the Classes shall give and receive, in the course of their Collegiate-life those tokens of respect which tend to the preservation of due subordination.

VII. It shall be the duty of the Senior-Class to inspect the lower Classes and expecially of the Freshman Class; and to instruct them in the Customs of the College, and in that graceful and decent behaviour toward Superiors, which politeness and a just and reasonable subordination require.

Chapter III.

Of the Religious Worship and Order of the College: and on Monitors.

I. It shall be the duty of the President, Professors, and Tutors, diligently to inspect and watch over the manners and behaviour of the Students, and in all proper methods both by example and precept, to recommend to them virtuous and blameless life, and a diligent attention to the publick and private duties of religion.

II. The President, or in his absence, one of the Professors, or one of the Tutors, shall pray, every morning and evening in the Chapel, and read a Chapter, or some suitable portion of scripture. And every undergraduate Student shall be obliged to attend, upon the penalty of six & a quarter Cents for every instance of absence, and of three Cents for being tardy, or egressing, without a sufficient reason.

III. Monitors shall be appointed by the President, who shall be furnished with bills, in which they shall note down those, who are absent from, come late to, or egress from, prayer or other public exercises, on which the Students are by law obliged to attend; which bills they shall deliver to the President, a Professor or a Tutor, whenever they shall be required.

Chapter IV.

Of the Course of Academic Literature and Instruction in the College.

I. The President, Professors and Tutors shall instruct the undergraduate Students in the learned languages, and liberal arts and sciences, and the whole course of academic Literature.

II. The Senior Class shall be under the especial instruction of the President: Each Tutor shall take the care of, and instruct the particular class committed to his charge by the President: The Professors shall deliver public, and private lectures and give instruction to the Classes and Students, in the several branches of Science which they severally profess, under the direction of the President.

III. The established course of study in the College shall be as follows, viz.

The first or Freshman Class shall study Virgil, Cicero's Oratore, Greek Testament, Arithmetic, Bookkeeping and practice Elocution. The second class shall read Homer, Homer's Iliad, Algebra, Geometry, Mensuration of Superfices and Solids, the ascertaining of heights and distances, Conic Sections, Plane and Spherical Trigonometry, Navigation, Surveying, Geography, Composition, English Grammar, and practise Public Speaking. The third Class shall study Astronomy, determinations of Geographic Longitudes and Latitudes by Observations of Eclipses, and the Lunar Observation, and use of the Celestial Globe, Natural & experimental Philosophy. Chemistry. Botany. Cicero de Oratore, Logic. Priestly's lectures on History. Forensic Disputation. Composition and public Speaking. The fourth Class shall study, Rhetoric, Laws of Nature and Nations, the Constitution of the United States, & the Constitution of the individual States. Moral Philosophy. Forensic disputations and Compositions.

IV. If any student shall appear on examination deficient in those branches of knowledge, which, according to the regulary course of literature in the College, he hath been pursuing, it shall be the duty of the President or his Tutor, to admonish him of such deficiency that he may be incited to apply with greater diligence to study: And it, notwithstanding at the next succeeding public examination holden after an interval of at least six months, he shall appear so deficient as to be unfit for his standing, and unable with profit and reputation to pursue his studies with his Class, he shall be degraded by the President, Professors and Tutors, to the next lower class or dismissed from the College.

V. If any Scholar shall frequently neglect the public exercises, or if he shall spend the hours of study in idleness, and manifest a prevailing inclination to a dissolute behaviour; or if he entices others from their studies and draw them into bad practices, he shall be dismissed from the College.

VI. On the Wednesday before the twentieth of March annually, the Senior Sophisters shall be examined, under the direction of the President, by the Professors, Tutors and other Gentlemen of Liberal education, who may be present, as to their knowledge and proficiency in the learned languages, and the liberal Arts & Sciences; and being found well skilled in them, and the whole course of academic literature, shall be advanced to the standing of Candidates for the degree of Bachelor of Arts; and having made all necessary preparation for commencement, the President may give them leave of absence from the College, untill the Saturday before the Commencement.

Chapter V.

Of Vacations, and of Absence from the College.

I. There shall be two Vacations annually. The first, six weeks immediately after commencement: The Second, Six weeks from and after the first Wednesday in December.

II. The President shall appoint some suitable person, who, during the vacation, shall take care of and prevent damages from being done to the College, or to any of the Appertenances belonging to it. And such person shall have a reasonable compensation made him by the Board of Trustees.

III. No undergraduate shall reside in the College during any of the Vacations, without the knowledge and permission of the President.

IV. Immediately upon the expiration of every vacation, the undergraduate Students shall assemble at the College; and if any such Student shall not return to the College at the end of a Vacation, or of the time of absence allowed him by the President, Professor or a Tutor, and shall send no sufficient excuse, he shall be fined twenty five Cents for every days absence; and if he shall not return to the College nor send a sufficient reason before the end of the quarter, and the fine shall be charged in the quarter-Bill, it shall not be taken off upon excuse, unless it shall amount to more than fifteen dollars.

Chapter VI.

Of the Location of the Students.

I. The President shall have authority to locate the Students in the Chambers and Studies of the College; and if any Student shall refuse to dwell in the Chamber assigned to him by the President, he shall be dismissed from the College; and if any Student shall remove from his own into any other Chamber then his own, he may be fined, or punished in some other way as the circumstances of the case may require.

II. If the College chambers shall not be sufficient to receive all the Students, the President and a Majority of the Prudential Committee shall give liberty to so many as necessity shall require, to reside among the Inhabitants of Athens of a good moral Character: in which case a preference shall be allowed to such Students as belong to the place, when it shall be requested by them, their Parents, or Guardians, that they may reside in the families to which they belong.

III. All Scholars, living out of the College, and in Athens, shall be subject to the same laws and rules, in their chambers, as those, who reside in the College.

Chapter VII.

Of College Damages, and the Assessment of them.

I. When any damage shall be found done to any Chamber or any Study in the College, the person or persons to whom such Chamber or Study is assigned and belongs, shall make good the same, unless such damage shall have happened, while they were absent, in Vacation, or to any parts of the College, or the appurtenances thereof, at any time the same shall be assessed upon all the Undergraduate Students, and charged in their quarter-Bills: Provided always, if the person or persons, who were principals or accessories in doing any such damages, shall be discovered, he or they shall make full satisfaction for the same, and if they shall have done intentionally by a scholar or scholars, they shall each be liable to a fine not exceeding five dollars, and to any other College punishment which the circumstances of the offence shall require.

II. The President shall estimate all damages of broken glass, at the end of every quarter, and the same assess upon the Students, according to law, and charge in their quarter-Bills.

Chapter VIII.

Of Crimes and Misdemeanors.

I. If any Scholar shall be guilty of blasphemy, robbery, fornication, theft, forgery, or any other crime, for which an infamous punishment may be inflicted by the laws of the State, he shall be expelled.

II. If any Scholar shall give or accept a Challenge to be duel, he shall be immediately expelled.

III. If any Scholar shall assault, strike, or wound the President, a Professor or a Tutor—or shall disignedly break their doors or windows, he shall be expelled.

IV. If any Scholar shall be guilty of prophaneness—of fighting, or quarrelling—if he shall break open the door of a fellow Student—if he shall go more than two miles from Athens without leave from the

President, a Professor or a Tutor,—if he shall disturb others by noisiness, loud talking or singing during the time of study,—if he shall ring the Bell without order of permission—if he shall play at billiards, Cards or any unlawful game—if he shall associate with vile, idle or dissolute persons, or shall admit them into his chamber,—if he shall instigate or advise any Student to a refractory or stubborn behaviour—he shall for either of these Offences be punished by fine, admonition, or rustication, as the nature and circumstances of the case may require.

V. Whereas the laws of the College are few and general and cases may occur, which are not expressly provided by Law; in all such cases the president, Professors and Tutors shall proceed according to their best discretion, and may punish a Scholar by infliction of a fine or any other College censure, according to the nature and circumstances of his crime.

Chapter IX.

Of the Library; of the Museum; of the Philosophical Chamber and Apparatus.

I. No person, except the President, the Members of the Senatus Academicus, Professors, Tutors, Secretary, resident, Graduates, and Senior and Junior Sophisters shall have the liberty of taking books out of the Library, but by permission from the President: Provided, that no Student shall take more than three Books, out of the Library at one time.

II. The Librarian shall enter in a bill, the title and size of every book borrowed out of the Library, the name of the person, who borrowed it, and the time when it was borrowed and returned; for which a reasonable compensation shall be paid by the Students.

III. The Philosophical chamber, the Apparatus Room, and Apparatus shall be under the care of the President, and the Professor of Mathematics and Natural Philosophy, who shall be the keeper of the Museum.

Chapter X.

Of Commons.

I. The Steward appointed by the Board of Trustees, shall, when required by the President provide in the College-Hall, victuals, after the manner of living in common Families, for all the Professors and Tutors, Graduates and undergraduates, who reside in the College; and shall at all times cause the tables to be decently spread, and attended, at such a price as shall be fixed by the President and Board of Trustees. And if any Student, residing in the College refuses to be in commons he shall be dismissed from the College.

Chapter XI.

Of College Dues, and Quarter-Bills.

I. The College-Year shall begin at the Commencement evening. The first quarter shall end on the first Wednesday in August; the second on the first Wednesday in November; The third on the first Wednesday in February. And the fourth at the Commencement which shall be on the first Wednesday in May annually. The President may vary the endings of the three first quarters for a few days sooner or later at his discretion.

II. Towards the end of each quarter, the President shall cause to be written out a bill, with a duplicate thereof, containing the following sums, which shall be paid quarterly by each Student into the College Treasury, viz., for Tuition six dollars; for a chamber in the College One dollar; and for ordinary repairs and other Contingent charges fifty Cents; for sweeping, living out of College twelve & a half Cents; and for sweeping, and making beds, living in College fifty Cents.

III. The President having approved and signed the said bills, shall deliver one of them to the Treasurer of the College, and keep the other himself; and thereon take a writing signed by the Treasurer acknowledging his receipt of the other bills, and that he will be accountable to the President and Board of Trustees for the whole sum therein contained. And the Treasurer shall collect the same of the Students, and shall hold it subject to the order of the Board of Trustees.

IV. Toward the end of each quarter the Steward shall write a bill of the several Sums, payable to him for Commons at the price stated by the President and Board of Trustees, with a duplicate thereof, both which bills he shall present to the President; and the President having approved and Signed them, shall deliver one of them to the Steward, and keep the other himself, and thereon take a writing signed by the Steward, acknowledging the receipt of the other bill, which he shall be authorised to collect of the Students, and apply to his own use, and if he shall not be able to collect the Sums of Money due on said bills, without a suit, he shall have a right to use the bond given to the

Treasurer and Board of Trustees, at admission: provided he shall give sufficient security to the Treasurer to indemnify them.

V. The several Sums, charged in the quarter-Bills shall be considered as due, and payable as soon as the bills are made up according to law; and the Treasurer shall be authorised to demand the same immediately on the bills being delivered to him for collection, with lawful interest for all the time afterwards, during which they shall remain unpaid. And wherever bonds are entered for a Student by any person or persons, not resident in this state, it shall be the duty of the Treasurer, in case any quarter-bill of such Student shall remain unpaid for the term of three Months after it shall become due, to notify the President thereof; and it shall thereupon be the duty of the President to require other bonds for such Student from some person or persons resident in this State; and on a noncompliance with such requisition, such Student shall be dismissed.

VI. In case of the absence, sickness or any other incapacity of the President; and also in case the President's Office shall be vacant, the Professors and Senior Tutor at the College shall be authorised and required to do every thing relating to the quarter-bills of the Treasurer, and Steward, which by law the President is authorised and required to do.

Chapter XII.

Of Commencement and Academical Degrees.

I. No Scholar may expect the honor of the first degree, who hath not attended and performed the course of Academical exercises, as appointed by law, for the space of four years; except such as have been regularly admitted to an advanced standing, nor unless he shall also have produced on the day before the Commencement, certificated from the Treasurer, Steward and Librarian that he has paid to them their respective dues.

II. No candidate for the Second degree may expect the honor of the same, unless he shall have preserved a good moral character, and previously to the Commencement shall have signified to the President, his desire of the same.

III. All candidates for either degree shall be personally present, unless, in any instance, the President and Board of Trustees shall judge it proper to offer the honor of a degree upon an absent Candidate.

IV. All academical honours shall be given by the President with the consent of the Board of Trustees; and the candidates for the first or a second degree, shall each for the same, pay the President four dollars.

V. The Candidates for either degree, shall perform the public exercises which shall have been previously appointed for them by the President; and no public exhibition shall be made without such appointment, nor without having been previously approved by the President. The President shall begin and close the business and public entertainments of the day with prayer.

VI. There shall be no parade, illumination or fireworks at the time of the Commencement, but by the permission and under the direction of the President.

VII. No Scholar shall attend the instructions of any person who may undertake to teach any language, art, or science, in Athens, unless such person shall [have] liberty of teaching granted him by the President or Board of Trustees, and if any undergraduate shall transgress this law, he shall be punished by fine or otherwise, according to the Circumstances of the case.

VIII. That the Students may, as far as possible, be saved from the disgrace of public and known punishment, it is declared to be the duty of the President, Professors and Tutors carefully and critically to watch over and inspect the conduct and Manners of the Students at all times, and when necessary to admonish them in a private manner.

IX. The foregoing laws shall be subject to such alterations and amendments as may at any time be found necessary.

X. These laws shall be printed and each Student furnished with a Copy thereof, nor shall any Student be subject to the penalties, punishments or censures herein contained, until at least ten days after he shall have been furnished with a Copy as above-mentioned.

Made, enacted, and Ordained at Louisville, the Twelfth day of November, in the Year of Our Lord One thousand eight hundred and three, and of the Independence of the United States of America the Twenty eighth.

Jho. Milledge Governor,
and President of the Senatus Academicus

Attest.

J. Hamill Secy
of the University.

–Minutes of the Senatus Academicus, November 12, 1803, Vol. I, 1799-1803, pp. 39-57. Verified typescript copy in the library of the

University of Georgia. Copy of that copy in the Southern Historical Collection, the University of North Carolina.

7. Commencement exercises at the University of Georgia, 1804

The President presented a Diploma which he had issued, directed to Addin Lewis and others, authorizing them to examine the Candidates for degrees at the approaching commencement, with their report thereon, whereupon Resolved, That the President shall this day confer the degree of Bachelor of Arts on the young Gentlemen whose names are underwritten viz. Gibson Clarke, Augustine Smith Clayton, Thomas Irwin, Jeptha Vining Harris, Jared Irwin, William Henry Jackson, James Wayne Delton Jackson, Robert Rutherford and William Williamson, alumni of this University—and that Ebenezer Harlow Cumming Bachelor of Arts of the College of Hambden Sydney be admitted ad eundem; and that Elijah Clarke, William Prince, John Forsyth, and Henry Meigs be respectively admitted to the degree of Master of Arts.

The Board then accompanied the students in procession to attend the commencement, when the following exercises were performed viz.

Sacred Music.

A Prayer by the Revd. Mr. Marshall.

A Salutory Oration by William H. Jackson.

An oration in favor of liberty, and the superior advantages possessed by the United States over the Government of Europe by Jeptha Vining Harris.

An Oration in praise of virtue and the necessity of enforcing it by example—by Thomas Irwin.

A Poem descriptive of the means by which the Lands on the Oconee were obtained— The former possessors described and contrasted with the present, and a prediction of its future greatness by Augustine S. Clayton.

A dialogue between Messrs. Williamson, Mr. Jackson & Harris.

An Oration exciting to gratitude to France for her assistance during the revolutionary war, and the Cession of Louisiana by Jas. W. D. Jackson.

An Oration on the dignity of Man, and exhorting to agriculture and a knowledge of the Arts and Sciences by Robert Rutherford.

An Oration in praise of a representative government and the Sciences by William Williamson.

A Dialogue between Messrs. Jared Irwin, James W. D. Jackson Rutherford and Clayton.

A disquisition on Taste by Ebenezer Harlow Cumming of Hambden Sydney College.

A Valedictory Oration by Gibson Clarke.

The President in conformity to the preceding resolution conferred the respective degrees on the Gentlemen therein mentioned.

A concluding Prayer by the Revd. Mr. Hull.

The Board returned to the college.

The Board has with pleasure and satisfaction beheld the great and rapid improvement in science of the students at the University, and felicitate themselves on the prospect of the institution becoming conspicuously and eminently useful to the community.

The Board adjourned until six o'Clock tomorrow Morning.—Minutes of the Board of Trustees, 1794-1817, Vol. I, 83-84. Original in the General Library, the University of Georgia. Photocopy in the Southern Historical Collection, the University of North Carolina.

8. Proposal for establishing a university in Virginia by subscriptions, lottery and luxury tax, 1805

Your petitioners approach the legislature, with hopes of awakening its attention, because one sustains & the other sweetens human life; and because one is the tutelar interest of the state, and the other its political soul.

A single fact will demonstrate their intimate connexion, and close affinity. By the official returns of the exports of the two countries, those of the United States appear to have exceeded those of Great Britain in the year 1803, in relation to the numbers of people; even allowing to Britain a re-exportation due to her foreign possessions, and confining the United States to native commodities. It is republicanism, which, within twenty years, has enabled us to overtake a start of centuries, in the arts of industry.

By saving her, agriculture will flourish. She was never saved by factitious wealth or exclusive knowledge; by the quackery of oracle, or the patriotism of privilege.

Some diffusion of knowledge, is admitted to be necessary for her existence; and in Virginia, the government diffuses none.

Hence, about five hundred of our children, at an expense of four hundred dollars each, are annually sent to other countries, to find, what they cannot find at home; and many return, fraught with the most pernicious prejudices. This annual drain of cash is equal to a capital of four millions. Yet half a million would save it. By laying out that sum in an university, the whole expense would be reimbursed to the state, in somewhat above two years, if extraneous educations should not increase; but as these daily accumulate, the annual loss will presently amount to the whole sum sufficient to establish an university. By investing half a million once, in providing for the education of our children at home, we shall therefore save an accumulating capital of half a million annually, to invigorate agriculture and industry.

If institutions for education, patronized by governments, are errors, why are our children forced abroad to such? Is it not better to erect them at home, and instill into our children our own principles, than to send them abroad, to bring back such as other governments may instill?

Your petitioners, pleased with the theory of equalizing knowledge by the education of a whole nation, have delayed to remind the legislature of the subject, from a hope of seeing this theory carried into practice. But it has not been effected in the United States, or in any other part of the world.

An impracticable design, can no longer be a good reason for defeating what is practicable. At least, a refusal to place a good education within the reach of a considerable portion of the people, for the purpose of giving a bad one to all, would be unjust, unless that purpose was fulfilled. Will the legislatures do nothing for republicanism, under pretense of doing every thing? The same theory inculcates a community of knowledge, and a community of property. Is one part of it attainable without the other? Can we equalize knowledge without equalizing wealth? Moral machines are like physical. A wheel may work well in one, which would shatter another. If ballancing knowledge by sharing it equally, should not be a project exactly as speculative as an Agrarian law, it could yet be easily proved, that an Agrarian law, & an equal division of knowledge, are moral wheels constructed upon principles so similar, that neither could work well without the other; nor in union with the inequalities of knowledge or wealth, produced by fair commerce or honest industry.

Not a theoretical, but an attainable diffusion and balance of knowledge and wealth, should guide patriots. The wealth out of the hands of a government, is the balance against the wealth within them. Such also is the attainable balance of knowledge; and it becomes more necessary, as governments are enriched by charter patronage. Not bad, but the best educations, can create a balance on the side of the people, against the talents collected into governments, and rich corporations. Such only are safe centinels to watch power and alarm nations. They ought to be too wise to be deceived, and too numerous to be corrupted. By an intercourse with men but thus educated, the people will require more wisdom than from any system for bestowing narrow educations; because a cheap university, by pouring into society a far greater body of learned men, furnishes a band of patriots, who must teach the ignorant to defend their rights, for the sake of preserving their own. Neither this, nor a balance of knowledge in relations to other states, so important to Virginia, is attainable, by making learned men rare, or teaching all the people to read and write.

Our present policy splits real estates by laws of inheritance; accumulates facitious wealth by charters; and makes the best educations dear and rare, by a necessity for seeking them abroad. Thus, in a short time, a monopoly of wealth and knowledge, will be opposed to a scattered, unchartered, needy and ignorant landed interest. On the contrary, the best educations ought to be cheapened for agriculture, as the laws by dividing inheritances, diminish its ability to buy them; to sustain her against charter accumulations of privilege and wealth and to preserve the most faithful ally of republican government by making a right to keep a gun, dear in England, the rich became sole proprietors of the game. So they will monopolize good educations here from the same course.

The dereliction of education by the legislature, will expose it to the occupancy of some adventurer. Will it be seized by a monied aristocrat, from its costliness; or by an ambitious religious sect, as a medium for sowing with missionaries (in imitation of the Jesuits) its designs throughout the union? Or will such factions unite? Can a dereliction constitute the freedom of education, when an university, governed by the legislature, would be open to all parties; and a dereliction, will condemn knowledge to become the test of one?

The ingenious theory before attended to, contends that governments ought not to meddle with education; but it does not approve and unite with this opinion, modes or gratifying avarice and ambition by law. It does not advise us to swallow the poison and neglect the antidote. This is inevitable death. To feed avarice and ambition by artificial accumulations, to leave education dear, and thus to weave knowledge into a wreath for the brow of monopoly, is a system, immeasurably distant from the theory, whence an enemy has been drawn, against cherishing knowledge by law.

Education is an instrument which will be used to sustain or to destroy governments, of the most powerful nature. If free governments throw it away, it will be seized and used by some tyrannical principle. In their custody, it is secured against misapplication, by the same responsibility which secures life and property.

A mode of government will probably cause a school to flourish, which causes a nation to flourish. Can a school flourish without government, whilst no other community can; or can aristocratical form, which are bad for nations, be good for colleges? Will irresponsibility, which paralyzes duty in one case, invigorate it in the other? Personal genius and virtue may bestow temporary success upon bad principles, but good principles only can produce permanent good effects.

Your petitioners therefore implore the legislature, to set about the establishment of a college, by law and by example; upon a scale sufficiently plentiful and liberal, to educate the children of the state at home, in the most perfect manner.

Half a million of dollars will probably suffice. It is far less than Virginia pays for funding, for banking, or for Louisiana; and it will save her annual cent: per cent: in money, besides the returns in science and republican principles, with all their effects; to neither of which any of these pecuniary expenditures pretend.

To raise a fifth of this sum, it is proposed that the legislature open a subscription by law; that they resort in addition to an annual lottery, excluding lotteries for any other purpose; and that they provide for a deficiency by a tax upon pleasure horses, carriages, or other subjects.

Thus the poor will have secured to them the blessing of a moderate government without cost; and the contributions of the rich, for the sake of their own liberty and property, and the happiness of their children, will even bring back to them pecuniary profit. By making the subscriptions payable when one hundred thousand dollars are subscribed, even this mode of contribution may become very general, and tolerably equal among the wealthy.

If the government of the university is made accountable to the Legislature, an annual election of governors, will create an honorary degree; the discharge of which will be invigorated, as being a road to public favor, so as to prepare candidates for office, by habits of virtue and patriotism.

A site may be selected in one of the middle counties, near to fuel, wood, limestone and provisions, as far from the vices of towns; which may be kept at a distance by law, and by the purchase of a large tract of land; and the necessary professions and trades, as tenants, may be made subservient to collegiate morals.

Your petitioners, conscious that neither can flourish without the other; that agriculture will become a slave, if republicanism should perish; and that republicanism will perish, divided by charter interests; unless a vast accession of knowledge is infused into the agricultural interest, to regulate and check the vast accession of wealth bestowed upon exclusive privilege; the enemy of republicanism; doubt not of the same care of their welfare, which has often excited, and would upon this occasion kindle, the gratitude and filial piety for the Legislature of Virginia.

The writer of this essay, knows of about fifty youths sent out of the state for education. He solicits those who are willing to patronize an university by subscription, to communicate the sums they will subscribe to the Editor of the Enquirer. On this part, he will subscribe two thousand dollars, and personally claim this engagement, if the undertaking is set on foot. For this purpose, a law empowering those, who will, to form themselves into a society, to appoint commissioners for soliciting subscriptions, and to provide a mode of bringing them into the treasury, when they shall amount to a certain sum, will be necessary.—*The Richmond Enquirer*, December 6, 1805.

9. Charter of the University of Orleans, 1805

Whereas the independence, happiness and grandeur of every republic depend, under the influence of Divine Providence, upon the wisdom, virtue, talents and energy of its citizens and rulers.

And whereas, science, literature and the liberal arts contribute in an eminent degree, to improve those qualities and acquirements.

And whereas learning hath ever been found the ablest advocate of genuine liberty, and the best supporter of rational religion, and the source of the only solid and imperishable glory which nations can acquire.

And forasmuch as literature and philosophy furnish the most useful and pleasing occupations, improving and varying the enjoyments of prosperity, affording relief under the pressure of misfortune, and hope and consolation in the hour of death.

And considering that in a commonwealth, whose humblest citizen may be elected to the highest public office, the knowledge which is requisite for a magistrate should be widely diffused.

Sec. 1. *Be it therefore enacted by the governor of the territory of Orleans, by and with the advise and consent of the legislative council thereof,* That an university be and is hereby instituted within this territory, to be called and known by the name or stile of "The University of Orleans;" that the regents thereof shall consist of the governor of this territory, the judges of the superior court thereof, the judge of the court of the United States for the district of Orleans, the mayor and the recorder of the city of New-Orleans, the president of the legislative council for the time being, who shall always be regents of the said university in virtue of their respective offices; and the following persons, to wit: The rev. Patrick Walsh, Paul Lanuffe, Joseph Faurie, Peter Derbigny, Lewis Kerr, Joseph Saul, Dr. Fortin, Dr. Robelot, Dr. Montegut, Dr. LeDuc, Dr. Dow, James Brown, Edward Livingston, James Workman, Evan Jones, Mons. Bore and Mons. Detrehan; and that the places of such of the said regents as are not hereby declared to be regents in virtue of their office, and who shall resign or die, shall from time to time be supplied by the legislature of this territory; that the said regents, as soon as may be, after the passing of this act, shall convene at such time and place as the governor shall appoint, and by plurality of voices, by ballot, choose a chancellor and vice-chancellor, to continue in office during the pleasure of said regents; that the said chancellor, or in his absence from the said meeting, the vice-chancellor, or in case both be absent, then the senior regent present, (and whose seniority shall be decided by the order in which the regents are named or appointed) shall preside, and in case of division, have a casting voice at all meetings of the said regents: that all meetings of the said regents after the first, shall be held at such time and place as the chancellor, or in case of his death, absence from the territory, or resignation of both of them, then at such time and place as the senior regent present in the territory shall appoint, and it shall be the duty of the chancellor, vice-chancellor or senior regent, as the case in virtue of the above contingencies may be, to order and call a meeting of the said regents, whenever and as often as three regents shall in writing apply for and request the same, such order or call to be published in one or more of the public newspapers in the city of New-Orleans, at least fifteen days prior to such meeting; and further, that any nine of the said regents meeting at the time and place so ordered, shall be a quorum, and be enabled to transact the business which by this act they shall be authorised or directed to do and transact: that the said university shall be and hereby is incorporated, and shall be known by the name of "The University of Orleans," and by that name shall have perpetual succession, and power to sue and be sued, and to hold, possess and enjoy property real and personal.

Sec. 2. *And be it further enacted*, That the said corporation shall appoint by ballot a treasurer and a secretary, to continue in office during the pleasure of the corporation; that the treasurer shall keep fair and true accounts of all monies by him received and paid out, and that the secretary shall keep a fair journal of all the meetings and proceedings of the corporation, in which the yeas and nays on all questions shall be entered, if required by any of the regents present; and to all the books and papers of the corporation every regent shall always have access, and be permitted to take copies of them.

Sec. 3. *And be it further enacted*, That the said regents shall as speedily as may be, establish a college within the limits of the city of New-Orleans, for the instruction of youth in the Latin, Greek, English, French, and Spanish languages, as well as in the sciences, philosophy and literature: the name and title of which said college shall be "The College of New-Orleans." That the said regents shall appoint for the said purpose and to preside over and govern the said college, a president and four professors, namely, one professor for the Latin and Greek languages, logic and ancient history; one other professor for the English, French, and Spanish languages, rhetoric and modern history; one other professor for mathematics and natural philosophy; and one other professor for moral philosophy, and the law of nature and nations: that it shall be the duty of the said president and professors to instruct and give lectures to the students of the said college, according to such plans of education as the said regents may approve and direct in the branches of learning above mentioned; that the said president and professors, or a majority of them, shall be called and stiled "The faculty of the College," which faculty shall have the power of enforcing the rules and regulations adopted by the said regents for the government and discipline of the said college, and of granting and confirming, by and with the consent of the said regents, such degrees in the liberal arts and sciences, to such students of the college, who by their proficiency in learning, the said professors shall think entitled to them, as are usually granted and conferred in other colleges in Europe and America; and to grant to such graduates, diplomas or certificates under the common seal of the said university, to authenticate and perpetuate the memory of such graduations; and the said president and professors shall hold their offices during good behavior.

Sec. 4. *And be it further enacted*, That the said regents shall as speedily as may be, establish within each county of this territory, one or more academies for the instruction of youth, in the French and English languages, reading, writing, grammar, arithmetic and geography; that the said regents shall appoint for each of the said academies a discreet person duly qualified to be master thereof, whose duty it shall be to instruct the pupils placed under his care according to the plan of education adopted and promulgated by the said regents, and to enforce the rules ordained by the said regents for the government and discipline of the said academies.

And whereas the prosperity of every state depends greatly on the education of the female sex, insomuch that the dignity of their condition is the strongest characteristic which distinguishes civilized from savage society.

Sec. 5. *Be it further enacted*, That the said regents shall establish such a number of academies in this territory as they may judge fit, for the instruction of the youth of the female sex, in the English and French languages, and in such branches of polite literature, and such liberal arts and accomplishments as may be suitable to the age and sex of the pupils.

Sec. 6. *And be it further enacted*, That it shall be the duty of the said regents, and they are hereby authorised and required as soon as may be, to erect, purchase or hire, as they may deem most expedient for carrying the purposes of this act into effect, suitable buildings for the seminaries and establishments contemplated by this act, to make ordinances for the government and discipline thereof; to establish plans of education therefor, which plans shall embrace each and every of the languages, sciences and branches of learning herein before directed to be taught in the said college and academies respectively; to regulate the admission of students and pupils into the same; to elect and appoint persons of suitable learning and talents to be the president and professors of the said college, and the masters and instructors of the said academies, to agree with them for their salaries and emoluments, to visit and inspect the said college and academies, and examine into the state of education and discipline therein, and make a yearly report thereof to the legislature: and generally to do all lawful matters and things whatsoever necessary, for the maintaining and supporting the establishments aforesaid: *Provided, however*, That no ordinances shall be of force which shall be repugnant to the provisions of this act, the laws of the territory or of the United States.

Sec. 7. And for the more extensive communication of the useful knowledge, *Be it further enacted*, That as soon as may be, after the establishment of the said college and academies, the said regents shall establish in each county of this territory, (except as is hereafter provided for) and in such place in each county as may be most generally convenient and accommodating to the inhabitants thereof, one public library to consist of such works in the French and English languages, as the said regents shall approve of and select: that the said regents shall appoint trustees in each county for preserving the said libraries, and shall make the proper rules and ordinances for that purpose; and also for regulating the manner in which persons may be admitted to read in the said libraries, and in which the books thereof may be lent out; and that the said regents may appropriate and contribute a reasonable sum out of the funds of the said university, for improving and augmenting the public library of the city of New-Orleans, instead of establishing a distinct library therein.

Sec. 8. *And be it further enacted*, That for the establishment and support of the institutions contemplated by this act, there shall be raised annually a sum not exceeding fifty thousand dollars by two lotteries, the first of the said lotteries to be set on foot as speedily as may be after the passing of this act, and that the regents of the said university shall appoint five discreet persons to be managers of the said lotteries, each of whom shall give security to be approved of by the said regents, in such sum as they shall direct, conditioned for the faithful discharge of the duty required of such manager by this act, and the said managers shall have power to adopt such schemes as to them may seem proper to sell the said tickets, and to superintend the drawing of the said lotteries and the payment of the prizes; and that as often as the said managers shall receive the sum of one thousand dollars, they shall deposit the same in the Louisiana Bank, and the said managers and regents shall render an account of their proceedings therein at the next session of the legislature after each drawing, and it shall be the duty of the governor of the territory from time to time, to call on the said managers and regents, and enforce the execution of the provisions of this act.—*Acts Passed at the First Session of the Legislative Council of the Territory of Orleans*, pp. 304-20.

10. North Carolina's "Dartmouth College Case," 1805

The Trustees of the University of North Carolina v. Foy and Bishop. From Wilmington.[1]

Section 41 of the Constitution declares that "schools shall be established by the Legislature for the convenient instruction of youth, with such salaries to the masters, paid by the public, as may enable them to instruct at low prices, and all useful learning shall be duly encouraged and promoted in one or more universities." In obedience to this injunction of the Constitution, the Legislature established an university, and in 1789 granted to the Trustees of the University "all the property that had theretofore or should thereafter escheat to the State." In 1800 the Legislature repealed this grant. This repealing act is void, it being in violation of section 10 of the Bill of Rights, which is a part of the Constitution, and declares "that no freeman ought to be taken, imprisoned or disseized of his freehold, liberties or privileges, or outlawed or in any manner destroyed or deprived of his life, liberty or property, but by the law of the land."

This was an action of ejectment brought to recover the possession of certain escheated lands in the district of Wilmington. The defendants pleaded in bar of the act of 1800, entitled "An act to repeal so much of the several laws now in force in this State as grants power to the Trustees of the University of North Carolina to seize and possess for the use of the said university any escheated or confiscated property." To this plea the plaintiff demurred, and the defendants having joined in demurrer, the case was sent to this Court for the opinion of the judges.

Locke, J., delivered the opinion of the Court. The Legislature of North Carolina in 1789 granted to the Trustees of the University "all the property that has heretofore or shall hereafter escheat to the State." And by another act, passed in 1794, they also granted "the

1. The decision in this case was cited by Daniel Webster in the famous Dartmouth College Case decided in 1819, "as most fit to be followed on this occasion." See below and also Edgar W. Knight, "North Carolina's 'Dartmouth College Case,'" *Journal of Higher Education,* XIX (March, 1948), 116-22. For a controversy involving Liberty Hall Academy (now Washington and Lee University) in Virginia, see James M. Hutcheson, "Virginia's 'Dartmouth College Case,'" *Virginia Magazine of History and Biography,* LI (July, 1943).

confiscated property then unsold." By an act passed in 1800 they declared, "that from and after the passing of this act, all acts and clauses of acts which have heretofore granted power to the Trustees of the University to seize and possess any escheated or confiscated property, real or personal, shall be and the same is hereby repealed and made void.

"*And be it further enacted*, That all escheated or confiscated property which the said trustees, their agents or attorneys, have not legally sold by virtue of the said laws shall from hence revert to the State, and henceforth be considered as the property of the same, as though such laws had never been passed."

The Trustees of the University in pursuance of the powers vested in them by the act of 1789, have brought this suit to recover the possession of a tract of land escheated to the state before the passing of the repealing act in the year 1800. The defendants have pleaded this repealing act in bar, by which they allege the power of the trustees to support this action is entirely destroyed. It is therefore now to be considered how far the trustees have title under the act of 1789, and, in the next place, how far they are divested of that title by the repealing act of 1800.

To determine the first question, it may be necessary to take into view the objections stated to the title of the trustees, independent of the operation of the repealing act, and these are two: first, that no title to escheated lands vests in the State until an inquisition or office found; and, secondly, that if the State had title, yet the trustees have derived none by the act of 1789, because the State attempted to convey the right by act of Assembly and not by grant, as required by section 36 of the Constitution. With regard to the first objection, the Court think it a sufficient answer to say that on this subject the law has been supposed to be long settled, as this objection has been made in almost every suit heretofore brought by the Trustees of the University, and always overruled. The Court approve of the decisions upon this point, and will observe the ancient and wise maxim "*stare decisis*."

As to the second objection, the words of the Constitution are, "All commissions and grants shall run in the name of the State of North Carolina and bear test and be signed by the Governor," etc. It seems to be a fair and clear exposition of this part of the Constitution to say that when the State conveys land by grant, the grant shall have the requisites prescribed, to wit, run in the name of the State, bear teste and be signed by the Governor, etc., and that all grants otherwise authenticated shall be void. It became necessary that the officer whose duty it shall be to sign and authenticate grants should be pointed out, and that their form and substance should be ascertained, in order to give uniformity to such grants and to avoid that variety which would be produced by the judgment of different officers. But the Court sees nothing in this clause restricting the Legislature to this single mode of conveyance; they are left free from any control in the mode or manner of transferring their property, unless they should adopt the one pointed out in the Constitution, and then the form and ceremony are prescribed. This opinion is warranted not only by the expressions contained in the clause itself, but by the many and repeated acts of Assembly passed, since the making of the Constitution, for the purpose of transferring property. Many of these acts have been mentioned and referred to by the counsel for the lessors of the plaintiff. We are therefore of opinion that the land in question vested in the State without an inquisition or office found, and that the Legislature were competent to pass the interest in the same to the Trustees of the University by the act of 1789; and that the trustees have a good and valid title, unless the operation of the repealing act of 1800 has destroyed it.

The operation of this act is next to be considered; and it may be necessary to premise that the people of North Carolina, when assembled in convention, were desirous of having some rights secured to them beyond the control of the Legislature, and these they have expressed in the Bill of Rights and the Constitution. The preamble to the Constitution states, among other things, that "We, the representatives of the freemen of North Carolina, chosen and assembled in Congress for the express purpose of framing a constitution, under the authority of the people, most conducive to their happiness and welfare, do declare, etc." Section 13 directs the General Assembly to elect several officers of State. Section 15 directs the election of a Governor. Section 38 directs that there shall be a sheriff, coroner or coroners and constables in each county. It became necessary for the Legislature to appoint these officers or to pass such laws as would secure to the people such officers as would carry this form of government into effect. The framers of this instrument appear to have been well acquainted with the importance and necessity of education, and lest this object might escape the attention of the Legislature or be by them neglected, section 41 declares, "That a school or schools shall be established by the Legislature for the convenient instruction of youth, with such salaries to the masters paid by the public as may enable them to instruct at low prices; and all useful learning shall be encouraged and promoted in one or more universities." By this section as strong an injunction was imposed on the Legislature to establish an university as by the preceding clauses to appoint the several officers of government; these objects seem to be regarded by the framers of the Constitution with equal solicitude; they have, therefore, in the same imperative style declared that there shall be an university, and that there shall be a Governor, leaving to the Legislature to make such appropriations and create such funds for the endowment of the institution as would be sufficient to effect the purposes for which it should be established. In 1789 the Legislature obeyed this constitutional injunction and made an appropriation of escheated lands, and appointed trustees for the management of the concerns of the institution. By the act of 1800 the Legislature declared that this property should be taken from the trustees and revert to the State. Is, then, this last act authorized by the Constitution, or does it destroy a right which that instrument gave to the people, a right highly esteemed in all civilized nations, that of educating their youth at a moderate expense? a right of acquiring knowledge and good morals, which have always been deemed most conducive to the happiness and prosperity of the people?

Some light will be thrown upon this subject by examining the nature of corporations: how property can be taken from them, and how they can be dissolved. Corporations are formed for the advancement of religion, learning, commerce or other beneficial purposes. They are either aggregate or sole, and created by grant or by law. When they are once erected, they acquire many rights, powers, capacities, and some incapacities as, first, to have perpetual succession; and, therefore, all aggregate corporations have necessarily the power of electing members in the room of those who die, to sue and be sued and to do all other acts as natural persons. Second, to purchase lands and to hold them for the benefit of themselves and successors. Fourth, to have a common seal. Fifth, to make by-laws for the better government of the corporation. These corporations cannot commit crimes, although their members may in their individual capacity. The duties of those bodies consist in acting up to the design for which they were instituted. Let us next inquire how their corporate property can be taken from them and how they may be dissolved. A member may be disfranchised or lose his place by his own improper conduct, or he may resign. A corporation may be dissolved by act of Parliament, which is boundless in its operation; by the natural death of all its members, in case of an aggregate corporation; by surrender of its franchises into the hands of the King, which is a kind of suicide; by forfeiture of its charter through negligence or abuse of its franchises, in which case the law judges the body politic to have broken the condition on which it was incorporated, and therefore the incorporation to be void; and the regular course is to bring an information in the nature of *a quo warranto*, to inquire by what authority the members now exercise their corporate power, having forfeited it by such and such proceedings. None of these prerequisites have been done in the present case. We are then led to inquire into the soundness of an argument greatly relied on by the defendant's counsel, that those who create can destroy. The Legislature have not pretended to dissolve the corporation, but to deprive them of a part of the funds that were deemed to be vested in them and to transfer those funds to the State. In England the King's consent to the creation of any corporation is absolutely necessary, either given expressly by charter or by act of Parliament, where his assent is a necessary ingredient or implied by prescription. The King may grant to a subject the power of erecting a corporation; and yet it is the King that erects—the subject is but the instrument. Where there is an endowment of lands, the law distinguishes and makes two species of foundation: The first, *fundatio incipiens*, or the corporation; in which sense the King is the founder of all colleges and hospitals; the other, *fundatio proficiens*, or the dotation of it, in which sense the first gift of the revenues is the foundation, and who gives them is the founder. The Constitution directed the General Assembly to establish this institution and endow it; then it would seem from the principle upon which all this doctrine is predicated, that the Constitution and not the Legislature had erected this corporation; the Legislature being only the agent or instrument, whose acts are valid and binding when they do not contravene any of the provisions of the Constitution. We view this corporation as standing on higher grounds than any other aggregate corporation; it is not only protected by the common law, but sanctioned by the Constitution. It cannot be considered that the Legislature would have complied with this constitutional requisition, by establishing a school for a month or any determinate number of years, and then abolishing the institution; because the people evidently intended this university to be as permanent as the Government itself. It would not be competent for the Legislature to declare that there should be no public school in the State, because such an act would directly oppose that important clause in the Constitution before mentioned. But if the Legislature can deprive the university of the appropriated and vested funds, they can do that which will produce the same consequences; for, deprive the institution of funds already vested and refuse to make any additional appropriations, and there never can exist in the State a public school or schools; and thus the Legislature may indirectly effect that purpose which, if expressed in the words before mentioned, they could not do. Besides, when the Legislature have established an university, appointed trustees and vested them with property which they were to hold in trust for the benefit of the institution, have they not discharged their duty as the agents of the people and transferred property, which is afterwards beyond their control? From that moment the trustees became in some measure the agents of the people, clothed with the power of disposing and of applying the property thus vested to the uses intended by the people, but over which the power of the Legislature ceased with the discharge of the constitutional injunction; unless it might be necessary in the course of time to make other or further appropriations to continue and support the institution; and this we consider to be their duty at all times, when such necessity shall exist, that the expectation of the people, as expressed in the Constitution, may not be disappointed.

But one great and important reason which influences us in deciding this question is section 10 of the Bill of Rights, which declares "that no freeman ought to be taken, imprisoned or disseized of his freehold, liberties or privileges, or outlawed or exiled, or in any manner destroyed or deprived of his life, liberty or property, but by the law of the land." It has been yielded on the part of the defendant that if the Legislature had vested an individual with the property in question, this section of the Bill of Rights would restrain them from depriving him of such right; but it is denied that this section has any operation on corporations whose members are mere naked trustees, and have no interest in the donation, and especially on a corporation erected for a public purpose. It is also insisted that the term, "law of the land," does not impose any restrictions on the Legislature, who are capable of making the law of the land, and was only intended to prevent abuses in the other branches of Government. That this clause was intended to secure to corporations as well as to individuals the rights therein enumerated, seems clear from the word "*liberties*," which peculiarly signifies those privileges and rights which corporations have by virtue of the instruments which incorporate them, and is certainly used in this clause in contradistinction to the word "*liberty*," which refers to the personal liberty of the citizen. We therefore infer that by this clause the Legislature are as much restrained from affecting the property corporations as they are that of a private individual, unless the "law of the land" should receive the construction contended for on the part of the defendant. It is evident the framers of the Constitution intended the provision as a restraint upon some branch of the Government, either the executive, legislative, or judicial. To suppose it applicable to the executive would be absurd on account of the limited powers conferred on that officer; and from the subjects enumerated in that clause, no danger could be apprehended from the Executive Department, that being entrusted with the exercise of no powers by which the principles thereby intended to be secured could be affected. To apply to the judiciary would, if possible, be still more idle, if the Legislature can make the "*law of the land*." For the judiciary are only to expound and enforce the law, and have no discretionary powers enabling them to judge of the propriety or impropriety of laws. They are bound, whether agreeable to their ideas of justice or not, to carry into effect the acts of the Legislature as far as they are binding or do not contravene the Constitution. If, then, this clause is applicable to the Legislature alone, and was intended as a restraint on their acts (and to presume otherwise is to render this article a dead letter), let us next inquire what will be the operation which this clause will or ought to have on the present question. It seems to us to warrant a belief that members of a corporation as well as individuals shall not be so deprived of their liberties or properties, unless by a trial by jury in a court of justice, according to the known and established rules of decision derived from the common law and such acts of Legislature as are consistent with the Constitution. Although the trustees are a corporation established for public purposes, yet their property is as completely beyond the control of the Legislature as the property of individuals or that of any other corporation. Indeed, it seems difficult to conceive of a corporation established for merely private purposes. In every institution of that kind the ground of the establishment is some public good or purpose intended to be promoted; but in many the members thereof have a private interest, coupled with the public object. In this case, the trustees have no private interest beyond the general good; yet we conceive that circumstances will not make the property of the trustees subject to the arbitrary will of the Legislature. The property vested in the trustees must remain for the uses intended for the university, until the judiciary of the country in the usual and common form pronounce them guilty of such acts as will, in law, amount to a forfeiture of their rights or a dissolution of their body. The demurrer must therefore be allowed, and the plea in bar overruled.—A. D. Murphey (reporter), *Cases Argued and Determined in the Supreme Court of North Carolina*, 1804-1810, Vol. V, 57 ff. Justice Locke delivered the opinion of the court. Justice Hall dissented. For a decision of the Supreme Court of Alabama holding the University of that State to be a public corporation see Trustees of the University of Alabama *v.* Winston, 5 Stewart and Porter (Alabama, 1833), 17-39.

11. The Legislature of North Carolina re-enacts the law providing for the support of the University of that State by escheats, 1805

Be it enacted by the General Assembly of the State of North Carolina, and it is hereby enacted by the authority of the same, That an act entitled "An act to repeal so much of the several laws now in force in this state as grants powers to the Trustees of the University of North Carolina to seize and possess for the use of the said university any escheated and confiscated property," so far as relates to the escheated property, be and the same is hereby repealed and made void.—*Laws of North Carolina*, 1805, p. 2. The act restored the law of 1789, which had provided for the support of the University of North Carolina by escheats, following decision of the Court of Conference in North Carolina's "Dartmouth College Case" given above.

12. Students and graduates of the University of South Carolina, 1805-1860

Year	Graduates	Students
1805	—	30
1806	1	57
1807	4	93
1808	31	107
1809	18	92
1810	25	105
1811	25	118
1812	34	171

Year	Graduates	Students
1813	33	141
1814	44	149
1815	38	134
1816	37	108
1817	27	113
1818	35	107
1819	30	107
1820	28	110
1821	27	88
1822	24	76
1823	8	65
1824	19	108
1825	32	115
1826	28	114
1827	13	114
1828	20	87
1829	28	97
1830	37	115
1831	38	114
1832	33	108
1833	37	86
1834	22	52
1835	12	70
1836	11	114
1837	40	155
1838	37	153
1839	22	160
1840	37	168
1841	51	169
1842	42	150
1843	30	134
1844	37	134
1845	33	122
1846	31	137
1847	35	171
1848	32	221
1849	64	237
1850	63	195
1851	46	184

Year	Graduates	Students
1852	46	199
1853	24	122
1854	21	190
1855	66	195
1856	33	180
1857	21	158
1858	44	201
1859	39	184
1860	38	170

—Green, *op. cit.*, 436-38.

13. Extracts from the minutes of the faculty of South Carolina College, 1805-1811

The South Carolina College
January 10th AD. 1805.

This being the day appointed by the Board of Trustees for the opening of the South Carolina College, and the commencement of its operations, the Faculty held a meeting.

William Harper and Wesley Harper were examined and admitted to the Sophomore Class. Charles M. DeWitt, Thomas W. Robertson, John N. Davis, James Goodwin, John T. Goodwin, John Mayrant, and Benjamin Waring were admitted to the Freshman Class.

The South Carolina College Jany 12th 1805

The Faculty met and examined Isaac Smith, but found him deficient in qualifications.

The South Carolina College Jan. 14th 1805

The Faculty examined and admitted George W. Glenn into the Sophomore Class, and Henry Taylor into the Freshman Class.

The South Carolina College Jan. 16th 1805

The Faculty having examined John Caldwell and William Davis, admitted the former into the Sophomore, and the latter into the Freshman class.

The S. C. College Jan. 22nd 1805

William Goodwin and Powell McRae were examined by the Faculty and admitted into the Freshman class.

The S. C. College Jan. 31st 1805

At a meeting of the Faculty this day, Anderson Crenshaw was admitted to the Junior Class.

The S. C. College Feb. 4th 1805

William Waring was this day permitted to join the Freshman Class.

The S. C. College Feb. 6th 1805

Robert Reid was examined and admitted into the Freshman Class.

The S. C. College Feb. 7th 1805

The Faculty examined and admitted into the Freshman Class, Benjamin Heriot.

The S. C. College Feb. 20th 1805

The Faculty, after the customary examination, admitted Charles Course into the Freshman Class.

The S. C. College 21st of March 1805

John M'Iver has this day been admitted by the Faculty into the Freshman Class.

The S. C. College April 1st 1805

The Faculty examined Josiah Evans, and permitted him to enter the class of Freshmen.

The S. C. College April 18th 1805

Isaac Smith was re-examined for admittance into the Freshman class, and permitted to enter.

The S. C. College 2nd May 1805

At a meeting of the Faculty; Resolved that an examination of the students be held on the eleventh day of July next.

The S. C. College May 11th 1805

George Davis was, at this meeting of the Faculty admitted into the Freshman class.

The S. C. College June 10th 1805

The Faculty examined and admitted William Neisbit into the Freshman Class.

The S. C. College July 11th 1805

The Faculty met in the Chapel at nine o'clock in the morning, and examined the Sophomore class in the different studies which they have pursued, since their former examination. In the opinion of the Faculty the class has made good progress in its studies.

The S. C. College July 11th 1805

The Faculty having examined the Freshman class were satisfied with the proficiency of the class in general, but were sorry to find, in a few, a culpable deficiency. Those few were particularly admonished.

The S. C. College Oct 14th 1805

At a meeting of the Faculty, Thomas Palmer was admitted into the Freshman Class.

The S. C. College Oct 16th 1805

At a meeting of the Faculty: Resolved that a public Exhibition of Declamations and Dialogues, by the junior, sophomore and freshman classes, be held on the evening of the fourth of December.

The S. C. College Nov. 27th 1805

The Faculty completed, this day, the examination which they had commenced on the twenty fifth inst.

The result was, that the several classes acquitted themselves in so satisfactory a manner, that they were each permitted to rise to the next higher grade.

The S. C. College Dec. 11th 1805

The Faculty having examined and admitted into the Freshman class James Dinkins, permitted him to return to Camden, and defer joining the class till the sixth of January.

The S. C. College Dec. 30th 1805

The Faculty having met, examined and admitted into the junior class Walter Crenshaw, and into the Sophomore class John M'Iver the elder, and Nathaniel Ware.

The S. C. College Jany. 9th 1806

Derrill Hart was this day examined and admitted by the Faculty into the Freshman class:

Thomas Gaillard was likewise admitted into the same class:—And James Gaillard, William Jones and Charles Stephens were admitted into the Sophomore Class.

The S. C. College Feb 7th 1806

At a meeting of the Faculty holden this day William Davis of the Sophomore class was called before the Board to give an account of his behaviour in the Chapel during the devotional exercises of the last evening [illegible] his conduct had been highly [illegible] designed to show disrespect [illegible] who was present, it was Resolved by the Faculty after maturely deliberating on the circumstances of the case, that Davis should be suspended for the term of three months:—Then to be restored on the condition of producing, from a reputable instructor, a certificate of his good moral conduct and diligent attention to study, during that period.

The S. C. College March 10th 1806

At a meeting of the Faculty, Richard Hutson was examined and permitted to join the Freshman class.

The S. C. College April 3rd 1806

The Faculty admitted into the Freshman Class Barnaby Branford.

The S. C. College April 4th 1806

Resolved by the Faculty of the College that a general examination of the students be held on the first Monday in May.

The S. C. College Dec. 1st 1806

The general examination of the classes was holden by the Faculty and other literary gentlemen, on the last week in November, after which, they were allowed to rise each to the next higher grade without any individual exceptions.—William Brantley of North Carolina who was at the same time examined with the (then) Sophomore Class, being found qualified was admitted, with them, into the Junior Class.

The S. C. College Dec. 4th 1806

Elias Dubose of Darlington, was, at a meeting of the Faculty, admitted, this day, into the Sophomore Class.

The S. C. College Dec. 17 1806

The Faculty met and admitted John Gill of the Bethel Academy, into the Junior Class.

The S. C. College Jan 4th 1807

Stephen Miller was admitted into the Junior Class.

The S. C. College Jan 5th 1807

This day, was admitted, by the Faculty, into the Junior class, John Murphy of North Carolina; and into the Sophomore Class John Lide, of Darlington.

The S. C. College Jan 11th 1807

John B. Muldrow of Darlington was examined and admitted into the Freshman Class.

The S. C. College June 1st 1807

The Faculty met in the Library to inspect the Monitors' Bills of the past month, and to deliberate on the concerns of the institution.— Agreed that it would be proper for the President, after evening prayers, to address the students on the subject of their inattention to neatness in dress and their indecorum at mealtimes and during Chapel devotion.— Agreed Thos Gill of the junior class have permission to be absent from College, during the remainder of the present session, in consideration of ill health.—

Resolved, that agreeably to the College Laws, Ch. 10th, Sec. 3rd. the following provisional rules for the government of the students until the next meeting of the Board of Trustees, be proposed to the standing Committee for their concurrence. viz.

1st. No student shall go beyond the limits of the Town of Columbia, without special permission from an officer of College.

2d. The Steward, at meal times, shall be invested with a similar authority, for the preservation of order, to that of the other officers.

The S. C. College Monday June 22nd 1807

The Faculty met this morning pursuant to their adjournment, and resumed the business of the last meeting. The principal offenders having acknowledged their fault and expressed their penitence, Resolved That only their conduct shall be animadverted upon with severity by the President after evening prayers; but without a particular mention of their names.

One of the youths concerned, who was called on for a witness, having, on Saturday, refused to answer the questions proposed to him, openly avowing his determination not to give evidence in the manner required by the laws of College (Ch. 6—sec. 7), was allowed the intervening time for reflection.— Being called on today, and still continuing obstinate, Resolved That unless he relents before Evening prayers, and voluntarily come forward with acknowledgement, he shall then be publicly and severely reprimanded and his name, offence and punishment be recorded.

The first resolve was executed; but the execution of the last was omitted: the subject of it having acknowledged his error to the President, and promised in future to obey the law.

The S. C. College July 15th 1807

The Faculty assembled in the Chapel.— In the morning they examined the Junior Class in geometry. In the afternoon, the Soph. C. in Arithmetic and Algebra.

The S. C. College July 16th 1807

The Soph. C. was examined in Homer's Iliad and Morses Geography:— The Freshman C. in the 12th Book of the Aeneid with the application of the principles of Prosody; also in Cicero's Orations. The Greek Testament and Murray's Eng. Grammar.

The S. C. College July 17th 1807

The Professors and Tutors met this morning at the Chapel to publish the result of the Examination and dismiss the Students.

The result agreed upon was, in substance, as follows. The Juniors have in general acquitted themselves in such a manner as to give tolerable satisfaction and to preclude the necessity of passing any particular censures.— With regard to those who were placed on a conditional standing at the last Examination, the Faculty perceive no reason for alleviating that condition, and therefore think proper to continue them in the same situation.

The Sophomore Class has not in the opinion of the Faculty made so great proficiency, in the mathematical branches, as they had a right to expect. In Homer, a number did themselves credit. In the Geographical examination they find nothing to censure, as it respects the class at large. . . .

Concerning their attainments in Mathematics however, it is but justice to a majority of the class to remark, that their progress has been impeded by the backwardness of a few; who, requiring common attention from the Professor, prevented him from forwarding the others with the desired rapidity.

The Freshman Class has, in general, given satisfaction in Virgil and Cicero.– In English Grammar they succeeded tolerably well; but the Faculty recommend some further attention to it during the vacation. In Greek, the Faculty cannot think the class sufficiently versed.– They must therefore strongly recommend it to the class in general, but especially to some of the younger ones, to be more assiduous in their attention to that Branch of learning.

The foregoing result was communicated to the students, after morning prayers, by Professor Park; after which, and some suitable remarks, the College Exercises were formally declared to be suspended until the first Monday in October.

The S. C. College Oct 17th 1807

The Faculty met at Tenement No 3 Room No 3.– John D. Murphy and Benjamin Whitner, from the Hopewell Academy, Pendleton, presented themselves for admission. After perusing the recommendations which they produced, and asking some questions, it was concluded that, for the present, they be allowed to recite with the Sophomore Class agreeably to Chapter 1st Sec 15th of the Laws.

The S. C. College October 20th 1807

The Faculty met at Tutor Herbemont's room, in pursuance of the President's summons.

Complaint had been made that Powell McRea, James Goodwin and John Mayrant had recently been engaged in disorderly behaviour, at one of the inns of this town, at an unseasonable hour of the night; that they had, either as principals or seconds been implicated in a duelling [illegible] proceeded to a neighboring district, where they were about to perform the last deed, when they were prevented by the interposition of the Civil Authority.

The above mentioned young gentlemen were separately examined, and made among others, the following acknowledgements.– McRea acknowledged that as a second he had been the bearer of a challenge from a citizen of Georgia to Goodwin. Goodwin acknowledged that he had accepted the challenge, and taken steps to comply with it. Mayrant acknowledged that he had consented to be the second of Goodwin, and begun to act in that capacity.

After mature deliberation, it was unanimously resolved that the following sentence of suspension be read this day at the evening prayers.

Sentence

Passed upon James Goodwin, Powell McRea, and John Mayrant of the Junior Class, in the Chapel of the South Carolina College, October 20th AD 1807.

At a meeting of the Faculty of the South Carolina College, held on the twentieth day of October in the year of our Lord one thousand, eight hundred and seven:

Whereas it has appeared in evidence to this Board as well as by confession, that James Goodwin, Powell McRea, and John Mayrant of the Junior Class were, on the eighteenth instant implicated in riotious conduct at a public house in this town followed by an engagement in duelling contrary to the peace and good order of the community, disgraceful to the literary institution of which they are members, and in open violation of its positive laws:

Resolved therefore that the said James Goodwin, Powell McRea, and John Mayrant be, and they are hereby suspended from all connection with this college; and that the nature of their respective offences be reported to the next meeting of the Board of Trustees.

The above sentence was pronounced by President Maxcy at the time appointed, and accompanied by a forcible, solemn, and eloquent address to the assembled college.

The S. C. College Dec. 16th 1807

A meeting of the Faculty was held this day at Tutor Hooker's Room. It having clearly appeared that Wm. Davis of the Senior Class has never attended to the duties of College since the public examination and has, for much the greatest part of the time, been absent from his room in study hours, both by night and by day. Resolved unanimously that he be degraded from his standing in the Senior class, and that his degradation be announced by the President after evening prayers.

The S. C. College Jan. 4th 1808

The Faculty held a meeting in the Library to consider the state of College, and particularly to devise means for preventing still further the frequenting of taverns by the students.

The S. C. College Feb. 1st 1808

The Faculty met at Tutor Herbemont's room this morning where they commenced and continued through the greatest part of the day a close examination of the students, relative to the outrages committed at the Steward's House and other places on Sat and Sunday night.

Feb. 2nd 1808

The business of yesterday was today resumed. In the course of the inquiry, several things transpired which fixed a strong suspicion on certain individuals, but there was no evidence which in the opinion of the Faculty, would justify a public punishment.

The South Carolina College Feb. 5 1808

At a meeting of the Faculty held this day: Whereas great irregularities have, at various times, but especially of late, taken place, which, in nearly every instance, that has come within the knowledge of the Faculty, has originated in drinking at taverns, and whereas the practice of visiting such places is still kept up by a number of the students, notwithstanding the express prohibition of the Laws, the repeated public charges and private remonstrances of the President, and the exertions of the Faculty, by mild means, to prevent it:

On motion of Professor Perrault, Resolved That we will, by severe means, endeavor to enforce that law of college which forbids the frequenting of taverns; and that any student, who shall be found drinking at such places, shall be suspended.

Resolved That the President, this evening publish to the assembled College the foregoing resolution.

The South Carolina College March 4th 1808

The meeting of the Faculty was held at the Library: President Maxcy in the chair.

The attention of the board was called to the case of Samuel B. Canbey of the Sophomore class, against whom were laid several charges of misdemeanor. Strong presumptive evidence appeared of his being engaged in an assault on the windows of the Steward's House, and in the destruction of some of the furniture about the College well, on the night of the 29th ult. It also appeared that he had, within a day or two, taken fish from a fish seller, in a private manner, without liberty, and without a compensation. It further appeared that he had, at various times, but particularly at one of the recitations, within a few days, treated an officer of College, with open, designed, and pointed disrespect.

The faculty, therefore, taking these circumstances into consideration, and calling to mind that this student was under the necessity of being censured for delinquency at the last examination; that he has constantly neglected his studies since that time; that he has, through most of the winter, been characterized by rashness of behaviour; that he has repeatedly given to the Faculty collectively and to several members of the Faculty individually promises of reformation, and has repeatedly violated those promises, and slighted their friendly advice; and believing him, while here, a detriment to the College, and no advantage to himself, resolved to suspend him at once, and to hold another meeting tomorrow or at some other more convenient time, to review the evidence to deliberate farther on the subject, and to determine on the nature of his sentence. Adjourned to 9 o'clock tomorrow.

The S. C. College 5th of March 1808

The Faculty assembled agreeably to adjournment. Canbey, being summoned, before the Board, the President, after some remarks, stated the grounds of accusation against him, and the nature of his offences, and concluded by ordering him to depart immediately from the precincts of College.

The S. C. College March 9th 1808

At a meeting of the Faculty held this evening at the President's house:

Resolved that Samuel Boykin Canbey be, and he is hereby suspended from College and debarred its privileges for the term of four months.

Resolved that the condition of his re-admittance to the Sophomore Class, at the termination of that period, shall be the passing of a satisfactory examination before the Faculty, and the production of a testimonial of good behaviour and a certificate from some reputable instructor of his having faithfully pursued those branches of study on which his class shall have been employed.

The S. C. College March 28th 1808

The Faculty held a meeting in the Library to enquire into some irregularities which took place on Saturday night, and having ascertained that two of the Seniors and three of the Sophomores were at a negro house of ill fame, where dancing and drinking were going on, at a late hour, they were severally summoned before the Faculty and admonished....

The South Carolina College Ap. 4th 1808,

At a meeting of the Faculty of the South Carolina College legally held in the College Library on Monday the fourth day of April in the year of our Lord One Thousand Eight Hundred and Eight:

The Reverend President Maxcy in the Chair:

Whereas John Y. Goodwin of the Senior Class, and James E. Dinkins of the Junior Class did, on Sunday morning last, so far lose sight of the laws of God, the rules of civil society and the statutes of this institution, as to engage in the barbarous, wicked and ungentlemanly act of Duelling:

Resolved, therefore, unanimously, that the said John Y. Goodwin and James E. Dinkins be, and they are hereby suspended from all connection with this college, debarred from all its privileges, and peremptorily ordered to depart from its precincts within twelve hours from this time.

Resolved, likewise, that the nature of their offences be exhibited before the Board of Trustees, and their names reported for expulsion.

The So: Car: College Apr. 8th 1808

The Faculty devoted this day to a serious consideration of the general state of College, and particularly of the result of the late examination. It was agreed by all that the examination of the classes was in its result, in many respects totally unsatisfactory.

It was apparent from the awkward manner in which a number acquitted themselves, that gross indeed, and almost unpardonable must have been their negligence.

Admonition, advice and remonstrance had been repeatedly used, and as repeatedly disregarded. The necessity of vigor was therefore manifest; and vigor in the present instance, the Faculty determined to try. It was of course Resolved that, considering the inattention of Powell McRea of the Senior Class, to his studies, his persistence in habits of dissipation, and the very little hope, which there is, of his deriving any advantage from his college life, a letter be directed to his father recommending to him to procure the dismission of his son.

Whereas Derrill Hart has been, for many weeks past, very remiss in his attention to college duties, frequently out at late hours of the night, often at taverns, and in some instances under the influence of liquor, and whereas he absented himself from one part of the Examination, and in the other part was found totally deficient.– Resolved therefore that Derrill Hart of the Junior Class be, and he is hereby degraded to the Sophomore Class.

John Stark having been equally irregular and discovering at the examination equal ignorance of his studies, Resolved that John Stark of the Junior Class be, and he is hereby degraded to the Sophomore Class.

Curtis Patrick having been equally inattentive to his studies and other collegiate duties and having without any permission been absent from the examination, Resolved that Curtis Patrick of the Junior Class be, and he is hereby degraded to the Sophomore Class.

John McRea having for sometime past been unjustifiably negligent in his studies, and appearing shamefully ignorant of the examination, Resolved that John McRea of the Sophomore Class be, and he is hereby placed on a conditional standing.

In addition to the above censures which were announced in public, the Faculty called before them several of the Sophomore Class to admonish them for their deficiency.

They also passed and published a resolution withholding their approbation from the manner in which the Sophomore Class in general appeared at their examination.

Resolved that Tutor Hooker, in the name of the Faculty, respectfully request Mr. O'Hanlon of Columbia not to entertain the students of College at late hours of the night, and not to suffer them to drink or gamble at any hour.

Resolved that hereafter those students who may be absent from the general examinations, whether with permission or without, shall, whenever they return, undergo a private examination: and that President Maxcy do, at some convenient times, make known this resolve to the students.

The South Carolina College April 13. 1808

At a legal meeting of the Faculty held this day: Whereas John Stark of the Sophomore Class did on the eighth instant, in the view of several of his fellow students, by opprobrious language and menacing gestures notoriously insult one of the officers of this institution, giving him, among other indecencies the shameful epithet of "*infernal liar*", exhibiting conduct unbecoming him as a young gentleman, and directly opposite to that deference and respect for his officers which is enjoined by the laws.

Resolved therefore that the said John Stark be, and he is hereby suspended from his standing in College.

Resolved likewise that his offence be stated, and his name reported to the Board of Trustees for expulsion.

The S. C. College April 18, 1808

The Faculty having taken into consideration the case of John Stark of the Sophomore Class who was suspended on the 13th of April: Resolved, in consequence of his acknowledgements to Professor Perrault and assurances of future good behaviour—in consideration of its being the first instance of an offence of this kind—and in consideration of the very honorable ground which his father has taken for his restoration to the college in consistency with its honor and its interests—that John Stark be permitted to resume his standing in the Sophomore class from which he was suspended.

Resolved further that if he shall steadily and faithfully pursue his studies and strictly conform to the laws until the ensuing commencement, the Faculty will ask leave to withdraw the report made to the Trustees.

The S. C. College April 19, 1808

The Faculty met at Tutor Hubemont's room and called to account several students who had left the College Commons, and were boarding in town.

A much greater degree of regularity than usual having, for some weeks past, reigned in the affairs of College, the Faculty were happy to find it unnecessary, at the present meeting to extend their animadversions to others objects, and therefore soon adjourned.

The South Carolina College June 9th 1809

The Faculty met in the Library to take into consideration the unpardonable deficiency manifested for a few weeks past by the students in their attention to the duties of College. Several were called up and admonished by the President. It was then resolved by the Faculty that they should meet once a week during the present term for the purpose of inspecting the Monitors Bills, that those students who persevered in their deficiency without assigning reasonable excuses, should be publicly admonished or dismissed from the College, as the case might require.

The S. C. College Feb. 21st 1810

The Faculty having assembled, continued their inquiries. Whereas sufficient evidence has been produced that on Friday night last Wm. Wade of the Senior class was concerned in making a festive entertainment at the house of an infamous mulatto woman—that he carried a pistol with which he intended to defend property not his own—that he actually threatened to take the lives of some who entered the house. For these reasons besides a peculiar obstinacy discovered in Wade in presence of the Faculty—Resolved, that Wm. Wade be and is hereby suspended from all the privileges of the College until the first of May next—Resolved, that if he shall then produce sufficient evidences of his good behaviour & be able to pass a satisfactory examination, he shall be readmitted into the College—

Resolved that he be ordered forthwith to leave the precincts of College & that if he disobey any of these resolves or refuse to comply with the terms of his suspension he shall be reported to the Trustees as the law directs—

The following resolves were then passed by the Faculty. That if any student shall be absent from his room without special liberty after 11 o'clock at night, or shall be found walking beyond College grounds after half past nine o'clock in the evening, or shall be detected in visiting houses occupied by negroes or persons of bad fame, or shall clandestinely enter the enclosure or house of any persons in, or near Columbia, or commit depredations on their property, such student shall be forthwith suspended from the College.

Likewise that particular admonition be publicly given to those students who have lately been concerned in some of the irregularities and enormities above mentioned.

The S. C. College April 18th 1811

At a regular meeting of the Faculty—Whereas James N. Mayrant did a few evenings since notoriously trample on the authority of the Faculty, & set the laws of College as well as the laws of God at defiance by wantonly & profanely whistling aloud in the Chapel during evening prayers. It is also well known to the whole College that notwithstanding the repeated admonitions given by the officers of College Mayrant has time after time behaved in a rude disorderly & insulting manner at the Commons particularly by wantonly destroying the Stewards furniture—In addition to these considerations Mayrant has most shamefully neglected the exercises & duties of College and thereby become unpardonably deficient. It is therefore the unanimous opinion of the Faculty that the good of the College requires that Mayrant should no longer be a member of it whereupon

Resolved that James N. Mayrant be and he is hereby suspended from the college and ordered forthwith to leave its precincts.

Resolved that he be reported to the Trustees of the College as the law directs for expulsion.

The S. C. College June 27th 1811

The Faculty having this day closed the examination of the several classes in college met in the library to form the result. It was agreed that with two exceptions the members of the several classes should be allowed to hold their respective standings. With regard to Pepoon & Hirons of the junior class it was resolved that for their unpardonable inattention to the duties of College, & their general deficiency in their studies, but particularly in Euclids' Elements, they be placed on a conditional standing, & be required to make up their deficiencies during the ensuing vacation in order to regain a full standing. It was likewise determined by the faculty that those members of the junior class unavoidably deficient in Euclid & Algebra, & also those of the sophomore class in Algebra be required to make up their deficiencies during the vacation.—In the South Caroliniana Library, the University of South Carolina. Photocopies in the Southern Historical Collection, the University of North Carolina.

14. Honor roll at the University of South Carolina, 1806-1861

(V., Valedictory; S. Salutatory.)

The valedictory was first honor until after 1821.

1807—Walter Crenshaw, v.; John Caldwell, s.
1808—James R. Gregg, v.; John Murphy, s.
1809—Jas. L. Petigru, v.; Alexander Bowie, s.
1810—James Dillett, v.; William Lowry, s.
1811—B. J. Earle, v.; William Arthur, s.
1812—H. L. Pinckney, v.; John B. O'Neall, s.
1813—George McDuffie, v.; John G. Creagh, s.
1814—Hugh S. Legare, v.; Henry Trescott, s.
1815—Elijah Gilbert, v.
1816—D. L. Wardlaw, v.; Henry A. Gibbes, s.
1817—Charles Fishburn, v.; Archibald Baynard, s.

1818—Francis H. Wardlaw, v.; Josiah J. Kilpatrick, s.
1819—Thomas H. Taylor, v.; C. G. Memminger, s.
1820—James Terry, v.; Richard Yeadon, s.
1821—Basil Manly, v.; Amzi W. Alexander, s.
(From this time the salutatory was declared by the board of trustees to be the first honor.)
1822—Wm. J. Wilson, s.; J. W. Grant, v.
1823—Wm. F. Colcock, s.; Robert Spenser, v.
1824—Richard T. Brumby, s.; James W. Daniel, v.
1825—Randall Hunt, s.; T. J. Withers, v.
1826—Edmund Bellinger, s.; R. G. Quarles, v.
1827—This year twenty-four seniors were expelled and no honors were awarded.
1828—Nicholas Summer, s.; Hiram McKnight, v.
1829—Lewis R. Gibbes, s.; W. J. Boone, v.
1830—B. F. Johnston, s.; John A. Mills, v.
1831—James H. Thornwell, s.; Richard S. Gladney, v.
1832—Joseph W. Lesesne, s.; Nelson Mitchell, v.
1833—James Simons, s.; Elisha Hamlin, v.
1834—C. P. Sullivan, s.; M. L. Bonham, v.
1835—William Blanding, s.
1836—J. Pearson, s.; A. Simkins, v.
1837—John N. Frierson, s.; D. W. Ray, v.
1838—A. Gregg, s.; E. Bellinger, v.
1839—Isaac M. Hutson, s.; David E. Frierson, v.
1840—Haskell S. Rhett, s.; Thomas M. Hanckel, v.
1841—Wm. J. Rivers, s.; Robert B. Boylston, v.
1842—Wm. P. Starke, s.; J. M. Landrum, v.
1843—S. J. Barnett, s.; C. D. Melton, v.
1844—P. H. Nelson, s.; J. H. Carlisle, v.
1845—Robert Garlington, s.; Thomas B. Fraser, v.
1846—E. L. Patton, s.; A. A. Morse, v.
1847—Thomas Frost, s.; John S. Green, v.
1848—James P. Adams, s.; L. S. Blanding, v.
1849—C. H. Simonton, s.; T. J. Glover, v.
1850—J. H. Rion, s.; Robert W. Barnwell, v.
1851—J. H. Elliott, s.; J. R. Chalmers, v.
1852—J. H. Hudson, s.; D. H. Porter, v.
1853—J. I. Middleton, s.; C. E. Leverett, v.
1854—James Lowndes, s.; Benjamin R. Stuart, v.

1855—C. W. Boyd, s.; W. L. Trenholm, v.
1856—G. M. Fairlee, s.; H. Covington, v.
1857—W. H. White, s.; E. L. Rivers, v.
1858—Edward H. Buist, s.; Grimke Rhett, v.
1859—Wm. Thomas Cleveland, s.; Wm. E. Boggs, v.
1860—Thomas M. Logan, s.; Alexander C. Haskell, v.

There were no commencement exercises in December, 1861.
—Green, *op. cit.*, 432-33.

15. A State University is Proposed for Virginia, 1806

On Tuesday Mr. Semple asked for leave to bring in a bill, to establish "the University of Virginia." Much, he observed, had been already done to improve the face of our country; and multiply the productions of the earth. Surely it was time to do something for its people; something that might conduce to the improvements of man, and multiply that most valuable of all productions: an enlightened understanding.

The advantages of education were not to be denied, if it was considered in regard to the morals of a nation. Ignorance was the parent of vice, and it would be idle to expect men to do what was right, until they knew what was really so. Considered in regard to a republican government, the wisdom of the people must be considered as its firmest support. The very existence of that form of government depended upon the people having information enough to penetrate into the designs of the rich and the powerful. It is wisdom alone that constitutes the check upon all those active powers, which are striving to overthrow the liberties of the people.

It would be impracticable perhaps to introduce *at once* into the commonwealth a general system of education. Difficulties might at present exist which would require the hand of time to remove. But was this any reason, why the legislature should sink into complete listlessness? It was time to set about the work: other legislatures taking it up, *where* they left it, might contribute to enlarge the system.

Mr. Semple explained the details of this project; it was desirable (he thought) that the University should be established in some county, that was below the South-West mountain, in a central situation, recommended by the salubrity of the climate, and the cheapness of provisions. It should be far removed from every scene of bustle, dissipation, and vice. To support this institution, it was contemplated to raise the sum of 500,000 dols. At least *one fifth* of this sum was to be collected by voluntary contributions: 30,000 dols. every year by a lottery, and the state should pledge itself to authorize no other, until this plan was accomplished; and the rest of the capital, by a tax to be laid upon such articles as are principally in the hands of the rich. *Three-fifths* of this capital were to be employed in conducting the institution; *two-fifths* in purchasing a proper scite, and in erecting the necessary buildings. In the purchase of the scite, he conceived that the land attached to it should be in so large a body as to keep at a distance, by the jurisdiction to be given to the University, every person that might injure the morals of the pupils, at the same time to admit of a certain number of lots being leased out for the benefit of the institution.

Mr. Semple hoped that leave would be given to bring in the bill.

Leave was accordingly given, and Messrs. Semple, Tazwell, Smythe (of Wythe), Harvie, Miller (Northumberland), Jones (Nottoway), Wooding, Reeder, Moore, Minor, Garland, Harrison (Amelia), and Carter Harrison were appointed a committee to bring in the bill.

Mr. Semple then asked leave to bring in a bill "to open a subscription for the benefit of the University of Virginia." Referred to the same select committee.—*The Richmond Enquirer*, January 16, 1806.

16. Some duties of the faculty of South Carolina College, 1806

The Faculty shall examine all applicants for admission to the College, and determine on their qualifications, they shall appoint the time, place, and mode of recitation, and other exercises for each class, or individual student; and with the concurrence of the standing committee, may make provisional rules and regulations, for the government of the students, in the recess of the board of trustees, subject to the control of the board.

The Faculty shall keep a register, in which shall be entered the names of all the students admitted; and in successive columns shall be noted their progress through the classes, marks of distinction conferred upon them, departure, dismission or graduation. To which shall be added an alphabetic index. They shall also keep a book in which shall be minuted all their transactions; and the register and minute books of the Faculty, shall be laid before the trustees at their meetings in Columbia; and may, at all times, be inspected by any individual trustees, or member of the state government.

The President and professors shall, during every session of the College, constantly devote themselves to the instruction and government of the students. They shall constantly attend the devotional exercises of the chapel, and the President shall perform prayers, morning and evening. In his absence the officers shall perform in rotation.—Green, *op. cit.*, 216-17.

17. William E. Parker is graduated from the University of Tennessee, 1806

Wm. E. Parker was examined on Virgil and Rhet., Horace and Logic, Geog. 7. Gr. Test., Lucien, Math's, Ethics, Nat'l Phil'y and A. Hor., 7, at dif't ex's and approved, graduated on the 18th day of Oct., 1806.

S. C.
Nov. 25th, 1806.

—Note by President Samuel Carrick, of Blount College, 1806, in Moses White, *Early History of the University of Tennessee*, 15. White says that Parker "was unquestionably the first student to be graduated at a college in Tennessee."

18. Thomas Jefferson recommends du Pont de Nemours for president of the University of New Orleans, 1806

I sent M. Briot's letter to the Philosophical society, having as you are sensible, no time to give to objects of that nature. Since Orleans has been established under a government of it's own, it's legislature has begun a scheme for an academy, and I suppose Congress will endow it with lands. I apprised Govr. Claiborne of the advantages the institution would derive from placing you at it's head. He is fully sensible of it, and will pay due attention to it when the scheme is advanced to maturity.—Thomas Jefferson to du Pont de Nemours, February 12, 1806. Given in Dumas Malone (ed.), *Correspondence Between Thomas Jefferson and Pierre du Pont de Nemours, 1798-1817*, p. 89.

19. The curricula of South Carolina College, 1806, 1836, 1860

LATIN

1806		1836	1860
Freshman:	Virgil (Bucolics and Georgics) Cicero De Oratore.	Horace (complete)	Livy, Bk. XXI Horace (except Ars Poetica).
Sophomore:	Horace	Tacitus (Histories, Germania, Agricola). Juvenal (six satires).	Tacitus (Germania, Agricola). Select Satires of Juvenal and Persius.

	1806	1836	1860
Junior:	Cicero De Oratore	Cicero De Oratore. Juvenal (four satires).	Cicero's De Officiis or Lucan's Pharsalia. Horace's Arts Poetica.
Senior:	Palladius De Re Rustica.	Select Latin.	Terence's Andria. Plautus's Captivi.
		GREEK	
Freshman:	New Testament. Xenophon's Cyropedia.	Xenophon's Anabasis (six bks.) Homer (eleven bks.)	Homer's Iliad completed (eighteen bks.)
Sophomore:	Homer's Iliad.	Homer (ten bks.)	Demosthenes's De Corona and selections from historians and orators.
Junior:	Longinus's Sublimitate.	De Homer (two bks.) Demosthenes.	Aeschylus, Septem, Sophocles, Oed. Tyr., Euripides, Medea.
Senior:	Demosthenes, Select Orations.	Greek Dramatists.	Pindar, Plato, Aristotle (selections).
		MATHEMATICS	
Freshman:	Arithmetic.	Bourdon's Algebra to equations of 3rd degree, ratio and proportion, infinite series, logarithms, Legendre's plane geom.	Rev. of Algebra (in theory of logarithms), Arith., Theoretical (Loomis), Geometry (Loomis).
Sophomore:	Vulgar and decimal fractions, Algebra.	Legendre's solid geometry.	Plane Trig. Conic Sections.
Junior:	Geometry, theoretical and practical.	Desc. Geom., Conic Sections, Analyt. Geom., Fluxions, Quadrature, Curvature, etc.	Spherical Trig. Analytical Geom. (Davies) Lectures on Differential and Integral Calculus.
Senior:	Parts of higher Math.		
		ENGLISH	
Freshman:	Eng. Grammar.	Blair's Lectures and Rhetorical exercises.	
Sophomore:	Sheridan's Lectures on Elocution.		Elocution.
Junior:		Elements of Criticism Rhetoric.	Whateley's Rhetoric. Elements of Criticism.
Senior:			Criticism and Elocution.

President Maxcy taught Belles Lettres, as did President Preston. The subject was attached to one of the chairs, Logic for the most part.

HISTORY

	1806	1836	1860
Freshman:		Tyler's History.	Ancient History.
Sophomore:			History of Middle Ages. History of Bible.
Junior:			Political Philosophy.
Senior:	Millot's Elements of History.	History, Political Economy.	Political Economy, Political Ethics.

By 1838 Professor Lieber had introduced History into the junior and senior classes. In 1847 the sophomores studied History of the Middle Ages; the juniors studied Modern History, this last being changed to Political Philosophy in 1849. History of the Bible, Connexion of Sacred and Profane History, came in for the first time in 1859.

LOGIC.

From the beginning in the junior class.

MORAL PHILOSOPHY.

From the beginning in the junior year.

METAPHYSICS.

Always in the senior year.
—Green, *op. cit.*, 181-82.

20. Laws on misdemeanors and criminal offenses at South Carolina College, 1807

1. If any student shall be guilty of any blasphemy, robbery, duelling, fornication, forgery, or any such atrocious crime, he shall be expelled.

2. All the students are strictly forbidden to play at cards, or any unlawful game; to use profane or obscene language; to strike or insult any person; to associate with persons of known bad character; to visit taverns without liberty; to appear in indecent dress, or in woman's apparel; to lie, steal, get drunk, or be guilty of other gross immoralities. If any student shall transgress in any of these respects, he

shall be admonished, suspended, degraded or expelled, as the case may require.

3. No student may keep in his room any kind of firearms or gun powder; nor fire any in or near the College, in any manner whatever; and any student who shall violate this law, shall be liable to admonition, suspension or expulsion.

4. If any student shall wilfully insult or strike any of the officers of the College, he shall be suspended or expelled.

5. All the students are strictly forbidden to play on any instrument of music in the hours of study, and also on Sundays; and shall abstain from their usual diversions and exercises on those days.

6. If any student shall refuse to open the door of his room, when required to do it by one of the Faculty, he shall be liable to public admonition; and the Faculty, when they shall think it necessary may break open any room in the College at the expense of those by whom they are refused admittance.

7. If any student shall refuse to give evidence respecting the violation of any of the laws of the College, when required by the Faculty, he shall be admonished or suspended.

8. No student is permitted to make a practice of entertaining company in his room, especially in the hours of study.

9. All students are strictly forbidden, without previous liberty obtained of a member of the Faculty, to bring any spiritous liquor into the College; and if any student, by bringing spiritous liquor into the College, shall be the occasion of riotous conduct or tumult, he shall be liable to admonition or suspension.

10. No student shall make any festival entertainment in the College, or in the town of Columbia, or take part in any thing of the kind, without liberty previously obtained of the President.

11. All the students are required to be particularly careful respecting fire, especially when they are obliged to go from their rooms; or in carrying it through the entries; and they are strictly forbidden to smoke segars or pipes in any part of the College, except their own rooms.

12. If any students shall enter into a combination to oppose the authority of the Faculty, or to impede the operation of the laws, they shall be punished by admonition, suspension or expulsion; and if any student shall express a determination not to submit to the laws, he shall be immediately suspended from the College; and be reported to the trustees.—Green, *op. cit.*, 220-22.

21. Charter of a college in East Tennessee, 1807

WHEREAS it is provided by an act of the Congress of the United States, entitled, "An Act to authorize the State of Tennessee to issue grants to certain lands therein described, and to settle the claims to the vacant and unappropriated lands within the same," passed the eighteenth day of April, one thousand eight hundred and six, that there shall be one hundred thousand acres of land laid off on the south side of Holston and French Broad, and west side of Big Pigeon rivers, to which the Indian claim had been estinguished; and that the proceeds of the sales of the said one hundred thousand acres of land should be appropriated in such way by the legislature of this state that the profits thereof should be applied to the support of two colleges in this state, the one in East and the other in West Tennessee, to be established by the legislature of this state; And whereas it is expedient that this General Assembly should establish a college in East Tennessee, capable of receiving that part of said donation, designed by said act to be given to the college to be established in East Tennessee aforesaid: Therefore,

1. *Be it enacted by the General Assembly of the State of Tennessee*, That there shall be thirty persons appointed by this General Assembly, who shall be, and hereby are constituted a body-politic and corporate, by the name of the "Trustees of East Tennessee College." And by that name shall have perpetual succession and a common seal. And the said trustees, and their successors, by the name aforesaid, shall be endowed with, and receive in such manner as the General Assembly of this state may from time to time direct, that part of the donation aforesaid, which was designed for the college in East Tennessee; and they shall by the name aforesaid, be capable in law, to purchase, receive and hold to them and their successors forever, or for any less estate, any lands, tenements, goods, or chattels, which shall be given, granted, or devised to them or purchased by them to the use of said college, and to use and dispose of the same, in such manner as to them shall seem most advantageous for the use of said college. The said trustees and their successors by the name aforesaid, may sue and be sued, plead and be impleaded, in any court of law or equity in this state or elsewhere.

2. *Be it enacted*, That no less than seven of said trustees shall constitute a board, to determine upon any matter relative to said college,

nor shall any of the real or personal estate belonging to said college be disposed of or appropriated at any session of said board, except a states session; nor shall any president or professor in said college, ever be chosen, except at a stated session of the board; but temporary appointments which shall expire with the next stated session after they are made, may be made at an adjourned or called session of the board.

3. *Be it enacted*, That the said trustees at their stated sessions, shall have full power and authority to elect a president, such professors, tutors, and other officers in said college, as they may judge necessary, and to make such by-laws, rules and regulations for the government of said college, and the promotion of education therein, as in their opinion may be expedient or necessary; *Provided*, such by-laws, rules and regulations are not inconsistent with the constitution and laws of the United States, or of this state.

4. *Be it enacted*, That upon the death, removal out of the county in which he resides, or resignation of any of the said trustees, the vacancy thereby occasioned, shall be supplied, by the remaining trustees appointing some other person, a resident of the same county, in which the one deceased, resigned or removed, resided; which appointment shall remain until the expiration of the next session of the General Assembly; within which time, the General Assembly shall supply such vacancy.

5. *Be it enacted*, That the said trustees shall have two meetings of their board in each year, at the place where said college is established, to commence on the first Thursday of April, and the first Thursday of October, in each year; and at either of said sessions, the board may adjourn to any day they may judge expedient; and when, in the opinion of the president and any two trustees of said college, a called session may be necessary, they may call the same. And at any stated session, the board of trustees shall have power to remove the president, professors, or any other officer of said college; and to fix and regulate their respective salaries. And the president and professors of said college, with the advice and consent of a majority of the board, shall have full power and authority, at any stated session of the said board, to confer on any student in said college, or any other person they may think proper, the degrees of Bachelor of Arts, Master of Arts, or any other degree known and used in any college or university, in any of the United States. At every meeting of the board of trustees, when there is a president of the college present, he shall

be president of the board, but shall in no wise have a vote, when there is no president present, the board may appoint one of their own body to act as president.

6. *Be it enacted*, That each of said trustees, before acting in his appointment, shall before some judge or justice of the peace, take an oath, faithfully, honestly and impartially to discharge the duties of his said appointment; and that in all votes by him to be given as a trustee of said college, he will so vote, as in his judgment will best promote the interest of said college, and education therein.

7. *Be it enacted*, That said trustees shall have full power to sell, exchange, assign, transfer or convey any of the real or personal estate of said college by deed or otherwise, except the proceeds of the sales of an moiety of said one hundred thousand acres of land, with which the said college is endowed by this act, at any stated session of said trustees, provided a majority of the acting trustees shall be privy to, and join in the same. And said trustees, at their first stated meeting, or at some adjournment of the same, shall appoint one of their own body, secretary; and one other of their own body, treasurer; and said treasurer before entering on the duties of office shall enter into bond, with approved security, in the sum of one hundred thousand dollars, to the governor for the time being, and his successors in office, conditioned for the safe keeping, paying, settling and accounting for all moneys by him received, on account of said college.

8. *Be it enacted*, That said college be established on ten acres of land, within two miles of Knoxville, conveyed in trust, for the use of said college, by Moses White, at a place called the Rocky or Poplar Spring.—Edward Scott, *Laws of Tennessee*, I, 1047.

22. Tennessee exempts from taxation lands of the University of North Carolina, 1807

Section 2. *Be it enacted*, That all those lands within the limits of this state, which have been devised or given by any person or persons to the trustees of the University of North-Carolina, or to any other person or persons for the use of said University, shall be, and the same hereby are exempted from the payment of any state, county or other tax, nor shall the said lands or any part thereof, be liable to the payment of any tax, nor shall the said trustees, or any other person in whom the title to such lands may be, be ever liable to return a list of such lands, or to pay any tax of any description therefor, so long as said lands are held for the use of said University.

Section 3. *Be it enacted*, That from and after the passing of this act, all the lands within the limits of this state, which hath been appropriated for the use of schools, or which are held by any person or persons in trust for the use of any college, academy, or other seminary of education in this state, shall be, and the same hereby are exempted from the payment of any state county or other tax; nor shall any person or persons be bound to return any list of any such lands nor be liable to pay any tax therefor.—*Acts of Tennessee*, 1807. Passed November 30, 1807.

23. The trustees of the University of Georgia have to adjust salaries of the faculty, 1808

Upon taking into view the scarcity of money at this period, and the small number of students at Franklin College, Resolved, that the salaries of the Officers from this time be as follows, to wit, The President, fifteen hundred dollars P annum. The Master of the Grammar school six hundred dollars, and the Professor of the french language four hundred dollars.—Minutes of the Trustees of the University of Georgia, 1794-1817, Vol. I, 152. Original in General Library, the University of Georgia. Photocopy in the Southern Historical Collection, the University of North Carolina.

24. The trustees of the University of Georgia order repairs to the buildings, 1808

The prudential Committee having reported verbally that they have examined the rooms of the college, and the situation of the house, and that they find many of them foul and much out of repair—It is ordered, that Mr. Hull Chairman of the prudential Committee be requested to employ some fit and proper person or persons to clean and scour out the rooms, and make such repairs as may be deemed necessary—to have good strong locks put upon the doors, glass in the sashes, and the windows fastened down so as prevent them from being opened from without, and that hereafter all the rooms, not in the immediate occupation of some one or more of the tutors, or students be locked up and the keys thereof kept by the President, except when the Rooms are opened once each month to be aired, or whenever the said Chairman shall apply for them. And be it further resolved that the President draw on the Treasurer for the sum of One hundred dollars payable to said Chairman, to enable him to carry into effect the foregoing resolution.—*Ibid.*, I, 141.

25. Extracts from the minutes of the trustees of the University of Tennessee, 1808-1829

Document no. 1—April 7, 1808

At a meeting of the Trustees of East Tennessee College at the Court House in Knoxville on the first Thursday in April 1808, being the seventh day of said Month

Present John Cocke, Archibald Roane, John Kennedy, Francis A. Ramsey, Richard Mitchell, Arthur Crozier, John Crozier, John Williams and Thomas Emmerson.

The Oath [1] required by the Act of Assembly was administered to the members present by John Hillsman Esquire a Justice of the Peace for the County of Knox—

On Motion General John Cocke was appointed President pro: Tem:—

Thomas Emmerson was appointed Secretary

John Crozier was elected Treasurer and entered into Bond with Security as required by Law—

A Communication from the Rev. Samuel Carrick President of Blount College was received and read—

On Motion, Resolved that the Rev. Samuel Carrick be appointed President of East Tennessee College pro: Tem: who shall hold his Office untill a permanent Appointment shall be made, and shall be allowed a Salary at the Rate of Four hundred and fifty Dollars pr. Annum—

Resolved that in Case the Number of Students shall in the Opinion of the President require an Assistant Tutor he be Authorized to procure one, and that he render an Account of the Expence incurred thereby to the Trustees at their next Meeting.

On Motion Resolved that the President continue to carry on the business of Tuition at the Place heretofore known by the Name of

1. "*Be it enacted,* That each of said trustees, before acting in his appointment, shall before some judge or justice of the peace, take an oath, faithfully, honestly and impartially to discharge the duties of his said appointment; and that in all votes by him to be given as a trustee of said college, he will so vote, as in his judgment will best promote the interest of said college, and education therein." Scott, *Laws of Tennessee,* I, 1047.

Blount College, under the Rules and Regulations heretofore adopted by the Trustees of Blount College, which Rules and Regulations are hereby adopted and Shall continue in force untill the Next stated meeting of this Board.

Resolved that the Board of Trustees will at their next stated meeting proceed to make a permanent Appointment of a President of the College.

Resolved that the Secretary be directed to cause the foregoing resolution to be published in the Newspapers printed in Knoxville for four weeks, together with a Notice of the Time and place of Meeting and a list of the Names of the Trustees.

Resolved that the Treasurer furnish the Necessary books for keeping the Records and Accounts of the Board and that he render his Account therefor to the Next Meeting—

On Motion the Board Adjourned untill the next stated meeting—

October, 1808

At a meeting of the Board of Trustees of East Tennessee College at the House formerly called Blount College on the first Thursday in October 1808—

Present The Rev. Samuel Carrick, President John Kennedy, John Williams, John Crozier, Archibald Roane, Francis A. Ramsey, Arthur Crozier, and Thomas Emmerson—

The following members to wit, George W. Campbell, John Rhea, James Reece, Major Lea, Hopkins Lacey, Robert Gant, and John Lowry appeared, and the Oath required by Law having been administered to them by Francis A. Ramsey Esquire a Justice of the Peace for the County of Knox, they took their Seats—

A Communication from the President inclosing his Account against the Trustees was received and read—

On Motion Resolved that the President to be elected be allowed Four Hundred and fifty Dollars as his Salary for the ensuing year—

The Board proceeded to the Election of a President, Mr. Lea and Mr. Reece were appointed Tellers; On Counting the Ballots, it appeared that the Rev. Samuel Carrick was unanimously elected—

Ordered, that the Treasurer pay to the President, the Sum of one hundred and Seventy four Dollars and forty five Cents, being the Balance due him as pr. his Account rendered—

Ordered, that Messrs Williams, Roane and Emmerson, be Appointed a Committee to draw up such rules and regulations for the Government of the College as they may deem Necessary, and that they report the same to the Board—

Ordered, that the rules for the Government of the College, heretofore adopted, be continued in force untill altered or Amended by the Board of Trustees—

On Motion Adjourned untill the next stated meeting—

October 5, 1820

At a meeting of the Trustees of East Tennessee College at Knoxville on the first Thursday of October 1820 being the 5th day of said month.

Present Messrs	John Crozier	Arthur Crozier
	F. A. Ramsey	Wm. B. Lenoir
	Major Lea	Enoch Parsons
	John Williams	John Sutherland Junr
	Robert King	William C. Myeratt

The Oath required by the act of Assembly was administered to John Sutherland Jr., Wm. B. Lenoir, Robert King, Enoch Parsons, William C. Myeratt by Francis A. Ramsey a justice of the peace for Knox County, who thereupon severally took their seats as Trustees of said College—

On motion Major Lea Esqr was appointed President Pro: tem:—

William C. Myeratt was appointed Secretary in the room of Thomas Emmerson—

The board proceeded to elect a President when the Reverend David A. Sherman was unanimously chosen who on being notified thereof, appeared and took his seat accordingly—

On motion It was ordered that Francis A Ramsey John Sutherland Junr. and William C. Myeratt be a committee to inquire into the state of the funds, the Library and other real or personal property belonging to East Tennessee College, and also to procure if practicable the record of the proceedings of former meetings of said Trustees and report thereof to the next adjourned meeting of the Board—

On motion Ordered that Col. John Williams Gen. Enoch Parsons and John Sutherland Jr. be appointed a committee to confer with the board of Trustees of Hamden Sidney Academy and know whether a union can be effected as to the two institutions and their funds and to report thereof to the next adjourned meeting of the board—

On motion Resolved unanimously that East Tennessee College be put into immediate operation with the Students now belonging to Hamilton Sidney Academy, under the care and management of the Reverend David A Sherman—

Ordered that the Rev. David A Sherman, Col. John Williams and Francis A Ramsey be a committee to draft rules for the regulation of East Tennessee College and submit the same to the next adjourned meeting of this board—

On motion of Col F A Ramsey It is Ordered by the board, That the meetings and adjournments of the board of Trustees of East Tennessee College be hereafter Opened and concluded by prayer—

The Board adjourned to meet again on Tuesday the 10th instant, at 12 O Clock.

At an adjourned meeting of the Trustees of East Tennessee College at Knoxville On Tuesday the 10th day of October 1820 Present

The Rev. David A Sherman
John Crozier
F. A. Ramsey
John Williams
Wm. B. Lenoir
Enoch Parsons
John Sutherland Jr
William C. Mynatt

Col. John Williams, Gen. Enoch Parsons and John Sutherland Jr. made the following report, in obedience to an Order of the board at their last meeting, which report was received and ordered to be recorded and is in the words & figures following—

In a conference between a committee of the Trustees of East Tennessee College and a committee of the Trustees of Hamden Sidney Academy for the purpose of ascertaining whether a temporary union of the two institutions can take place—

The Committees above mentioned do agree that the Trustees of Hamden Sidney Academy shall continue to conduct and regulate the admission of students and the manner of teaching in said Academy as at the Commencement of the present session—

The Trustees of said Academy shall superintend the Collection of tuition money, as respects the College for the present session and permanently for the Academy and pay the same over to the President as heretofore—

The Trustees of the College shall regulate the admission of students into the College, the price of tuition and the manner of teaching, they shall also attend the examinations of the students and the conferring of degrees and shall likewise manage the College funds.

It is further agreed that Only the students in the first branch in said Academy shall be admitted into East Tennessee College and the Trustees of said Academy agree that they will continue the Rev. D. A. Sherman President of said Academy—

The Trustees of the College agreed that the price of tuition in the College for the present session shall not exceed the price paid by the students in the first branch in said Academy at the commencement of the present session—It is further agreed that the above agreement shall be continued untill the Trustees of either institution give the other thirty days notice of their desire to abandon the same—

The above basis of an agreement the Committees submit to the respective boards of Trustees for their adoption—

signed John Williams Chairman
for the Committee of the
College

Joseph C. Strong Chairman
of the Committee for the
Academy

Resolved unanimously that the Rev. D. A. Sherman, President, &c prescribe rules regulating the of tuition and other rules necessary for the government of East Tennessee College untill the next stated meeting of the Board of Trustees—

The board proceeded to elect a Professor of the Mathematics and natural Philosophy when Mr. Daniel E. Watrons was unanimously chosen—Francis A Ramsey, John Sutherland & W. C. Mynatt a committee appointed at the last meeting of the board of Trustees to inquire into the state of the funds belonging to East Tennessee College &c. Report that said College have $8,350 in Bank stock in the Bank of the State of Tennessee at Knoxville that the dividends on said stock up to the first day of July 1820 amounted to the sum of $990.. . 56 cents—Said committee also report that they have procured the book containing the records of the proceedings of former meetings of the Board of Trustees of this College—that they have not been able to ascertain as to other property of said College and ask leave to suspend their report or that subject untill the next stated meeting of the board, which was allowed—

Ordered that

Francis A Ramsey and John Sutherland be appointed a Committee to settle and direct the payments of all sum or sums of money that is due by the East Tennessee College and report the same to the next stated meeting of the board—

It is ordered by the board that the Secretary publish in some newspaper printed in Knoxville at least four weeks prior to the next stated meeting of the board, the names of the Trustees of said College and instruct their attendance thereat—And that a similar publication be made prior to each stated meeting of the Board—

Board adjourned untill next stated meeting.

October 11, 1821

East Tennessee College

At an adjourned meeting of the Board of Trustees on Thursday the 11th day of October 1821. Present the Reverend David A. Sherman

John Crozier	John Sutherland Jr.
Major Lea	William Park
Robert King	Matthew Nelson
Edward Scott	William C. Mynatt Trustees

Matthew Nelson was duly qualified as one of the Trustees of said College and took his seat accordingly.

The Board ordered that the following rules be adopted for the Government of said college and ordered the same to be recorded—

The Laws of East Tennessee College

Chap. 1

Of the government of the College

The government of the College shall be vested in the President, Professors and Tutors or such officers as shall be duly elected qualified and introduced into office and shall be styled the Faculty of the College—

2. The President shall have power to direct in all matters relating to the College; to govern the Students, and to punish all crimes and offences, committed by them against the laws of the College, except in cases referred by law to the Faculty or Trustees—

3. The Professors & Tutors, severally, shall have power to govern the undergraduate students, and to punish them for any crime, except in cases referred by law to the Faculty or Trustees; Provided that they

may not, in any case, proceed contrary to the advice and direction of the President—

4. The President, at his discretion shall have authority to appoint a meeting of the Faculty. All matters, which by law are referred to the Faculty, shall be brought before such meetings and determined by the major part of the members present, whereof the President shall be always One, and concurring in such determination: And when the members present shall be equally divided the President shall have a casting vote—

5. Every judgment for expulsion, dismission for fault, suspension, public admonition, and sending a student home, shall be by the Faculty, except in cases provided for by the State Legislature, and every judgment for expulsion and dismission, shall be in writing and published before the assembled students in such manner as the President shall direct—copies of all such judgments on application to the President shall be given to all concerned—And if any student shall apprehend himself aggrieved by any such judgment he shall have liberty at any time after the same shall have been given of applying to the President, by a petition in writing, for a new Trial; And on such petition the President shall order a new trial to be had—Should the student his parent or guardian prefer making an appeal to the Trustees, to a new trial before the Faculty, or should he feel aggrieved by the wrath of such new trial before the Faculty, he shall have the liberty of bringing a petition to the Trustees for relief, which petition he shall lodge with the President and the President shall, as speedily as may be, lay the same before the Trustees at a meeting warned in the manner directed in the act of incorporation, unless a stated session of the Trustees shall be at hand—

Chap. 2

Of admission into the College—Manners

1. No candidate shall be permitted to attend the Collegiate exercises untill he shall have been regularly examined and approved, nor untill he shall have complied with the conditions prescribed in the 4th article of this chapter and in chapter nine—

2. Every candidate for admission into the College shall produce satisfactory evidence of a good moral character—

3. No student shall be admitted as a member of this College from any other College unless he produce a certificate from the proper au-

thority that he has been subject to no College censure; except on a hearing the Faculty or Trustees shall deem it consistent with the interest of the College to admit him—

4. No candidates name shall be registered untill he shall have subscribed the following engagement—I, AB. on condition of being admitted as a member of East Tennessee College promise on my faith and Honor, to observe all the laws and regulations of the College, particularly that I will avoid using profane language, gaming, and all indecent behaviour and disrespectful conduct to the Faculty of the same; as Witness my hand—

5. Every student not belonging to the Town of Knoxville shall be placed under the guardianship of a patron approved by the Faculty, such patron to be chosen by the parent or legal guardian of the student or appointed by the President, and no student shall contract any debt without a written permission from his patron, on penalty of being privately dismissed—

6. Masters & Bachelors of Arts, who shall signify to the President their purpose of residing in the Town of Knoxville, with a [purpose] of pursuing literature under his direction, and under government of the College, and give sufficient bond to the President and Fellows for the payment of their term Bills shall be considered as resident graduates and students of the College—

7. When any of the Faculty is present each student shall enter the College with his head uncovered, and shall immediately take his seat and attend to his studies in silence—

8. If the students shall be assembled in the College Hall, when any member of the Faculty shall first enter they shall all rise and receive him with respect. The same rule shall be observed at the entrance and departure of any respectable stranger in the course of the day—

Chap. 3

Religious order and worship

1. It shall be the duty of the Faculty diligently to inspect and watch over the manners and behaviour of the students and in all proper methods by example and precept to recommend to them a virtuous and blameless life and a diligent attention to the public and private duties of religion—

2. The President, or in his absence one of the Professors or one of the Tutors, shall pray every morning and if convenient in the evening

in the College and read a chapter or some suitable portion of Scripture; unless a sermon or some other theological discourse shall be delivered. And every undergraduate student shall be obliged to attend unless he can render a sufficient excuse for absence—

3. The President is desired frequently to deliver, in the College, Lectures or dissertations on such religious moral and other subjects as he shall judge proper for the instruction of the College; which being publickly appointed, every student shall attend—

4. It is enjoined upon all the students to observe the Lords day as holy and sacred to the duties of religion and if any student shall profane the said day by making indecent noises or disturbance or shall behave indecently or profanely at the time of public worship or at prayer in the College he may be punished by admonition or otherwise, as the nature and demerit of the crime shall require—

Chap. 4

Of the course of Academic Literature and instruction in the College—

1. The Faculty shall instruct the undergraduate students in the three learned Languages, the liberal arts and the whole course of Academic Literature.

2. The President with the advice of the Professors and Tutors shall appoint all classical exercises and examinations and the authors which shall be read and recited by the respective classes. And it shall be the duty of the President annually at the commencement to lay before the Trustees the state and method of instruction, the authors recited, and the progress of literary improvement in the College—

Each Professor shall at his discretion, deliver, occasionally public Lectures in the College—

The students are required universally to assemble at each Lecture according to the direction of the Professors; and shall by them be required to account for absence and any other negligence—

Each student shall take notes of the several heads of the instruction delivered at each Lecture; and shall be examined by the Professors concerning the knowledge which he has gained from the preceding lecture—

3. The classes shall dispute before the President or their Tutor at least once a fortnight and on Wednesdays in the afternoon the students shall declaim in the College agreeably to the direc-

tions of the Faculty and each one whenever required shall deliver his declamation to the President or to his Tutor, fairly written with his name subscribed—The President may appoint a monitor who shall previously notify those who are to declaim and at the time of declaiming deliver a catalogue of them to the President, Professor or Tutor—

4. If any student shall be absent from any lecture recitation, disputation or other classical exercise duly appointed, he may be admonished: and every student who shall be absent from an examination appointed by the Faculty shall receive such college punishment as the nature of the offense might require—

5. Students who do not intend to graduate may be permitted to join any class for which the Faculty may judge them qualified—

6. Till circumstances allow different arrangements the President and visiting Officers shall divide among them the branches of education to be taught at this institution—

7. A limited number of indigent young men may be allowed tuition gratis on exhibiting satisfactory testimony of indigence and good character—the number to be fixed annually, or for each Session by the Trustees—

Chap. 5

Of Vacations and of absences from the College

1. There shall be two vacations annually to consist of four weeks each and to commence immediately after each public examination—

2. Immediately upon the expiration of every vacation the undergraduate students shall assemble at the College. If any student shall voluntarily absent himself from the College without a just and reasonable excuse when by law he ought to be present the Faculty shall have power at their discretion to correct such disobedience as the nature of the case may require—

Chap. 6

Of College damages and the assessment of them.

1. When any damage shall be found done, except by the inevitable providence of God, to any chamber or study in the College the same shall be assessed upon all the undergraduate students, and charged in their term Bills. Provided always, if the person or persons who were principals or accessories in doing any such damages shall be discovered, he or they shall make full satisfaction for the same; and if they shall

have been done intentionally by any student or students they shall each be liable to any college punishment which the circumstances of the offense shall require—

2. The President shall cause to be estimated all damages of broken glass at the end of every term, and the same to be assessed upon the students according to law and charged in their term Bills.

3. To ascertain other damages done to the College buildings and appurtenances, there shall be annually, at commencement, three persons, who shall be called Inspectors of the College, and any two of them have power to act, whose duty it shall be to inspect and estimate all damages done to the College buildings and appurtenances whenever they shall be required by the President— And all estimates of damages, particularly stated the Inspectors shall deliver to the President in writing with their names subscribed; which estimate with a reasonable compensation to the Inspectors for their trouble shall be the rule by which the undergraduates shall be assessed and charged respectively by the President for damages in the term Bill next after estimates shall have been made—

4. All damages estimated by the Inspectors of the College shall by order of the President be immediately repaired when practicable; And when in the opinion of the Inspectors it shall be expedient that any damage done to the College or to any of the appurtenances thereof should be repaired before an estimate of such damage is made the President shall order the repairs to be made; and provided the repair is full and complete, the actual expence shall be a   to the Inspectors in the estimate of the damage otherwise it shall be assessed according to their discretion—

5. Whenever, in the opinion of the Inspectors of the College it shall be necessary that the College or any of the public chambers or entries thereof should be whitewashed or cleansed the same shall be done by order of the President under the direction of the Inspectors or some one of them, the expence of which shall be paid out of the College Treasury.

Chap. 8.

Of commencement and Academical degrees

1. The commencement shall be on the first Thursday of October annually—

2. No student may expect the honor of the first degree, unless he

stand approved examinations on all the branches of study pursued in the College, and shall have been approved as a candidate for the same; And also have, on the day before the commencement, produced a certificate from the Treasurer that he has paid to him his due—

3. No candidate for the second degree may expect the honor of the same unless he shall have preserved a good moral character, and previous to the commencement signified to the President the desire of the same—

All candidates for either degree shall be personally present unless in any instance the President and Trustees shall judge it proper to confer the honor of degree upon an absent candidate, in which case he shall pay into the College Treasury one dollar, or such greater sum as the President and Trustees shall appoint—

4. All academical honors shall be given by the President with the consent of the Trustees; And the Candidates for a first or second degree, shall each, for the same pay to the President four dollars—

5. Students who do not wish to pursue all the branches of education taught in the College, shall, on leaving the institution be entitled to a certificate or Diploma from the President and Trustees stating the branches of education he has pursued and his proficiency in them— No student, however shall be entitled to this privilege whose conduct shall not have been good and his proficiency respectable—

Chap. 4

Of College dues and term or session Bills

1. Every student shall on his admission to the College and before he is allowed to recite, produce to the President or his proper instructor, a certificate from the Treasurer, that he has paid in advance half the sum required for tuition for a session. Provided that when more than half a session shall have expired before such student shall be admitted, he shall be charged for such part of the session only as shall remain—

Board adjourned untill Saturday the 20th instant

A. Sherman—President

Attest
William C. Mynatt Secy

At a meeting of the Board of Trustees of East Tennessee College on the 20th day of October 1821. Present the Rev. David A. Sherman President—

April 25th 1829

Robert King, James King, William C. Mynatt, William Park, S. D. Jacobs, D. P. Armstrong, & H. A. M. White Trustees

Ordered that the Treasurer pay to the Revd. Charles Coffin seven hundred and fifty dollars for his services as President for the last session ending the 1st April inst.

Ordered that the Treasurer pay to the Rev. Stephen Foster three hundred dollars for his services as Professor in the College for the last session ending the 1st April inst.–

The committee appointed at the last meeting to examine the account of the Treasurer report "that they have examined the acts. of Robt. King Esq. Treasurer of East Tennessee College and find them correct, leaving a balance in his hands of four hundred and thirty two dollars and seven & ¼ cts.

Saturday May 2nd 1829

The Board met pursuant to adjournment–present Revd. Charles Coffin President, W. B. A. Ramsey Secty.– Robert King–Pryor Lea–W. B. Reese–S. D. Jacobs–D. P. Armstrong–H. A. M. White –W. Park–& R. G. Dunlap Trustees– Ordered that Mr. James Ledford be employed for the present session, as an instructor in the Preparatory School at the compensation of one hundred and fifty dollars.

Ordered that the price of tuition in the College and Preparatory School be the same the present, it was the last, session.

Upon an investigation of the case of G. W. Gale, who had appealed to the Board from the judgment of the faculty in refusing to admit him as a student of the College, it is considered by the Board that an appeal is authorized in all such cases, and that the said G. W. Gale be admitted as a student, upon his complying with the laws in such cases made and provided.

Ordered that the secretary correspond with P. M. Miller Esq. in relation to a suit commenced in the Chancery Court of the Western District of Tennessee, by James Neal and Daniel W. Ragsdale, against the President and Trustees of East Tennessee College and John P. McLemone.

Ordered that the secretary be authorized to lease out the old college building and lot to Isaac Lewis for an indefinite term of time, upon his agreeing to quit and give possession of the same after ten days notice to that effect, and keeping the same in good order–

The Board adjourned without day

Saturday May 9th 1829 called meeting Present Rev. Charles Coffin President S. D. Jacobs pro tem, Robert King, James King, William Park, D. P. Armstrong, H. A. M. White & William C. Mynatt Trustees—

The following was adopted as the course of studies in the College—Requisitions for admission into the Freshman class—Mornays English Grammar—Arithmetic—Worcesters Geography—Adams latin Grammar—Liber Primus—Viri Romae—Virgil—Cicero, Select Orations—Sallust—Danas Latin Tutor—Hackenbergs Greek Grammar—Jacobs Greek Reader—Freshmans class 1st Term—Adams Roman Antiquities—Livy—Graca Majora begun—Algebra begun—Translations & Composition alternately each every four weeks, through the year Declamation. Parsing in English—2nd Term Cicero De Oratione—Graca Majora continued—Algebra continued—History—Sophomore class 1st Term—Horace—Euclid 6 Books—Blair's Lectures—Days Plane Trigonometry—Surveying and Navigation—Essays and Forensic disputations, alternately once a fortnight, through this and remaining years—Declamations & English parsing—2nd Term—Graca Majora continued—mensuration—Guaging—Spherical Trigonometry—Hodges Logic—Junior class 1st term—Duttons conic sections—Tacitus—Chemistry—Paleys Natural Theology—2nd Term—Graca Majora continued—Enfields Natural Philosophy—Paleys Evidences—Paleys Moral Philosophy—Senior class 1st Term—Graca Majora concluded—Locke, Hidges, Brown—Vattels Law of Nations 2nd Term—Buttens Analaogy—Political Economy—Greek Testament or Hebrew or French Language, at the option of the student—Recitations in the Bible once a week by all the students in each class—

The following law was also adopted and passed in lieu of the 4th section of Chap. 4, which is hereby repealed—

Documents 27-28

May 9th 1829

Every student deficient in any College exercise, may be required to make amends for his deficiency, by extraordinary study and recitation at a time appointed by his Instructor, and if any one shall refuse to comply with this rule or be habitually guilty of idleness, and deficiency, he may be dismissed or expelled. The following was adopted and enacted in lieu of Section 8 of Chap. 1st which section is hereby repealed.

Every judgment for expulsion; for refusing an applicant admission into College, on account of character and not literary qualifications; dismission for fault; suspension and sending a student home, shall be by the Faculty, except in cases provided for by the State Legislature; and every judgment shall be in writing, and be published before the assembled students in such manner as the President shall direct—copies of all such judgments shall on application be given by the President to all persons concerned—and if any student or applicant for admission into college shall apprehend himself aggrieved by any such judgment he shall have liberty at any time, after the same shall have been given of applying to the President by a petition in writing, for a new trial; and on receiving any such petition, the President shall order a new trial to be had— Should the student or applicant or his Parent or Guardian, prefer making an appeal to the Trustees to a new trial before the Faculty, or should he feel aggrieved by the result of such new trial before the Faculty he shall have the liberty of bringing a petition to the Trustees for relief, which petition he shall lodge with the President, and the President shall as speedily as may be, lay it before the Trustees at a meeting warned in the manner directed by the act of incorporation, unless a stated session of the Trustees shall be at hand. The following was added to Chap. 2 Section 2 and adopted as part of the laws—unless he has come ignorant of the requisition and nothing appears to his prejudice; in which case he shall be admitted into College on probation. The following laws were also adopted. Every registered student shall be required to possess at all times a correct copy of the laws of college—the price of a printed copy shall be 12½ cents.

Every registered student shall be considered a member of College until he shall have taken a degree or been discharged honorably with a regular certificate from the President or sent away in dis[grace].

The following was adopted and enacted in lieu of the 7th section of Chap. 7th which section is hereby repealed—

Any student who shall have been inexcusably absent, shall be admonished; and if he shall habitually absent himself he may be dismissed in disgrace, or expelled—

The Board adjourned without day

—Minutes of the Board of Trustees, the University of Tennessee. Microcopy in the Southern Historical Collection, the University of North Carolina. Used by permission of the University of Tennessee.

26. The President of the University of Georgia is instructed to admonish some students for killing hogs, 1809

The Board of Trustees having perused the minutes of evidence made by the President of the College upon an enquiry had by the authority of the same, into certain charges exhibited against some of the students for killing hogs the property of Mr. Danl. W. Easly, and they having been requested by the authority aforesaid to express their opinion upon the said evidence, and also as to the steps proper to be taken thereupon do Resolve that the evidence appears to them sufficient against John Davis, Yelverton King and James Thweat, & advise that the said persons be by the President publickly admonished in the college chapel.–Minutes of the Trustees of the University of Georgia, 1794-1817, Vol. I, 161. Original in the General Library, the University of Georgia. Photocopy in the Southern Historical Collection.

III

1811–1820

1. Recipients of the Master of Arts degree in the College of South Carolina, 1812-1860

This list of the recipients of the second degree, with the year in which it was conferred, is taken from the minutes of the board of trustees and of the faculty.

1812, Robert W. Gill, 1809.
Benjamin F. Whitner, 1809.

1814, William Brantley, 1808.

1836, Napoleon Gustavus Rich, 1833.
William Blanding, 1835.
Mathias Clark (graduated in 1835, so that he must have taken the degree in residence.)
David Johnson, Jr. (who also graduated in 1835).

1837, C. K. Johnson (?)
William E. Martin, 1834.
Peter C. Gilliard, 1834.
Frederick Belser, 1834.

1839, James A. Marshall, 1838.
Isaac Foreman, 1836.

1840, Charles Kershaw, 1835.
John D. Wilson, 1837.
James N. Frierson, 1837.
Edwin DeLeon, 1837.
John A. Leland, 1837.
James W. McCants, 1837.
Samuel J. Chapman, 1837.

1841, David J. Williams, 1837.

1842, John Jacob Seibles, 1836.

1843, Six resident graduates, but the minutes of the trustees are silent in regard to those who received the A. M. degree, and the minutes of the faculty are lost.

1846, Robert Boyce, 1845.
James H. Carlisle, 1844.
J. Thornton Carpenter, 1845.
Henry C. Davis, 1844.
Wyatt J. Goin, 1845.
Theodore S. Gourdin, 1845.
Thomas B. Fraser, 1845.
William J. Hand, 1829.
Arthur P. Hayne, 1841.
George W. Landrum, 1845.
John H. Logan, 1844.
William J. Rivers, 1841.
Thomas J. Workman, 1843.

1847, Julius Anderson, 1846.
William B. Carlisle, 1841.
Henry McIver, 1846.
Henry T. Moore, 1846.
Christopher G. Hume, 1845.
Robert H. Reid, 1846.
Ephriam M. Seabrook, 1844.
William B. Wilson, 1846.

1849, William H. Talley, 1848.
William B. Telford, 1847

1850, William H. Parker, 1846.
Paul H. Seabrook, 1847.

1851, S. M. G. Gary, 1847.
Robert Henry, Jr., 1848.
John K. Jackson, 1846.
Rufus K. Porter, 1849.
Henry S. Williams, 1850.

1852, John Douglass, 1843.
Thomas T. Dill, 1845.

1853, James H. Rion, 1850.
Horace H. Sams, 1850.

1854, Henry Buist, 1847.
E. S. J. Hayes, 1850.
Eugene McCaa, 1852.
J. Felix Walker, 1850.

1855, Alfred B. Brumby, 1851.
James C. Calhoun, 1852.
J. Wood Davidson, 1852.

1856, H. Walker Adams, 1852.
Josiah Bedon, 1855.
Henry M. Clarkson, 1855.
William B. Culp, 1854.
Charles E. Fleming, 1855.
Alfred Wallace, 1855.

1857, John G. Scarborough, 1854.

1858, Alexander C. Elder, 1855.

1859, George E. Coit, 1856.
Harris Covington, 1856.
George M. Fairlee, 1856.
William Royal, 1841.

1860, Henry C. Mitchell, 1857.

—Green, *op. cit.*, 433-36. The second or master's degree was slow to develop as an earned or degree in course. For a long time it was and occasionally even nowadays is given as an honorary degree. Samuel Eliot Morison in *Three Centuries of Harvard* reported "it was a saying that all a Harvard man had to do for his Master's degree was to pay five dollars and stay out of jail."

2. A petition from the Trustees of Albemarle Academy to the General Assembly of Virginia, 1815

A PETITION of the Trustees of Albemarle Academy, praying to be authorized by law to demand and receive certain moneys which have arisen on the sale of the two glebes of the parishes of St. Ann and Fredericksville in the said county, with the interest or profits thereon; and also, annually, from the President and Directors of the Literary Fund, a dividend of the interest or profits of that fund, proportioned every year to the ratio which the contributions of the said county shall have borne to those of the rest of the State in the preceding year; praying, also, the General Assembly to reduce the number of visitors, to provide for their appointment and succession, and for that of such other officers as they may think necessary; to define their powers and duties, to lay down such fixed principles for the government and administration of the said institution as may give it stability;

to change its name to that of the *Central College*; and to make such amendments to the act for the establishment of public schools, passed on the 22d day December, 1796, as may facilitate its commencement and lighten its execution in the said county.

Ordered, That the said petition be referred to the Committee of Propositions and Grievances; that they do examine the matter thereof, and report the same, with their opinion thereupon, to the House.

Resolved, As the opinion of this Committee, that so much of the petition of the Trustees of the Albemarle Academy as prays for certain amendments to the act establishing the same, is reasonable.

Resolved, As the opinion of this Committee, that so much of the said petition as prays that all moneys now appropriated to the literary fund, within the said county, may hereafter be vested in the said Trustees, for the use of the said Academy, be rejected.

The said resolutions being twice read, were, on questions severally put thereupon, agreed to by the House.—*Journal of House of Delegates*, 1815-1816, pp. 23, 38, 56.

3. Thomas Jefferson to Joseph C. Cabell on the petition, 1815

...Could the petition which the Albermarle academy addressed to our legislature have succeeded at the late session a little aid additional to the objects of that would have enabled us to have here immediately the best seminary of the US. I do not know to whom P. Carr (President of the board of trustees) committed the petition and papers; but I have seen no trace of their having been offered. Thinking it possible you may not have seen them, I send for your perusal the copies I retained for my own use. They consist 1. of a letter to him, sketching at the request of the trustees, a plan for the institution. 2. One to Judge Cooper in answer to some observations he had favored me with, on the plan. 3. A copy of the petition of the trustees. 4. A copy of the act we wished from the legislature. They are long. But, as we always counted on you as the main pillar of their support, and we shall probably return to the charge at the next session, the trouble of reading them will come upon you, and as well now as then. The lottery allowed by the former act, the proceeds of our two glebes, and our dividend of the literary fund, with the reorganization of the institution are what was asked in that petition. In addition to this if we could obtain a loan for 4. or 5. years only, of 7. or 8000 D. I think I have it now in my power to obtain three of the ablest characters in the world to fill the higher professorships of what in the plan is called the IId or General grade of education, three such characters as are not in a single university of Europe and for those of languages & Mathematics, a part of the same grade, able professors doubtless could also be readily obtained. With these characters, I should not be afraid to say that the circle of the sciences composing that 2d or General grade, would be more profoundly taught here than in any institution in the US. and might I go further.

The 1st or Elementary grade of education is not developed in this plan; an authority only being asked to it's Visitors for putting into motion a former proposition for that object. For an explanation of this therefore, I am obliged to add to these papers a letter I wrote some time since to Mr. Adams, in which I had occasion to give some account of what had been proposed here for culling from every condition of our people the natural aristocracy of talents & virtue, and of preparing it by education, at the public expence, for the care of the public concerns. This letter will present to you some measures still requisite to compleat & secure our republican edifice, and which remain in charge for our younger statesmen. On yourself, Mr. Rives, Mr. Gilmer, when they shall enter the public councils, I rest my hopes for this great accomplishment, and doubtless you will have other able coadjutors not known to me.—Paul Leicester Ford (ed.), *The Writings of Thomas Jefferson.* IX, 500-1.

4. President Jonathan Maxcy of South Carolina College praises the institution for "order, peace, and industry," 1816

I have spent nearly thirty years in College business, and I can say with truth, that I never knew an instance in which a College was conducted with such order, peace, and industry, as this has been during the past year. We have had no difficulty, except in a few cases, from the resort of certain individuals to taverns and other places of entertainment.—Green, *op. cit.*, 30, 31.

5. Jefferson's reply to Governor Plumer of New Hampshire on the Dartmouth College Case, 1816

Monticello, July 21, 1816

I thank you, Sir, for the copy you have been so good as to send me, of your late speech to the legislature of your State, which I have read a second time with great pleasure, as I had before done in the public papers. It is replete with sound principles, and truly republican. Some articles, too, are worthy of peculiar notice. The idea that institutions established for the use of the nation cannot be touched nor modified, even to make them answer their end, because of rights gratuitously supposed in those employed to manage them in trust for the public, may perhaps be a salutory provision against the abuses of a monarch, but is most absurd against the nation itself. Yet our lawyers and priests generally inculcate this doctrine, and suppose that preceding generations held the earth more freely than we do; had a right to impose laws on us, unalterable by ourselves, and that we, in like manner, can make laws and impose burdens on future generations, which they will have no right to alter; in fine, that the earth belongs to the dead and not the living. I remark also the phenomenon of a chief magistrate recommending the reduction of his own compensation. This is a solecism of which the wisdom of our late Congress cannot be accused. I, however, place economy among the first and most important of republican virtues, and public debt as the greatest of the dangers to be feared. We see in England the consequences of the want of it, their laborers reduced to live on a penny in the shilling of their earnings, to give up bread, and resort to oatmeal and potatoes for food; and their landholders exiling themselves to live in penury and obscurity abroad, because at home the government must have all the clear profits of their land. In fact, they see the fee simple of the island transferred to the public creditors, all its profits going to them for the interest of their debts. Our laborers and landholders must come to this also, unless they severely adhere to the economy you recommend. I salute you with entire esteem and respect.—A. E. Bergh (ed.), *The Writings of Thomas Jefferson*, XV, 46-47.

6. THE PRESIDENT AND DIRECTORS OF THE LITERARY FUND OF VIRGINIA REPORT ON "THE ESTABLISHMENT OF AN UNIVERSITY," 1816

The next subject, to which the President and Directors of the Literary Fund beg leave to call the attention of the legislature, is the establishment of an University, to be called "*The University of Virginia*."— The advantages, that will result from the establishment of such an institution, are incalculable. At present, a great proportion of our youth are sent out of the state, and sometimes out of the United States, for the acquisition of science in general, or with a view to a proficiency in some of the learned professions. Large sums of money are thus annually sent away, which, if expended here for the same object, would support a liberal and extensive scheme of public instruction, and contribute in other respects greatly to the prosperity of the country. Our being tributary to a large amount to other states is, however, a small evil, compared to others we may experience. The young men of our country, by leaving their own state before their judgments are formed, will frequently acquire elsewhere habits and opinions uncongenial with those of their fellow-citizens. Estranged by absence from the customs and principles of their parents and their ancestors, they return in some degree aliens to their native land. Every enlightened statesman must consider the education of the youth of a country, as intimately and inseparably connected with its prosperity. It is a high and solemn duty, which the government is bound by every consideration of patriotism and interest to discharge. How afflicting, then, must it be to every Virginian, who is alive to the honour and happiness of his country, to reflect, that so large a portion of our youth should seek in other states, and amongst strangers, that instruction which they ought to have found at home.

The term University comprehends the whole circle of the arts and sciences, and extends to the utmost boundaries of human knowledge. The President and Directors have resorted to every source of information on this branch of the subject, which the shortness of the time, and their other avocations of a public and imperious nature, would permit. So far as they have been able to inform themselves of the constitutions of colleges in the United States, or those in Europe, they are inclined to believe that scarcely any two institutions of this kind agree in the course of instruction they pursue, or in the distribution of the sciences amongst the various professors. In some colleges, most attention is bestowed on subjects which are neglected in others; and the modes of imparting instruction, and the rules and discipline of various colleges, are essentially dissimilar. The system of instruction, which is adopted in any country, ought certainly to have relation to the peculiar situation of the people amongst whom it is to operate. In the populous countries of Europe, where labor is cheap, where all the active professions are over-stocked, and where there are multitudes of persons who devote themselves to literary and scientific pursuits, or the cultivation of the arts, human knowledge, which is derived from books, must necessarily have attained a higher degree of perfection, than in a country yet in its infant state, where every man is engaged in the exercise of a trade or profession, or in pushing his fortune by enterprise and industry. Here the population is thin, and we find very few who devote themselves exclusively to scientific researches. In European countries too, colleges and universities being old establishments, perfected by the experience of ages, and enriched by large and successive endowments, they can be carried on upon a scale which would be wholly incompatible with the means of a state which is making its first effort to establish such institutions. Nor, are the kinds of studies which are adapted to the wants of European countries, precisely those which are suited to the situation of our own. Some of the arts and sciences which contribute to the ornament of society, and are peculiar objects of pursuit in older countries, must be postponed, at least, to the cultivation of those which are essential to the welfare of the community. Not that these should be proscribed in our institutions, but attended to as secondary to such as are more useful and important in their nature. It would be a fatal error in us, in the formation of the system now to be adopted, to attempt to commence on too large a scale. It is the part of wisdom to begin with moderation, and to improve as it advances, rather than, by an unnatural or gigantic effort, to exhaust its own powers, and bring on premature debility and decay. If we proceed with caution; if we keep in view the situation of the country, and the extent of our means: if those means receive improvements, of which they are susceptible; and the legislature still extends to the Literary Fund their fostering care and protection, it is confidently believed, that the period is not distant, when the anticipations of the enlightened friends of public instruction will be realized. The President and Directors of the Literary Fund, upon the best consideration they can give the subject, recommend as follows:

1. That there shall be appointed by the legislature five commissioners, who shall purchase, or accept, in some central and healthy part of the commonwealth, to be designated by the legislature, such a quantity of land, as will be not only sufficient for the use of the University, but to prevent establishments in its neighborhood that would endanger the morals of the students, or their being seduced from their studies. Provided, that, before the bargain for the same be binding on the state, it shall be sanctioned by the executive; and that the said commissioners shall proceed to contract for, and cause to be erected, under the control of the executive, all the necessary buildings for an university, to be called the University of Virginia, the expense of erecting which buildings, and of the land, if purchased, shall be paid for out of the Literary Fund.

2. That, when said buildings are complete, the said commissioners

shall purchase, for the use of the said university, all necessary furniture, to be paid for out of the Literary Fund, subject to the control of the President and Directors thereof.

3. That, as soon as the said buildings shall be finished, the governor, with the advice of the council of state, shall proceed to appoint fifteen visitors, who shall serve one year; after which, the said governor and council shall annually make a similar appointment of the same visitors, or others, which said fifteen visitors, the two senior judges of the court of appeals, the governor for the time being, and one of the Directors of the Literary Fund, to be annually designated by the board, shall be visitors of the University of Virginia; shall have the power to make all bye laws, rules and regulations for the government of the said university and the good order of the same, as to them shall seem fit, provided they are not inconsistent with the laws of this commonwealth; and that they shall have power to appoint the president and professors, hereinafter provided for, and to have a general superintendance and control of the said university.

4. That there shall be appointed by the visitors, nine professors of said university, one of whom shall act as president, but shall discharge the duties of one of the professorships. That the said Professorships shall consist of the following: 1st. A Professor of Moral Philosophy, Rhetoric and Belles Lettres. 2d. A Professor of Law and Police. 3d. A Professor of Mathematics. 4th. A Professor of Natural Philosophy. 5th. A Professor of Anatomy and Medicine. 6th. A Professor of Military Science. 7th. A Professor of Ancient and Modern Languages. 8th. A Professor of the Fine Arts. 9th. A Professor of Chemistry. That there be paid quarter yearly to the said President and Professors reasonable salaries, out of the Literary Fund. That the said visitors shall keep a regular journal of their proceedings, in which they shall state particularly the manner in which the University is conducted; the rules they may adopt for its government; the progress which is made in science therein, and every thing of importance connected therewith, to be annually submitted to the General Assembly.

5. That there be educated, boarded and clothed, at the public expense, to be paid out of the Literary Fund, ten young men, to be selected by the visitors from the candidates in the academies, before spoken of. Each young man so educated, shall remain four years at said university; and in case of vacancies, they shall be supplied by the choice of the visitors, out of the academies aforesaid. Each of whom so educated shall be bound to serve four years in either of the academies,

as principal or assistant teachers, if required. That the visitors of the said university shall supply the said scholars, who are to be educated at the public expense, with the necessary cloathing, books and stationary, to be paid for out of the Literary Fund.

6. That there be established on the foundation of said university seven fellowships, which are to be filled by the appointment of the visitors, out of the most learned and meritorious of those who have graduated at said university, who shall receive annually reasonable and moderate salaries out of the Literary Fund, and shall be obliged to serve four years as principal teachers in one of the academies, if required so to do.

There are two things recommended in the above plan, which demand some explanation. The first is the recommendation of a Professor of Military Science, and the second the adoption of fellowships, on the foundation of the university. In relation to the first, the President and Directors of the Literary Fund beg leave to remark, that there is a great want of Military Science in our country. That, though the government of the United States have the power to establish Military Schools, and have established one, yet that is not commensurate with the wants of the country; nor does it preclude the necessity, or lessen the duty of the states, to impart to their citizens such a share of the military art, as may be highly essential in time of war, when the safety of the state may be endangered.— In free governments, great reliance is placed in the first stages of war, indeed through all time of a defensive war, on militia. In republics, every soldier is a citizen, which renders it a solemn duty that, to a certain extent, every citizen should be a soldier. It is not enough, that every man understands that the country ought to be preserved independent; that he possesses certain rights which are sacred and imprescriptible; there is an obligation on him, to place himself in a situation, and obtain that knowledge, which shall enable him to preserve the high privileges he possesses, and transmit them unimpaired to posterity. This power, military science confers. For, though valor and patriotism will do much, yet they will do much more when combined with discipline and military information. An occasion now offers of communicating to the youth of our country, upon whom we must rely as its defenders, the principles of military science, to a considerable extent. It is not expected that the lectures, or instruction of a professor, can alone make an officer. But they may lay a foundation of knowledge, which will be highly useful in the formation of the military man. It is believed that the Professor of Military Science, would embrace in his course of instruction, amongst others, the following objects: Engineering and Gunnery; The formation and laying off of camps; The means of preserving the health of soldiers; Camp discipline and police; The apparatus of war; The formation of arsenals and magazines; Fortification. It would be useful also, if the Professor of Military Science, should have authority to employ, as auxiliary to his professorship, a fit person to instruct the students in the manual exercise the use of the broad sword, fencing, and the elements of military tactics, so as to enable them to understand and to direct, or perform the more simple evolutions. These athletic and manly exercises, might be used in the intervals of study, and whilst they would win our youth from habits of dissipation, give grace and agility to the body, and preserve their health, they would familiarize them with military ideas, and the use of arms.

The recommendation of the establishment of fellowships is founded on a wish to encourage the ardent pursuit of science in such young men, who, though destitute of the means of obtaining an education, have been selected for their talents, and instructed and supported at the public expense. It is to them we ought to look, as the source which is to supply us with teachers and professors; and thus by the service they will render in imparting instruction to the youth of the country, they will amply repay what that country has done for their benefit. Besides, it is a consideration of great importance, that you create a corps of literary men, who, enabled by receiving a decent competence, to devote their whole time to the pursuits of science, will enlarge its boundaries, and diffuse through the community a taste and relish for the charms of literature. The effect produced by concentrating at one place many literary men, whose co-operation, as well as whose collisions, will excite a generous spirit of emulation, is incalculable.

In recommending the establishment of new schools, academies, and an university, the president and directors confine themselves within the limits of the resolution of the general assembly. But, in enquiring into the best means to advance by new institutions the cause of public instruction, we must not be unmindful that we have at present in the state, various academies and a college. Several of these academies are believed to be respectable; and the propriety of including them in the general system, by imparting to them a portion of the Literary Fund, has been already suggested. In relation to the college of William and Mary, it affords the President and Directors great pleasure to be enabled to state, that they have every reason to believe that this institution affords at present strong evidence of prosperity; that the professorships are filled with ability; and that the students are numerous, and increasing daily. The commonwealth is greatly interested in the welfare of this institution, and ought to count largely on the assistance it will afford in diffusing the benefits of science and literature amongst our citizens. The funds of this college are believed to be ample for its ordinary expenditure: but if any assistance is required, the President and Directors recommend to the General Assembly to appropriate an adequate sum, out of the Literary Fund.

The President and Directors have submitted to the legislature what they consider the best organization of schools, &c. for this commonwealth; but they are not so sanguine as to believe that it can be carried into effect at once to its full extent, without a considerable augmentation of their funds. It is, therefore, respectfully referred to the legislature to decide, whether it would not be better to execute the system by degrees; to extend its operation, as the fund may be increased; and in its application always to keep in view the ultimate completion of the whole. With these impressions, it is recommended, that the product of the fund be immediately applied to the establishment of a school in each township, as indicated by the foregoing plan; that an academy be then established in each district; and that, after the accomplishment of these objects, the surplus that may remain, be applied to found and support the University of Virginia. In order to expedite the operation and perfection of the system, it is earnestly recommended to the General Assembly to augment the fund, by additional appropriations. In recommending to commence with Primary Schools, the President and Directors have been influenced by no consideration but a belief that the greatest public benefit would be thereby derived. It is supposed that no fewer than twenty thousand of the youth of this state may receive instruction in these schools at the same time. The President and Directors cannot believe that an object of so much importance ought to be postponed for any other. But they trust that, from their preference of these, no inference will be drawn of their entertaining opinions unfavorable to the other branches of the system; or, that their execution should be delayed one moment beyond the period when it may be practicable.

The President and Directors of the Literary Fund have endeavored to obtain, by a correspondence with some of the most enlightened citizens of the United States, particularly of those who have had most experience in conducting literary institutions, such information as would enable them to report a system of rules and regulations for the government of the University, Academies and Schools. Though they have been favored with answers from some of the gentlemen alluded to, they do not think they have sufficient data as yet to comply with that part of the resolution of the General Assembly. The nature of the rules will depend in some degree on the principles of the system the legislature shall adopt. It is believed by the President and Directors, that it would be best to leave this part of the subject to the visitors of the university, when appointed, who, as it is presumed they will be citizens selected for their wisdom and their experience, can, by comparing the various systems now in force in the different colleges in the union, extract from them such provisions as will be adapted to the situation of our university, and contribute to its prosperity. If it should, however, be the opinion of the legislature that it is expedient for the President and Directors of the Literary Fund to perform that duty, they will do it in the best manner they can, as soon as they can collect the necessary materials for the purpose. All which is respectfully submitted.—*Sundry Documents on the Subject of a System of Public Education for the State of Virginia*, Richmond, 1817, pp. 27-34.

7. The first stone of Central College, Virginia, is laid, 1817

We understand, that agreeably to appointment the first stone of the Central College was laid, at Charlottesville, on Monday last (the 6th.) and that with all the ceremony and solemnity due to such an occasion. The Society of Free Masons, and a large company of citizens, attended. The scene was graced by the presence of Thomas Jefferson and James Madison, late Presidents of the United States, and of James Monroe, the actual president.—*Richmond Enquirer*, October 17, 1817. For a list of subscriptions to Central College, see Nathaniel Francis Cabell (ed.), *Early History of the University of Virginia, As Contained in the Letters of Thomas Jefferson and Joseph C. Cabell* (Richmond: J. W. Randolph, 1856).

8. Extracts of minutes of the Board of Visitors of the University of Virginia during the rectorship of Thomas Jefferson, 1817-1826

At a meeting of the Visitors of the Central College held at Charlottesville, on the 5th day of May, 1817, on a call by three members, to wit: John Hartwell Cocke, Joseph C. Cabell and Thomas Jefferson.

Present, James Monroe, James Madison, John H. Cocke and Thomas Jefferson.

The records of the trustees of the Albemarle Academy, in lieu of which the Central College is established, were received from their secretary by the hands of Alex. Garrett, one of the said trustees.

Resolved, that Valentine W. Southall be appointed secretary to the Board, and that the records be delivered to him.

The Board proceeded to the appointment of a proctor, and the said Alexander Garrett was appointed, with a request that he will act as treasurer also until a special appointment can be made.

The Board being informed that at a meeting which had been proposed for the 8th day of April last at Charlottesville, and at which the three members only, who called this present meeting had attended, the said members had visited and examined the different sites for the college within a convenient distance around Charlottesville, had deemed the one offered them by John Perry about a mile above the town to be the most suitable, and offered on the most reasonable terms, and had provisionally authorized a purchase of certain parcels thereof for the site of the said college and its appendages, and the members now present having themselves proceeded to the said grounds, examined them and considered the terms of the said provisional purchase, do now approve of the said grounds as a site for the said college and its appendages, and of the terms of purchase, which they hereby confirm and ratify. And they accordingly authorize their proctor above named to proceed to a regular conveyance thereof to himself and his successors in trust for the said college.

The act establishing the Central College having transferred to the same all the rights and claims existing in the Albemarle Academy and its trustees, and having in aid of the subscriptions and donations, obtained or to be obtained, and of the proceeds of the lottery authorized by law, specially empowered this college, by its proper officers, to demand and receive the moneys which arose from the sales of the glebe lands of the parishes of St. Anne and Fredericksville, or such part thereof as belongs to the county of Albemarle or its citizens, in whatever hands they may be, to be employed for the purposes of this college, ordered that the proctor enquire into the state of said property, and report the same to this Board; and that in the meantime, he be authorized to demand and receive so much of the said moneys as may be requisite to pay for the land purchased from the said John Perry, and to make payment accordingly.

In view of a plan presented to the trustees of the Albemarle Academy for erecting a distinct pavilion or building for each separate professorship, and for arranging these around a square, each pavilion containing a school-room and two apartments for the accommodation of the professor, with reasonable conveniences, the Board determined that one of these pavilions shall now be erected; and they request the proctor, so soon as the funds are at his command, to agree with proper workmen for the building of one of stone or brick below ground, and of brick above, of substantial work, of regular architecture, well executed, and to be completed, if possible, during the ensuing summer and winter; that the lot for the said pavilions be delineated on the ground of the breadth of — feet with two parallel sides of indefinite length, and that the pavilion first to be erected be placed on one of the lines so delineated, with its floor in such degree of elevation from the ground as may correspond with the regular inclined plane to which it may admit of being reduced hereafter.

And it is further resolved, that so far as the funds may admit, the proctor be requested to proceed to the erection of dormitories for the students adjacent to the said pavilion, not exceeding ten on each side, of brick, and of regular architecture, according to the same plan proposed.

The Board, proceeding to consider the plan of a lottery prepared by the trustees of the Albemarle Academy, approve of the same, and resolve that it be carried into execution and without delay, by the proctor and by such agents as he shall appoint, and that the moneys to be received for tickets by those entrusted with the sale of them, be from time to time, and at short periods, paid into the hands of the proctor, and by him deposited in the Bank of Virginia in Richmond, with which bank it is thought expedient that an account should be opened with him in trust for the Central College.

Resolved, that a subscription paper be prepared, and placed in such hands as the proctor shall deem will be most likely to promote it with energy and success, in which shall be different columns, to wit: one for those who may prefer giving a donation in gross, another for those who may be willing to give a certain sum annually for the term of four years, and a third for donations in any other form. And that the moneys subscribed be disposed of as they are received by the proctor, in the manner above prescribed for those received on the lottery.

Resolved, that Thomas Jefferson and John H. Cocke be a committee on the part of the Visitors with authority, jointly or severally, to advise and sanction all plans and the application of moneys for executing them which may be within the purview and functions of the proctor for the time being.

Th. Jefferson,
James Monroe,
James Madison,
J. H. Cocke.

May 5, 1817.

July 28, 1817.

At a called meeting of the Visitors of the Central College, held at the house of Mr. Madison in Orange, Thomas Jefferson, James Madison, John Hartwell Cocke, and Joseph C. Cabell, being present.

The plan of the first pavilion to be erected, and the proceedings thereupon, having been stated and agreed to,

It is agreed that application be made to Dr. Knox, of Baltimore, to accept the professorship of languages, belles-lettres, rhetoric, history and geography, and that an independent salary of four hundred dollars, with a perquisite of twenty-five dollars from each pupil, together with chambers for his accommodation, be allowed him as a compensation for his services, he finding the necessary assistant ushers.

Alexander Garrett requesting to resign the office of proctor, it is agreed that Nelson Barksdale of the county of Albemarle, be appointed his successor.

It is also agreed that it be expedient to import a stone-cutter from Italy, and that Mr. Jefferson be authorized and requested to take requisite measures to effect that object.

James Madison,
J. H. Cocke,
Joseph C. Cabell,
Th. Jefferson.

At a meeting of the Visitors held at Charlottesville 7th October, 1817:

On information of the amount of the subscription to the Central College, known to be made, and others understood to be so, the Board resolves that the pavilion now erecting be completed as heretofore directed, with the twenty dormitories attached to it, and that two other pavilions be contracted for and executed the next year with the same number of dormitories to each; that one of these be appropriated to the professor of languages, belles-lettres, rhetoric, oratory, history and geography, one other to the professor of chemistry, zoology, botany, anatomy; and the third, until otherwise wanted, for a boarding-house, to be kept by some French family of good character, wherein it is proposed that the boarders shall be permitted to speak French only, with a view to their becoming familiarized to conversation in that language.

The Board is of opinion that the ground for these buildings should be previously reduced to a plain, or to terraces as it shall be found to admit with due regard to expense; that the pavilions be correct in their architecture and execution, and that where the family of a professor requires it, two additional rooms shall be added for their accommodation.

On information that the Reverend Mr. Knox, formerly thought of for a professor of languages, is withdrawn from business, the order of July 20 is rescinded, and it is resolved to offer, in the first place, the professorship of chemistry, etc., to Dr. Thos. Cooper of Pennsylvania, adding to it that of law with a fixed salary of 1,000 dollars and tuition fees of twenty dollars from each of his students, to be paid by them; and to accede also to the conditions stated in his letter of September 16 to Th. Jefferson; and that he be advised with as to a qualified professor of languages; or such other measures be taken to obtain one as shall be found most advisable; that the professor of languages should be engaged to take place on the 1st of April, and Dr. Cooper, as soon as a pavilion for him can be erected, or as he can otherwise accommodate himself with lodgings.

Resolved, that every student shall be required to pay sixty dollars per annum tuition fees, of which twenty dollars shall be paid to each professor he attends, and the surplus thereof, if any, to remain for the use of the college, and that fifteen dollars be paid moreover for each dormitory by the students occupying them.

Resolved, that any deficiency in the moneys paid or payable by subscription or otherwise, in or before April next, to pay for the pavilions and dormitories, the first year's salaries to the two professors aforesaid and other necessary expenses, shall be obtained, if practicable, by negotiations with the banks on a pledge of the future instalments of subscriptions, and of the college property as security, and that of the latter instalment the sum of 25,000 dollars shall be disposed of as shall hereafter be directed, either to the Commonwealth or the banks of some other safe moneyed institution, or an interest sufficient to pay the annual salaries of the two professors aforesaid forever,

Resolved, that the proctor be authorized to hire laborers for levelling the ground and performing necessary services for the work or other purposes.

James Madison,
James Monroe,
David Watson,
J. H. Cocke,
Jos. C. Cabell,
Th. Jefferson.

October 7, 1817.

At a meeting of the Visitors, 8th October, 1817:

Certain letters from Dr. Thos. Cooper to Th. Jefferson, dated September 17 and 19, received since the meeting of yesterday, being communicated to the Board of Visitors, and taken into consideration with his former letter of September 16, they are of opinion that it will be for the interest of the College to modify the terms of agreement which might be generally proper, so as to accommodate them to the particular circumstances of Dr. Cooper, and to reconcile his interests to an acceptance of the professorship before proposed to him. They, therefore, resolve:

1. That the expenses of transporting his library and collection of minerals to the College shall be reimbursed to him.

2. That, however disposed they would be to purchase for the College his collection of mineral subjects, his philosophical and chemical apparatus, the extent of their funds is as yet too little ascertained to authorize engagements for them; but that an interest of six per cent per annum on a fair valuation should be paid for the use of them in his own hand, until it can be seen that the other more indispensable calls on the funds of the college will leave them competent to the purchase.

And, ultimately, should nothing short of the immediate purchase of these articles be sufficient, then we are of opinion that their purchase be made, and the ready money, if required, be obtained from the bank as proposed in the resolution of yesterday for other pecuniary deficiencies.

3. That the expense in articles consumed necessarily in a course of chemical lectures shall be defrayed by the College.

4. That the branches of science proposed for Dr. Cooper be varied and accommodated in his case, as it is expected they must be in others, to the particular qualifications of the professor.

5. That the committee of superintendence of the proceedings of the proctor in the execution of his functions heretofore appointed, are authorized to take such measures as they think best for providing the necessary apartments for the use of the chemical and mineralogical purposes.

Resolved, that Alexander Garrett be appointed treasurer for the College.

Joseph C. Cabell,
J. H. Cocke,
James Monroe,
Th. Jefferson, for himself and for James Madison, who assented to all the articles but was obliged to depart before they could be copied and signed.

October 8, 1817.

Resolved, that the Board concurs in the opinion of the Visitors of the Central College expressed in their resolution of February 26, that it is expedient that the funds of the University be diverted as little as possible to the general engagement of the professors required for the institution, until provision be made of buildings for their accommodation, and for dieting and lodging the students; and that the measures adopted by them for the buildings of the present year be approved and pursued.

That Dr. Thomas Cooper of Philadelphia, heretofore appointed professor of chemistry and of law for the Central College, be confirmed and appointed for the University, as professor of chemistry, mineralogy and natural philosophy, and as professor of law also, until the advance of the institution and increase of the number of students shall render necessary a separate appointment to the professorship of law; that in addition to his permanent salary of 1,500 dollars he shall receive such sums during the first and second years as, with his salary and his tuition fees, shall amount, in the whole, to not less than 3,500 dollars a year, to commence on the first Monday of April of the ensuing year, 1820, or so soon after as he shall arrive at the University.

That the expense of removing his philosophical apparatus, his library and collection of minerals to the University be reimbursed to him; that until he shall have fifty students of chemistry, the expense in articles consumed necessarily in the course of chemical lectures be defrayed by the University, not exceeding 250 dollars in any course.

That the offer of his philosophical apparatus at the price it cost him, be accepted, and that also of 2,500 specimens of his collection of minerals, labelled and arranged in pasteboard cases, to be selected from his whole collection, for the use of the University, at the price of fifty cents each, by John Vaughan, Professor Patterson and Zaccheus Collins, with a suspension of payment, however, of the principal of these purchases until the more urgent provisions for the accommodation of the professors and students shall enable the school of the University to be opened generally, and with the payment, in the meantime, of interest at the rate of six per centum per annum on their amount.

Considering the importance, and the difficulty also at this time, of procuring American citizens, of the first order of science in their respective lines, to be professors in the University, the committee of superintendence are hereby jointly instructed and authorized, should any such offer, not to lose the opportunity of securing them for the University, by any provisional arrangements they can make within the limits of the salary and tuition fees before stated, and even with such reasonable accommodations as the case may require, suspending, however, their actual engagement until a meeting of the Visitors, and reserving to them the right of approval or rejection.

Resolved, that the said committee be jointly authorized to purchase, at a fair valuation or reasonable price, of John Perry, if a fit occasion occur, such portion of his land lying between the two parcels heretofore purchased of him, as may conveniently unite the whole in one body; provided the payment be deferred until it can be received of the sixth instalment of subscriptions, or of the public endowment for the third year of the institution.

The Board proceeded to the appointment of the committee of superintendence, and John H. Cocke and Thos. Jefferson were appointed, with authority, jointly or severally, to direct the proceedings of the agents of the institution, but jointly only to call a special meeting of the Board.

Resolved, that the course of authenticating the proceedings of the Board be by the signature of the secretary, and counter-signature of the rector, or if there be no secretary, or not present, then by that of the rector alone.

And the Board adjourned.

Th. Jefferson, Rector.

March 29, 1819.

At a meeting of the Visitors of the University of Virginia, at the said University on Monday, the 4th of October, 1819, present, Thomas Jefferson, Robert Taylor, James Madison, Chapman Johnson and John Hartwell Cocke.

Resolved, that instead of the hotel, which had been directed to be built in this present year by the Visitors of the Central College at their meeting of February 26, and approved by this Board on the 29th of March last, the erection of an additional pavilion by the committee of superintendence, is approved; as also their engagements for two other additional pavilions and dormitories, in anticipation of the funds of the ensuing year.

Resolved, that, for the accomplishment of the buildings commenced, and for all other lawful expenses and disbursements on behalf of the University, the bursar be authorized, with the approbation of a member of the committee of superintendence, to draw on the President and directors of the Literary Fund, for the whole, or any part of the public donation charged on that fund, for the ensuing year, 1820, so soon as the same shall become payable.

It is the opinion of the Board that at least three other pavilions, making ten with those in hand, five hotels, and additional dormitories, in number depending on that of the students who shall apply for admission into the University, with their appendages, will be necessary for the proper accommodation of the whole number of professors contemplated by the legislature; and that the proctor, under the direction of the committee of superintendence, be required to make an estimate of the whole expense of completing such buildings, distinguishing the expense of each, and that such estimate should accompany the report of this Board to the president and directors of the Literary Fund.

Resolved, that as the stone in the neighborhood of the University is not found capable of being wrought into capitals for the columns of some of the pavilions, and it may be necessary to procure elsewhere proper stone or marble, and to have capitals executed here or elsewhere, the proctor be authorized to take such measures relative thereto, and to make such arrangements for their execution, either by the two Italian artists engaged for that purpose, or by others, or compromise with them, as the committee of superintendence shall approve.

It appearing to the Board that the buildings and the funds of the University will not be in a condition to justify the commencement of any of its schools during the next spring, and that, therefore, the duties of the professorships to which Dr. Thomas Cooper was appointed must be deferred, the committee of superintendence is instructed to communicate that fact to Dr. Cooper, to arrange with him the terms on which the delay may be made, consistent with his convenience, and conformable to an honorable fulfillment of our engagements with him; and to report their proceedings to the Board at their next meeting.

An inventory of the property conveyed by the proctor of the Central College to the president and directors of the Literary Fund, a statement of the funds in money and credits of the said College, conveyed to the use of the University, with the accounts of the disbursements, and of the funds in hand, from the close of the preceding accounts to the last day of September in this present year, as furnished by the bursar and proctor, and a draught of a report of the same, and of the condition of the University, being proposed to the Board, the same, after consideration and amendment is agreed to....

At a meeting of the Visitors of the University of Virginia at the said University, on Monday the 2d of April 1821, present, Th. Jefferson, rector; James Breckenridge, Chapman Johnson and James Madison.

A letter having been received by the rector from Thomas Appleton, of Leghorn, stating the prices at which the Ionic and Corinthian capitals wanting for the pavilions of the University may be furnished there in marble, and these prices appearing to be much lower than they would cost if made here in stone, resolved, that it be an instruction to the committee of superintendence to procure the said capitals in marble from Italy.

Resolved, as the opinion of this Board, that it is expedient to procure the loan of 60,000 dollars, or so much thereof as may be necessary, as authorized by the late act of the general assembly, concerning the University of Virginia, and that the committee of superintendence be instructed to negotiate the same with the president and directors of the Literary Fund of preference, or if not to be obtained from them, then with others, according to the authorities of the said act.

Resolved, that it is expedient to proceed with the building of the library on the plan submitted to the Board: provided the funds of the University be adequate to the completion of the buildings already begun, and to the building the western range of hotels and dormitories, and be also adequate to the completion of the library so far as to render the building secure and fit for use; and that it be an instruction to the committee of superintendence to ascertain as accurately as may be the state of accounts under the contracts already made, the expenses of completing the buildings begun and contemplated. And not to enter into contracts for the library until they are fully satisfied that without interfering with the finishing of all the pavilions, hotels and dormitories, begun and to be begun, they have funds sufficient to put the library in the condition above described.

And the Board adjourns without day.

Th. Jefferson, Rector.

October 2, 1820.

At a meeting of the Visitors of the University of Virginia, by special call, on Thursday the 29th of November, 1821, at the University, two members only attending, to wit: Thomas Jefferson and Chapman Johnson, they adjourned to the next day.

November 30, present, Thomas Jefferson, Chapman Johnson, James Madison and John Hartwell Cocke.

The Board being informed that of the 60,000 dollars permitted to be borrowed from the Literary Fund by the act of the last general assembly, the sum of 29,100 dollars only has as yet been obtained, and that there is uncertainty as to the time when the balance may be obtained, they deem it expedient that the annuity of 15,000 dollars, receivable on the 1st of January next, be applied to the accomplishment of the buildings and other current purposes, in the first place, and that, should further sums be wanted before the receipt of the balance of the said loan, the committee of superintendence be authorized to borrow from the bank to the amount of that balance, to be replaced by the said balance when received.

Resolved, that the superintending committee be authorized to have an engraving made of the ground-plat of the buildings of the University including the library, and so many copies struck off for sale as they shall think proper, and also to engage a good painter to draw a perspective view of the upper level of buildings, to be engraved, yielding to him, for his trouble, the patent right, and paying his reasonable expenses coming, staying and returning, should it be required.

A proposition having been received to join with other seminaries in a petition of Congress, for a repeal of the duty on imported books, resolved, that this Board will concur in such a petition and a form being prepared and approved, and a form also of a letter to our senators and representatives in Congress requesting them to present and advocate the said petition, the rector is desired to authenticate and forward the same.

A form of a report, as annually required to be made to the president and directors of the Literary Fund, on the funds and condition of the University, was then proposed, amended and agreed to in the following words:

To the president and directors of the Literary Fund:

In obedience to the act of the general assembly of Virginia, requiring that the rector and Visitors of the University of Virginia shall make report annually to the president and directors of the Literary Fund (to be laid before the legislature at their next succeeding session), embracing a full account of the disbursements, the funds on hand, and a general statement of the condition of the said University, the said rector and Visitors make the following report:

At their meeting in April last, the attention of the Visitors was first drawn to the consideration of the act of the late general assembly, which authorized the Literary Board to lend, for the use of the University, a further sum of 60,000 dollars from such moneys as should thereafter come to their hands. And taking such view as could then be obtained of the expenses already incurred for the lands, buildings and accessory purposes, for the accommodation of the professors and students of the University, so far as already completed, or in a state of advancement, and the further expenses still to be incurred necessarily to complete those accommodations, they concluded it to be for the benefit of the institution to obtain the said loan.

A meeting of the rector and Visitors of the University of Virginia was held at the University on 7th April, 1823, at which were present, Thomas Jefferson, James Madison, Chapman Johnson, George Loyall and Joseph C. Cabell.

It was resolved, that the loan of sixty thousand dollars, which the president and directors of the Literary Fund were authorized by an act of the last general assembly to make to the University, be accepted, and that the rector be authorized to execute the proper bonds, and to take the necessary steps for drawing the money, and that it be drawn in the following time and sums: that is to say thirty thousand dollars immediately, and the remaining thirty thousand dollars on the first day of January next; or in such other sums, and at such other times, as the president and directors of the Literary Fund and the executive committee of the University may agree upon.

It was resolved that the charges of Mr. Coffee for materials, packages, etc., be allowed him.

An anonymous letter, supposed to be in the handwriting of James Oldham, a carpenter, formerly employed at the University, which bears date 18 January, 1822 (by error as is supposed for 1823), and addressed to Thomas Griffin, Esq., a member of the legislature of Virginia, containing various charges, of misconduct, against Arthur S. Brockenbrough, the proctor of the University, having been laid before the Board by the said Brockenbrough, and the Board thinking that if the said James Oldham will avow himself the author of this letter, and profess himself willing to afford any evidence of these charges, they ought to be investigated.

Therefore, resolved, that the executive committee be charged with the duty of calling on the said Oldham, to declare whether he is the author of the letter aforesaid, and is willing to give any information as to the charges therein mentioned, and if he avow himself the author, and willing to give the information, then that they enter into the investigation thereof, upon evidence taken in such mode as they may prescribe, and report thereon to this Board at their next meeting.

Resolved, that the executive committee be authorized and required to employ from time to time an accountant, to settle and state the accounts of the University and to report thereon to the Board, at each meeting, and that they allow to the said accountant a reasonable compensation for his service.

Resolved, that Joseph C. Cabell and John H. Cocke, or either of whom may act, be appointed a committee to settle and report to the Board the accounts of the bursar and proctor of the University, with authority, if they deem it expedient, to require a statement thereof by the accountant.

The Board adjourns indefinitely.

Th. Jefferson, Rector.

April 7, 1823.

Wednesday, April 7, 1824.

Joseph C. Cabell attended with the members present on Monday.

In the University of Virginia shall be instituted eight professorships, to wit: 1st, of ancient languages; 2d, modern languages; 3d, mathematics; 4th, natural philosophy; 5th, natural history; 6th, anatomy and medicine; 7th, moral philosophy; 8th, law.

In the school of ancient languages shall be taught the higher grade of the Latin and Greek languages, the Hebrew, rhetoric, belles-lettres, ancient history and ancient geography.

In the school of modern languages shall be taught French, Spanish, Italian, German and the English language in its Anglo-Saxon form; also modern history and modern geography.

In the school of mathematics shall be taught mathematics generally, including the high branches of numerical arithmetic, algebra, trigonometry, plane and spherical geometry, mensuration, navigation, conic sections, fluxions or differentials, military and civil architecture.

In the school of natural philosophy shall be taught the laws and properties of bodies generally, including mechanics, statics, hydrostatics, hydraulics, pneumatics, acoustics, optics and astronomy.

In the school of natural history shall be taught botany, zoology, mineralogy, chemistry, geology and rural economy.

In the school of anatomy and medicine shall be taught anatomy, surgery, the history of the progress and theories of medicine, physiology, pathology, materia medica and pharmacy.

In the school of moral philosophy shall be taught mental science generally, including ideology, general grammar, logic and ethics.

In the school of law shall be taught the common and statute law, that of the chancery, the laws feudal, civil, mercatorial, maritime and of nature and nations; and also the principles of government and political economy.

This arrangement, however, shall not be understood as forbidding occasional transpositions of a particular branch of science from one school to another in accommodation of the particular qualifications of different professors.

In each of these schools instruction shall be communicated by lessons or lectures, examinations and exercises, as shall be best adapted to the nature of the science, and number of the school; and exercises shall be prescribed to employ the vacant days and hours.

The professors shall be permitted to occupy, rent free, a pavilion each, with the grounds appropriated to it. They shall also receive from the funds of the University such compensation as shall have been stipulated by the agent or fixed by the Board; and from each student attending them tuition fees as hereinafter declared.

The professors shall permit no waste to be committed in their tenements, and shall maintain the internal of their pavilions, and also the windows, doors and locks external during their occupation, in as good repair and condition as they shall have received them.

The collegiate duties of a professor, if discharged conscientiously, with industry and zeal, being sufficient to engross all his hours of business, he shall engage in no other pursuits of emolument unconnected with the service of the University without the consent of the Visitors.

Every student shall pay to the professor whom he attends, if he attends but one, fifty dollars the session of ten months and a half; if two, thirty dollars each, if three or more, twenty-five dollars each—and these payments shall be made in advance, and before his admission into the school. And they shall maintain their dormitories in the condition in which they shall receive them in like manner as is required of the professors. The proctor shall in duty attend in both cases to the observance of this requisition.

Although, as before expressed, the Board is in the expectation that they may be able, either immediately or at no distant period, to establish eight professorships; yet some uncertainties in the state of their funds, and other considerations render it prudent, for the present, to establish seven only; and the school of anatomy being that which it will be most expedient to postpone, they instruct their agent accordingly to make no engagement for an anatomical professor, or a provisional one only, subject to the future determination of the Board. They deem it also expedient that professors of law and moral philosophy shall be taken from among the citizens of the United States.

Considering as satisfactory the qualifications and character of George Blaettermann, of the city of London, recommended to them as professor of modern languages, the agent is authorized to engage him for that professorship, unless circumstances unknown to this Board should, in his judgment, furnish cause to decline that engagement, and to proceed to procure one who may merit more unexceptionably the approbation of the Board.

The Board then proceeded to the appointment of a professor, and Francis Walker Gilmer was appointed to the professor of law, or of moral philosophy, at his election, to be signified to the rector.

The executive committee are authorized to appoint a collector of the arrears of subscriptions, and are required to take measures as may be necessary to effect a speedy collection.

An act of the last assembly having appropriated to the University, for the purchase of a library and apparatus, the sum of 50,000 dollars out of the first moneys that may be received from the government of the United States on account of the claim of this Commonwealth for advances and expenditures during the late war, having also authorized a contingent loan to that amount, by board of public works, on the credit of the appropriation so made, and it being proper to provide for the receipt and disposal of this money, and for the negotiations of the authorized loan to such extent as may be advisable, the Board doth therefore, resolve:

First, that as soon as the money so appropriated, or any part thereof, shall be payable, it be paid to the bursar of the University, or to his order; that so much thereof as may be required by the executive committee, not exceeding 20,000 dollars, be placed by him in Europe under the control of the agent hereby deputed to that country, to be employed in the purchase of such books and apparatus as may be deemed most useful for the commencement of the several schools in the University; and the balance of the money which may be received by the bursar be deposited in bank, subject to the future orders of the Board.

Secondly, that the executive committee be authorized, if they deem it expedient, in anticipation of the money to be received from the General Government, to negotiate a loan with the board of public works for any sum not exceeding that hereby directed to be placed under the control of the agent in Europe; and to pledge the money so to be received from the General Government for the payment of the interest and refunding the principal of the loan; and any money so borrowed by the executive committee shall be placed under the control of the agent in Europe, in lieu of that mentioned in the first resolution, and for the purpose therein specified.

And the Board adjourned without day.

Th. Jefferson, Rector.

At a meeting of the Visitors of the University, October 4th, 1824, present, Thomas Jefferson, James Madison, James Breckenridge, John H. Cocke, George Loyall and Joseph C. Cabell.

Punishment for major offences shall be expulsion, temporary suspension, or interdiction of residence or appearance within the precincts of the University. The minor punishment shall be restraint within those precincts, within their own chamber, or in diet, reproof by a professor, privately or in presence of the school of the offender, or of all the schools, a seat of degradation in his school-room of longer or shorter duration, removal to a lower class, dismission from the school-room for the day, imposition of a task; and insubordination to these sentences shall be deemed and punished as contumacy.

Contumacy shall be liable to any of the minor punishments.

The precincts of the University are to be understood as co-extensive with the lot or parcel of its own grounds on which it is situated.

The major punishments of expulsion from the University, temporary suspension of attendance and presence there, or interdiction of residence or appearance within its precincts, shall be decreed by the professors themselves. Minor cases may be referred to a board of six censors, to be named by the faculty, from the most discreet of the students, whose duty it shall be, sitting as a board, to inquire into the facts, propose the minor punishment which they think proportioned to the offence, and to make report thereof to the professors for their approbation, or their commutation of the penalty, if it be beyond the grade of the offence. The censors shall hold their offices until the end of the session of their appointment, if not sooner revoked by the faculty.

Inattendance on school, inattention to the exercises prescribed, and misbehavior or indecorum in school shall be subject to any of the minor punishments; and the professor of the school may singly reprove, impose a task, or dismiss from the room for the day.

Habits of expense, of dissoluteness, dissipation, or of playing at games of chance, being obstructive to the acquisition of science by the student himself and injurious by example to others, shall be subject in the first instance to admonition and reproof to the offender, and to communication and warning to the parent or guardian, and, if not satisfactorily corrected, to a refusal of further continuance at the University.

No student shall make any festive entertainment within the precincts of the University, nor contribute or be present at them, there or elsewhere, but with the consent of each of the professors whose school he attends, on pain of a minor punishment.

No student shall admit any disturbing noises in his room, or make them anywhere within the precincts of the University, or fire a gun or pistol within the same, on pain of such minor sentence as the faculty shall decree or approve. But the proper use of musical instruments shall be freely allowed in their rooms, and in that appropriated for instruction in music.

Riotous, disorderly, intemperate or indecent conduct of any student within the precincts shall be punished by interdiction of a residence within the precincts; and repetitions of such offences, by expulsion from the University.

Fighting with weapons which may inflict death, or a challenge to such fight, given or accepted, shall be punished by instant expulsion from the University, not remissible by the Faculty; and it shall be the duty of the proctor to give information thereof to the civil magistrate, that the parties may be dealt with according to law.

Offences cognisable by the laws of the land shall be left to the cognisance of the civil magistrate, if claimed by him, or otherwise to the judgment of the faculty; all others to that of the faculty. And such of these as are not specially designated in enactments of the Visitors may be subjected by the faculty to any of the minor punishments permitted by these enactments.

Sentences of expulsion from the University (except in the case of challenge or combat with arms) shall not be final until approved by the Board of Visitors or, when they are not in session, by a majority of them, separately consulted. But residence within the precincts, and attendance on the schools may be suspended in the meantime.

No student shall, within the precincts of the University, introduce, keep or use any spirituous or vinous liquors, keep or use weapons or arms of any kind, or gunpowder, keep a servant, horse or dog, appear in school with a stick, or any weapon, nor while in school, be covered without permission of the professor, nor use tobacco by smoking or chewing, on pain of any of the minor punishments at the discretion of the faculty, or of the board of censors, approved by the faculty.

All damages done to instruments, books, buildings or other property of the University by any student, shall be made good at his expense; and wilful injury to any tree, shrub or other plant within the precincts, shall be punished by fine, not exceeding ten dollars, at the discretion of the faculty.

When a professor knocks at the door of a student's room, any person being within, and announces himself, it shall be opened, on pain of minor punishment; and the professor may, if refused, have the door broken open; and the expenses of repair shall be levied on the student or students within.

At the hour appointed for the meeting of every school, the roll of the school shall be called over, the absentees and those appearing tardily, shall be noted, and if no sufficient cause be offered, at the rising of the school, to the satisfaction of the professor, the notation shall stand confirmed, and shall be given in to the faculty, the presiding member of which for the time being shall, on the 15th day of May, August and December, or as soon after each of these days as may be, transmit by mail a list of these notations to the parent or guardian of each delinquent.

When testimony is required from a student, it shall be voluntary, and not on oath. And the obligation to give it shall—(if unwilling to give it, let the moral obligation be explained and urged, under which every one is bound to bear witness, where wrong has been done, but finally let it)—be left to his own sense of right.

Should the religious sects of this State, or any of them, according to the invitation held out to them, establish within, or adjacent to, the precincts of the University, schools for instruction in the religion of their sect, the students of the University will be free, and expected to attend religious worship at the establishment of their respective sects, in the morning, and in time to meet their school in the University at its stated hour.

The students of such religious school, if they attend any school of the University, shall be considered as students of the University, subject to the same regulations, and entitled to the same rights and privileges.

The room provided for a school-room in every pavilion shall be used for the school of its occupant professor, and shall be furnished by the University with necessary benches and tables.

The upper circular room of the rotunda shall be reserved for a library.

One of its larger elliptical rooms on its middle floor shall be used for annual examinations, for lectures to such schools as are too numerous for their ordinary school room, and for religious worship, under the regulations allowed to be prescribed by law. The other rooms on the same floor may be used by schools of instruction in drawing, music, or any other of the innocent and ornamental accomplishments of life; but under such instructors only as shall be approved and licensed by the faculty.

The rooms in the basement story of the rotunda shall be, one of them for a chemical laboratory, and the others for any necessary purpose to which they may be adapted.

The two open apartments, adjacent to the same story of the rotunda, shall be appropriated to the gymnastic exercises and games of the students, among which shall be reckoned military exercises.

A military instructor shall be provided at the expense of the University, to be appointed by the faculty, who shall attend on every Saturday from half after one o'clock to half after three P.M., and shall instruct the students in the manual exercise, in field evolutions, manoeuvres and encampments. The students shall attend these exercises, and shall be obedient to the military orders of their instructor. The roll shall be regularly called over by him at the hour of meeting, absences and insubordinations shall be noted, and the list of the delinquents shall be delivered to the presiding member of the faculty for the time being to be animadverted on by the faculty, and such minor punishment imposed as each case shall, in their discretion, require. The school of modern languages shall be pretermitted on the days of actual military exercise.

Substitutes in the form of arms shall be provided by the proctor, at the expense of the University; they shall be distinguished by numbers, delivered out, received in and deposited under the care and responsibility of the instructor, in a proper depository to be furnished him; and all injuries to them by a student shall be repaired at the expense of such student.

Work-shops shall be provided, whenever convenient, at the expense of the University, wherein the students who choose, may exercise themselves in the use of tools, and such mechanical practices as it is convenient and useful for every person to understand, and occasionally to practice. These shops may be let, rent free, to such skillful and orderly mechanics as shall be approved by the faculty, on the condition that they will permit the use of their tools, instruments and implements, within the shop, to such students as shall desire and use the permission discreetly, and under a liability for any injury they may do them; and on the further condition, if necessary, of such mechanics receiving instruction gratis in the mechanical and philosophical principles of his art, so far as taught in any of the schools.

The Board then proceeded to consider the draught of a report to be made, as required by law, to the president and directors of the

Literary Fund and before concluding it finally, they adjourned to to-morrow morning.

March 5, the Board met according to adjournment, present the same members as yesterday.

Resolved, that on payment of the said sum of 50,000 dollars by the General Government, a sum not exceeding 6,000 dollars thereof be advanced on loan to the building fund of the University for the purpose of finishing the interior of the library-room.

For the use and care of the library the Board now establishes the following regulations:

The professors of the University shall at all times have free use of the books of the library, in confidence that they will not keep them out longer than while in actual use, and leaving with the librarian a note of the books borrowed.

Books may be lent to the students of the University, by the librarian, and by no other person, on a written permit from a professor whom such student attends, specifying the day beyond which they will not be retained. But it is meant that the books lent are for reading only, and not for the ordinary purpose of getting lessons in them as school books.

No student shall carry any book borrowed from the library, out of the precincts of the University; nor shall any student be permitted to have more than three volumes in his possession at any time.

If a student shall not return a borrowed book on or before the day limited in his permit, he shall receive no other until it be returned; and he shall pay, moreover, for every week's detention beyond the limitation, ten cents for a 12mo. or book of smaller size, twenty cents for an 8mo., thirty cents for a 4mo. and forty cents for a folio.

Not every book in the library shall be free to be lent to students, but such only as shall not be expressly prohibited by the faculty on account of their rarity, value or liableness to injury.

No student shall ever be in the library but in presence of the librarian, or of some professor whom he attends, nor shall be allowed to take any book from the shelves, nor remain in the room to read or consult any book, but during such presence.

If any student deface, injure, or lose any book of the library, he shall pay the value of the book if defaced, double value if injured, and threefold, if lost; and shall be suspended from the privilege of borrowing during such term as the faculty shall adjudge.

On some one day of every week during term, and during one hour of that day (such day and hour to be fixed on by the faculty) the librarian shall attend in the library, to receive books returned, and to lend such others as shall be applied for according to rule. And at some one hour of every day (to be fixed by the faculty) the librarian shall attend, if requested by any such professor, such book or books as he may require, and to receive any he may have to return.

The librarian shall make an entry of every book lent, and cancel the same when returned, so that it may always be known in what hands every book is.

Strangers whom the librarian may be willing to attend, may visit the library; but, to prevent derangement of the books, they are to take no book from the shelf, but in his presence. They may also be permitted to consult any book, to read in it, make notes or quotations from it, at the table, under such accommodations and arrangements as the librarian shall prescribe, on his own responsibility.

Resolved, that the salary of the librarian be raised to the sum of 150 dollars.

Tuesday, October 4.

The Board met according to adjournment. Present the same members as yesterday.

On complaint from the faculty of certain riotous proceedings of some of the students on the nights of September 30 and October 2, and of insults on some of the professors, the whole of the students were called before the Board of Visitors, they were exhorted to state to the Board the facts which had taken place within their knowledge, whereupon fourteen of them came forward and acknowledged that on the night of the second they had masked and disguised themselves and gone out on the lawn where they had made some noise, but denied they had committed any trespasses or insults on the professors, and on their engaging to appear before the board of the faculty and to repeat to them the information now given, they were dismissed.

The Board receives from Messrs. Key and Long a written declaration that in consequence of the transactions which had taken place, and particularly of a remonstrance of the day before subscribed by sixty-five students, they could no longer remain in their present situations, that they had lost all confidence in the signers of that remonstrance, and cannot and will not meet them again.

The Board adjourned to to-morrow.

Wednesday, October 5.

The Board met according to adjournment. Present the same members as yesterday.

Resolved that the 47th enactment be amended, by inserting after the word "chewing" the words "or smoking."

No student shall appear out of his dormitory masked or disguised in any manner whatever, which may render the recognition of his person more difficult, on pain of suspension or expulsion by the faculty of professors.

Intoxication shall, for the first offense, be liable to any of the minor punishments, and any repetition of the offence to any of the major punishments.

Resolved, that the 40th enactment be amended, by inserting after the word "dissipation," the words "of profane swearing."

No person who has been a student at any other incorporated seminary of learning shall be received at this University, but on producing a certificate from such seminary or other satisfactory evidence to the faculty with respect to his general good conduct.

The professors being charged with the execution of the laws of the University, it becomes their duty to pursue proper means to discover and prevent offences. Respect from the student to the professor being at all times due, it is more especially so when the professor is engaged in his duty. Such respect, therefore, is solemnly enjoined on every student, and it is declared and enacted, that if any student refuse his name to a professor, or being required by him to stop, shall fail to do so, or shall be guilty of any other disrespect to a professor, he shall be liable to any of the punishments, minor or major.

Thursday, October 6.

The Board met according to adjournment. Present the same members as yesterday.

Resolved, that Mr. Johnson, Mr. Cabell, and Mr. Loyall be appointed a committee, whose duty it shall be to consider and enquire what system may be digested for the better government of the University; that they be especially charged with the duty of considering how far it may be practicable and prudent to connect with the University a court having cognisance over misdemeanors committed within the precincts of the University, and over those committed by members of the University, within the county of Albermarle, and that they report thereupon to the next meeting of the Visitors.

Resolved, that for the purpose of receiving the report of the committee appointed by the preceding resolution, and of acting thereupon, and for the transaction of such other business as may then require attention, an extra meeting of the Board be held on the second Monday in December next.

A communication from the faculty of professors is received in the following words, to wit: "University of Virginia. Ordered, that Wilson Miles Carey having, on the night of the 1st instant, resisted the authority of a professor, used violence against him, and excited others to follow his example, and for abusive epithets concerning the said professor, be expelled from the University."

Another communication from the said professors is received in the following words, to wit: "University of Virginia. Ordered, that William L. Eyre having, on the night of the 1st instant, promoted a riot by repeatedly using indecent and approbrious language respecting some of the professors during the disturbance of the night in question, and having refused to give his name when called upon by two professors, be expelled from the University. Copied from the minutes of the faculty. Robert Dunglison, secretary. George Tucker, chairman, 1825, October 6." Resolved, that the said sentence is unanimously approved by the Board of Visitors.

A third communication from the said professors is also received in the following words, to wit: "University of Virginia. Ordered, that Robert A. Thompson having, on the night of the first instant, armed himself with a stick for the purpose of resisting the authority of two professors, be expelled from the University. Copied from the minutes of the faculty. Robert Dunglison, secretary. George Tucker, chairman, October 6, 1825." Resolved, that the said sentence is approved by the Board of Visitors.

A letter is received from T. H. Key and George Long in these words, to wit: "To the rector and Visitors of the University of Virginia: Gentlemen, The undersigned professors of the University of Virginia hereby tender to you the resignation of their respective chairs. T. H. Key, George Long. October 6, 1825."

Resolved, that Chapman Johnson, Joseph C. Cabell and John H. Cocke be a committee to communicate to Professors Key and Long the objections which occur to the Board to the resignation of their offices as proposed in theirs of this day, and to confer with the said professors on the subject of that letter.

Resolved, that the said committee do make known to the faculty of professors the proceedings which have been had upon their communication of the second day of this month, relative to the disorders in the University, which have lately occurred, and that they also make known to them the names of those students who voluntarily acknowledge themselves present and agents in some of the transactions complained of.

The Board adjourned to to-morrow.—A. A. Lipscomb (ed.), *The Writings of Thomas Jefferson*, Vol. XIX, 361 ff.

9. Authority for appointing "The Board of Commissioners for the University of Virginia," 1818

Be it further enacted, That there shall be established in some convenient and proper part of the State, a University, to be called "The University of Virginia," wherein all the branches of useful science shall be taught. In order to aid the Legislature in ascertaining the permanent site of the said University, and in organizing it, there shall be appointed, without delay, by the Executive of this Commonwealth, twenty-four discreet and intelligent persons, who shall constitute a Board to be called "The Board of Commissioners for the University." One member of the said Board shall be appointed from each of the senatorial districts, as they were arranged by an act of the last session of the Legislature. If any person so appointed shall fail or refuse to act, his place shall be supplied from the same district, by appointment of the President and Directors of the Literary Fund. The said Board shall meet on the first day of August next, at the tavern in Rockfish Gap on the Blue Ridge, for the purpose of performing the duties hereby assigned to them. At least three-fourths of the whole number shall be necessary to form a Board for the transaction of business; but any smaller number may adjourn from day to day, until a quorum shall attend. The said Board, when assembled, shall have power to adjourn from time to time, and from place to place, until their duties shall have been performed. It shall be their duty to enquire and report to the Legislature at their next session:

First—A proper site for the University.

Secondly—A plan for the building thereof.

Thirdly—The branches of learning which should be taught therein.

Fourthly—The number and description of professorships; and

Fifthly—Such general provisions as might properly be enacted by the Legislature, for the better organizing and governing the University.

The said Board are also authorized and required to receive any voluntary contributions, whether conditional or absolute, whether in land, money, or other property, which may be offered, through them, to the President and Directors of the Literary Fund, for the benefit of the University; and to report the same to the Legislature at their next session. The members of the said Board of Commissioners shall be allowed for their services the same pay and traveling expenses, as are allowed to members of the General Assembly, to be ascertained and certified by the Board, and paid out of the literary fund.

Be it further enacted, That as soon as the site of the said University shall be ascertained by law, there shall be appropriated out of the revenue of the literary fund, the sum of fifteen thousand dollars per annum, for the purpose of defraying the expenses of procuring the land and erecting the buildings, and for the permanent endowment of the said University; *provided, however*, that the appropriation hereby made to the University, shall in no manner impair or diminish the appropriations hereinbefore made to the education of the poor in the several counties or corporations.

Be it further enacted, That the University aforesaid shall be under the government of thirteen Visitors, to be appointed by the President and Directors of the Literary Fund, and to hold their offices for seven years, and until their successors shall be appointed, unless sooner displaced by the said President and Directors. All vacancies in the office of Visitor, by death, resignation, or removal out of the Commonwealth, or failure to act, for the space of one year, shall be supplied by the said President and Directors.

The said Visitors shall appoint one of their own body to be Rector, and they shall be a body corporate, under the name and style of "The Rector and Visitors of the University of Virginia;" and, as such, they may have and use a common seal, receive and hold property for the benefit of the University, sue and be sued, implead and be impleaded. They shall have power to appoint a clerk for their own body, and allow him a reasonable compensation for his services; to appoint and remove the professors and teachers, and all other officers of the University; to regulate their salaries and fees, and to make all such by-laws and regulations as may be necessary to the good government of the University, and not contrary to the laws of the land. But the said Rector and Visitors shall at all times conform to such laws as the Legislature may from time to time think proper to enact for their government; and the said University shall in all things, at all times, be subject to the control of the Legislature.

This act shall commence and be in force from and after the 1st day of March.—Cabell, *op. cit.*, pp. 430-32.

10. Thomas Jefferson sends to the Speaker of the House of Delegates the Report of the "Board of Commissioners" of the University of Virginia, November 20, 1818

Monticello Nov. 20. 1818

Sir

The Commissioners appointed under the act of the last General assembly for appropriating a part of the revenue of the literary fund and for other purposes, met according to law, at the Rockfish gap, on the 1st day of August last, and having continued their session by adjournments until the 4th day of that month, agreed to a Report, which being signed in Duplicate, individually and unanimously, by all the members who attended, they instructed me to transmit to the Speakers of both houses of legislature. In obedience to that instruction I now inclose one of the sd original reports, with a copy of their journal, and of the documents exhibited and left in their possession.

Some of the outstanding subscription papers therein mentioned, have been returned with additional subscriptions to the amount of 2650 Dollars and an additional purchase has been made of 48 ¾ acres of land adjoining the site of the Central College, necessary to the probable extent of buildings should that be adopted, as proposed by the Report, for the site of the University; which circumstances having taken place since the date of the Report. I have deemed it a duty to mention as supplementary to it.

I have the honor to be with sentiments of the highest respect and consideration, Sir

Your most obedient
and most humble servant
Th: Jefferson

—Original in Virginia State Library; typescript copy in the Southern Historical Collection, the University of North Carolina.

11. Report of the Rockfish Gap Commission appointed to fix the site of the University of Virginia, 1818

The Commissioners for the University of Virginia, having met, as by law required, at the tavern, in Rockfish Gap, on the Blue Ridge, on the first day of August, of this present year 1818, and having formed a board, proceeded on that day to the discharge of the duties assigned to them by the act of the Legislature entitled an "act appropriating part of the revenue of the literary fund, and for other purposes" and having continued their proceedings by adjournment from day to day to Tuesday the 4th day of August, have agreed to a report on the several matters with which they were charged, which report they now respectfully address and submit to the Legislature of the State.

The first day enjoined on them was to enquire and report a site, in some convenient and proper part of the State, for an university, to be called the "University of Virginia." In this enquiry, they suppose that the governing considerations should be the healthiness of the site, the fertility of the neighboring country, and its centrality to the white population of the whole state: for altho the act authorized and required them to receive any voluntary contributions whether conditional or absolute, which might be offered through them to the President & Directors of the literary fund, for the benefit of the University, yet they did not consider this as establishing an auction, or as pledging the location to the highest bidder.

Three places were proposed, to wit Lexington, in the county of Rockbridge, Staunton, in the county of Augusta, and the Central College, in the county of Albermarle. Each of these was unexceptionable as to healthiness & fertility. It was the degree of centrality to the white population of the State which alone then constituted the important point of comparison between these places; and the Board, after full enquiry, & impartial & mature consideration, are of opinion that the central point of the white population of the State is nearer to the Central College than to either Lexington or Staunton by great & important differences, and all other circumstances of the place in general being favorable to it as a position for an university, they do report the Central College, in Albemarle, to be a convenient & proper part of the State for the University of Virginia.

2d. The Board having thus agreed on a proper site for the University to be reported to the Legislature, proceed to the second of the duties assigned to them, that of proposing a plan for its buildings; and they are of opinion that it should consist of distinct houses or pavilions, arranged at proper distances on each side of a lawn of a proper breadth, & of indefinite extent, in one direction, at least, in each of which should be a lecturing room with from two to four apartments for the accommodation of a professor and his family: that these pavilions should be united by a range of Dormitories, sufficient each for the accommodation of two students only, this provision being deemed advantageous to morals, to order, & to uninterrupted study; and that a passage of some kind under cover from the weather should give a communication along the whole range. It is supposed that such pavilions on an average of the larger and smaller will cost each about $5,000, each dormitory about $350, and Hotels of a single room for a Refectory, & two rooms for the tenant necessary for dieting the students will cost about $3,500 each. The number of these pavilions will depend on the number of professors, and that of the Dormitories and Hotels on the number of students to be lodged and dieted. The advantages of this plan are, greater security against fire & infection; tranquillity and comfort to the Professors, and their families thus insulated; retirement to the students, and the admission of enlargement to any degree to which the institution may extend in future times. It is supposed probable that a building of somewhat more size in the middle of the grounds may be called for in time, in which may be rooms for religious worship under such impartial regulations as the visitors shall prescribe, for public examinations, for a Library, for the schools of music, drawing, and other associated purposes.

3. 4. In proceeding to the third and fourth duties prescribed by the legislature of reporting "the branches of learning, which shall be taught in the University, and the number and description of the professorships they will require" the commissioners were first to consider at what point it was understood that university-education should commence? Certainly not with the Alphabet, for reasons of expediency & impracticability, as well as from the obvious sense of the Legislature, who, in the same act make other provision for the primary instruction of the poor children, expecting doubtless, that, in other cases, it would be provided by, the parent, or become perhaps subject of future, and further attention for the legislature. The objects of this primary education determine its character & limits.– These objects would be,

To give to every citizen the information he needs for the transaction of his own business.

To enable him to calculate for himself, and to express & preserve his ideas, his contracts & accounts, in writing.

To improve by reading, his morals and faculties.

To understand his duties to his neighbors, & country, and to discharge with competence the functions confided to him by either.

To know his rights; to exercise with order and justice those he retains; to choose with discretion the fiduciary of those he delegates; and to notice their conduct with diligence with candor & judgment.

And, in general, to observe with intelligence and faithfulness all the social relations under which he shall be placed.

To instruct the mass of our citizens in these their rights, interests and duties, as men and citizens, being then the objects of education in the primary schools, whether private or public, in them should be taught reading, writing & numerical arithmetic, the elements of mensuration, (useful in so many callings) and the outlines of geography and history, and this brings us to the point at which are to commence the higher branches of education, of which the legislature require the development: those for example which are to form the statesmen legislators & judges, on whom public prosperity, & individual happiness are so much to depend:

To expound the principles and structure of government, the laws which regulate the intercourse of nations, those formed municipally for our own government, and a sound spirit of legislation, which banishing all arbitrary and unnecessary restraint on individual action shall leave us free to do whatever does not violate the equal rights of another.

To harmonize and promote the interests of agriculture, manufactures & commerce and by well informed views of political economy to give a free scope to the public industry.

To develop the reasoning faculties of our youth, enlarge their minds, cultivate their morals, and instill into them the precepts of virtue and order:

To enlighten them with mathematical and physical sciences, which advance the arts, and administer to the health, the subsistence and comforts of human life;

And generally, to form them to habits of reflection and correct action, rendering them examples of virtue to others, and of happiness within themselves.

These are the objects of that higher grade of education, the benefits and blessings of which the legislature now propose to provide for the good & ornament of their country the gratification and happiness of their fellow citizens, of the parent especially & his progeny on which all his affections are concentrated.—

In entering on this field the commissioners are aware that they have to encounter much difference of opinion as to the extent which it is expedient that this institution should occupy. Some good men and even of respectable information consider the learned sciences as useless acquirements; some think that they do not better the condition of man; and others that education like private & individual concerns, should be left to private individual effort; not reflecting that an establishment, embracing all the sciences which may be useful & even necessary in the various vocations of life, with the buildings & apparatus belonging to each, are far beyond the reach of individual means, & must either derive existence from public patronage or not exist at all. This would leave us then without those callings which depend on education, or send us to other countries, to seek the instruction they require. But the Commissioners are happy in considering the statute under which they are assembled as proof that the legislature is far from the abandonment of objects so interesting. They are sensible that the advantages of well directed education, moral, political & economical are truly above all estimate. Education generates habits of application, of order and the love of virtue; and controuls, by the force of habit, any innate obliquities in our moral organization. We should be far too from the discouraging persuasion, that man is fixed, by the law of his nature, at a given point: that his improvement is a chimera, and the hope delusive of rendering ourselves wiser, happier or better than our forefathers were. As well might it be urged that the wild & uncultivated tree, hitherto yielding sour & bitter fruit only, can never be made to yield better: yet we know that the grafting art implants a new tree on the savage stock, producing what is most estimable both in kind & degree. Education, in like manner engrafts a new man on the native stock, & improves what in his nature was vicious & perverse, into qualities of virtue & social worth; and it cannot be but that each generation succeeding to the knowledge acquired by all those who preceded it, adding to it their own acquisitions & discoveries & handing the mass down for successive & constant accumulation, must advance the knowledge & well-being of mankind; not *infinitely*, as some have said, but *indefinitely*, and to a term which no one can fix or foresee. Indeed we need look back half a century, to times which many now living remember well, and see the wonderful advances in the sciences and arts which have been made within that period. Some of these have rendered the elements themselves subservient to the purposes of man, have harnessed them to the yoke of his labours, and effected the great blessings of moderating his own, of accomplishing what was beyond his feeble force, & of extending the comforts of life to a much enlarged circle, to those who had before known its necessaries only. That these are not the vain dreams of sanguine hope, we have before our eyes real & living examples. What, but education, has advanced us beyond the condition of our indigenous neighbors? And what chains them to their present state of barbarism and wretchedness, but a bigotted veneration for the supposed superlative wisdom of their fathers and the preposterous idea that they are to look backward for better things and not forward, longing, as it should seem, to return to the days of eating acorns and roots rather than indulge in the degeneracies of civilization. And how much more encouraging to the achievements of science and improvement, is this, than the desponding view that the condition of man cannot be ameliorated, that what has been must ever be, and that to secure ourselves where we are, we must tread with awful reverence in the footsteps of our fathers. This doctrine is the genuine fruit of the alliance between Church and State, the tenants of which, finding themselves but too well in their present condition, oppose all advances which might unmask their usurpations, and monopolies of honors, wealth and power, and fear every change, as endangering the comforts they now hold. Nor must we omit to mention, among the benefits of education, the incalculable advantage of training up able counsellors to administer the affairs of our country in all its departments, Legislative Executive and Judiciary, and to bear their proper share in the councils of our national Government; nothing, more than education, advancing the prosperity, the power, and the happiness of a nation.

Encouraged therefore by the sentiments of the Legislature, manifested in this statute, we present the following tabular statement of the branches of learning which we think should be taught in the University, forming them into groups, each of which are within the powers of a single professor:

I Languages antient
Latin
Greek
Hebrew

II Languages Modern
French
Spanish
Italian
German
Anglo-Saxon

III Mathematics Pure
Algebra
Fluxions
Geometry elementary
Transcendental
Architecture Military Naval

IV Physico-Mathematics
Mechanics
Statics
Dynamics

Pneumatics
Acoustics
Optics
Astronomy
Geography

V Physics or Natural Philosophy
Chemistry
Mineralogy

VI Botany
Zoology

VII Anatomy
Medicine

VIII Government
Political economy
Law of nature & nations
History (being interwoven with Politics & Law)

IX Law Municipal

X Ideology
General Grammar
Ethics
Rhetoric
Belles Lettres & the fine arts

Some of the terms used in this table being subject to a difference of acceptation, it is proper to define the meaning and comprehension intended to be given them here—

Geometry elementary is that of straight lines and of the circle
Transcendental, is that of all other curves; it includes of course *Projectiles*, a leading branch of the military art.

Military Architecture, includes Fortification, another branch of that art.

Statics respect matter generally, in a state of rest, and include Hydrostatics, or the laws of fluids particularly, at rest or in equilibrio.

Dynamics, used as a general term, include
Dynamics proper, or the Laws of *solids* in Motion; and
Hydronamics, or Hydraulics, those of fluids in motion.

Pneumatics teach the theory of air, its weight, motion, condensation, rarefaction, &c.

Acoustics or Phonics, the theory of sound.

Optics the Laws of light & vision.

Physics or Physiology in a general sense, mean the doctrine of the physical objects of our senses.

Chemistry, is meant, with its other usual branches, to comprehend the theory of agriculture.

Mineralogy, in addition to its peculiar subjects is here understood to embrace what is real in geology.

Ideology is the doctrine of thought.

General Grammar explains the construction of Language.

Some articles in this distribution of sciences will need observation. A professor is proposed for antient Languages, the Latin, Greek and Hebrew, particularly, but these languages being the foundation common to all the sciences, it is difficult to foresee what may be the extent of this school. At the same time no greater obstruction to industrious study could be proposed than the presence, the intrusions, and the noisy turbulence of a multitude of small boys: and if they are to be placed here for the rudiments of the languages, they may be so numerous, that its character and value as an University, will be merged in those of a Grammar school. It is therefore greatly to be wished, that preliminary schools, either on private or public establishment, could be distributed in districts through the state, as preparatory to the entrance of students into the University. The tender age at which this part of education commences, generally about the tenth year, would weigh heavily with parents in sending their sons to a school so distant as the central establishment would be from most of them. Districts of such extent as that every parent should be within a day's journey of his son at school, would be desirable in cases of sickness, and convenient for supplying their ordinary wants, and might be made to lessen sensibly the expense of this part of their education. And where a sparse population would not, within such a compass, furnish subjects sufficient to maintain a school, a competent enlargement of district must, of necessity, there be submitted to. At these District schools or colleges, boys should be rendered able to read the easier authors, Latin and Greek. This would be useful and sufficient for many not intended for an University education. At these too might be taught English grammar, the higher branches of numerical arithmetic, the geometry of straight lines and of the circle, the elements of Navigation, and Geography to a sufficient degree, and thus afford to greater numbers the means of being qualified for the Various Vocations of life, needing more instruction than merely menial or praedial labor; and the same advantages to youths whose education may have been neglected until too late to lay a foundation in the learned languages. These institutions, intermediate between the primary schools and University, might then be the passage of entrance for Youths into the University, where their classical learning might be critically completed, by a study of the authors of highest degree and it is at this stage only that they should be received at the University— Giving then a portion of their time to a finished knowledge of the Latin and greek, the rest might be appropriated to the modern languages, or to the commencement of the course of science for which they should be destined. This would generally be about the fifteenth year of their age, when they might go with more safety and contentment to that distance from their parents. Until this preparatory provision shall be made, either the University will be overwhelmed with the grammar school, or a separate establishment, under one or more ushers, for its lower classes, will be advisable, at a mile or two distant from the general one; where too may be exercised the stricter government necessary for young boys, but unsuitable for youths arrived at years of discretion.

The considerations which have governed the specification of languages to be taught by the professor of modern languages were that the French is the language of general intercourse among nations, and as a depository of human science, is unsurpassed by any other language living or dead; that the Spanish is highly interesting to us, as the language spoken by so great a portion of the inhabitants of our continents, with whom we shall probably have great intercourse ere long; and is that also in which is written the greater part of the earlier history of America. The Italian abounds with works of very superior order, valuable for their matter, and still more distinguished as models of the finest taste in style and composition: and the German now stands in a line with that of the most learned nations in richness of erudition and advance in the sciences. It is too of common descent with the language of our own country, a branch of the same original Gothic stock, and furnishes valuable illustrations for us. But in this point of view the Anglo-Saxon is of peculiar value. We have placed it among the modern languages because it is in fact that which we speak, in the earliest form in which we have knowledge of it. It has been undergoing, with time, those gradual changes which all languages, antient and modern, have experienced: and even now needs only to be printed in the modern character and orthography, to be intelligible in a considerable degree to an English reader. It has this value too above the Greek and Latin, that while it gives the radix of the mass of our language, they explain its innovations only. Obvious proofs of this have been presented to the modern reader in the disquisitions of Horn Tooks; and Fortescue Aland has well explained the great instruction which may be derived from it toward a full understanding of our antient common law on which as a stock our whole system of law is engrafted. It will form the first link in the chain of an historical review of our language through all its successive changes to the present day, will constitute the foundation of that critical instruction in it, which ought to be found in a seminary of general learning and thus reward amply the few weeks of attention which would alone be requisite for its attainment, a language already fraught with all the eminent science of our parent country the future vehicle of whatever we may ourselves achieve and destined to occupy so much space on the Globe, claims distinguished attention in American education—

Medicine, where fully taught is usually subdivided into several professorships, but this cannot well be without the accessory of an hospital, where the student can have the benefit of attending clinical lectures & of assisting at operations of surgery. With this accessory, the seat of our University is not yet prepared, either by its population, or by the numbers of poor, who would leave their own houses, and accept of the charities of an hospital. For the present, therefore we propose but a single professor for both medicine & anatomy. By him the elements of medical science may be taught, with a history & explanations of all its successive theories from Hippocrates to the present day: and anatomy may be fully treated. Vegetable pharmacy will make a part of the botanical course, & mineral & chemical pharmacy of those of mineralogy & chemistry. This degree of medical information is such as the mass of scientific students would wish to possess, as enabling them, in their course thro life, to estimate with satisfaction the extent & limits of the aid to human life & health, which they may understandingly expect from that art: and it constitutes such a foundation for those intended for the profession, that the finishing course of practice at the bed-sides of the sick, and at the operations of surgery in a hospital, can neither be long nor expensive. To seek this finishing elsewhere, must therefore be submitted to for a while.

In conformity with the principles of our Constitution, which places all sects of religion on an equal footing, with the jealousies of the different sects in guarding that equality from encroachment & surprise, and with the sentiments of the legislature in favor of freedom of religion manifested on former occasions, we have proposed no professor of Divinity: and tho rather, as the proofs of the being of a god, the creator, preserver, & supreme ruler of the universe, the author of all the relations of morality, & of the laws & obligations these infer will be within the province of the professor of ethics; to which adding the developments of these moral obligations, of those in which all sects agree with a knowledge of the languages, Hebrew, Greek and Latin, a basis will be formed common to all sects. Proceeding thus far without offence to the Constitution, we have thought it proper at this point to leave every sect to provide, as they think fittest, the means of further instruction in their own peculiar tenets.

We are further of opinion that, after declaring by law that certain sciences shall be taught in the University, fixing the number of professors they require, which we think should, at present, be ten, limiting (except as to the professors who shall be first engaged in each branch) a maximum for their salaries, (which should be a certain but moderate subsistence, to be made up by liberal tuition fees, as an excitement to assiduity,) it will be best to leave to the discretion of the visitors, the grouping of these sciences together, according to the accidental qualifications of the professors; and the introduction also of other branches of science, when enabled by private donations, or by public provision, and called for by the increase of population, or other change of circumstances; to establish beginnings, in short, to be developed by time, as those who come after us shall find expedient. They will be more advanced than we are, in science and in useful arts, and will know best what will suit the circumstances of their day.

We have proposed no formal provision for the gymnastics of the school, altho a proper object of attention for every institution of youth. These exercises with antient nations, constituted the principal part of the education of their youth. Their arms and mode of warfare rendered them severe in the extreme. Ours on the same correct principle should be adapted to our arms & warfare: and the manual exercise, military manoeuvres, and tactics generally should be the frequent exercises of the students, in their hours of recreation. It is at that age of aptness, docility & emulation of the practices of manhood, that such things are soonest learnt and longest remembered. The use of tools too in the manual arts is worthy of encouragement, by facilitating, to such as choose it, an admission into the neighboring workshops. To these should be added the arts which embellish life, dancing, music, & drawing; the last more especially, as an important part of military education. These innocent arts furnish amusement & happiness to those who, having time on their hands, might less inoffensively employ it: needing, at the same time, no regular incorporation with the institution, they may be left to accessory teachers, who will be paid by the individuals employing them; the University only providing proper apartments for their exercise.

The fifth duty prescribed to the Commissioners is to propose such general provisions as may be properly enacted by the legislature, for the better organizing & governing the University.

In the education of youth, provision is to be made for 1. tuition. 2. diet. 3. lodging: 4. government: and 5. honorary excitements. The first of these constitutes the proper functions of the professors. 2. The dieting of the students should be left to private boarding houses, of their own choice, and at their own expense; to be regulated by the visitors from time to time, the house only being provided by the University within its own precincts, and thereby of course subjected to the general regimen, moral or sumptuary, which they shall prescribe. 3. They should be lodged in dormitories, making a part of the general system of building. 4. The best mode of government for youth in large collections, is certainly a desideratum not yet attained with us. It may be well questioned whether *fear* after a certain age, is a motive to which we should have ordinary recourse. The human character is susceptible of other incitements to correct conduct, more worthy of employ, and of better effect. Pride of character, laudable ambition, & moral dispositions are innate correctives of the indiscretions of that lively age; and when strengthened by habitual appeal & exercise, have a happier effect on future character, than the degrading motive of *fear*. Hardening them to disgrace, to corporal punishments, and servile humiliations, cannot be the best process for producing erect character. The affectionate deportment between father and son offers in truth the best example for that of tutor & pupil; and the experience & practice of* other countries, in this respect, may be worthy of enquiry & consideration with us. It will be then for the wisdom & discretion of the Visitors to devise & perfect a proper system of government, which, if it be founded in reason & comity, will be more likely to nourish, in the minds of our youth, the combined spirit of order & self respect, so congenial with our political institutions, and so important to be woven into the American character. 5. What qualifications shall be required to entitle to entrance into the University, the arrangement of the days & hours of lecturing for the different schools, so as

* A police exercised by the students themselves, under proper direction has been tried with success in some countries, and the rather as forming them for initiation into the duties and practices of civil life.

to facilitate to the students the circle of attendance on them; the establishment of periodical and public examinations, the premium to be given for distinguished merit; whether honorary degrees shall be conferred; and by what appellations; whether the title to these shall depend on the time the candidate has been at the University, or, where nature have given a greater share of understanding, attention, and application; whether he shall not be allowed the advantages resulting from these endowments, with other minor items of government, we are of opinion, should be entrusted to the visitors; and the statute under which we act, having provided for the appointment of these, we think they should moreover be charged with the erection, preservation & repair of the buildings, the care of the grounds & appurtenances and of the interests of the university generally: that they should have power to appoint a Bursar, employ a Proctor & all other necessary agents; to appoint & remove professors, two thirds of the whole number of visitors voting for the removal: to prescribe their duties & the course of education, in conformity with the law: to establish rules for the government & discipline of the students not contrary to the laws of the land: to regulate the tuition fees, & the rent of the dormitories they occupy: to prescribe & control the duties & proceedings of all officers, servants & others with respect to the buildings, lands, appurtenances & other property & interests of the university: to draw from the literary fund such monies as are by law charged on it for this institution: and in general to direct & do all matters & things which, not being inconsistent with the laws of the land, to them shall seem most expedient for promoting the purposes of the said institution; which several functions they should be free to exercise in the form of by laws, rules, resolutions, orders, instructions or otherwise as they should deem proper.

That they should have two stated meetings in the year, and occasional meetings at such times as they should appoint, or on a special call with such notice as themselves shall prescribe by a general rule; which meetings should be at the University, a majority of them constituting a quorum for business; and that on the death or resignation of a member, or on his removal by the President & Directors of the Literary Fund, or the Executive, or such other authority as the legislature shall think best, such President & Directors, or the Executive, or other authority, should appoint a successor.

That the said visitors should appoint one of their own body to be Rector & with him be a body corporate, under the style & title of the Rector & visitors of the University of Virginia, with the right as such, to use a common seal; that they should have capacity to plead and be impleaded in all courts of justice, and in all cases interesting to the University, which may be the subjects of legal cognizance & jurisdiction; which please should not abate by the determination of their office, but should stand revived in the name of their successors, and they should be capable in law and in trust for the University, of receiving subscriptions and donations, real and personal, as well from bodies corporate, or persons associated, as from private individuals.

And that the said Rector and Visitors should at all times conform to such laws, as the legislature may, from time to time, think proper to enact for their government; and the said University should in all things, & at all times be subject to the control of the legislature—

And lastly the Commissioners report to the Legislature the following conditional offers to the President and Directors of the Literary Fund for the benefit of the University.

On the condition that Lexington, or its vicinity shall be selected as the site of the University, and that the same be permanently established there within two years from the date, John Robinson of Rockbridge county, has executed a deed to the President and Directors of the Literary Fund, to take effect at his death, for the following tracts of land, to wit,

400 acres on the North fork of James River known by the name of Hart's bottom purchased of the late Gen. Bowyer.
171 acres adjoining the same purchased of James Griggsby.
203 acres joining the last mentioned tract, purchased of William Paxton.
112 acres lying on the North river, above the lands of Arthur Glasgow conveyed to him by William Paxton's heirs.
500 acres joining the lands of Arthur Glasgow, Benjamin Camden and David Edmonson.
545 acres lying in Pryor's gap, conveyed to him by the heirs of William Paxton deceased.
260 acres lying also in Childer's gap purchased of Nicholas Jones.
500 acres lying on Buffalo, joining the lands of James Johnston.

340 acres on the Cowpasture river conveyed to him by General James Breckenridge, reserving the right of selling the two last mentioned tracts, and converting them into other lands contiguous to Hart's bottom, for the benefit of the University.

Also the whole of his Slaves amounting to 57 in number. One lot of twenty two acres joining the town of Lexington to pass immediately, on the establishment of the University, together with all the personal estate of every kind, subject only to the payment of his debts, and fulfilment of his contracts.

It has not escaped the attention of the Commissioners that the deed referred to is insufficient to pass the estate in the lands intended to be conveyed, & may be otherwise defective; but if necessary this defect may be remedied before the meeting of the Legislature which the Commissioners are advised will be done.

The Board of Trustees of Washington College have also proposed to transfer the whole of their funds, viz, 100 shares in the funds of the James River Company, 31 acres of land on which their buildings stand. Their philosophical apparatus; their expected interest in the funds of the Cincinnati Society; the libraries of the Graham and Washington Societies; and $3,000 in cash, on condition that a reasonable provision be made for the present professors. A subscription has also been offered by the people of Lexington and its vicinity amounting to $17,878, all which will appear from the deed and other documents, reference thereto being had.

In this case also, it has not escaped the attention of the Commissioners, that questions may arise as to the power of the trustees to make the above transfers.

On the condition that the Central College shall be made the site of the University, its whole property real and personal in possession, or in action is offered. This consists of a parcel of land of 47 acres, whereon the buildings of the college are begun, one pavilion and its appendix of dormitories being already far advanced, and with one other pavilion, and equal annexation of dormitories, being expected to be compleated during the present season. Of another parcel of 153 acres near the former, and including a considerable eminence very favorable for the erection of a future observatory of the proceeds of the sales of two glebes amounting to $3,280 86 cents; and of a subscription of $41,248 on papers in hand, besides what is on outstanding papers of unknown amount, not yet returned. Out of these sums are to be taken however, the cost of the lands, of the buildings, and other works done, and for existing contracts. For the conditional transfer of these to the President and Directors of the Literary Fund, a regular power signed by the subscribers and founders of the College generally, has been given to its Visitors and Proctor, and a deed conveying the said property accordingly, to the President and Directors of the Literary Fund, has been duly executed by the said Proctor, and acknowledged for record in the office of the clerk of the county court of Albermarle.

38 executed by the said Proctor and acknowledged for record in the Office of the clerk of the county court of Albe-marle

Signed and certified by the members present, each in his proper handwriting this 4th day of August 1818.

Th: Jefferson
Creed Taylor
Peter Randolph
Wm. Brockenbrough
Archd. Rutherford
Arch'd Stuart
James Breckinridge
Henry E. Watkins
James Madison
Armistead T. Mason
H. Holmes

Phil. C. Pendleton
Spencer Roane
John M. C. Taylor
J. G. Jackson
Thos. Wilson
Phil. Slaughter
Wm. H. Cabell
Nathl. H. Claiborne
Wm. A. G. Dade
[illegible]

Signatures of the Commissioners appointed to fix the site for the University of Virginia, August 4, 1818. Known as the Rockfish Gap Commission.

Signed and certified by the members present, each in his proper handwriting, this 4th day of August, 1818.

TH: JEFFERSON
CREED TAYLOR
PETER RANDOLPH
WM: BROCKENBROUGH
ARCHd. RUTHERFORD
ARCH: STUART
JAMES BRECKENRIDGE
HENRY E. WATKINS
JAMES MADISON
ARMISTEAD T. MASON
H. HOLMES
PHIL: C: PENDLETON
SPENCER ROANE
JOHN M. C. TAYLOR
J. G. JACKSON
THOs. WILSON
PHIL SLAUGHTER
WM. H. CABELL
NAT. H. CLAIBORNE
WM. A. C. DADE
WILLIAM JONES

—This important document may be found in several places, including Roy J. Honeywell, *The Educational Work of Thomas Jefferson* (Harvard University Press, 1931), Appendix J, pp. 248-60; Cabell, *op. cit.*, 432-47. The original manuscript in Jefferson's handwriting is now in possession of the Virginia State Library. Photocopy of the original is in the Southern Historical Collection, the University of North Carolina.

12. Congressional objections to the proposal to grant public lands for the endowment of state universities, 1819

Mr. Poindexter, from the Committee on Public Lands, to whom was referred a resolution instructing said committee to inquire into the expediency of appropriating one hundred thousand acres of land to each State, for the endowment of a university in each State, reported:

That they are fully impressed with the propriety and importance of giving every encouragement and facility to the promotion of learning, and the diffusion of knowledge over the United States, which can be done without a violation of the principle of the constitution, and the system of policy heretofore adopted for the advancement of the general welfare. The proposition under consideration is, whether it be or be not expedient to authorize a grant of one hundred thousand acres of land to each State in the Union, making it the whole two million three hundred thousand acres, to be vested in bodies corporate, created by the several States having the care and management of their respective universities. Your committee have no specific knowledge of the necessity which exists for this appropriation, in reference to any particular State whose resources may not be adequate to the support of literary institutions, as no petitions or memorials have been referred to them on the subject. In the absence of these it is fair to presume that the internal wealth and industry of the population, composing the several States, have been found sufficient to answer all the purposes of public education and instruction, so far as they have deemed it prudent and necessary to apply the means they possess to those objects. But if the aid of the General Government should, at any time, be required to enable a particular State, or every member of the Union, to carry into effect a liberal and enlarged system of education, suited to the views, capacities, and circumstances, of all classes of society; and if it should be thought wise and constitutional to extend to them the national bounty, the donation of extensive tracts of lands in the unappropriated Territories of the United States appears to your committee to be the most exceptionable form in which the requisite assistance could be granted. To invest twenty-three corporations, acting under State authority, with a fee simple estate in two million three hundred thousand acres of land, to be located in the Western States and Territories, would put it in their power to impede the settlement of that section of the Union by withholding these lands from market; to interfere with the general regulations now in force for the disposal of the public lands; to divide settlements which would otherwise be contiguous; and, consequently, to lessen the value of the lands offered for sale by the United States in the neighborhood of these large grants, which may remain unoccupied for any length of time, at the discretion of the Legislature of the State to which the donation is made. Your committee are of opinion that, besides these strong objections to the donations proposed in the resolutions submitted to their consideration, it does not comport with sound policy, or the nature of our republican institutions, to grant monopolies of large and extensive tracts of the public domain, either to individuals or bodies corporate. The lands of the United States ought, as far as practicable, to be distributed in small quantities among the great body of the people for agricultural purposes; and this principle ought in no instance to be violated, where the grantee is exempted from the payment of a valuable consideration to the Government. Your committee are sensible that it may be found necessary and useful, for the promotion of learning in this growing republic, either to endow a national university, or to extend its benevolence in a reasonable and proper proportion to individual States; but, in either case, they are of opinion that the requisite aid should be given in money and not in the mode pointed out in the resolution referred to them. They, therefore, recommend the following resolution to the House: *Resolved,* That it is inexpedient to grant to each State one hundred thousand acres of land for the endowment of a university in each State.—*American State Papers, Public Lands,* III, 363.

13. Charter of the University of Virginia, 1819

1. *Be it declared by the General Assembly of Virginia,* That the conveyance of the lands and other property appertaining to the Central College in the county of Albemarle, which has been executed by the proctor thereof, under authority of the subscribers and founders, to the President and Directors of the Literary Fund, is hereby accepted, for the use, and on the conditions in the said deed of conveyance expressed.

2. *And be it enacted,* That there shall be established, on the site provided for the said college, an University, to be called, *The University of Virginia;* that it shall be under the government of seven visitors to be appointed forthwith by the Governor, with the advice of Council, notifying thereof the persons so appointed, and prescribing to them a day for their first meeting at the said University, with supplementary instructions for procuring a meeting subsequently, in the event of failure at the time first appointed.

3. The said visitors, or so many of them as, being a majority, shall attend, shall appoint a rector, of their own body, to preside at their meetings, and a secretary to record, attest, and preserve their proceedings, and shall proceed to examine into the state of the property conveyed as aforesaid; shall make an inventory of the same, specifying the items whereof it consists; shall notice the buildings and other improvements already made, and those which are in progress; shall take measures for their completion, and for the addition of such others, from time to time, as may be necessary.

4. In the said University shall be taught the Latin, Greek and Hebrew languages, French, Spanish, Italian, German and Anglo-Saxon, the different branches of mathematics, pure and physical; natural philosophy; the principles of agriculture; chemistry; mineralogy, including geology; botany; zoology; anatomy; medecine; civil government; political economy; the law of nature and nations, munici-

pal law; history; ideology; general grammar; ethics; rhetorick; and belles lettres; which branches of science shall be so distributed, and under so many professors, not exceeding ten, as the visitors shall think proper and expedient.

5. Each professor shall be allowed the use of the apartments and accommodations provided for him, and those first employed, such standing salary as the visitors shall think proper and sufficient, and their successors such standing salary, not exceeding one thousand dollars, as the visitors shall think proper and sufficient, with such tuition fees from each student, as the visitors shall from time to time establish.

6. The said visitors shall be charged with the erection, preservation and repair of the buildings, the care of the grounds and appurtenances, and of the interests of the University generally: they shall have power to appoint a bursar, employ a proctor, and all other necessary agents; to appoint and remove professors, two thirds of the whole number of visitors voting for the removal; to prescribe their duties, and the course of education, in conformity with the law; to establish rules for the government and discipline of the students, not contrary to the laws of the land; to regulate the tuition fees, and the rent of the dormitories occupied; to prescribe and control the duties and proceedings of all officers, servants and others, with respect to the buildings, lands, appurtenances and other property, and interest of the University; to draw from the Literary Fund such monies as are by law charged on it for this institution; and, in general, to direct and do all matters and things which, not being inconsistent with the laws of the land, to them shall seem most expedient, for promoting the purposes of the said institution; which several functions they shall be free to exercise in the form of by-laws, rules, resolutions, orders, instructions, or otherwise, as they shall deem proper.

7. They shall have two stated meetings in every year; to wit, on the first Mondays of April and October; and occasional meetings at such other times as they shall appoint, or on a special call, with such notice as themselves shall prescribe by a general rule; which meetings shall be at the University; a majority of them constituting a quorum for business; and on the death, resignation of a member, or failure to act for the space of one year, or on his removal out of the Commonwealth, or by the Governor, with the advice of Council, the Governor with like advice shall appoint a successor.

8. The said rector and visitors shall be a body corporate, under the style and title of *The Rector and Visitors of the University of Virginia*, with the right as such, to use a common seal; they shall have capacity to plead and be impleaded in all courts of justice, and in all cases interesting to the University, which may be subjects of legal cognizance and jurisdiction; which pleas shall not abate by the determination of their office, but shall stand revived in the name of their successors; and they shall be capable in law, and in trust for the University, of receiving subscriptions and donations real and personal, as well from bodies corporate, or persons associated, as from private individuals.

9. And the said rectors and visitors shall, at all times, conform to such laws as the Legislature may, from time to time, think proper to enact for their government; and the said University shall, in all things, and at all times, be subject to the control of the Legislature. And the said rector and visitors of the University of Virginia shall be, and they are hereby required to make report annually, to the President and Directors of the Literary Fund (to be laid before the Legislature at their next succeeding session), embracing a full account of the disbursements, the funds on hand, and a general statement of the condition of the said University.

10. The said board of visitors, or a majority thereof, by nomination of the board, shall, once in every year at least, visit the said University; enquire into the proceedings and practices thereat; examine the progress of the students, and give to those who excel in any branch of science, there taught, such honorary marks and testimonies of approbations as may encourage and excite to industry and emulation.

11. On every twenty-ninth of February, or, if that be Sunday, then on the next, or earliest day thereafter, on which a meeting can be effected, the Governor and Council shall be in session, and shall appoint visitors of the said University, either the same or others, at their discretion, to serve until the twenty-ninth day of February next ensuing, duly, and timely notifying to them their appointment, and prescribing a day for their first meeting at the University; after which, their meetings, stated and occasional, shall be as herein-before provided: *Provided*, That nothing in this act contained shall suspend the proceedings of the visitors of the said Central College of Albemarle; but for the purpose of expediting the objects of the said institution they shall be authorised under the control of the Governor and

Council, to continue the exercise of their functions, and fulfil those of their successors, until the first actual meeting of their said successors.

12. *And be it further enacted*, That the additional sum of twenty-thousand dollars shall be, and the same is hereby appropriated to the education of the poor, out of the revenue of the Literary Fund, in aid of the sum heretofore appropriated to that object, and to be paid in the same manner, and upon the same conditions in all respects, as is prescribed by the fourth section of the act, entitled, *An act appropriating part of the revenue of the Literary Fund*, and for other purposes passed the twenty-first day of February, eighteen hundred and eighteen.

13. This act shall commence and be in force from and after the passing thereof.—*Acts of the Commonwealth of Virginia*, 1818. Charter enacted January 25, 1819.

Sir Monticello Mar. 11. 19

I yesterday recieved your favor of Feb. 23 covering the appointment of the 13th of the same month with which you have been pleased to honor me as a Visitor of the University of Virginia. impressed with the important effect which well conducted education will produce on the character and happiness of my native state, and ambitious for it's reputa[illegible] and prosperity I accept the charge willingly, and will endeavor to supply by zeal the defects of which I am sensible in the high qualifications required by an institution of such future augury. I pray you to accept the assurance of my highest respect and esteem.

His Excellency Th: Jefferson

Governor Preston.

Thomas Jefferson's acceptance of appointment as member of the Board of Visitors of the University of Virginia March 11, 1819.

14. Thomas Jefferson accepts membership on the Board of Visitors of the University of Virginia, 1819

Monticello Mar. 11. '19

Sir

I yesterday received your favor of Feb. 27. covering the appointment of the 13th of the same month with which you have been pleased to honor me as a Visitor of the University of Virginia. Impressed with the important effect which well conducted education will produce on the character and happiness of my native state, and ambitious for its reputation and prosperity I accept the charge willingly, and will endeavor to supply by zeal the defects of which I am sensible in the high qualifications required by an institution of such future augury. I pray you to accept the assurance of my highest respect and esteem.

Th: Jefferson

His Excellency
Governor Preston.

–*Calendar of Virginia State Papers and Other Manuscripts*, Vol. X, 482.

15. Daniel Webster cites the North Carolina case of 1805 to support his argument in the Dartmouth College Case decided by the Supreme Court of the United States in 1819

In *University v. Foy* the Supreme Court of North Carolina pronounced unconstitutional and void a law repealing a grant to the University of North Carolina: although that University was originally erected and endowed by a Statute of the State. The case was a grant of lands, and the court decided that it could not be resumed. This is a grant of the power and capacity to hold lands. Where is the difference of the cases, upon principles?–4 Wheaton, U. S., 571.

When the court in North Carolina declared the law of the state, which repealed a grant to its university, unconstitutional and void, the legislature had the candor and the wisdom to repeal the law. This example, so honorable to the state which exhibited it, is most fit to be followed on this occasion. And there is good reason to hope that a state which has hitherto been so much distinguished for temperate councils, cautious legislation, and regard to law, will not fail to adopt a course which will accord with her highest and best interest, and, in no small degree, elevate her reputation. It was for many obvious reasons most anxiously desired that the question of the power of the legislature over this charter should have been finally decided in the state court. An earnest hope was entertained that the judges of that court might have viewed the case in a light favorable to the rights of trustees. That hope has failed. It is here that those rights are now to be maintained, or they are prostrated forever.—Stephen K. Williams, *Cases Argued and Decided in the Supreme Court of the United States, 1815-19*, Book 4, Lawyers' Edition, p. 598.

16. Thomas Jefferson regrets that George Ticknor of Harvard does not accept a professorship at the University of Virginia, 1819

...I am glad to learn that Mr. Ticknor has safely returned to his friends; but should have been much more pleased had he accepted the Professorship in our University, which we should have offered him in form. Mr. Bowditch, too, refuses us; so fascinating is the *vinculum* of the *dulce natale solum*. Our wish is to procure natives, where they can be found, like these gentlemen, of the first order of requirement in their respective lines; but preferring foreigners of the first order to natives of the second, we shall certainly have to go for several of our Professors, to countries more advanced in science than we are...—Letter to John Adams. Given in Bergh, *op. cit.*, XV, 204-7.

17. Moses Waddel becomes president of the University of Georgia, 1819

The Rev. Moses Waddel, D.D. appointed to the Presidency of Georgia University, entered on the duties of his office on the 21st of May last. "The Missionary" (an excellent Christian journal just commenced in that state) remarks, that the energy and integrity of this gentleman's character, the competency of his skill and abilities, regulated by an ardour of feeling, and an accuracy of judgment rarely united in the same person, offer the most decisive pledge of prosperity to the institution, and most fully realize the anxious expectations of the community.—*The Virginia Evangelical and Literary Magazine*, II, (1819), 339-40.

18. Collegiate rules at Harvard, at the University of Virginia, and at the University of South Carolina, 1820, 1825, 1848

To prevent those tumults and disorders which are frequent at entertainments, and to guard against extravagance and needless expenses, no undergraduate shall make any festive entertainments in the College, the town of Cambridge, or the vicinity, except at Commencement and at public Exhibitions, with the permission of the President, under a penalty, for making or being present at such, not exceeding eight dollars. (Harvard)

No student shall make any festival entertainment in the college, or in the town of Columbia or take part in anything of the kind, without liberty previously obtained of the President. (South Carolina)

No student shall make any festive entertainment within the precincts of the University, nor contribute to, or be present at them there or elsewhere but with the consent of each of the Professors whose school he attends, on pain of a minor punishment. (Virginia)

No student shall keep a gun or pistol, or any gunpowder in the College or town of Cambridge; nor shoot, fish, or scate over deep waters, without leave from the President, or one of the Tutors or Professors, under the penalty of fifty cents. And if any scholar shall fire a gun or pistol within the College walls, yard, or near the College, or near houses, or behind fences or inclosures, in the town, he shall be fined not exceeding one dollar, or suffer other college punishments. (Harvard)

No student may keep in his room any kind of firearms or gun powder; nor fire any in or near the College, in any manner whatever; and any student who shall violate this law, shall be liable to admonition, suspension, or expulsion.

All the students are strictly forbidden to play on any instrument of music in the hours of study, and also on Sunday; and shall abstain from their usual diversions and exercises on those days. (South Carolina)

No student shall admit any disturbing noises in his room, or make them anywhere within the precincts of the University, or fire a gun or pistol within the same, on pain of such minor sentences as the Faculty shall decree, or approve; but the proper use of musical instruments, shall be freely allowed in their rooms, and in that appropriated for the instruction in music. (Virginia)

The students, when required, shall give evidence respecting the breach of any laws; shall admit into their chambers any of the officers, or, when sent for by them, shall immediately attend . . . or be punished by one of the high censures. . . . If entrance into a room be refused, an executive officer may break open any study or chamber door. (Harvard)

If any student shall refuse to open the door of his room, when required to do it by one of the Faculty, he shall be liable to public admonition; and the Faculty, when they shall think it necessary, may break open any room in the college at the expense of those by whom they are refused admittance. (South Carolina)

When a professor knocks at the door of a student's room, any person being within, and announces himself, it shall be opened on pain of a minor punishment; and the Professor may, if refused, have the door broken open; and the expenses of repair shall be levied on the student or students within. (Virginia)—See Honeywell, *op. cit.*, 279-80; *Enactments of the Rector and Visitors of the University of Virginia*, 1825; *Laws of Harvard College*, 1820; and Green, *op. cit.*, p. 220 ff.

19. Charter of the University of Alabama, 1820

1. A SEMINARY of learning is hereby established, to be denominated, "The University of the State of Alabama."

2. Three commissioners shall be appointed by the governor, within each county wherein any of the lands reserved by the United States for a seminary of learning may be situated, who shall enter into bond with sufficient security to the governor, and his successors in office, for the faithful performance of their duty, whose duty it shall be to lease the said lands, which leasing shall be for the term of one year from the first day of January next; and shall be done at public auction, offering the said lands in convenient tracts, and in such way as may be deemed most advantageous to the state, and also giving advertisement in the nearest public paper, of the lands so to be offered, at least two weeks previous to the offering of the same: *Provided*, That no improved land shall lease for a less price than two dollars per acre, for the said term of one year.

3. The said commissioners are authorized and required, as soon as may be, to employ the county surveyor, or some suitable surveyor, to admeasure the improved land as aforesaid, and to make report of the condition of the same, under the direction of said commissioners, to be returned to them with a plat of the said improved lands; the expense to be paid out of the rent of the lands.

4. It shall be the duty of the commissioners appointed by virtue of the second section of this act, to take bond with sufficient security for every such lease, payable to the governor and his successors in office, and to deposit the same with the comptroller, and to take cove-

nants from the several lessees against the commission of waste, or the expiration of the lease; and it shall also be the duty of the commissioners to visit the several tracts reserved within their counties respectively, at least once in every period of six months, for the purpose of preventing waste or trespasses from being committed; and it shall be their duty to give information of all waste or trespasses on said lands, to the solicitor of the circuit in which such lands shall be, whose duty it shall be to presecute the same.

5. Any person or persons who may unlawfully enter upon and destroy any timber or improvements, on any of the lands granted to this state for a seminary of learning, shall, on indictment and conviction, be fined in treble the amount of the damages, to be assessed by a jury, which fine shall be applied to the fund hereinbefore provided for the purposes of the said university.

6. The same proceeding may be had, and before the same jurisdiction, for enforcing the payment of any of the bonds or securities, that may be taken in virtue of this act, as is authorized by law in the case of defaulting collectors of the public taxes, and it shall be the duty of the officer who prosecutes for the state, for the recovery of the revenue against defaulting collectors, to prosecute for the recovery of the arrears of rent under this act.

7. All prosecutions under this act, shall be carried on as other prosecutions, in the name of the State of Alabama; and it shall be the duty of the solicitors of the several circuits, upon information of said commissioners, to prosecute such offenders, and to receive the fines imposed by this act, and pay the same into the public treasury.

8. The governor, *ex officio*, together with twelve trustees, two of whom shall be elected from each judicial circuit by joint ballot of both houses of the general assembly, and who shall continue in office for the term of three years, shall constitute a body politic and corporate in deed and in law, by the name of *The Trustees of the University of Alabama*, and by that name they and their successors shall have perpetual succession, and be able and capable in law, to have, receive, and enjoy, to them and their successors, lands, tenements, and hereditaments, of any kind or value, in fee or for life, or for years, and personal property of any kind whatsoever, and also all sums of money of any amount whatsoever which may be granted or bequeathed to them, for the purpose of promoting the interest of the said university.

9. The trustees of the said university shall and may have a common seal for the business of themselves and their successors, with

liberty to change or alter the same from time to time, as they shall think proper; and by their aforesaid name, they and their successors shall be able to sue and be sued, plead and be impleaded, answer and be answered, defend and be defended, in all courts of law and equity within this state; and to grant, bargain, sell, or assign any lands, tenements, goods, or chattels, in such manner as is hereinafter specified; and to act and to do all things whatsoever for the benefit of the said institution, in as ample a manner as any person, or body politic or corporate, can or may do by law.

10. No misnomer of the University of Alabama shall defeat or annul any gift, grant, devise, or bequest to the same: *Provided,* The true intent of the parties shall sufficiently appear upon the face of the gifts, grants, wills, or other writing, whereby any estate or interest was intended to pass to the said university; nor shall any misuser, or nonuser of the rights, liberties, privileges, jurisdiction, and authorities hereby granted to the said university, create a forfeiture thereof.

11. The trustees, or so many as shall be fixed on by their by-laws, shall have full power by the principal or professors of the said university, to grant or confer such degree or degrees in the arts or sciences to any of the students of the said university, or persons by them thought worthy, as are usually granted and conferred in other universities in the United States, and to give diplomas or certificates thereof, signed by them and sealed with the common seal of the trustees of the university, to authenticate and perpetuate the memory of such graduation.

12. No person shall be excluded from any liberty, liberties, immunity, office, or situation in said university, on account of his religious persuasion, provided he demean himself in a sober, peaceable, and orderly manner, and conform to the rules and regulations thereof.

13. The governor shall be *ex officio* the president of the board of trustees: *Provided however,* That in case he should not attend the meetings of the said trustees, the trustees shall elect a president *pro tempore,* who shall preside at such meetings.

14. The said trustees shall have power, and it is hereby declared to be their duty, upon a notice from the president of the board, to examine and report to the legislature, at their next session, such place or places, having a due regard to health and the fertility of the surrounding country, as shall appear to them most suitable for the location of the university; and the legislature shall, at the session when such report shall be made, proceed by joint ballot of both houses of

the general assembly, to make a choice of the site for the university, which choice, when so made, shall not be subject to any alteration thereafter.

15. The site thus selected by the legislature, shall be exempted from sale: *Provided,* The same shall have been granted to this state, by an act of the Congress of the United States for a seminary of learning; and if the same shall not have been granted to this state as aforesaid, the trustees shall have full power to purchase the site thus selected.

16. The trustees shall have the entire control over the site thus selected for the university, and may lay off and sell such lot or lots to such persons, and upon such conditions, as they may think proper.

17. The trustees shall, so soon as the selection shall have been made as aforesaid, contract with a suitable person or persons for the erection of such buildings as they may deem necessary, for the purpose of carrying this act into complete effect.

18. Every trustee elected or appointed by the provisions of this act shall, before entering on the duties assigned him as trustee, take and subscribe the following oath, before some judge or justice of the peace, to wit: "I, ———— ————, do solemnly swear, (or affirm), that I will faithfully discharge the duties assigned me as trustee, to the best of my skill and ability, without partiality or affection: So help me God."

19. The proceeds arising from the sales of the said lands, shall be paid over to the trustees, and shall be by them vested in such funds as they may direct: *Provided,* It shall be their duty to report annually to the legislature the financial situation of the institution: *And provided further,* That the capital stock arising from the sale of the lands as aforesaid, shall not be reduced in any manner whatever.

20. The laws now in force relative to the leasing of the said lands shall continue in force until the said lands shall be sold: *Provided,* That if they shall be sold previously to the first day of January, one thousand eight hundred and twenty-three, the lessee shall not be deprived of the benefit of remaining on the same until that time, and of receiving the growing crop.

21. The said trustees shall have the power to contract for the necessary buildings, and to do every other act necessary to carry this act into complete effect.

22. This act shall be deemed a public act, and judicially taken notice of without special pleading, and the same shall be liberally

construed, for fully carrying into effect the beneficial purposes hereby intended.

23. It shall be the duty of the general assembly to fill all vacancies in the board of trustees, which shall happen by the expiration of the term of service, death, resignation, or otherwise, at the next session after such vacancy shall happen: *Provided,* That should any vacancy happen during the recess of the general assembly, the board of trustees shall have the power to fill the same by an election, which shall continue until vacated by an election to be made by the general assembly, at their next session.

24. At the expiration of the term for which the present trustees are elected, the legislature shall proceed to the election of two trustees from each judicial circuit, who, together with the governor, shall form the board of trustees.

25. There shall be a stated annual meeting of the trustees, to be held at the time of conferring degrees, and the president of the university, together with two of the trustees, or three of the trustees without the president, shall have full power to call an occasional meeting of the board, whenever it shall appear to them necessary: *Provided,* That reasonable notice by mail or otherwise be first given to all the other trustees, specifying the cause or causes of such meeting: *And provided also,* That no business shall be transacted by the board, other than that specially assigned as the cause of the meeting, unless at least seven of the board shall concur therein.

26. At all meetings of the trustees, a majority shall be capable of doing and transacting all the business and concerns of the university, except such as is herein excepted: they shall have the power of electing all the necessary and customary officers of said institution: of fixing their several salaries, and of removing any of them for neglect or misconduct in office, a majority of the whole number of trustees concurring in said removal: *Provided,* That no permanent election of any officer shall be made, or salary be fixed, at any other than the stated annual meetings of the trustees; but all elections which shall be made at any called meeting, shall expire at the end of the next stated meeting: they shall have the power of prescribing the course of studies to be pursued by the students, and of framing and enacting all such ordinances and by-laws as shall appear to them necessary for the good government of the university, and of their own proceedings: *Provided,* The same be not repugnant to the laws of the United States and of this state.

27. The head of the said university shall be styled the President, and the instructors, the Professors; and the president and professors, while they remain such shall not be capable of holding the office of trustees; and the president and professors, or a majority of them shall be styled "The Faculty of the University;" which faculty shall have the power of enforcing the ordinances and by-laws adopted by the trustees for the government of the students, by rewarding or censuring them, and finally by suspending such of them as, after repeated admonitions, shall continue disobedient or refractory, until a determination of the board can be had. And it shall be in the power of a majority of the trustees present, at a stated meeting, to expel any student or students.

28. The title of the lands which this state has received as a donation from the Congress of the United States, for a seminary of learning is hereby vested in the said trustees and their successors in office, to be appropriated in the manner hereinafter directed, to wit: the said lands shall be sold at public auction at such times and places as the said trustees shall direct, or have by ordinance heretofore directed, at a price not less than seventeen dollars per acre; one fourth part of the purchase money shall be paid down at the time of the sale; one eighth part in one year thereafter, with interest at the rate of six per cent. per annum; one eighth part in two years after said sale, with interest as aforesaid; and the residue of the purchase-money shall be paid at the expiration of eight years after said sale, with interest as aforesaid, payable annually, to commence at the day on which the third payment shall become due: *Provided*, That the said trustees shall have power to lay off town lots at any place they may deem expedient, and to dispose of the same on such terms and under such regulations as they shall prescribe; *Provided*, That the said lots, when so laid off, shall not sell for a less sum than the minimum price herein expressed. And each purchaser shall, moreover, at the time of said purchase, execute his bonds, payable to the said trustees and their successors in office conditioned for the true and punctual payment of the purchase-money and interest thereon, according to the terms of said sale.

29. The said trustees, upon receiving from any purchaser of any tract or parcel of land which may be sold as aforesaid, the one-fourth part of the purchase-money so required to be paid as aforesaid, and the bonds conditioned as aforesaid, duly executed, shall issue to said purchaser, a certificate under the seal of the trustees, that the purchase

of such tract of land has been made by the purchaser, that he has paid one fourth part of the purchase-money, and that he has given bonds according to law, and declaring that upon the punctual payment of each and every one of the remaining installments, with the interest thereon, the amount of each of which shall be specified in such certificate, they will convey such tract of land to such purchaser, his heirs or assigns; and should such purchaser assign such certificate, the assignee shall possess all the rights which may have been vested in his assignor: *Provided*, That the purchaser of any tract of land aforesaid, his heirs or assigns, shall have the liberty at any time within the period of credit hereinbefore given, if the land shall not have been forfeited, of paying to the said trustees the whole amount of principal and the interest then due upon said purchase; upon which payment, the said trustees shall convey to such purchaser, his heirs or assigns, a title in fee simple to said land.

30. Should any purchaser of any tract of land as aforesaid, the heirs or the assignees of such purchaser, fail to make punctual payment of the amount of the principal and interest, or of interest which may become due on said tract of land, the said tract of land shall be absolutely forfeited to the said trustees, with the money paid thereon; and the said trustees are authorized, after the expiration of three months from the time of said forfeiture, to dispossess any person or persons who may be in possession of such tract of land, by the writ of unlawful detainer, saving, in every case of a forfeiture, the growing crop to the occupant: *Provided nevertheless*, That if the said trustees shall, within the said period of three months, institute a suit upon the bond given for the said purchase, in that case the said forfeiture shall not accrue until a failure of said suit to coerce the payment of the money due as aforesaid; which failure shall be ascertained by a return of *non est inventus* to a *capias ad respondendum*, or of *nulla bona* to a *fieri facias*.

31. At the expiration of the term of credit, or within three months thereafter, hereinbefore prescribed, upon the sales of said lands, the purchaser, his heirs or assigns, shall have the right, upon the payment of all interest then due upon said purchase, and upon surrendering up the certificate of purchase, to convert said purchase into a lease for ninety-nine years, renewable for ever, upon condition that the lessee, his heirs, executors, administrators, or assigns, shall pay to the said trustees, interest at six per centum per annum, upon the amount of

the original purchase-money due at the time of converting said sale into a lease.

32. Upon the election as aforesaid of any purchaser, his heirs or assigns, of any tract of land sold as aforesaid, to convert said sale into a lease as aforesaid, the said trustees shall execute to such lessee a deed of lease, specifying the terms thereof as aforesaid, which lease shall be assignable by said lessee, and the said assignee shall possess all the rights which may have been vested in his assignor.

33. The said trustees shall forever have the right to distrain any personal estate belonging to the lessee, his heirs, assigns, or the tenant in possession of any tract of land so leased, for the payment of the interest as it shall become due on said lease, in such manner as shall be prescribed by law: and the personal estate of said lessee, his heirs, assigns and the tenant in possession, shall always be liable in preference of other debts, for the payment of the interest due on the lease; and upon a failure of payment of the whole, or any part of the interest due on said lease, upon a *distringas* for that purpose to be issued, the lessee, his heirs, or assigns, shall forfeit all right and interest in and to the land so leased, together with all sums of money which may have been paid for the purchase and lease of the same; and all lands thus forfeited, shall be sold by the trustees to the highest bidder, at public auction for ready money, two months public notice being first given of the time and place of such sale, and after paying the amount due upon the original purchase, together with all interest due to the said trustees, up to the time of sale, with costs and expenses of sale—the remainder, if any, shall be paid to the lessee, his heirs, executors, administrators or assigns, who may be entitled to receive the same; and the person purchasing according to the provisions of this section, shall inure to all the equity, and be subject to the same rules as are hereinbefore prescribed for original purchasers or lessees; *Provided*, That all land forfeited by a failure of the payment of either the purchase-money or interest, shall never be sold for a less sum than is due and unpaid on said land, agreeably to the terms of the original sale or lease, (as the case may be), and all forfeited lands which may be offered for sale, and shall not bring the amount due on account of the purchase-money and interest, shall for ever remain the property of the trustees, and their successors in office, subject to the same rules and regulations as other lands belonging to the state university.

34. The said trustees shall have power to rent, from year to year, such part of the lands as shall not be sold at the public sales, as afore-

said, in such manner as they shall by ordinance prescribe, and the moneys which shall be due thereon, shall be recoverable in such manner as shall be prescribed by law.

35. It shall be the duty of the trustees, whenever a sale of lands is to take place, to appoint three of their own body, who, or any one of whom, together with such other trustees as may attend, shall be superintendents of said sale; and in case there shall be a failure of the agent to attend and conduct the sale, the trustees so attending, shall have power to appoint another agent, and to take his bond and approve of his security; and the board of trustees shall have power at all times, when they may deem it expedient, to remove any agent, and appoint another in his place.

36. The estate, both real and personal, of the said corporation shall be free and forever exempt from taxes, and the persons of all officers, servants, and students belonging to said university, shall during their continuance, there, be exempt from taxes, serving on juries, working on roads, and ordinary military duty.

37. There shall also be established three branches of said university for female education, to be located at such places as may be deemed by the legislature most for the public good; and the legislature shall proceed to locate and fix the sites of said branches, at the same time, and by the same manner of election that the site of the principal university is to be located; and said branches shall each be governed by twelve directors, to be elected annually by the board of trustees; and the government thereof shall in all respects be according to the by-laws of the university, framed and ordained for that purpose; *Provided*, that not more than one hundred thousand dollars shall be appropriated by said trustees for the purpose of erecting buildings for said branches.

38. A sum not exceeding fifty thousand dollars in the discretion of the trustees, of the moneys which may be received from the first payments of the lands sold, is hereby appropriated and set apart, for the erection of the necessary buildings of the said university; and the interest arising from the last payments, to be made upon the sales of the lands as hereinbefore provided to be sold, shall be set apart and vested, as the same may be received, in the stock of the United States, and applied exclusively to sinking the amount of money hereby appropriated to the erection of the buildings as aforesaid, until the amount so invested shall be equal to the sum which may be so ex-

pended, after which the same shall be considered as capital stock, and shall never thereafter be diminished.

39. The residue of the sum, after deducting the sum which may be expended in the erection of the buildings as aforesaid, which may be received from the payments on the sales of the lands, shall be invested by the trustees without delay, as the same shall be in such stocks of the United States, as the trustees may think most profitable: *Provided*, That a sum not exceeding one hundred thousand dollars, may, in the discretion of the board, be invested in a State Bank, if one shall be established, or in stock of the state, should such be created, and the sum so invested shall be considered capital stock, and shall never be diminished.

40. The interest to be paid by the purchasers of the lands, or the lessees as aforesaid, or which shall be received from the stock which shall be purchased, as herein before directed, or so much thereof as may be necessary, shall be appropriated by the trustees, to discharge the current expenses of the university, and the trustees shall report to the general assembly once in each year, the state of the funds committed to their charge, with such recommendations, with regard to the improvement thereof, as to them shall seem advisable.

41. It shall be the duty of the treasurer and comptroller of public accounts, to deliver over to the treasurer of the board of trustees, on his application, all sums of money and notes, and bonds which may be in possession of either of them, and which they have received from the rent of lands hereby vested in the trustees, or which they may hereafter receive, and the treasurer of the trustees shall give his receipt for the same; and the moneys so received shall be subject to the order of the trustees; and the trustees are hereby authorized to sue for and collect all sums which are now due, or which may hereafter become due from the notes or bonds which shall be so received by the treasurer of the said trustees, to be by them appropriated to the use of the university: *Provided*, That any moneys that are now in the hands of the treasurer or comptroller of public accounts, belonging to the State University, shall be subject to the call of the trustees, until the treasurer of the board of trustees shall be duly authorized to receive said moneys.

42. The trustees shall also have the power to sue for and collect all sums of money which are now due, or which may hereafter become due from such persons as have occupied or hereafter shall occupy any

of the lands hereby vested in said trustees, without a lease from said trustees.

43. The trustees of the state university are hereby allowed the sum of three dollars each, for each day they may be engaged in their duties as trustees aforesaid; also the sum of three dollars for every twenty-five miles travelling to and from the place of their meeting.

44. Said allowances shall be paid out of the university funds: *Provided*, That trustees who are members of the legislature, shall not receive any pay for their services as trustees, whilst they are in attendance as members of the legislature.

45. The office of the present trustees of the university of the state of Alabama, shall expire from and after the passage of this resolution; and the trustees to be elected at the present session of the legislature, shall continue in office for the term of three years; and all trustees thereafter to be elected shall continue in office for the like period; and all appointments to fill vacancies shall expire at the time of the next periodical election for trustees.

46. It shall be the duty of the treasurer of this state, to receive and safely keep, all moneys that may be paid over to him by order of the board of trustees, subject to their order; *Provided*, That the bond now required of the treasurer of this state for the faithful discharge of the duties of his office, shall be given in the penalty of one hundred thousand dollars, which shall operate as security for the safe keeping, as well of any funds belonging to the university of this state, that may be at any time deposited in the treasury of this state, as of moneys paid into or deposited in the said treasury on other accounts: *Provided also*, That the board of trustees be requested to inform the general assembly during the next session, of the amount of money paid over to the treasurer, the time when so paid over, and how long it remained in his care–so as to enable them to allow such additional compensation to said treasurer as they may deem just and proper.

47. In all suits or actions brought by or against the trustees of the university of Alabama, in any court of law or equity in this state, it shall not be necessary for their attorney or counsellor to produce the seal of the said trustees of the university of Alabama, or a power of attorney under the seal of the said corporation, to authorize them to appear and prosecute any suit or action in behalf of said trustees; and the courts of law and equity aforesaid, shall, in all cases, recognize their attorney or counsellor in the same manner as in suits between individuals.

48. The president of the board of trustees of the university, is hereby required to vest in the stock of the state, upon the same terms as the stock has heretofore been invested, what money is now in the treasury, arising from rents, interest, and sale of university lands.

49. The president of the board of trustees of the university, is hereby required to vest in the stock of the state upon the same terms as the stock has heretofore been vested, the amount of capital belonging to the university, which is now in the treasury, or which may be received during the present year.

50. The funds arising by the sale of the lands granted by the United States, for the support of a seminary of learning in this state, which have heretofore been vested as capital stock in the Bank of the State of Alabama, shall form a part of the capital of said bank, and the certificates of state stock issued by the governor, and the president and directors of said bank, to the trustees of the university of Alabama, for the moneys thus vested, shall be obligatory on the state in the same manner as though they had been issued by authority of law; and all moneys hereafter recovered as aforesaid, with the exception of the interest which may accrue and be collected on outstanding bonds, where the land has been sold on a credit, shall in like manner be vested as capital in said bank, and the faith and credit of the state are hereby pledged, for the safety of the funds thus vested and provided to be invested, in the same manner as is provided in the first section of an act entitled an act to establish the Bank of the State of Alabama, approved December the twentieth, eighteen hundred and twenty-three.

51. The investments hereafter made of the funds of the university in state stock and the investments made by this act, shall, when taken together, never exceed three hundred thousand dollars.

UNIVERSITY LANDS.

1. The governor is hereby authorized to appoint three commissioners in each county, within which any portion of the two townships of land granted by congress for a seminary of learning may have been or shall be reserved, whose duty it shall be to let or lease the same; which leasing may be done either publicly or privately, as the said commissioners may deem most advantageous to the state; *Provided*, That said lands be first offered for public leasing, in convenient tracts, until the first day of January, eighteen hundred and twenty-one.

2. All bonds and notes given for any such lease, shall be made payable to the governor for the use of this state, and may in his name be sued and recovered; and all sums of money arising from such leases, shall be set apart, for the purposes of the seminary of learning aforesaid.

3. In all cases where any of the lands granted to this state by act of congress for the purpose of a seminary of learning, may be cultivated by any person, who may not have rented the same, either at public auction or by private contract, of the commissioners appointed to rent the same, he, she, or they shall be bound, and are hereby made liable to pay the minimum price per acre as fixed by law, for every acre so cultivated; and the commissioners appointed to rent the same respectively, are hereby required to transmit to the comptroller of public accounts, a list of the names of the person or persons who may cultivate any of the lands aforesaid, describing the same by range, township, section, &c., together with the number of acres so cultivated by each person, who is hereby authorized to collect the same, in the same manner as is prescribed by law for the collection of money due the state.

4. If any person or persons shall unlawfully enter upon, and cut down, carry away or destroy any tree or trees, on any of the lands vested by law in the trustees of the university of the state of Alabama, every such person or persons, being lawfully convicted thereof, before a justice of the peace, shall forfeit and pay to the said trustees the sum of ten dollars for every tree so cut down, carried away, or destroyed; and moreover, shall be committed to the jail of the county in which such offence has been committed, there to remain until he or they shall pay the fine and costs assessed against him or them: unless such person or persons so convicted, shall execute to the said justice a bond with good security, payable to the trustees for the amount assessed as aforesaid, within fourteen days thereafter, which bond shall have the effect of a judgment; and should the same not be punctually paid, it shall be the duty of such justice to issue an execution thereon against such obligor or obligors and their securities, or their executors or administrators jointly; and all money received by such justice, in pursuance of the provisions of this act, shall be paid over by said justice, or his successors in office, as the case may be, to the trustees of the University of Alabama.

5. If any person or persons shall unlawfully enter upon, and destroy, or remove, any improvements situate on the lands vested as

aforesaid in the trustees of the University of Alabama, or unlawfully enter upon and commit any trespass, or trespasses, not provided for by the first section of this act, such person or persons so unlawfully entering upon, and destroying or removing such improvement, or committing such trespass or trespasses, shall be proceeded against and punished in the manner as described by the fifth section of an act entitled "An Act to establish a State University."

6. The trustees aforesaid shall have power to appoint such number of persons as they may deem expedient, residing near the said lands, for the purpose of protecting the same from trespasses, and to make them a reasonable compensation.—Aikin, *A Digest of the Laws of the State of Alabama*, pp. 427-36.

20. Jefferson to Joseph C. Cabell, 1820

Monticello, Jan. 22.20.

Dear Sir,—I send you the inclosed as an exhibit to our enemies as well as friends. Kentucky, our daughter, planted since Virginia was a distinguished state, has an University with 14. professors & upwards of 200 students. While we, with a fund of a million & a half of Dollars ready raised and appropriated, are higgling without the heart to let it go to it's use. If our legislature does not heartily push our University, we must send our children for education to Kentucky or Cambridge. The latter will return them to us fanatics & tories, the former will keep them to add to their population. If however we are to go a begging any where for our education, I would rather it should be to Kentucky than any other state, because she has more of the flavor of the old cask than any other. All the states but our own are sensible that knowlege is power. The Missouri question is for power. The efforts now generally making all the states to advance their science is for power, while we are sinking into the barbarism of our Indian aborigines, and expect like them to oppose by ignorance the overwhelming mass of light & science by which we shall be surrounded. It is a comfort that I am not to live to see this. Our exertions in building this year have amounted to the whole of the public annuity of this year, for which therefore we have been obliged to draw to relieve the actual distresses of our workmen; the subscriptions come in slow & grudgingly. You know that we are to pay Dr. Cooper 1500 D. in May, and his family will depend on it for subsistence in his absence. We have been obliged therefore to set apart, as our only sure dependence, 6. subscriptions on the punctuality of which we can depend, to wit, yours, Mr. Madison's, Genl Cocke's, Mr. Diges's and John Harrison's, & mine, which exactly make up the money. Affectly yours.—Ford, *op. cit.*, X, 154-55.

21. A TRAVELER COMMENTS ON THE UNIVERSITY OF VIRGINIA, *c.* 1820

We shortly afterwards passed through Charlottesville.... Here we saw an extensive university, which the state is erecting under Mr. Jefferson's auspices, and to which it is intended to invite the *ablest professors which Europe can supply*.—Adam Hodgson, *Remarks During A Journey Through North America in the Years 1819, 1820, and 1821*, pp. 213-14.

IV

1821–1830

1. Two weaknesses of southern colleges and universities, 1821

While on the subject of North Carolina, we cannot resist the inclination which we feel to bring forward one or two other particulars, which exhibit the present condition and future prospects of this state in a most favourable light. In an ardent and increasing zeal for the establishment of schools and academies for several years past, we do not believe it has been outdone by a single state. The academy at Raleigh was founded in 1804, previously to which there were only two institutions of the kind in the state. The number at present is nearly fifty, and is rapidly increasing. Great pains are taken to procure the best instructors from different parts of the country, and we have the best authority for our opinion, that in no part of the Union are the interests of education better understood, and under better regulations, than in the middle counties of North Carolina. The schools for females are particularly celebrated, and are much resorted to from Georgia, South Carolina, and Virginia. In the year 1816, the number of students at academies, within the compass of forty miles, amounted to more than one thousand. This space comprized the counties of Warren, Granville, Orange, Wake, Franklin, and two or three others adjoining. All the useful and ornamental branches of knowledge are taught at most of these institutions.

The University of North Carolina, which is at Chapel-Hill in Orange county, was incorporated about thirty years ago, but did not go into active operation for nearly ten years after. It is at present flourishing, contains more than a hundred students, and promises to become a useful and important institution. It is under the direction of fifty-five trustees, a number, which we think five times too large. We believe few circumstances have contributed more to retard the success of many of our southern colleges, than this propensity, which seems to be almost universal, of appointing at the outset a multitude of trustees. By this means, many are chosen to the office, who are not qualified; individual responsibility is weakened; no one feels the necessity of acting with much energy in a concern, which is entrusted to so many others; and finally nothing is done. Another practice, which is followed in some of the states, must effectually stop the progress of any literary institution. We mean the custom of making the professors' salaries depend on the annual grants of the legislature. Under such circumstances, they are subject to have their salaries reduced, or to be turned out of their places, by the whim or caprice of a party. The only security for stability in the internal government of an institution, and for having professors of high qualifications, is thus destroyed.—*North American Review*, XXX, New Series No. V. (January, 1821), 33-34.

2. JEFFERSON WRITES GLOOMILY TO CABELL ON THE LEGISLATIVE ATTITUDE TOWARD THE UNIVERSITY OF VIRGINIA, 1821

Monticello, January 31, 1821.

Dear Sir,

Your favors of the 18th and 25th came together, three days ago. They fill me with gloom as to the dispositions of our legislature towards the University. I perceive that I am not to live to see it opened. As to what had better be done within the limits of their will, I trust with entire confidence to what yourself, General Breckenridge, and Mr. Johnson shall think best. You will see what is practicable, and give it such shape as you think best. If a loan is to be resorted to, I think sixty thousand dollars will be necessary, including the library. Its instalments cannot begin until those of the former loan are accomplished; and they should not begin later, nor be less than thirteen thousand dollars a year. (I think it safe to retain two thousand dollars a year for care of the buildings, improvement of the grounds, and unavoidable contingencies.) To extinguish the second loan, will require between five and six instalments, which will carry us to the end of 1833, or thirteen years from this time. My individual opinion is, that we had better not open the institution until the buildings, library and all, are finished, and our funds cleared of incumbrance. These buildings once erected, will secure the full object infallibly at the end of thirteen years, and as much earlier as the legislature shall choose. And if we were to begin sooner, with half funds only, it would satisfy the common mind, prevent their aid beyond that point, and our institution, remaining at that for ever, would be no more than the paltry academies we now have. Even with the whole funds we shall be reduced to six Professors. While Harvard will still prime it over us with her twenty Professors. How many of our youths she now has, learning the lessons of anti-Missourianism, I know not; but a gentleman lately from Princeton told me he saw there the list of the students at that place, and that more than half were Virginians. These will return home, no doubt, deeply impressed with the sacred principles of our Holy Alliance of restrictionists.

But the gloomiest of all prospects, is in the desertion of the best friends of the institution, for desertion I must call it. I know not the necessities which may force this on you. General Cocke, you say, will explain them to me; but I cannot conceive them, nor persuade myself they are uncontrollable. I have ever hoped, that yourself, General Breckenridge, and Mr. Johnson, would stand at your posts in the legislature, until every thing was effected, and the institution opened. If it is so difficult to get along with all the energy and influence of our present colleagues in the legislature, how can we expect to proceed at all, reducing our moving power? I know well your devotion to your country, and your foresight of the awful scenes coming on her, sooner or later. With this foresight, what service can we ever render her equal to this? What object of our lives can we propose so important? What interest of our own which ought not to be postponed to this? Health, time, labor, on what in the single life which nature has given us, can these be better bestowed than on this immortal boon to our country? The exertions and the mortifications are temporary; the benefit eternal. If any member of our college of Visitors could justifiably withdraw from this sacred duty, it would be myself, who *quadragenis stipendiis jamdudum peractis*, have neither vigor of body nor mind left to keep the field: but I will die in the last ditch, and so I hope you will, my friend, as well as our firm-breasted brothers and colleagues, Mr. Johnson and General Breckenridge. Nature will not give you a second life wherein to atone for the omissions of this. Pray then, dear and very dear Sir, do not think of deserting us, but view the sacrifices which seem to stand in your way, as the lesser duties, and such as ought to be postponed to this, the greatest of all, Continue with us in these holy labors, until, having seen their accomplishment, we may say with old Simeon, "*Nunc dimittas, Domine*." Under all circumstances, however, of praise or blame, I shall be affectionately yours.

Th: Jefferson

—Thomas Jefferson Randolph (ed.), *Memoir, Correspondence, and Miscellanies from the Papers of Thomas Jefferson*, pp. 340-41.

3. Thomas Jefferson to General Breckenridge, deploring the delay in opening the University of Virginia, 1821

Monticello, February 15, 1821

Dear Sir,

I learn with deep affliction, that nothing is likely to be done for our Universtiy this year. So near as it is to the shore than one shove more would land it there, I had hoped that would be given; and that we should open with the next year an institution on which the fortunes of our country may depend more than may meet the general eye. The reflections that the boys of this age are to be the men of the next; that they should be prepared to receive the holy charge which we are cherishing to deliver over to them; that in establishing an institution of wisdom for them, we secure it to all of our future generations; that in fulfilling this duty, we bring home to our own bosoms the sweet consolation of seeing our sons rising under a luminous tuition, to destinies of high promise; these are considerations which will occur to all; but all, I fear, do not see the speck in our horizon which is to burst on us as a tornado, sooner or later. The line of division lately marked out between different portions of our confederacy, is such as will never, I fear, be obliterated, and we are now trusting to those who are against us in position and principle, to fashion to their own form the minds and affections of our youth. If, as has been estimated, we send three hundred thousand dollars a year to the northern seminaries, for the instruction of our own sons, then we must have there five hundred of our sons, imbibing opinions and principles in discord with those of their own country. This canker is eating on the vitals of our existence, and if not arrested at once, will be beyond remedy. We are now certainly furnishing recruits to their school. If it be asked what are we to do, or said we cannot give the last lift to the University without stopping our primary schools, and these we think most important; I answer, I know their importance. Nobody can doubt my zeal for the general instruction of the people. Who first started that idea? I may surely say, Myself. Turn to the bill in the revised code, which I drew more than forty years ago, and before which the idea of a plan for the education of the people, generally, had never been suggested in this State. There you will see developed the first rudiments of the whole system of general education we are now urging and acting on: and it is well known to those with whom I have acted on this subject, that I never have proposed a sacrifice of the primary to the ultimate grade of instruction. Let us keep our eye steadily on the whole system. If we cannot do every thing at once, let us do one at a time. The primary schools need no preliminary expense; the ultimate grade requires a considerable expenditure in advance. A suspension of proceeding for a year or two on the primary schools, and an application of the whole income, during that time, to the completion of the buildings necessary for the University, would enable us then to start both institutions at the same time. The intermediate branch, of colleges, academies, and private classical schools, for the middle grade, may hereafter receive any necessary aids when the funds shall become competent. In the mean time, they are going on sufficiently, as they have ever yet gone on, at the private expense of those who use them, and who in numbers and means are competent to their own exigencies. The experience of three years has, I presume, left no doubt, that the present plan of primary schools, of putting money into the hands of twelve hundred persons acting for nothing, and under no responsibility, is entirely inefficient. Some other must be thought of; and during this pause, if it be only for a year, the whole revenue of that year, with that of the last three years which has not been already thrown away, would place our University in readiness to start with a better organization of primary schools, and both may then go on, hand in hand, for ever. No dimunition of the capital will in this way have been incurred; a principle which ought to be deemed sacred. A relinquishment of interest on the late loan of sixty thousand dollars, would so far, also, forward the University without lessening the capital.

But what may be best done I leave with entire confidence to yourself and your colleagues in legislation, who know better than I do the conditions of the literary fund and its wisest application; and I shall acquiesce with perfect resignation to their will. I have brooded, perhaps with fondness over this establishment, as it held up to me the hope of continuing to be useful while I continued to live. I had believed that the course and circumstances of my life had placed within my power some services favorable to the outset of the institution. But this may be egoism; pardonable, perhaps, when I express a consciousness that my colleagues and successors will do as well, whatever the legislature shall enable them to do.

I have thus, my dear Sir, opened by bosom, with all its anxieties, freely to you. I blame nobody for seeing things in a different light. I am sure that all act conscientiously, and that all will be done honestly and wisely which can be done. I yield the concerns of the world with cheerfulness to those who are appointed in the order of nature to succeed them; and for yourself, for our colleagues, and for all in charge of our country's future fame and fortune, I offer up sincere prayers.

Th: Jefferson

–*Ibid.*, pp. 341-43.

4. THOMAS COOPER OF THE COLLEGE OF SOUTH CAROLINA TO JAMES MADISON, 1821

Columbia, S. Carolina, March 12, 1821.

Dear Sir

When I first engaged to act as chemical Professor at the South Carolina College, I refused to contract for a longer period than a twelvemonth, expressly on account of my engagement in Virginia. At my departure from this place last autumn, I refused making any promise to return here on a permanent engagement, untill I had an opportunity of ascertaining the prospects of the Charlottesville University. In the mean time, a Dr. Porter came here, on invitation of some of the Trustees, recommended by Professor Silliman of Yale College to take the chair of Chemistry should I decline it.

When I returned here, I passed thro' Virginia, & staid a week at Monticello. Mr. Jefferson told me, he was quite uncertain whether the Virginia legislature would afford sufficient aid to the Charlottesville institution to enable it to go on: that it was a very unpropitious time to make the application owing to the losses the state had lately incurred: that if they should refuse the necessary aid, the Buildings might remain unoccupied for seven years to come.

I found Governor Randolph also in great doubt whether any thing would be done by the Legislature or not. I returned with this hopeless kind of information to Columbia. I found there the Trustees desirous of retaining me, but hesitating about my election for another limited period: Dr. Porter meanwhile ready for the Chair, as my Suppleant, should I relinquish it.

I was not able to waste any more time indefinitely, my family were anxious to join me somewhere. I had no encouragement to go to your State, and I was compelled to accept of the chemical Chair on the conditions of permanent residence, and removing my family here. I have done so; and I consider myself as fixed in this place.

Since I have been here, the Trustees have influenced the Legislature to add 100 Dlrs to my salary as mineralogical Professor, and have since elected me President of the College for a period, which will end at my option or my demise.

Under these circumstnces, I feel myself bound in honour to recommend if I can an efficient Professor Chemistry & Mineralogy to your Institution; and under that obligation I write now.

Mr. Lardner Vanuxem, now with me here as an assistant, was formerly a student of mineralogy and Chemistry for two years in Philadelphia, and since that time for 3 years with exemplary industry at Paris, where he received the public compliment of approbation in the introductory lecture of the mineralogical professor in the School of Mines. His good character, talents, & merit are well known to Mr. Gallatin who will confirm this report.

I think I know every man in the United States who has pretensions to Chemical and mineralogical Knowledge. I speak with the utmost confidence, & without scruple, when I say, that Mr. Vanuxem has no equal among them. You *cannot* procure a person so well qualified in point of Knowledge. How he would perform as public lecturer I know not, but the necessary knowledge, as there is here. Mr. Vanuxem is about 30 Years of age: of a well known family in Philadelphia, his father a merchant of long standing there, attached to the Virginia politics, having a very large family natives of the United States. It is true I wish to render Mr. Vanuxem a service, but I have not the slightest motive to interest myself in his behalf, but his merit: and it is because I feel personally and anxiously concerned for the interest of the Virginia Institution, that you are now troubled with this detail from Dear Sir

Your obliged and faith-
friend and Servant
Thomas Cooper

–Edwin L. Green, *A History of the University of South Carolina*, pp. 334-36.

5. Bill of fare at the University of Georgia, 1821

Resolved, That for the purpose of giving general Satisfaction, the following Shall be established as a bill of fare for the Steward's Hall, viz.–

For Breakfast;

Good Coffee and Tea, corn and wheat bread well baked, butter, wholesome bacon or beef.

For Dinner;

Corn bread, wholesome bacon, including alternately all the parts of the hog usually preserved, with vegetables and fresh meat, either beef, mutton, lamb, shoat or poultry, and when fresh meat cannot be had, it may be Supplied by milk or molasses with a Second course of Confectionary–Molasses every other day, Soup two times a week and a course of Confectionary once–all of which Shall be well cooked and Served up in a neat cleanly manner.

For Supper;

Corn and wheat bread, good coffee and Tea or Coffee and milk, and butter.– Minutes of the Board of Trustees of the University of Georgia, Vol. 2, p. 256. Typescript copy in the General Library of the University of Georgia. Photocopy in the Southern Historical Collection, the University of North Carolina. Used by permission of the University of Georgia.

6. Rules on student conduct at the University of Tennessee, 1821

Chapter 7.

Of crimes and misdemeanors

1. Every student whether a graduate or undergraduate shall be subject to the laws & government of the College and show in speech and behaviour all proper tokens of Reverence & obedience to the Faculty of the College; and if any student shall transgress this law by treating them or any of them with reviling or reproachful language or by behaving contumaciously or contemptuously toward them or by being guilty of any kind of contempt of their persons or authority he may be punished by any censure, even to expulsion, as the nature & aggravations of his crime may require–

2. If any student shall be guilty of Blasphemy, Robbery, fornication, theft, forgery, duelling or any other crimes for which an infamous punishment may be inflicted by the laws of the state, he shall be expelled–

3. If any student shall assault, wound or strike the President, a Professor or tutor, or shall maliciously or designedly break their windows or doors he shall be expelled–

4. If any student shall be guilty of fighting striking quarrelling challenging, turbulent words or behaviour, wearing womens apparel, fraud, lying, defamation, or any such like crime, he shall be punished

by firm admonition or other College punishments suited to the nature and demerit of the crime—

5. If any student shall be guilty of an injury to a fellow-student or to any person within the Town of Knoxville, upon complaint & proof thereof made to the President, he shall with the advice of the Professors and Tutor give judgement thereon and order satisfaction to be made according to the nature of the offense or injury except on points in which the law of the land affords a sufficient remedy— If any student refuses to make such satisfaction he shall be publickly admonished and if after admonition he persists in such a refusal, he shall be dismissed—

6. If any student shall refuse to assist the President, or Professor or Tutor in suppressing any disorder, or to give his evidence respecting any matter under examination when in any of those cases required; or shall falsely declare himself ignorant of the matter, he may be punished by admonition, suspension or expulsion, as the circumstances of the crime may require; provided that no student shall be compelled to give evidence against himself—

7. If any student without leave obtained of the President or one of the Professors or of the Tutors, shall go out of the Town of Knoxville, or beyond the place allowed, or shall not return by the appointed time, he may be punished by firm admonition or otherwise according to the degree and circumstances of the offence—

8. Every student in studying time, shall abstain from hallowing, singing, loud talking, playing on a musical instrument and other noise in the College or the neighborhood—

9. If any student shall play at Billiards, cards or dice or any other unlawful game or at Backgammon or at any game for a wager, or shall keep in his chamber cards or other implements of gaming, he shall be punished for the first offence by admonition and for any subsequent offence may be suspended or sent home—

10. If any student shall venture any money or goods in any kind of Lottery, or chance game, not allowed by the laws of the land, he shall be punished by admonition or expulsion as the nature & circumstances of the crime may [require]—

11. If any combination or agreements to do any unlawful act, or to forbear compliance with any injunction from lawful authority in the College, shall be entered into by undergraduates; or if any enormity, disorder or act of disobedience shall be perpetrated by any undergraduate in consequence of such combination or agreements, in both

or either of those cases, such and so many of the offenders shall, upon due conviction, be punished with admonition, dismission, or expulsion according to the circumstances of their offences, or shall be judged necessary for the preservation of good order in the College–

12. Every student shall be answerable for all vicious, scandalous and immoral conduct during the several vacations in the same manner as in term time–

13. No student shall be questioned for any testimony he may give in regard to a violation of a law of this College: And in case any student shall so question his fellow students to ascertain whether he hath testified, or with an intent to bring him into contempt or shall endeavor to bring into contempt any student, because he has testified, the student so acting shall be deemed to have committed an offence, and may be proceeded against by the Faculty according to the aggravation of the Offence, even to dismission.–Minutes of the Board of Trustees, the University of Tennessee. Microcopy in the Southern Historical Collection, the University of North Carolina. Used by permission of the University of Tennessee.

7. Thomas Jefferson to Albert Gallatin on the University of Virginia, 1822

Our University of Virginia, my present hobby, has been at a stand for a twelve-month past for want of funds. Our last Legislature refused anything. The late elections give better hopes of the next. The institution is so far advanced that it will force itself through. So little is now wanting that the first liberal Legislature will give it its last lift. The buildings are in a style of purely classical architecture, and although not yet finished, are become an object of visit to all strangers. Our intention is that its professors shall be of the first order in their respective lines which can be procured on either side of the Atlantic. Sameness of language will probably direct our applications chiefly to Edinburgh.–Paul Leicester Ford (ed.), *The Writing of Thomas Jefferson*, X, 236.

8. Jefferson to Henry Dearborn on the University of Virginia, 1822

Our Virginia University is now my sole occupation. It is within sight of Monticello, and the buildings nearly finished, and we shall endeavor, by the best Professors either side of the Atlantic can furnish to make it worthy of the public notice. Strange as the idea may seem,

I sincerely think that the prominent characters of the country where you are could not better prepare their sons for the duties they will have to perform in their new government than by sending them here where they might become familiarised with the habits and practice of self-government. This lesson is scarcely to be acquired but in this country, and yet without it, the political vessel is all sail and no ballast. —*Ibid.*, pp. 237-38. For a strong plea for education in Virginia and high tribute to the educational services of Jefferson, see *Richmond Enquirer*, February 3, 1825, for article by "A Friend of Science," believed to be Joseph C. Cabell.

9. Thomas Jefferson to Thomas Cooper, 1822

Monticello, November 2, 1882

Dear Sir,—Your favor of October the 18th came to hand yesterday. The atmosphere of our country is unquestionably charged with a threatening cloud of fanaticism, lighter in some parts, denser in others, but too heavy in all. I had no idea, however, that in Pennsylvania, the cradle of toleration and freedom of religion, it could have arisen to the height you describe. This must be owing to the growth of Presbyterianism. The blasphemy and absurdity of the five points of Calvin, and the impossibility of defending them, render their advocates impatient of reasoning, irritable, and prone to denunciation. In Boston, however, and its neighborhood, Unitarianism has advanced to so great strength, as now to humble this haughtiest of all religious sects; insomuch that they condescend to interchange with them and the other sects, the civilities of preaching freely and frequently in each others' meeting-houses. In Rhode Island, on the other hand, no sectarian preacher will permit an Unitarian to pollute his desk. In our Richmond there is much fanaticism, but chiefly among the women. They have their night meetings and praying parties, where, attended by their priests, and sometimes by a hen-pecked husband, they pour forth the effusions of their love to Jesus, in terms as amatory and carnal, as their modesty would permit them to use to a mere earthly lover. In our village of Charlottesville, there is a good degree of religion, with a small spice only of fanaticism. We have four sects, but without either church or meeting-house. The court-house is the common temple, one Sunday in the month to each. Here, Episcopalian and Presbyterian, Methodist and Baptist, meet together, join in hymning their Maker, listen with attention and devotion to each others' preachers, and all mix in society with perfect harmony. It is not so in districts where Presbyterianism prevails undividedly. Their ambition and tyranny would tolerate no rival if they had power. Systematical in grasping at an ascendency over all other sects, they aim, like the Jesuits, at engrossing the education of the country, are hostile to every institution which they do not direct, and jealous at seeing others begin to attend at all to that object. The diffusion of instruction, to which there is now so growing an attention, will be the remote remedy to this fever of fanaticism; while the more proximate one will be the progress of Unitarianism. That this will, ere long, be the religion of the majority from north to south, I have no doubt.

In our university you know there is no Professorship of Divinity. A handle has been made of this, to disseminate an idea that this is an institution, not merely of no religion, but against all religion. Occasion was taken at the last meeting of the Visitors, to bring forward an idea that might silence this calumny, which weighed on the minds of some honest friends to the institution. In our annual report to the legislature, after stating the constitutional reasons against a public establishment of any religious instruction, we suggest the expediency of encouraging the different religious sects to establish, each for itself, a professorship of their own tenets, on the confines of the university, so near as that their students may attend the lectures there, and have the free use of our library, and every other accommodation we can give them; preserving, however, their independence of us and of each other. This fills the chasm objected to ours, as a defect in an institution professing to give instruction in *all* useful sciences. I think the invitation will be accepted, by some sects from candid intentions, and by others from jealousy and rivalship. And by bringing the sects together, and mixing them with the mass of other students, we shall soften their asperities, liberalize and neutralize their prejudices, and make the general religion a religion of peace, reason, and morality.

The time of opening our university is still as uncertain as ever. All the pavilions, boarding houses, and dormitories are done. Nothing is now wanting but the central building for a library and other general purposes. For this we have no funds, and the last legislature refused all aid. We have better hopes of the next. But all is uncertain. I have heard with regret of disturbances on the part of the students in your seminary. The article of discipline is the most difficult in American education. Premature ideas of independence, too little repressed by parents, beget a spirit of insubordination, which is the great obstacle to science with us, and a principal cause of its decay since the revolution. I look to it with dismay in our institution, as a breaker ahead which I am far from being confident we shall be able to weather. The advance of age, and tardy pace of the public patronage, may probably spare me the pain of witnessing consequences.

I salute you with constant friendship and respect.—*Ibid.*, pp. 242-44.

10. Jefferson to Thomas Cooper on collegiate discipline, 1822

The article on discipline is the most difficult in American education. Premature ideas of independence, too little repressed by parents, beget a spirit of insubordination which is the great obstacle to science with us and a principal cause of its decay since the revolution.—A. A. Lipscomb (ed.), *The Writings of Thomas Jefferson*, XV, 406. Jefferson's views on what is nowadays known as "student government" were set out in his Rockfish Gap Commission Report (see above), in the paragraph beginning: "In the education of youth, provision is to be made for . . ." where he urges appeal to honor and self-respect rather than to fear. For regulations at the University of Virginia see "Minutes of the trustees of Central College and the University of Virginia during the rectorship of Jefferson," above.

11. Regulation on students' walks on Sunday at the University of Georgia, 1822

The other proposition refers to the manner in which the students shall in future spend their Sabbath afternoons—whether they shall be compelled to attend divine service or be permitted to walk abroad on those evenings. The Senatus Academicus at their last meeting impliedly consented to the latter by confining their walks on that evening to one mile— So long then as this healthful and innocent indulgence is executed free from any conduct which is not violative of the laws of College, the Committee find no reason for making a change on that Subject. (1822)—Minutes of the Board of Trustees of the University of Georgia, Vol. 2, pp. 274-75. Typescript copy in the General Library of the University of Georgia. Copy in the Southern Historical Collection, the University of North Carolina. See E. M. Coulter, *College Life in the Old South* (New York: The Macmillan Company, 1928), pp. 77-115. "An incomplete record for a period of forty-three years prior to 1873 shows the following dismissals—no regard being had for the almost countless lesser punishments; idleness and neglect, 16; drunkenness, 27; disorderly conduct, 50; gambling, 4; playing cards, 4; fighting, 18; stabbing and shooting, 7;

disrespect to professors, 21; fighting chickens, 4; profanity, 1; cheating and lying, 1; indecency, 8; refusal to recite, 8; disturbing church, 3; and having firearms, 4." Coulter, *op. cit.*, 115.

12. An Act for the benefit of East Tennessee College, 1822

Sec. 1. *Be it enacted by the General Assembly of the State of Tennessee,* That the trustees of East Tennessee College be, and they are hereby authorised and empowered, to make sale of the Bank Stock which heretofore may have been purchased, with the interest of monie due the said Institution and vested in any of the Banks of this State, and the money arising from the sale of said stock the said trustees are hereby authorised to use, employ and appropriate in such manner as they may deem most conducive to the interest of said institution.

Sec. 2. *And be it enacted,* That the interest on College monies belonging to East Tennessee College, and which have been collected and deposited in pursuance of the acts of the General Assembly in such case made and provided, in any Bank or Banks of this State, shall henceforth be under the control of the trustees of East Tennessee College, to be appropriated by the said trustees in such manner only as shall benefit and advance the interests of said institution.

Sec. 3. *And be it further enacted,* That the said trustees, two-thirds concurring therein, shall have power and authority to sell and convey the lots and houses now designated by law as the site for the East Tennessee College, and the monies arising from the sale of said lots and houses shall be appropriated by the said trustees to the purchase of some other more eligible site for the said institution, in the vicinity of the town of Knoxville in the county of Knox, and in the erection of other buildings for said institution.—*Public Acts of the State of Tennessee,* Extra Session, July & August, 1822, pp. 104-5.

13. A legislative act of Tennessee on certain lands claimed by the University of North Carolina, 1822

Whereas the Trustees of the University of North Carolina have petitioned this General Assembly, that grants may be issued to them upon certain Military Warrants which have been issued by the State of North Carolina, and that their lands in this State may be exempted from the payment of taxes, and they have offered to give this State a fair equivalent for this exemption; and whereas great doubts exist as to the rights of the said Trustees to have grants issued to them upon said warrants, and it is desirable that their claims should be duly investigated by persons skilled in the law, and the said claims be finally adjusted and settled;

Sec. 1. *Be it enacted by the General Assembly of the State of Tennessee,* That it shall not be lawful for the Register of West Tennessee, the Governor and Secretary to issue any grant or grants to the President and Trustees of the University of North Carolina or their assigns upon any military warrants issued by the State of North Carolina to said President and Trustees until they shall be directed agreeably to the provisions of this act.

Sec. 2. *Be it enacted,* That the Governor of this State shall appoint two commissioners of competent legal knowledge, whose duty it shall be to investigate the title of the said President and Trustees to the said warrants, and to confer, and enter into, an arrangement with the said President and Trustees, or their agent or agents, touching and concerning the same, and for the exemption of the land of said President and Trustees within this State from taxation, and to do all acts and things necessary to adjust and settle the claims to the said warrants; and any agreement entered into by the said commissioners with the President and Trustees aforesaid, their agent or agents touching and concerning the said warrants, and touching and concerning the exemption of the lands of the said Trustees in this State from taxation, shall be binding on this State, which agreement, signed by the said commissioners, and the said Trustees, their agent or agents, shall be filed with the Secretary of State and by him published with the laws passed at the present session of this General Assembly: and the said commissioners, under the agreement which may be thus entered into, shall be, and they are hereby authorized to direct how said warrants shall be disposed of, and to whom grants thereon shall be issued, which direction shall be obligatory on the surveyors of the districts in which said warrants may be offered for location, the Register of West Tennessee, and Governor and Secretary of this State, *Provided,* that said warrants shall be located on lands west of Tennessee river, and if no agreement be entered into by them with the said President and Trustees, the issuing of grants upon the said warrants shall be and remain suspended until the further order of the General Assembly.

—*Ibid.,* pp. 8-9. It has been said that the history of education in Tennessee in the early times is the history of the public lands which is "the history of confusion." For the "compact" between Tennessee and the University of North Carolina, see the reference above, pp. 42-46.

14. Jefferson to Professor George Ticknor of Harvard on collegiate discipline, 1823

The rock which I most dread is the discipline of the institution, and it is that on which most of our public schools labor. The insubordination of youth is now the greatest obstacle in their education.—H. A. Washington (ed.), *The Writings of Thomas Jefferson*, VII, 300-2. In the same letter Jefferson wrote of the elective system: "I am not fully informed of the practices at Harvard, but there is one from which we shall certainly vary, although it has been copied, I believe, by nearly every college and academy in the United States. That is, the holding the students all to one prescribed course of reading, and and disallowing exclusive application to those branches only which are to qualify them for the particular vocations to which they are destined. We shall, on the contrary, allow them uncontrolled choice in the lectures they shall choose to attend, and require elementary qualification only, and sufficient age...."

15. The Board of Trustees of the South Carolina College seeks legislative aid for library, 1823

To the honourable the President and Members of the Senate of South Carolina:

Gentlemen,

The Trustees of the South Carolina college have requested me to apply to your honorable body for such an appropriation as may be consistent with the interests of the state, to increase the College library. It has been ten years, since any sum has been appropriated for this purpose. The present flourishing condition of the South Carolina College, the foster child of your liberal patronage, has assumed, and sustained an elevation of character among similar literary institutions flattering to the pride, and consoling to the feelings of every lover of his country.

Nevertheless, the increase of the Library has been slow; and certainly not proportioned to the intellectual demand. This arises from the inadequacy of the fund at present appropriated to the purchase of books; as that fund consists only of the residue of the *tuition fund* after all payments are made. The increased number of students, therefore, requires, a somewhat larger library, and altho' the number of books gradually grows greater, yet the proportion is not according either to the increased number of students, or to the increased demand of the lovers of reading.

The trustees of the South Carolina College also state that publications from France and England can at present be purchased *fifty per cent* cheaper than publications in the United States—as there is an express exception of the *duties* in favour of scientific and literary Institutions. They are also acquainted with a gentleman well qualified by his respectability and intelligence who will make any purchase, in conjunction with the Committee of the board, without charging any commissions. They therefore hope that your honourable body will make such further appropriations as may be deemed proper, for the advancement of learning, and the establishment of a library for the students.

John L. Wilson
President of the board of Trustees.

Columbia Dec. 9th 1823.

—Original manuscript is in the South Carolina Historical Commission; photocopy is in the Southern Historical Collection, the University of North Carolina.

16. Report of the committee of the trustees of South Carolina College to purchase books for the library, 1823

The Committee who were appointed by the Board of Trustees in Dec. last to purchase with the funds granted by the Legislature at their last Session Books for the Library of the South Carolina College Respectfully Report.

That in performance of the duty assigned them they in the first instance examined carefully the collection now in the Library of the College that their purchases might be made with a consistent reference to its present Condition.

That the Library appeared to possess a very good Collection of Modern works particularly in the English Language. That in History, Geography, Voyages and Travels, Politics & Belles Lettres its Collection is if not complete yet good—that it was deficient in classical Literature, in works of all kinds in foreign Languages and in most of the departments of Science.

Your Committee consulted with the faculty of the College, and at their Suggestion proceeded in the first place, to compleat the collection of ancient and Classical Literature, so far at least, as to procure one or two of the best critical Editions of every work. While the funds at their disposal would not permit them to purchase the rarer Editions, those distinguished particularly for Antiquity, as the Editio princeps of each author, or for the beauty of their Topography, it appeared to be important not only to the Character, but even to the utility of a National establishment that the most correct Editions, even if their reputation had enhanced their price, should be procured; they therefore ordered of every classical writer of Antiquity, that edition which secured most extensively the approbation of the Learned, and where the original work itself possessed distinguished Merit, two different but approved Editions have sometimes been procured. To these works have been subjoined as a necessary appendage, a number of treatises Illustrating the manners, customs, Arts, Sciences, Laws and Religion of ancient nations, works calculated to render more easy and more Satisfactory the study of Ancient History and Ancient Literature.

In the Library of a College, it was presumed that works treating on the fundamental principles of Language, works elucidating the History and elements of all Languages, ought to be found, many treatises therefore, on general philology, and the Grammars, and Dictionaries of most of the modern as well as the ancient Languages which have acquired the highest reputation have been added to the Collection. Thirteen hundred years have elapsed since the great Fabric of the Roman Power was subverted, and dismembered but some of its most important institutions have survived its power. In much the greater part of the civilized World the rights of persons and of property are still regulated by the profound Wisdom of the Roman Law and Nations in adjusting their claims and regulating their Maritime and international Law, still frequently submit to its equitable decisions and upon their municipal regulations few Nations principally of the Saxon race have departed in some respects from the principles of this code, it would seem still desirable that the opportunity of comparing their different systems of Jurisprudence should always exist. A compleat copy therefore of the Corpus Juris Civils with all of its supplements, and a few though a very few of its ablest commentations have been included in our order.

In science, some pains have been taken to collect the best Modern

Treatises particularly on astronomy, and the higher branches of the Mathematics.

In the important and daily increasing department of Natural History a few of the most valuable elementary works have been inserted. It is greatly to be regretted that in this department in which the most important treatises are too costly for the acquisition of private individuals, some public Collection could not be made.

To encourage the Educated youth of our Country to attend to those foreign Languages which are interesting from the excellency of the writers who have adorned them, or important from the increasing connection which the Nations who use them are likely to maintain with our own citizens, a small selection of the classic authors of France and Italy have also been ordered, a number of Spanish writers have also been procured, but in this language the works have chiefly been confined to those which relate to the discovery and early history of America.– Indeed in other languages pains have been taken to include many of the original writers on the early history of this continent.

Many miscellaneous works have also been included, either to fill up vacancies which were observed in our present collection, or on account of their intrinsic merit, perhaps also on account of their peculiarities– a few costly works which have been ordered on account of their beauty or their general interest will be found in the Catalogue.

From the best information that could be obtained, your Committee have reason to hope that the Books contained in their order, a copy of which accompanies this report, will (if they can be found) be all or nearly all procured by the funds at their disposal–and while they feel highly gratified at the liberality of the Legislature to this institution, they cannot help regretting that many departments of Literature and Science are still so incompletely filled in the Library of this College, it is an erroneous opinion that when there are more Books in a Library than even the most industrious Student could peruse in his life time there must therefore be as many as he can have occasion to use– Libraries, are the depositories of Knowledge. They should contain the opinion, the researches, the discoveries of the human race in every department of Literature, of Science or of all. Books are collected in them for consultation and reference. They should therefore comprehend all the pursuits of Man. In a College different Sciences requiring a very distinct course of study are always taught. Those who undertake to teach, must themselves learn, they are untrue to their own reputation if they do not keep their minds in a state of constant improvement. Those who are expected to instruct in the knowledge of the age, ought to have access to the Literature of the age. A Professor in some Sciences who performs his duty may have occasion in a single lecture to refer to fifty Authorities. In Speculative Sciences, where opinions are the result of abstract induction, a vigorous mind may surmount the want of such aid, and be itself its own instructor. But in those Sciences where knowledge consists in an accumulation of facts, he who has the opportunity of collecting and consulting most fully and freely the observations and discoveries of others, must require most knowledge, and where talents are equal, he must necessarily become the best instructor who has himself the most extensive means of acquiring information.

The order for Books was transmitted to Europe to Mr. Henry I. Nott according to the direction of the Trustees, as soon as they could be prepared. In the only Letter which has been received from Mr. Nott, he manifested the strongest disposition to promote the views of the trustees and of the Legislature, a knowledge of Books which was honorable to his age, and his pursuits and manifested an interest in the Commission entrusted to him which promises its successful accomplishment– The latest accounts which have been received of him, lead us to expect the daily arrival of a great part of the Collection ordered–

Signed Elliott Chairman
of the Committee

–Original manuscript is in the South Carolina Historical Commission; photocopy is in the Southern Historical Collection, University of North Carolina.

17. An act prescribing certain duties to the Trustees of East and West Tennessee Colleges, 1824

Section 1. *Be it enacted by the General Assembly of the State of Tennessee*, That should it at any time satisfactorily appear to the trustees of the East and West Tennessee Colleges, that it would not be inconsistent with the interest of the said colleges and academies, that the sale of said lands, or any part thereof, should be postponed to a further period than that fixed by law, it shall be lawful for the trustees of said colleges, both corporations concurring therein, to postpone the sale of said lands, or any part thereof, to a further day; and the sales thus made at the time to which said sales may be adjourned, shall be good and valid in law: *provided, however,* that the said trustees shall adopt the same rules in relation to the lands originally sold for the benefit of the colleges and academies, and the state.

Sec. 2. *Be it enacted,* That it shall be lawful for the trustees aforesaid, in any case where to them it shall appear right, to receive, from any person entitled to a part only of an original tract, the sum which each person may owe for his proportion of said original tract, and release such person from the residue of the money owing on the original tract: *Provided, however,* That no such power as is conferred by this section, shall apply to divisions of tracts which may take place after the passing of this act.

Sec. 3. *Be it enacted,* That if said trustees should postpone the sales of said lands, as provided for in this act, they shall, in all cases, require the payment in advance of all the interest which shall accrue during the period of postponement.—*Acts Passed at the Second Session of the Fifteenth General Assembly of the State of Tennessee,* 1824, pp. 33-34.

18. Thomas Jefferson Randolph reports on the embarrassed condition of his grandfather's estate, 1826

To the Rector and Visitors of the University of Virginia.

GENTLEMEN,

My grand-father, the late Thomas Jefferson, devised by his will, his library to the University of Virginia. He likewise suggested a wish that his bust, executed by Caracchi, with the pedestal and truncated column on which it stands, should be presented by his executor to that institution. It has ever been my most earnest desire to comply with all his wishes, and particularly with this; but the deeply embarrassed state in which his affairs were left, renders it extremely doubtful whether his property will be sufficient to meet claims upon it of a higher dignity. Under these circumstances, my duty as executor, compels me to withhold the payment of legacies until the debts are discharged.

The breaking up of his establishment, the sale of his effects, and the dispersion of his family, will leave the library exposed to injury. I must therefore ask to be allowed to deposit it at the University, in charge of your librarian, subject to my future order, should it become necessary to expose it to sale for the discharge of claims of a superior nature. The bust, not being mentioned in the will, but being the subject of an informal direction to his executor, cannot be deemed a specific legacy; and deeply mortifying as it is, he is compelled to offer it for sale with the residue of his property, in discharge of claims upon it.

Feelings of the most affectionate devotion to my grand-father's memory, would induce me as his executor to fulfil his wishes upon these points, at all risks but that of injustice to his creditors, and the fear that his memory might be stained with the reproach of a failure to comply with any of his engagements. An assurance is therefore given that when his debts are discharged, however much his family may be straitened in their circumstances, no considerations of pecuniary interest or of their individual distress, will bar immediate compliance.

Respectfully,
Th: J Randolph,
Executor of Th: Jefferson.

–*Journal and Documents of the House of Delegates*, 1826-27, p. 7.

19. Message of Governor John Tyler of Virginia on the loss of Jefferson, 1826

Fellow-Citizens of the Senate and of the House of Delegates:

I beg leave to be permitted to mingle my regrets with yours, at the loss, which this state has recently sustained, in the death of Thomas Jefferson; one of the most distinguished and beloved of her citizens; a loss, which is not only felt by Virginia, his native State, but will be acknowledged by the civilized world. It may well be questioned, whether there ever existed a civilian who, governed throughout by the purest motives, had conferred greater or more lasting benefits on his country or mankind. This State has especial reason for venerating his memory; since he essentially contributed to impress upon her institutions, the stamp of freedom which they bear, and so to shape her policy, as to wed her indissolubly to republican government. The Executive Department has fulfilled its duty towards his memory by decreeing such honors as fell within the limits of its power. Its omissions will be supplied by Legislative interposition. The honors paid to the illustrious dead are, for the most part, of rich desert, and tend to the preservation of high and honorable feeling. They form no idle pageant or heartless parade, but are decreed by the wise in politics for the benefit of posterity. Whether you shall direct a Statue, as has heretofore been done in the case of Gen. Washington, and to stand by the side of each other, or shall order a more proud and lofty monument to be erected to the memory of each, will be worthy of your serious deliberation.

While lamenting the loss which we have sustained in the death of that estimable citizen, we shall find abundant cause for the expression of our gratitude to an overruling Providence for the prosperity and happiness which has attended us as a nation. Amidst the trembling apprehensions of the friends of human liberty, and the gloomy predictions of the enemies of free government, we have completed, under circumstances highly auspicious, the fiftieth year of our existence. Our growth in population and wealth stands wholly unrivalled, while the future unveils the most cheering prospects. We have already verified the great truth, that man is capable of self-government, and are advancing, under Providence, with rapid steps to the fulfilment of a higher destiny than the annals of history have ever yet unfolded. Our form of government can no longer be considered an *experiment* in politics. Crowned with success, it stands forth an example to the world, and exhibits the proudest triumph of reason and philosophy. To perpetuate the blessings which we enjoy, so that generations, in endless succession, may possess the same high privileges with ourselves, cannot be other than the ardent wish of all—and it belongs, especially, to Legislators, by the adoption of wholesome and necessary laws, to throw around the public liberty, entrenchments, over which the evil propensities and passions of mankind cannot break. Much has been done by your predecessors to accomplish this most desirable object—and, as watchful guardians of the public good, I feel every assurance that you will labor assiduously in the same holy cause.

Among those subjects possessed of the most manifest importance, in the accomplishment of this end, is the organization of a system for the diffusion of general instruction among the great mass of the people. If the mind be set free from the bonds, in which ignorance would bind it, the body will sooner or later partake of its condition; and the most effectual mode of enslaving the one is by benighting the other. This is sufficiently evinced by the history of the world in all its stages. Not to go further, in search of an example, we might be content to refer to that period of English History, when under the early Kings, all the learning was confined to the Clergy; and it was denounced as an offence of high magnitude for any other than a Priest to be found in possession even of a Bible. This was the age of slavery, the offspring of mental ignorance and superstition. That age was succeeded by one of greater light and greater liberty; and, in all countries, the amelioration or debasement of man's condition, has been the constant attendant on the spread of intelligence, or the extinguishment of the lights of science. With us, new motives exist for so enlarging the means of instruction, as to embrace all the community. The happiness or misery of any individual is for the greater part, merely comparative, and what is true as to an individual is also true in regard to a community. Hence the great importance in a government like ours, which fears no comparison with any other that has ever existed, but claims a proud pre-eminence above them, that the mass of its citizens should be well informed. A government emphatically of the people, necessarily rests for its support and durability on them, and their general instruction becomes therefore a desideratum of the first importance: Otherwise, they are apt to be made the ready instruments in the hands of the designing for the overthrow of all that is dear and valuable. These truths have evermore been acknowledged, and your predecessors in the Legislative Hall, acting under their influence, have not been unmindful of the solemn duties which they imposed. The University at Charlottesville has commenced its career under circumstances the most flattering; and promises fully to crown the hopes and wishes of the State. It exists as a proud monument of Legislative wisdom, and excites to new exertions in the same generous cause of literature and science. Its immediate benefits must, however, be confined to a few; and I turn, therefore, with anxious solicitude to the examination of that system whose efforts are directed to the diffusion of information among the great body of the People. On this subject, and all others to which in the exercise of my duty under the Constitution I may advert, I shall speak openly and without reserve. We are fellow-laborers in the same common cause—the cause of our Country; and I should justly be esteemed as unworthy the station which I hold, did I cloak or dissemble my opinion on any question connected with the public good.—*Ibid.*, pp. 1-2.

20. Rector James Madison reports on the University of Virginia, 1826

In obedience to the law requiring that the Rector and Visitors of the University of Virginia, should make a report annually to the President and Directors of the Literary Fund (to be laid before the

Legislature at their next succeeding meeting) embracing a full account of the disbursements, the funds on hand, and a general statement of the condition of the said University, the said Rector and Visitors make the following

REPORT:

The first act required from the Board at their present meeting, was that of providing for the vacancy in the Rectorship, occasioned by a loss which clothed the whole land in mourning; and which has fallen with peculiar force on the institution committed to their care. To that lamented event, the Board cannot refer, without feeling that some tribute is due on their part, to the memory of a patriot and sage, so distinguished by his various and invaluable services to his country; and so eminently entitled to manifestations of grateful affection from every portion of its citizens. After discharging with a zeal which never abated, and with abilities which commanded universal admiration, all the labours imposed by a series of most important public trusts, he did not cease, in his retirement from them, to cherish that love of country and of liberty, which had been the ruling principle of his life. Reflecting more particularly, on the great truth, that as no people can be happy but with free government, so no government can long be free, without knowledge for its conservative element, he determined to close his illustrious career, by devoting the resources of his genius and his vast acquirements, to the erection of this monument to science and liberty; indulging to the last hour of his protracted existence, the gratifying confidence that under the auspices of the State to which it was dedicated, it would more than re-pay whatever might be done for it, by the lights it would diffuse, and the characters it would rear, for the service and the ornament of the republic.

With an origin so propitious, and the continued patronage of the State, the Board are encouraged to expect that no part of the promised blessings will be disappointed, in the progress of the University, to its destined usefulness.

Since the report last made, the acquisition of a Professor of Law has completed the number required for the existing arrangement: And the matriculated students have been increased to 177; the state of the schools being

In the school of		
	Ancient Languages,	107
	Modern Languages,	90
	Mathematics,	98
	Natural Philosophy,	43
	Natural History,	45
	Anatomy and Medicine,	16
	Moral Philosophy,	28
	Law (opened in July,)	26

This increase justifies the expectation, that additions to the number will continue to be made as the benefits of the institution shall be unfolded, and regulations for extending and ensuring them shall be suggested by experience. The enactments now made with this view, will be laid before the Legislature as soon as they shall be duly prepared for the purpose.

From a comparative view of the tasks of the Professors of Law, and of Moral Philosophy, it was found convenient and mutually agreeable to the parties, that the science of Political Economy should be taught in the school of the latter instead of the former.

On a further consideration of the most eligible period for the session of the University, it has been provided that the next session shall commence on the first of February, and terminate on the fourth of July; and that all future sessions shall commence on the twentieth of August in each year, and terminate on the fourth of July ensuing; but that there shall be one recess of all the schools, and no more during each session, to commence on the fifteenth and terminate on the thirty-first of December.

In pursuance of what communicated in the last report, the library room in the Rotunda has been nearly compleated, and the books put into it. Two rooms for the Professors of Natural Philosophy and of Chemistry, and one large Lecture room, have also been fitted for use. The work of the Anatomical Hall, is so far advanced that it may be used early in the next session. The Portico of the Rotunda has been finished, with the exception of the flight of steps, and the laying of the marble flags, which have been received and paid for. The work remaining to be done, is the finishing one other large oval room, one small one, and the entrance hall of the Rotunda, with the unfinished parts of the Portico, and about one-fourth of the Anatomical Hall. Some small additions are also necessary for the better accommodation of the Professors in their Pavilions, and of the students in their Dormitories, and for a few other minor objects.

The receipts by the collector of arrearages of subscriptions since the date of the last report, amount of $644 85, leaving a balance still due of $8161 68, of which $3661 68 are considered separate.

The accounts for the receipts, disbursements, and funds on hand for the year ending with the month of September, as rendered by the Bursar and Proctor, are given with this report, as is required by law.

In looking to the future, the Board notwithstanding their anxiety to bring the establishment into a complete state, without exceeding its current resources, find on comparing with these, the engagements and estimated demands for the present and the next year, that at the end of the next, an adverse balance will exist of not less than twenty thousand dollars; the extinguishment of which will require the estimated annual surplus of income thereafter, for a period of about seven years. In submitting this unavoidable result, the Board venture to hope that a favourable view will be taken by the General Assembly, of the advantage to the institution from a public liberation of its funds from the debts otherwise weighing upon them; and of the prospect thence opened of earlier enlargements of its scope of action and usefulness.

JAMES MADISON, *Rector.*

October 7th, 1826.

—*Ibid.*, pp. 2-3.

21. Jared Sparks comments on South Carolina College, Dr. Thomas Cooper and other members of the faculty, 1826

25th April, Tuesday. Arrived in Columbia at eleven in the morning, after a tedious and monotonous ride from Augusta,—pine barrens, unceasing sands, clouds of negroes where any vegetation appears. Edgefield is the only town on the route. Lexington is a small settlement amidst a waste of pines. Called on Dr. Cooper, President of Columbia College, and presented my letter of introduction; conversed with him a short time, and with Professor Nott; am to meet them again in the morning to be introduced to the proper person for giving me access to the papers in the Executive Department.

26th April, Wednesday. Dr. Cooper called at eight o'clock, and introduced me to Mr. McCord, a gentleman of the bar. Mr. McCord walked with me to the State House, and by his aid I was introduced to the keepers of the records and papers in the Executive Department, the Assembly, and Senate. Professor Nott likewise accompanied me. Proposed first to examine the papers in the Senate; and Professor Nott reconciled the keeper to this proposition by assuring him that he would remain with me during my investigations, and make himself responsible for the safe-keeping and proper treatment of the papers. Mr. Chapman, the keeper, seemed to regard me with suspicion, and looked at me as he would do at a land speculator who was in search of some mysterious document, and might do mischief by gaining too much knowledge. His scruples were happily quieted, however, by the plain statement of the case which I made to him, and by the interest shown in my behalf by the gentleman already mentioned. The result was, that all things were given in charge to Professor Nott, who remained with me in the Senate Chamber till two o'clock, aiding me in looking over the papers.

Dined with Mr. McCord, in company with a dozen gentlemen, among whom were Judges Nott, Johnson (of the upper country), and Colcock; also Mr. Preston, Mr. Desaussure, Mr. Butler, Mr. Bullard, and Holmes. Dr. Cooper came in after dinner. It was a very agreeable party. The conversation was that of men of intelligence, observation, and knowledge of the world. Professor Vanuxem, of the college, was of the party. Politics were duly considered. It was agreed that Everett's notions of slavery in his speech were calculated to make him popular at the South. The college in this place is flourishing by the patronage of the legislature. Money is often granted for the purchase of books, and there is at this time an appropriation of this sort. It is supposed that Professor Henry will go out to Europe to make the purchase.

27th April, Thursday. Devoted the wholeday to researches among the records in the State House, with as much success, on the whole, as I had reason to expect. Professor Nott has aided me. Passed the evening at President Cooper's in company with the professors and several gentlemen of Columbia. Dr. Cooper possesses a vast fund of knowledge on almost all branches of science and general literature. His mind is capacious, quick, and fertile. He is not a voluble talker, but he speaks to the point, clearly and appropriately. The conversation turned on Professor Stuart's article on the Hebrew Pentateuch in the last number of the "North American Review." Dr. Cooper expressed a decided disapprobation of the argument, said it was defective in many points, and proposed to reply to it, if I would insert a reply in the "Review." I declined on the ground that controversy is as far as possible excluded from the work.—Jared Sparks, *Journal of a Southern Tour in 1826*, given in Herbert B. Adams, *The Life and Writings of Jared Sparks,* I, 436-38.

22. Benjamin Silliman comments on Thomas Cooper, 1828

Dr. Cooper was well known as a sturdy sceptic in religion, and Mr. Maclure's [1] plans for education did not include the Bible. . . .

As the companion of Mr. Maclure in his last visit to New Haven, Dr. Cooper is entitled to be mentioned on this occasion, as well as on account of some friendly epistolary relations, for a time, subsisting between us. Dr. Cooper came out from England, I believe, with Dr. Priestly, or soon after, in 1794, during the exciting periods of the French Revolution. Dr. Cooper resided with Dr. Priestly at or near Northumberland on the Susquehannah River, and was familiar with his scientific pursuits; and being himself a man of science, he occasionally wrote to me, and always exhibited a vigorous and discriminating mind. I had never seen him before his visit to New Haven with Mr. Maclure in November 1828. On that occasion his manners were mild and conciliating, and his appearance was patriarchal and venerable, very different from what I had imagined it to be. Ten years after, 1839, my third edition of Bakewell's Geology appeared. In an appendix I had endeavored to reconcile the Mosaic history with geology, but this gave great offence to Dr. Cooper, who in a letter to me protested against my views, both scientific and moral, and he even wrote a considerable book, principally in opposition to me indeed, but still more to vituperate Moses or the author of the Pentateuch, whoever he might be. In the last letter which I received from him he reviled the Scriptures, especially of the Old Testament, pronouncing them in all respects an unsupported and, in some respects, a most detestable book. To this letter I made no reply, feeling that it was such a violation of gentlemanly courtesy when writing to one whose sentiments he knew to be so opposite to his own, that I thought it better to drop the correspondence, and I never heard from him again. While presiding over the College at Columbia, S. C., he made no secret of his infidelity, and the community in South Carolina was

1. William Maclure, distinguished geologist, was born in Scotland, resided some years in London where he made much money in business, then came to the United States where he began the exploration of the geology of this country, the results of which were "published in 1809 in the Transactions of the Philosophical Society of Philadephia."

divided into supporters and opponents of Dr. Cooper, until he was constrained to resign. One of his college faculty, Professor Gibbs, informed me that as he—Professor Gibbs—was passing the college grounds on Sabbath morning on his way to church, he met Dr. Cooper going to work in his laboratory, who said to him—"Come along with me and learn something that is true and worth knowing." —George P. Fisher, *Life of Benjamin Silliman, M.D., LL.D.* I, 285-87.

23. Rules on conduct of students College of East Tennessee, 1829

Of Punishments.

1. The administration of the government of this College shall ever be mild and equitable, and as nearly parental as the nature of the establishment will admit. The reformation of the offender shall be steadily and judiciously aimed at, as far as practicable; and no severe or disgraceful penalty shall be rewarded, except when the paramount interests of the Institution shall demand it, or when the flagitious character of the offence shall render it indispensable.

2. The punishments of the Institution being wholly of a moral kind, and addressed to the sense of duty, and the principles of honor, comprise two classes, the major and the minor punishments.

3. In the minor punishments are included, confession, private admonition or reprehension of a Student by an officer of the Institution; admonition before the Faculty of the College; public admonition of reprehension in the presence of the Students and Executive Committee; putting an offender in a state of probation, or rendering him liable to dismission in the presence of the Students and Executive Committee; and suspension. In cases of suspension, the Student is not allowed to go on with his Class, but is required to recite privately to some member of the Faculty.

4. The major punishments are, private and public dismission; rustication,[2] and expulsion. In cases of rustication the Student shall leave College for a time not less than two, nor more than six months.

5. The minor punishments shall be inflicted by the Faculty; the major, in all cases, by the Board of Trustees.

6. When, in the opinion of the Faculty, an offence is committed, rendering the offender liable to any of the major punishments, it shall

2. Rustication was an ancient form of collegiate discipline or punishment under which students delinquent in their academic duties were required to leave the campus and go to the country, sometimes with a tutor, to catch up with their work.

be the duty of the President to signify the same to the Executive Committee; who, after giving due notice to the Student so offending, are to call a session of the Board of Trustees; where he shall have a fair and impartial hearing; and, if found guilty, shall be subject to the punishment which the Laws of the Institution, in such cases, have provided.

Of Religious Duty, Moral Conduct and Misdemeanors.

1. The Students are to consider themselves, and each other, as young gentlemen, associated for the purposes of mutual improvement; and that it is their interest and their duty to demean themselves accordingly. All the Laws and regulations of this Institution have originated from a parental solicitude to promote their present comfort and advancement in knowledge, and their future usefulness and respectability in society; and they have deliberately acknowledged their obligation to obey these Laws; it is, therefore, confidently hoped, that few individuals will disappoint the reasonable expectations of their friends, and forfeit their title to the benefits and honors of the Institution.

2. As all experience has shewn, that no institution for education can enjoy permanent prosperity without the influence of religion; and as every Student is dependent upon Almighty God for his life and faculties, his privileges and opportunities; it is enjoined upon each one to cultivate a sacred sense of his correspondent obligations, to make it his habitual endeavor to conduct himself, at all times and in all places, with moral and religious propriety, and so to use all his advantages as to answer the great end of his creation.

3. It is enjoined upon every student to observe the Lord's Day as sacred to the duties of religion; and to attend public worship some where, if in his power. If any student shall profane the day by indecent noise or disturbance, or irreverent conduct at public worship, he may be punished by admonition, or otherwise, as the nature and demerit of the offence shall require.

4. The students shall be particularly careful, when the sacred Scriptures are read and prayers are offered in the College, to yield an orderly and serious attention to these duties, as of their own personal concern. Any frivolous or irreverent conduct, during these exercises, shall be subject to public admonition, and such further punishment as the aggravation of the offence may require.

5. The students are required to yield obedience to all the Laws and regulations of the College, and in speech and behaviour to treat the Instructors with respect and decorum. Any violation of this requirement, or opprobrious language and behaviour towards any member of the Faculty, shall subject the offender to reprehension, dismission or expulsion.

6. Any student who shall refuse to appear personally before an Officer of College, when sent for, who shall disobey the lawful commands of his Instructor, or be insubordinate under the censure and punishment of the Faculty, or any one of them, shall be judged guilty of contumacy, and may be admonished, rusticated, or expelled, according to the aggrevation of the offence.

7. It shall be the duty of each student, or of his Parent or Guardian, to procure seasonably, the necessary books. In all cases of failure, the President, in connexion with the Executive Committee, may procure them, and the Student shall be charged for them, in his bills at the Treasury. Where the failure arises through negligence, twenty-five cents per volume shall be added to the original cost.

8. If the scholarship or general conduct of any student be such, that it does not appear to comport with the interest of the Institution, or with his own interest to continue him in it; it shall be the duty of the President, having the advice of the Executive Committee, to inform his Parent or Guardian, that the continuance of such Student will be inexpedient; and to permit him to be withdrawn, without public censure or disgrace.

9. If any student be guilty of perjury, robbery, theft, forgery, or any other crime for which an infamous punishment may be inflicted by the laws of the State, he shall be expelled.

10. If any student shall possess or exhibit any indecent picture, or purchase, introduce or read in College any obscene books, or be guilty of lying, profaneness, intemperance, playing at cards or other unlawful games, or at any game for a wager, or of other gross immoralities or impieties, he shall be punished according to the heinousness of the offence, by admonition, suspension or expulsion.

11. If any student shall quarrel with, insult or abuse a fellow-student, he shall be admonished by the Faculty, and give satisfactory assurances of his future peaceable and orderly behaviour, or be subjected, according to the circumstances of the case, to a greater punishment.

12. If any student shall fight a duel, or send or accept a challenge to fight a duel, or carry such challenge, or be a second in a duel, or any wise aid or abet it, or abuse or ridicule a fellow-student for refusing to fight or be concerned in a duel, he shall be immediately expelled.

13. No student shall bring, or cause to be brought into College, any distilled or fermented liquors; nor any fire-arms or ammunition of any kind; nor a sword, dirk, sword-cane or any deadly weapon whatever, upon penalty of any minor punishment.

14. No student shall, on any occasion, associate with persons of notoriously bad character, under penalty of admonition, suspension or expulsion.

15. Every student shall preserve order and decorum in his own room, and shall be responsible for all disorder in it, unless he give information, when in his power, of the person or persons from whom it proceeded.

16. All writing, cutting or marking upon the walls, doors or furniture of the College, is strictly prohibited. Every student convicted of any one of these offences, shall, besides paying double the amount of damage done to the property, be subject to any minor punishment.

17. No shouting, loud talking, whistling, jumping, dancing or any other boisterous noise, shall be permitted in the entries or rooms of the College at any time. During the hours of study, especially, perfect silence must be maintained throughout the house. Any violation of this rule shall subject the offender to admonition.

18. If any clubs or combinations of the Students shall, at any time, take place, either for resisting the authority of the College, interfering with its government, or for concealing or executing any mischievous design, every Student concerned in such combination, shall be considered as guilty of the offence which was intended, and be subject to any minor or major punishment.

19. Every student shall be answerable for his moral conduct, during the several vacations, in the same manner as in term time.

20. Any student, absenting himself at one time more than two months, from the exercises of his Class, without leave, shall forfeit his standing, and no longer be regarded a member of College. Nevertheless, on affording to the Faculty satisfactory explanations, he may become a candidate for re-admission.

21. A student rusticated, dismissed or expelled, shall forfeit his Tuition fees.

22. It is to be regretted, that in almost all literary institutions, breaches of order and high misdemeanors are committed by the unworthy few who lurk among them unknown, and which render necessary the extension, to all, of processes afflicting to the feelings of those who are conscious of their own correctness, and who are above all participation in those vicious irregularities. While the offenders continue unknown the tarnish of their faults spreads itself over the worthy also, and confounds all in common censure. The Trustees are aware that a prejudice prevails, too extensively among the young and inexperienced, that it is dishonorable to bear witness one against another, and this sentiment is assiduously inculcated by the unworthy and the vicious. But this loose principle in the Ethics of school-boy combinations, is unworthy of mature and regulated minds, and is accordingly condemned by the laws of their country; which, in offences within their cognizance, compel those who have a knowledge of a fact to disclose it for the purposes of justice and for the general good and safety of society.

It is, therefore, ordered, that any Student refusing to give testimony, when called upon, against another Student, who is charged with an offence and then under examination for the same, shall be liable to any minor or major punishment; *Provided*, that no Student shall be compelled to criminate himself. The rules of evidence in the courts of justice shall be adhered to in all trials for offences.

23. If any student shall testify falsely against a Student on his trial for any offence, upon conviction thereof, he shall be dismissed.

24. Whereas, the Laws of the College are few and general, and cases may occur which are not expressly provided for by Law; in every such instance the delinquent may be proceeded against according to the nature and circumstances of the offence; and be subjected to any minor or major punishment.—*Laws of the College of East Tennessee, Enacted by the Board, October, 1829* (Knoxville, Tennessee: Printed by F. S. Heiskell, 1829). The only copy of these laws which we have seen is the property of Lawson McGhee Library, Knoxville. Microcopy is in the Southern Historical Collection, the University of North Carolina.

24. Some early resolutions of the trustees of the University of Alabama, 1829-1832

Resolved that the Salary of the Professors first to be appointed in the University of Alabama shall be $1500 per annum, together with such fees for Tuition as may be required by the Board of Trustees,[3] which they retain to themselves the power to fix at a moderate rate, provided however that the compensation to each professor shall not be less than $2000 annually. (January 5, 1829)

Resolved by the Board of Trustees that they will proceed in pursuance of an Act of Assembly to elect a head of the University of Alabama to be styled the President of the University of Alabama. (January 7, 1830)

Resolved That the salary of the adjunct Professor to the chair of Chemistry shall be established at one thousand dollars pr. annum. (January 7, 1830)

Resolved, That twenty thousand dollars be appropriated for the purpose of purchasing a Library and Chemical and Philosophical apparatus for the use of the University of Alabama, and that the President of the University be requested to proceed to the Northern States or to Europe for the purpose of purchasing the same as early as possible; and further, that the President of this Board be requested to solicit our Senators and Representatives in Congress to use their best exertions for the passage of a law authorizing the said Library, Chemical and philosophical apparatus if purchased in Europe to be imported free from duties. (January 13, 1830)

Resolved, That the sum of forty & 37 ½/100 dollars be allowed to James A. Bates for his expenses for candles furnished the Board of Trustees and attending the Board during their present Session as Door Keeper. (January 18, 1830)

Resolved by the President and Trustees of the university of Alabama, that ten thousand dollars of the funds appropriated at the last meeting of this Board for the purchase of a Chemical and Philosophical apparatus, together with a library, be subject to the order and control of Professor John F. Wallis of this University for the purpose of making purchase of a Philosophical and chemical apparatus, and if he shall deem it expedient to do so, he is authorized to visit Europe and remain absent until July next, for the purposes aforesaid—(July 1, 1830)

Be it ordained by the President and Trustees of the University of Alabama, that the President of the University of Alabama shall re-

3. The early meetings of the trustees were given over almost entirely to fiscal affairs, buildings, and the management of the university lands. The materials which follow are taken from the minutes of the trustees and the faculty in the Library of the University of Alabama. Typescript copy of the early materials are in the Southern Historical Collection, the University of North Carolina.

ceive a Salary of three thousand dollars per year payable quarterly.

Be it further ordained, that the salaries of the Professors of said University as heretofore fixed by ordinance of the Board shall be payable quarterly. (November 24, 1830)

Resolved that the board shall be furnished by the Steward of this University to the Students thereof who may choose to board with him at the rate of eighty dollars for the collegiate year.

And that all such Students as may pay for their board shall be required to board with the Steward—(December 20, 1830)

Resolved that the President of this Board be and he is hereby authorized and empowered to employ William McMillian as a librarian to the University untill the Faculty shall think proper to change such appointment and that he also be employed in the collection of Specimens of Natural History and shall have power to make him compensation at the rate of two hundred dollars pr. annum for the time he may be employed as such librarian or collector of specimens, and that the President of this Board at any time he may think proper shall have power to dismiss said McMillian from such employment paying him only for the time he may have been employed—(January 2, 1831)

Be it ordained by the Trustees of the university of Alabama that it shall be the duty of the President of the University of Alabama as soon as may be—to make out a list of all such Books as in his opinion may be necessary to form a library for the commencement of instructions in this university, calculated for the use of one hundred students, and forward one of such lists to Mr. David Woodruff of Tuscaloosa, one to Mr. Lowar and Hogan of Philadelphia, one to Mr. C. O. G. Carrill of New-York and to such other booksellers of Philadelphia, Newyork or Boston as he may think proper, and request them to inform him at what price or for what sum they will undertake to furnish the Books contained in the said list, and deliver them safely at the university.

And be it further ordained, that it shall be the duty of the President aforesaid as soon as answers may be received from the persons to whom lists shall have been furnished to accept the proposal of such person or persons as in his opinion will be most conducive to the interest of the university and to close a contract with such person or persons for the purchase of said Library and shall require such Bookseller to cause the books to be shipped immediately, directed to the Trustees of the university of Alabama, and delivered safely at the university, and to forward his or their bill for payment.

And be it further ordained that it shall be the duty of the President of the University, as soon as he may have closed a contract with any person or persons for the purchase of a Library as aforesaid to inform the President of the Board of Trustees of such contract, and of the sum, which he may have agreed to pay for such Library, and it shall be the duty of the President of the Board of Trustees as soon as he may be informed that the books for said Library have been safely delivered at the University to issue his Warrant upon the Comptroller of public accounts for the amount which shall have been agreed upon between the President of the University and such Bookseller or Booksellers or to cause payment to be made in any other manner that may have been agreed upon.

And be it further ordained that for the purpose of carrying this ordinance into effect, the sum of six thousand dollars of the University fund be and the same is hereby appropriated and placed subject to the Warrant or draft of the President of this Board. (January 3, 1831)

Resolution to provide for the printing and publishing of the Ordinances and Resolutions of the Board of Trustees.

Resolved by the President and Trustees of the University of Alabama, that it shall be the duty of the Secretary of the Board of Trustees, immediately after the adjournment of the present Session to contract for the printing and publishing of one hundred copies of the ordinances and Resolutions of a public and General nature which may have been passed by the Board of Trustees since the close of their annual session in the year 1826—(January 8, 1830)

Resolved that Fifty dollars be allowed William Mc Millian for services rendered the University in collecting Specimens of Natural History the year 1830—(January 15, 1831)

Resolved by the President and Trustees of the University of Alabama that a Teacher of French, Spanish and other Modern Languages be appointed in this University on a Salary of one thousand dollars, and the Faculty be requested to furnish to this Board at their next meeting, the name or names of individuals in their opinion qualified for that office, together with such testimonials as may be in their possession, as to their qualifications. (April 13, 1831)

Resolved by the President and Trustees of the University of Alabama that a Teacher of Elocution and of English literature be appointed on a Salary of one thousand dollars, and that the Faculty be requested to present to this Board at their next meeting, the name or names of individuals in their opinion qualified for that office, together with such testamonials as may be in their possession as to their qualifications. (April 13, 1831)

Be it ordained by the President and Trustees of the University of Alabama that the Teachers of Modern Languages and of Elocution &c. to be appointed by the previous resolutions of this Board during the present term shall be required to perform the duties of Tutors in the other departments under the direction of the President, whenever in his opinion they can be so engaged with advantage to the Institution. (April 14, 1831)

Resolved by the President and Trustees of the University of Alabama that fifteen hundred dollars be and the same is hereby appropriated for the purpose of paying for the Cabinet of Minerals purchased under the authority of the Board by the Faculty of the University from professor Nuttall. (December 30, 1831)

And be it further ordained that each member of the Faculty shall have under his special care a certain number of Students rooms, which he shall visit every night in the week and also every day in the week with the exception of the day time of Saturday and Sunday–Should any officer be necessarily prevented from attending to this duty, he shall procure some other member of the Faculty to visit the rooms in his place–and should any Student not be found in place, and not give within a sufficient time a satisfactory reason of his absence he shall be reported to the Faculty, and by them to the parent or guardian–and should such absences continue to occur during the hours of study, it shall be the duty of the Faculty after having tried admonition in vain to dismiss such Student from the institution.

And be it further ordained that each member of the Faculty shall as often as once in two months, report to the Faculty all the damages done in the rooms under his care, and the Faculty shall cause the necessary repairs to be made, and the amount to be charged to the authors when known, otherwise to the occupants of rooms. (January 17, 1832)–Minutes in the Library of the University of Alabama. Typescript copy in the Southern Historical Collection, the University of North Carolina.

V

1831–1840

1. James Breckenridge reports on the University of Virginia, 1831

In obedience to the law requiring the rector and visitors of the university of Virginia to make a report annually to the president and directors of the literary fund, to be laid before the legislature at their next succeeding meeting, embracing a full account of the disbursements, the funds on hand, and a general statement of the condition of the university, the rector and visitors make the following

REPORT:

In conformity to the provisions of the act of the general assembly, establishing the university of Virginia, which requires of the rector and visitors, that they should annually visit the institution for the purpose of enquiring into the proceedings and practices thereat, and of examining into the progress of the students, they held a stated annual meeting at the university, commencing on Monday the 11th July, 1831, and terminating on the 20th of that month.

During this session of the board, embracing the period of the public summer examination, the members were engaged in discharging such duties as the condition of the university, relative to its general economy and management, rendered incumbent on them, and in occasionally attending on the examinations of the several classes.

The results of these examinations were highly gratifying, and together with an increased number of successful candidates for those academic distinctions which constitute the appropriate rewards of merit in the student, give satisfactory proof that a large and respectable proportion of the youth who resort hither for instruction, have thus far fulfilled the hopes of their country, and the expectations of their friends. These, in gratifying numbers, are gathering the fruits of their industry, application and devotion to their studies, while they vindicate the judicious liberality of the state in the construction and endowment of the university. They testify, at the same time, to the general zeal and ability of the professors who guide and direct them.

The general management and economy of the institution have been such, during the past academic year, as in most respects to meet the approbation of the board. With a view, however, of rendering the police of the institution more efficient, they have deemed it expedient to abolish the office of assistant proctor, and to separate those of patron and proctor, heretofore united in the same individual.

The office of patron has been continued with Mr. Arthur S. Brockenbrough, with the permission to keep a bookstore within the precincts of the university, in some tenement rent free, to be designated by the executive committee of the board, with a view, particularly, of furnishing the requisite text books to the students, at a specified rate, to be regulated by the faculty.

The office of proctor, now embracing the duties formerly assigned to the assistant proctor, and aided in the discharge of some of them by the hotel-keepers and janitor, has been filled by the appointment of Mr. John A. Carr of Albemarle, a gentleman highly recommended to the board as possessing the requisite qualifications for its discharge.

Mr. John A. G. Davis, who at the last meeting of the board had consented, on their invitation, to fill for the limited term of twelve months, the chair of law, then vacant by the appointment of the former professor to a judicial office, has been appointed professor of law on a permanent footing.

In the recess of the board, their executive committee appointed Col. Colonna d'Ornano, to the place of tutor, in the school of modern languages. At the end of the session of the university which has just terminated, that gentleman intending to return to Europe, and the term of his temporary appointment having expired, the board have supplied his place by the permanent appointment of Mr. J. Hervé, recently of Richmond. Mr. Hervé is a native of France, recommended as well qualified for the duties of his appointment.

In addition to the honorary distinction of graduate in the several schools of the university already provided for by the board, the rector and visitors have deemed it expedient to authorize the higher degree of "master of arts," to be conferred on those who may be induced to appropriate a longer period to academic pursuits, to embrace an ampler course of study, and distinguish themselves by higher attainments in science.

The number of matriculates in the session of the university which has just terminated, is one hundred and thirty-three, precisely the same as of the preceding session; and they were distributed among the several schools, as follows:

In the school of

Ancient Languages,	57	Chemistry and Materia Medica,	37
Modern Languages,	46	Med. and Med. Jurisprudence,	29
Mathematics,	78	Anatomy and Surgery,	23
Natural Philosophy,	57	Moral Philosophy,	37
Law,	17		

The accounts of the receipts, disbursements and funds on hand, as rendered by the bursar and proctor, are given with this report as required by law.

JAMES BRECKENRIDGE, *Rector Pro Tem.*

July 20th, 1831.

—*Journal and Documents of the House of Delegates*, 1831-32.

2. The University of Alabama is reported in flourishing condition, 1831

This new and flourishing Institution, which was briefly mentioned in our number for July, has received its Apparatus and part of its Library from Europe. In addition to the usual collegiate course of study, it embraces a department for the modern languages, is open to students who wish to pursue merely a scientific and English course. The regular College charges, as well as board and incidental expenses, are moderate.—*American Annals of Education and Instruction for the Year 1831*, p. 546.

3. Extracts from the ordinances for the government of the University of Alabama, 1831

Chapter 1.

Sect. 1. Be it ordained by the President and Trustees of the University of Alabama that the annual Stated Meetings of the Board shall be on the third Wednesday of December. The Board may also be convened by the President of the University and four of the Trustees whenever they may think it necessary.

Sect. 2. And be it further ordained that at this annual Meeting a Committee shall be appointed to attend the next annual examination of the College classes, which examination shall commence on the second Wednesday of December. It shall be the duty of the aforesaid

Committee to report to the Board the progress of the Classes, and any other matters, which in their opinion may require attention.

Chapter 2.

The Faculty

Sect. 1. And be it further ordained that the Faculty consist of the President, Professors and other instructors. The Faculty are charged with the immediate Government and direction of the University. They shall enforce the by laws prescribed by the Trustees, and shall have authority to make any other regulations not contrary to them, which they may Judge necessary to the welfare of the Students. The President shall preside at meetings of the Faculty, who are to decide by the quarter number of votes, that of the President always being one to give validity to the decisions of the majority. The Faculty during the Session shall devote themselves to the instruction and discipline of the University; they shall reside on the College premises and occupy such rooms as may be designated at a meeting of the Faculty.

Sect. 2. And be it further ordained, that it shall be the duty of the President to attend the meetings of the Board of Trustees, to give necessary information, and to suggest any measures, which in his opinion will conduce to the prosperity of the University.

Sect. 3. And be it further ordained, that the President shall have power to visit the classes and any of the departments of the University and to give such directions and to perform such acts generally not inconsistent with the laws of the University as shall in his Judgment promote the interest of the Institution.

Sect. 4. And be it further ordained, that the President shall preside [at] commencements, examinations and exhibitions, and in case of the absence, sickness or death of the President, the Senior Professor, present, shall have all the powers of the President in the Government of the University, during such disability or untill the next meeting of the Board of Trustees.

Sect. 5. And be it further ordained, that he shall officiate in the usual devotional exercises, morning and evening, and in his absence the duty shall devolve on the other college officers.

Sect. 6. And be it further ordained that the Faculty shall hold frequent meetings to deliberate on the concerns of the college, to secure the most perfect uniformity of discipline, and to inflict necessary punishments.

Sect. 7. And be it further ordained that the Faculty shall distribute among themselves the various classes and exercises, and each member of the Faculty shall hear the recitations which may be thus assigned him.

Sect. 8. And be it further ordained that if the Scholarship or general conduct of any Student be such that it does not appear to comport with his own interest, or to the interest of the University to continue him in it, the Faculty are authorized to inform his parent or Guardian that the continuance of such Student will be inexpedient and to dismiss him without censure or disgrace.

Sect. 9. And be it further ordained that the Faculty shall appoint one of their number as Secretary to record their important acts, to send notices to parents or Guardians, and at the close of each Session to furnish the Trustees with an accurate list of all the Students who may have been connected with the College during the Session, with the dates of their admission and departure, and a specification of the sums which they ought respectively to have paid into the Treasury.

Sect. 10. And be it further ordained that the Faculty shall be authorized during the intervals of the slated meetings of the Board of Trustees to procure additional temporary instructors, or tutors, whenever they Judge the interest of the institution requires it—but such an arrangement shall continue in force only till the slated meetings of the Board.

Sect. 11. And be it further ordained that the salaries of the Faculty shall be paid quarterly, and the Comptroller is authorized to issue his warrant every quarter on the Treasurer, for the amount due to each college officer.

Chapter 3.

Admission into College

Sect. 1. And be it further ordained, that no Student shall be admitted to regular membership in this university, untill he has been on probation at least six months nor untill he has attained the age of fourteen.

Sect. 2. And be it further ordained, that there shall be four regular classes—the freshman—Sophomore—Junior, and Senior.

Sect. 3. And be it further ordained, that the requisits for admission into the Freshmen class, are an acquaintance with the English Grammar, a knowledge of Arithmetic, and Geography, and ability to commence the reading the higher Latin and Greek authors, and testimonials of good moral character—provided, however, that the Faculty shall have power for the first year to receive Students, in the Freshman class with less degree of preperation, if in their opinion it would be proper to do so, and provided further that no Student shall be admitted as a member of this university from any other institution, unless he produce a certificate from the proper authority of his regular and honorable dismission and standing.

Sect. 4. And be it further ordained that persons may be admitted to advance standing, or from any other college, provided they are found qualified, on examination for the Studies of the class which they propose to join.

Sect. 5. And be it further ordained, that the university shall be open to persons who are not candidates for a degree, and who desire to study in particular departments only, provided they are found qualified for the studies of the department which they wish to join.

Sect. 6. And be it further ordained, that no Student shall be admitted for a less time than one session, the tuition for which must be paid in advance to the Treasurer of the State, who is authorized to receive the same on the certificate of the President being presented that the Student is properly qualified for admission at the university.

Sect. 7. And be it further ordained, that each Student on admission, shall sign a promise to obey all the laws of the university of Alabama, and this shall be renewed at the beginning of each Session.

Chapter 4.

Literary Exercises

Sect. 1. And be it further ordained, that there shall be three recitations or lectures daily in each class, the first immediately after morning prayers, the second at eleven or twelve oclock, and the third one hour before evening prayers—on Saturday however there shall be only one morning exercise—and the Senior class shall be excused from recitation four weeks before commencement.

Sect. 2. And be it further ordained, that on the Twenty third of December, if it fall not on Sunday there shall be an annual exhibition, parts in which shall be assigned to Scholars of the two classes, reference being had in the selection to Scholarship, to general conduct, and to speaking talent—but nothing shall be spoken under any pretence at any exhibition or commencement which has not been approved by the President.

Sect. 3. And be it further ordained, that there shall be the last week of each Session or previous to every vacation or recess a public examination, to which the Trustees, the parents of the Students, literary and Scientific Gentlemen generally, are invited. The examination shall be conducted in the most thorough and exact manner, so as to exhibit as far as possible to the parents, Guardians, and friends of the institution the evidence of diligence, and acquirements of each individual.

Sect. 4. And be it further ordained, that the Senior class under the direction of the President, and each of the other classes under the direction of the Teacher of Elocution, and English literature, shall devote at least one half day in each week to translation, speaking, or composition, in such manner as the President shall prescribe.

Sect. 5. And be it further ordained, that the Students are forbidden during the time of Lecture, recitation, or devotional exercise, to whisper, to engage in any reading or making any manner of disturbance, or to use any text book in a recitation room, except in the Language department, unless required by the Teacher.

Sect. 6. And be it further ordained, that any student who fails to perform a public exercise assigned him shall be subject to punishment, according to the nature of the case.

Sect. 7. And be it further ordained, that every Student is required on the Sabbath to refrain from the usual exercises and divertions.

Sect. 8. And be it further ordained that the President is to direct at what time the bell is to be rung for college exercises, for study hours, meals and all other occasions.

Sect. 9. And be it further ordained, that for any absence from recitations or prayers, or tardiness at the same, for deficiency in a lesson, or neglecting to furnish a theme, or to declaim a Student is liable to admonition, and if such absence or deficiency be frequent, he shall be liable to higher punishments–no Student shall be absent from any exercise except by permission of the officer with whom that exercise is to be performed, unless he has obtained from the President leave of absence from College.

Sect. 10. And be it further ordained, that no absence from any literary exercise shall be considered as an excuse for want of preperation in the same at the daily reviews and at the public examinations: and every deficiency in any exercise whether by absence from it or an imperfect learning of the same, must be made up within a reasonable time, in order to the Student's retaining a standing in his class.

Sect. 11. And be it further ordained that no Student shall during Session time join or leave a class, or occupy, or leave a dormitory without permission from the Faculty or President.

Sect. 12. And be it further ordained, that every Teacher shall keep an exact roll of each class attending his instruction, which roll he shall call over at every recitation or lecture, carefully marking all absentees and the result shall be registered by the Secretary of the Faculty, in a Book kept for that purpose.—Minutes of the Trustees of the University of Alabama, in the library of that institution. Typescript copies in the Southern Historical Collection, the University of North Carolina.

4. Extracts from Thomas Cooper's defense of himself on charges of infidelity, 1831

On the present occasion, Dr. C. claims for himself, the same rights to which every other citizen is entitled under the Constitution, and no other; nor will he consent to renounce them, or any of them, come what, come may.

THERE are some preliminary observations bearing upon this question, that are worthy of remark. Who, and what description of persons are they, who exclaim against Dr. C. on this occasion? They are, *first*, the political opponents of the State Rights party, who have on this occasion called in the aid of the sectarians. It has been over and over declared by the opponents of Dr. C. and it is well understood, that this attack originated from his opposition to a favourite candidate and leader among that class of politicians, who are inclined to extend patience, forebearance, and submission, till resistance to oppression has become powerless and useless.

Secondly. The Clergy and leading members of the Calvinistic persuasion; all the citizens who are in favour of stopping the Sunday mails; who call for legislative interference in religious questions and controversies; and for penal laws against what they are pleased to call heresy and infidelity.

Thirdly. This is a renewed attempt, so often made, to bring the South Carolina College under Presbyterian influence and controul. An attempt that began with the institution of the College, and has continued ever since. The attack, utterly unprovoked by Dr. C. was commenced on him by a very early remonstrance of a Presbyterian meeting, against his election as President. It was followed up by a pamphlet issued against him, by a member of that persuasion at Charleston; by another of equal virulence, published by a Judge of the Federal Bench, resident in that city; by another of the same description, published against him by a reverend gentleman of the Presbyterian Church, in York district; by incessant attacks in the newspapers; by the Presentment of two Grand Juries against him for heterodoxy or infidelity. Against this system of persecution kept up for years, who can blame him, if he is tempted, at length, to defend himself by a fair and faithful exposition of the character of the assaults and the assailants, their objects and motives? These gentlemen have as much right to their creed as Dr. C. has to his; but neither of them has an exclusive right.

Fourthly. Dr. C's. opinions, known and published long before he came to South Carolina, are unpopular among the orthodox and religious party in this state; who doubtless entertain a conscientious objection to any President, whose sentiments on the subject of religion are widely different from their own. An objection which lay against any and every President from some quarter or other; and which in fact, renders it desirable that the President of the College should be of no particular description of religionists.

The present occasion has been seized upon by all these parties, to coalesce in a general outcry, which may remove an obstacle to their respective plans and wishes. A very *leading* inducement to the present attack, is, that it presents a plausible and favourable opportunity on the part of a particular description of religionists,

To put an interdict on the freedom of the press, and to prohibit the discussion of all questions that affect the interest of the Clergy.

To establish by precedent, the right of the Legislature to interfere in the decision of religious disputes, and the suppression of unpopular opinions.

To enact by direct or indirect legislation, a creed and test for the President of the College, which shall bring that institution, and ultimately every other seminary of education, under sectarian management and controul.

To pave the way for clerical influence on the election ground, to destroy the freedom of election, and procure the return of members of the legislature, on considerations founded on religious discriminations and preferences. It is a movement of the Rev. Dr. Ely's *Christian party in politics*, for many years in contemplation, and now avowedly instituted and organized for the declared purpose of controuling the civil government of the States, and of the United States.

The present attempt at religious persecution, and all the proceedings involved in it, will become a part of the legislative history of South Carolina; and will go far to decide among us the questions.

Whether the Constitution of the State is binding on the Legislature? Or whether the Legislature may obey it or disobey it, interpolate, amend, add to it, alter it or mould it into any form, or for any purpose of temporary convenience?

If the Constitution in whole or in part, is binding or not binding, as any legislature in its discretion may think proper, of what use is such a Constitution?

Whether in South Carolina, "*the freedom of the press, and the freedom of religious belief and profession without discrimination or preference*," are words of strict limitation, or expressions without force or meaning?

Whether, in South Carolina, there shall be a state religion: a religion enacted by the Legislature, to which a minority shall be bound to conform?

Whether the Clergy of the Calvinistic persuasion, shall forever hereafter possess themselves in South Carolina, of the exclusive management and controul of education throughout the state?

And whether any form of religion, or any doctrine which cannot support itself by the press, can be fairly entitled to legislative aid or protection?

It is high time these questions, and in particular the power of the legislature over the constitution, and the rule of constitutional construction, should be decided. Religious liberty is at least as valuable as civil liberty, and it is at this moment much more in danger. Admit but of one slight case of religious legislation, it will be a fact this year, a precedent the next, and settled law forever after.

Of the general accusations against Dr. Cooper, the sum and substance, the very pith and marrow of the controversy is no more than this: Dr. C. neither believes or professes the religious creed of his opponents, or their theory of clerical pretensions and claims. He appeals to the Constitution of the State; and demands for himself under that Constitution, the right of professing whatever opinion he holds to be true, be it what it may; and if necessary, of assigning publicly the reasons of his belief. He claims the same right of differing from others, that they claim of differing from him. If he tolerates what he considers as their heresies, they have no right of exclaiming against his. What part of the constitution establishes a legislative despotism over opinion? or an infallible judge of truth?

When the national legislature at Washington passes a law, its principles, its bearings, its tendencies, are open to the examination of any citizen, either for approval or objection—if the proceedings of Congress may be called up by means of the press, before the tribunal of the public, who are they, who claim an exemption from a similar appeal? If the Clergy are this privileged class—if *they* may demand the punishment of any men bold enough to doubt their opinions or pretensions, we may well ask, who confers on *them* this exclusive monopoly? Certainly not the Constitution of our own state, or of the United States.

Dr. Cooper's opponents say, that even if a private citizen may take this liberty, it ought not to be allowed to the President of the College, who ought not to be protected by the Constitution, or by the law, in professing infidel opinions. The question however, is, not what the framers of the Constitution ought to have done, but what they actually have done. If the Constitution as it now exists, includes him in its protection, the legislature cannot exclude him. If that Constitution is to be altered or amended, it must be done in the manner prescribed by the 11th Article, and in no other. As to infidel opinions, what competent authority has defined them?

The position then, taken by Dr. Cooper, and hereafter insisted on, is this:

That by the existing Constitution of South Carolina, the perfect freedom of the press, and the perfect freedom of religious profession, are guarantied forever, to all mankind: Religion, therefore, is, a prohibited subject: the Legislature cannot touch it, or act in any manner on any religious question, or in reference to any religious consideration or suggestion whatever; for it is not possible to legislate on the subject, without making some sort of discrimination or giving some kind of preference among religious opinions; but to do this, is absolutely forbidden by the Constitution, in words as strong as the language can supply.

The oath taken by every member, to defend, protect, and preserve the Constitution, extends equally to every part of it. What the Legislature cannot do, no agent of the Legislature can do.

No exception is made as to time; no provisional authority is delegated as to any future officer or contingency; no exception is made as to persons; *forever hereafter, within this state, to all mankind,* are the words. Where the constitution authorises no exception, the Legislature can make none.

Of the specific accusations against Dr. Cooper, he is accused of having published an anonymous pamphlet at Washington, in the year 1829, entitled, "A Letter to any Member of Congress." It appeared there, just before the Sunday Mail question was expected to be debated. It was unknown in South Carolina, till Gen. Blair made it known.

2. He is accused of having advanced similar doctrines in his Political Economy.

3. He is accused of having delivered opinions before the Students of the College, adverse to the Geology of the Book of Genesis, and the authority of Moses.

On the other hand, it has been distinctly and in express terms admitted by his opponents, and never denied, that however erroneous his opinions may be, his motives are honest and pure; that his talents and learning are undeniable; his moral conduct irreproachable; that he is mild in his manners, kind to the students, and faithful and diligent in the performance of his College duties. The objections to him relate to his speculative opinions on religious subjects, and to them exclusively. Here then, by common consent, is an attack against a citizen, not for error of conduct, but error of opinion! Is it not fair to ask, who has a right to judge of error of opinion? Does the Constitution, when it declares the freedom of the press inviolable, require a citizen before he proposes any opinion for public examination and discussion, to go before some infallible judge of truth and error, for a license to do so? Who is that judge? The Constitution has erected no POPE; no organ of infalibility but a FREE PRESS; neither can the Legislature, nor will they.

However, before these specific charges are distinctly replied to, it will be proper to lay down some general principles that may bear upon these questions, and for that purpose to refer more particularly to the Constitution of the State of South Carolina in the first place; and to the contract entered into between the Trustees of the College and Dr. Cooper in the second place. . . .

The Constitution is the contract of the people with each other, containing the terms and conditions on which they agree to unite as a political community. In this, their mutual compact, they have, by the above clause, formally rejected and discarded in plain and strong language, all denominations, descriptions, discriminations, and preferences depending on religious opinion. They have put no interdict on the perfect freedom of religious belief, profession, or discussion. By the Constitution, a man may not only believe, but *profess* that belief. They have excluded no officer of any description, present or future; no individual whatever, from the benefit of this constitutional privilege. It belongs, "*forever hereafter, in this state to all mankind*," without exception. The people met in convention, and agreed to unite in one community; not as Christians, Jews, Mahometans, or Pagans, but as men and citizens only; for the mutual enjoyment of the benefits of civil society; leaving and conceding to each other, the full and perfect liberty of opinion and profession on all religious subjects; still further guarantied by the perfect freedom of the press. All this is clear beyond denial from the words of the constitution, selected to express this right in the most ample manner.

This constitution is the law paramount of this state: to deprive any citizen of the benefits and provisions of this constitution, is an act of injustice. The legislature possesses no authority but what the constitution gives it; nor can it rightfully legislate away, or on any pretence, interpolate or change the provisions of the constitution, under whose authority alone, it holds all its own authority. The mode of altering the constitution, if needed, is specially described in Art. XI. No legislator, therefore, can join in enacting in any discrimination or preference, or erecting any civil disability in favour of, or against any person of any description, on religious pretences, without violating the constitution of the state, and disregarding the obligations of his own solemn oath, to preserve, protect and support it.

Dr. Cooper, for himself, and all other citizens of South Carolina, claims the benefit of this wise provision of the constitution, not as a favour but as a *right;* and he demands, what satisfactory reply can be made to this argument; and on what pretence he alone shall be excluded from the right granted by the constitution to "all mankind?" And by what authority the legislature can make an exception when the constitution makes none?

If the constitution of the state be not a deception on those who rely on it—a mass of words without meaning—if the oath taken to support this constitution, to protect and preserve it, be not a mere farce, a solemn mockery, an appeal to heaven, that has no binding force on the conscience, and that any motive of convenience may absolve—the argument might well rest here. The Legislature ought to say at once "the constitution gives us no authority to legislate on religious questions or pretences: this is a civil community not a religious one."

But a legislative body always consists of classes and descriptions of men divided according to the varieties of public opinion prevalent at the day. Let us appeal then to those who constitute our present legislature.

With what consistency can any *defender of State Rights* exclaim against the invasion of the Federal Constitution by the General Government, who in support of a religious persecution, invades without scruple the constitution of his own state? This will indeed open wide the flood-gates of implication and construction.

With what face can any *opponent of nullification* consent to nullify the constitution of his own state, and inflict punishment for mere differences of religious opinion; differences expressly protected, and no where excepted or prohibited by that constitution?

With what face can any *religious man* recommend to a member of the legislature, a deliberate violation of his oath? Is religion to be supported by perjury? By a deliberate breach of the most solemn religious obligations?

If these applications, pretensions, and persecutions about religious opinion are to be encouraged, where will they end? If the legislature may take upon them to decide any one religious controversy, they may decide any other, and assume all the powers of an ecclesiastical Synod. They should remember that their powers are political, not polemical.

Has the legislature, for instance, a right to decide that this is a christian community? Who gave them that right? Assuredly not the constitution. The elder Mr. John Adams, officially informed the Day of Algiers, that the constitution of the United States was *in no sense founded on the Christian religion;* and he was right. Our republics are civil and political, not religious communities.

When Dr. Cooper came to South Carolina, he looked at the constitution of the state, and found himself apparently protected by that supreme law of the land, in the full right and enjoyment of his opinions on religious subjects, and of professing them without liability to molestation on that account. After giving up his former profession, his honorable appointments in the University of Virginia and their advantages—after a dozen years residence in the diligent performance of his duties here—depending for his support on the situation he accepted in exchange for the emoluments he renounced—he finds himself on a sudden, subjected to discrimination and preference, to punishment by loss of character, of property and of station, amounting to utter destruction, because his religious opinions are considered as unpopular; and for no other cause or reason assigned or assignable! Let it be granted that the great majority of the citizens differ with him at present as to these opinions—what then? Where is it enacted among us that the religion of the majority shall be the established religion? Or has a minority no rights under the constitution? Is not this the consolidation argument of the present majority in Congress? An argument that has erected that body into an absolute despotism, has prostrated the influence of the south, annihilated her independence, despoiled her of her property, and reduced her to absolute vassalage!

Surely the constitutional rights of a citizen in South Carolina do not depend on sectarian licence or permission—on the breath of temporary popularity—on an outcry that would annihilate the liberty of the press, and compel every man who had a proposal to make for the good of his country, to make it with a halter round his neck, unless the more numerous party should previously approve of it! or are we forbidden here to speak of the clergy, but in conformity to leave from the Synod first had and obtained? No: the rights of the citizen are to be looked for in the Constitution, and no legislature can look out of it.

Let it be conceded for a moment, that the legislature may decide who is in the right, and who is in the wrong between religious disputants; and consider the dangerous extent to which such a doctrine will lead. The very proposal to do so, the calling upon the legislature to interfere in such a case, and to make a formal discrimination and preference between two sets of citizens, who have no other difference but a religious one, amounts to all intents and purposes, to a call on the legislature to establish and condemn religious opinions by law; that is, to set the dangerous precedent of connecting religion with politics, and enacting for so much sought for holy alliance between church and state! This is exactly what the Sunday Mail petitions are striving to bring about. This is the great object of Dr. Ely's CHRISTIAN PARTY IN POLITICS, not so much known among us as it ought to be.

The present application is in fact, an attempt among the leaders of a particular religious sect to prostrate the liberty of the press—to prohibit the discussion of any question they stand in fear of—to establish by legislative authority a "*discrimination and preference*," founded on religious belief—and to procure gradually the enactment of their creed as a test for the Presidency of the College. It is the desperate struggle of a clerical combination, working on the passions and prejudices of their well meaning, but unthinking adherents, to acquire political influence and power; and for this purpose, they ask of our legislators to disregard the constitution, to violate their oaths, to grant a prohibition monopoly in favor of certain religious tenets, and exclude from office all men, who do not belong to what is falsely called the predominant theological party: and they calculate that there is in the legislature, a timid and temporizing spirit that may be swayed by popular outcry: a calculation in which I trust they will be deceived. Nor is it by any means certain, that the prevailing sect of to day, will be such, half a dozen years hence. Wise men will hesitate, before they open the doors to let in an unceasing struggle among religious disputants for political power; striving for this purpose to influence electors out of doors, and the elected within.

It has been said, that if the President of the College be permitted to be an infidel, then is infidelity established by law. I will not stop to enquire what is infidelity; but if this reasoning be valid, then will an Episcopalian or Presbyterian President, give rise to the establishment of Episcopalianism or Presbyterianism by law. The true state of the case is, that neither the legislature, or the trustees, who are the agents of the legislature, have any right to enquire into, or to take cognizance of the religious belief of any of the Officers of the College. The constitution forbids them; their oaths forbid them; the interminable disputes and sectarian manouvrings among the Trustees, which such an investigation would bring into play, forbid them; and the temptations to hypocricy among candidates that it would hold out, must surely caution them against such a proceeding. The world has seen too much of religious tests and qualifications, to be blind at this day to their inefficacy and injustice. There never has been upon earth a source of irreligion and hypocrisy so productive as the Corporation and Test acts of Great Britian. In that country they have abolished them; have we any good reason for adopting them in this?

Infidelity: what is infidelity? is not that man an infidel to men, who refuses to believe what I believe? But in what part of the constitution, by what state law is infidelity defined or prohibited? Among the innumerable shades of belief and disbelief which honest men may conscientiously profess, where is the line to be drawn? Who can draw it? Whether this *can* be done or not, where *has* it been done in the laws of South Carolina? The legislature is now, for the first time, on the spur of the occasion, suddenly called upon to establish a new and undefined offence, and to punish it retrospectively with the loss of station and property, on purpose to reach Dr. Cooper, to convict him of this non-descript crime, and to remove him from office by an ex post facto law! Amid all the injustice which the fervor of clerical and political zeal may incite men to commit, I cannot yet believe that this persecution can succeed in South Carolina.

It seems to be taken for granted in the publications against Dr. Cooper, that it is the duty of the legislature to insist that the officers of the College shall be Christians. This is very disgraceful to writers who ought to know what the constitution contains. The legislature have just the same right to insist that they shall be Pagans or Mahometans. The constitution says, the legislature shall not interfere with religious profession or worship, or make any discrimination or preference on that account. It leaves every form of religion to stand or fall by its own intrinsic merits.

But suppose the legislature to insist that the President shall be of the Christian religion. What is the Christian Religion? Enquire of Dr. Ely, how many articles does its creed contain? Is it a Papist, a Quaker, an Arian, a Sabellian, an Universalist, a Socinian, a Christian? Is the whole of the Bible of divine inspiration? If not, how much of it? Are we bound by the historical part as well as the doctrinal? Where is the line to be drawn?

If Christianity be adopted it must be some one of the many forms and sects of Christianity: which of them is to be honoured by a preference?

No: the legislature cannot touch the subject of religion without violating the constitution, which they have SWORN to protect and preserve; for this plain reason, that they cannot, by any possibility legislate upon it, without making a forbidden discrimination and preference among the various forms of profession and worship.

Either the constitution is mere waste paper, or it is the Law paramount of this state; which as a derivative and subordinate power, the legislature is bound to preserve, protect, support and obey, in whole and in every part; nor can any alteration be made in it, but according to the prescribed forms of the XIth Article. Upon this firm ground, Dr. Cooper takes his stand: he claims for himself and for all his fellow citizens, equally interested in this question as he is, every right enumerated and guaranteed by the existing constitution. He denies the authority of the legislature to tamper with that constitution, or on any pretence whatever to interpolate an exception where the constitution contains none; nor can he yet believe they will be inclined to do so from any motive of short lived popularity, or from the instigation of men who are anxious to seize on every pretence for bringing about an alliance between sectarian societies, and the civil authorities.

It may be asked, suppose the opinions of the President of the College to be so unpopular that no citizen will send his son to be educated there—what are we to do in such a case? must we retain a man, who is an obstacle to the prosperity of the College?

It may be well enough to reply to this question, although the case has not occurred yet, nor is it likely to occur, notwithstanding the calumnies employed and the persevering efforts made to render Dr. C. and the South Carolina College unpopular. This outcry of unpopularity has been fraudulently excited on purpose to give colour to the attacks on the President; to force him out and to force some sectarian in. The real ground of all this rancorous opposition, is, that the College is not unpopular, but much otherwise.

But the objection is worth considering: *shall we retain an Officer in the College, whose religious opinions are prejudicial to the prosperity of the Institution?*

The first consideration manifestly is, does the constitution authorise the Legislature, or the Trustees to take any cognizance whatever of such an objection? The constitution says *you shall make neither discrimination or preference on this account:* and each legislator has declared upon oath that he will act accordingly.

Again. The South Carolina College is not, and under the present constitution never can be, a theological seminary; what then have the Governors of it to do with theological opinions or objections?

The next consideration is, can any religious denomination of students be excluded; whether Musselman, Jew, Papist, Socinian, Unitarian, Deist or Atheist? I apprehend not; yet, if it be determined that the Presidency shall be given to some form or sect of religionist, the prejudices of all the rest will be raised against him as strongly as in the supposed case of Dr. Cooper, and favouritism will be shewn to the favoured sect. Prejudices there always will be, because there will always be much ignorance in the community; and if no President must be elected until one perfectly unobjectionable on the score of religion can be chosen, none will ever be chosen.

Moreover, a President may have reputation and qualifications conducive to the prosperity of the College, and attractive to students, far more than to compensate any prejudice on the score of religious opinion. Students are sent here to acquire useful knowledge, not sectarian theology....

Dr. Cooper has nothing to recant. He disavows no opinion: he acknowledges no misconduct: he has no apology to make for the past: he enters into no promise or compromise for the future: he asks no favour: he demands for himself and for every other citizen, the constitutional *right* of believing what appears to him to be true, and of *professing* what he believes, let the subjects be what it may. He will not tamely surrender one tittle of the rights of the citizen under the constitution, attacked in his person; and if he is to suffer for defending them, be it so; he will abide the consequences. . . .

After a long life of observation and reflection, I am compelled to conclude, that for all these mischievous results of public ignorance, there is absolutely no remedy but a sedulous, anxious, and persevering care on the part of the government, to provide full and ample education at the public expense for every human creature in the community, willing to accept of the means, and to use them. Schools in every district as well as the State College, should be amply provided with qualified teachers, and the means of teaching, free of expense. Of all purchases, knowledge is the cheapest. Of all our public wants, knowledge is the greatest. There is scarcely no evil upon earth, whereat ignorance does not lie at the root. It is no exaggeration to say, that if political and constitutional knowledge among us, had been as much attended to ten years ago, as at present, imperfect as it still is, it would have saved to the State of South Carolina AT LEAST thirty millions of dollars! Even at this moment, the prosperity of the state is in danger of being crushed and prostrated for want of this knowledge diffused among the mass of the people. Something has been done, but much indeed remains.

T.C.

Pentateuch

The position that Dr. Cooper was compelled to take before his class, in justification of the geological position he adopted in conformity with the latest and best considered opinions of European geologists, was that however opposite they might appear to the statement in the book of Genesis and to the numerous geologists who felt themselves bound to conform to these statements, he was nevertheless at full liberty to adopt and insist on his own, inasmuch as the book of Genesis *as we now have it*, like all the other books of Moses as they are called, are not the writings of Moses, or have any reasonable claim to divine authority, if the bible itself is to be received as a book worthy of credit. To that book, and to that book alone, Dr. Cooper appealed; presuming that if the bible was open to others, it ought not to be closed to him. The position assumed by Dr. Cooper was,

THAT THE FIVE BOOKS OF MOSES AS THEY ARE CALLED (THE PENTATEUCH) WERE NOT WRITTEN BY MOSES IN THE STATE IN WHICH WE NOW HAVE THEM.

In advancing this opinion, Dr. Cooper has said nothing that has not been repeatedly urged before by very many learned and pious christians. In fact it is a position in perfect conformity to the *earliest, and the latest* opinions of the great majority of the christian world: and if any clergyman presumes to say that this has not been in the very earliest times, and is now a very common, and even prevailing opinion among learned and pious christians, he is either too grossly ignorant to be argued with or the means to deceive. As to the opinion itself, it is open to the refutation of those who think they can refute it....
—*The Case of Thomas Cooper, M.D. President of South-Carolina College; Submitted to the Legislature and the People of South Carolina, December, 1831* (Columbia, S.C.: Printed at the Times and Gazette Office). From the copy in the Hammond Collection, South Caroliniana Library, University of South Carolina. Typescript copy in the Southern Historical Collection, the University of North Carolina. Thomas Cooper, educator, scientist and political philosopher, was born in England and studied at Oxford. He was actively sympathetic with the French Revolution and came to this country in the early 1790's, practiced law and served as district judge in Pennsylvania, as professor of chemistry in Dickinson College in that state and in the University of Pennsylvania. Thomas Jefferson had high admiration for Cooper and got appointment for him as first professor of natural science and of law in the University of Virginia in 1819. (See minutes of the first meeting of the Board of Visitors, above). Jefferson said that Cooper was "acknowledged by every enlightened man who knows him, to be the greatest man in America, in the powers of mind and in acquired information" and his biographer Dumas Malone, describes him as "a pioneer in Southern education" and gives him "a conspicuous place in the history of the intellectual liberty in America." But Cooper was too liberal in religious matters for the conservative churchmen in the Old Dominion and because of bitter attacks on him by the clergy of that state he never assumed duties at the University of Virginia and Jefferson found it necessary to pay Cooper's salary for a year. Cooper went to Columbia as professor of chemistry and

political economy in South Carolina College (later the University of South Carolina), became acting-president of the institution in 1820 and president the following year. He served in this position until 1833 when he resigned the post. Shortly afterwards he lost his professorship because of increasing opposition to his very liberal views on religion, his annual lecture on the authenticity of the Pentateuch finally getting him into dire trouble. A legislative resolution that "it is expedient that the board of trustees of the South Carolina College do forthwith investigate the conduct of Doctor Cooper, and if they find that his continuance in office defeats the ends and aims of the institution that they be requested to remove him." The trial was held at the end of 1832 in the hall of the House of Representatives and Cooper made vigorous defense and was acquitted for lack of substantial proof although there was strong dissent from the decision. Opposition to Cooper continued, however, and finally there was a demand for the resignation of the entire faculty, some members of whom were re-engaged but Cooper was not among them. He spent the remainder of his life editing *The Statutes at Large of South Carolina.* See Edwin L. Green, *A History of the University of South Carolina,* Chapter III; Virginius Dabney, *Liberalism in the South,* 51-52, 72-73; Dumas Malone, *The Public Life of Thomas Cooper, 1783-1839* (New Haven: Yale University Press, 1926), Chapters X, XI.

5. The Faculty of the University of Alabama Keep Busy with Disciplinary Matters, 1831-1834

No student shall have or use, on the premises of the University, any spirituous or vinous liquors, or weapons or arms of any kind, or gun-powder, or keep a servant, horse or dog, or bring any stick into a public college room, or in such a room to use tobacco in any way, or to be covered without permission of the officer present—

The occupant of each room in College should be held responsible for all damages done in the rooms occupied by themselves, when the author of such damage is not known—

At the weekly stated meetings of the Faculty each Instructor shall hand in to the President, & to be filed with the secretary a list of all the students who have attended his respective classes during the week, with the absences & deficiencies, together with a statement of the length of each exercise, & of its nature; that is, whether it be a recitation by the student or a lecture by the Instructor, or a combination of both.

In the opinion of the Faculty, it will not be expedient to encourage the admission of students to this University under the age of 14—unless in some special cases, as where there are two brothers who have prosecuted their studies together one of whom may be over & the other under the required age—

In the opinion of the Faculty it will not be expedient to encourage the admission of students, who wish to prosecute the study of languages, unless they are sufficiently far advanced to join some one of the existing classes—

No female or servant be permitted for any reason whatever, to enter any of the College buildings; & should any student be found countenancing in any way a violation of this regulation he shall be dealt with, as the nature of the offense may require—

The study hours until altered shall be from 9 A.M. till one o'clock; from 2 P.M. till evening prayers; & from 7 P.M. till bed time, that during these hours every student will be expected & required to be in his own room quietly pursuing his studies, and every known violation of this regulation will subject the offender to censure, according to the nature of the case—provided, however, students may be allowed to play on musical instruments between the hours of 9 & 10 in the evening—

Any attempt of a student to enter a fellow student's room without consent, at any time, & particularly, during study hours will be regarded & treated as a misdemeanor—

Throwing out of the College windows any kind of filth or dirty water, be strictly forbidden, & that the students be expected to furnish every sleeping room with a chamber vessel which shall be emptied every morning by the College servant—

The following shall be the duties of the College servants—besides ringing the bell & sweeping daily the recitation rooms & the two entries in each dormitory, they shall perform the following services in the dormitories; to wit: make fires every morning, sweep the private rooms, make beds, carry out dirty water from the bed chambers, & furnish the students with clean water & on Wednesday & Saturday afternoons to brush their shoes—

Any student, not belonging to town who shall violate the laws by visiting town during the study hours, especially at night without permission shall be admonished for the first offence & liable to be reported to his parents or guardian & on a repetition of the offence shall be subject to such severe punishment as the Faculty may judge the case requires—

It shall be the duty of the Faculty to visit the rooms very frequently for the purpose of ascertaining any violations of the study hours—

Whereas it is ordained in the by-laws, that if the scholarship or general conduct of any student be such, that it does not appear to comport with his own interest or the interest of the University to continue him in it, the faculty are authorised to inform his parent or guardian that the continuance of such student will be inexpedient, & to dismiss him without censure or disgrace.—And whereas it appears, that the general conduct of Edward S. Stickney, Robert T. Ashurst, John J. Scott, & Wm. C. Ashe is not such as ought to be expected &— required in the members of a University, (notwithstanding the admonitions they have received):— Therefore resolved unanimously, that the aforesaid individuals be dismissed without censure or disgrace; and that their parents or guardians be furnished with a copy of this preamble & this resolution.

Resolved unanimously, that the following individuals, viz; Elijah H. Gordy & John H. Gindrat be suspended from this institution for the period of two months, in consequence of their disorderly conduct on the night of the twenty fourth instant, as in consequence of a want of satisfactory progress in their studies.

And whereas it appears that the scholarship & general conduct of Richard K. Harrison have not been such as ought to be expected & required from the member of a University, (notwithstanding the repeated admonitions, he has received):— Resolved therefore that the aforesaid R. K. Harrison be dismissed without censure or disgrace, & that his guardian be furnished with a copy of this resolution....

That the Librarian do not let out to the students any books containing valuable plates, or any translations of the College Text-Books, unless upon a special order of the President or one of the Professors.

That no student be allowed after the expiration of the legal time for keeping out a book, to take again the same book, if it be applied for by some other student.

That nothing be spoken on the College premises, upon a public occasion by a student, unless approved of by the President or by the Faculty.

That those who sleep and live in town be excused from morning prayers, provided they have no recitation before breakfast.

Resolved unanimously by the Faculty of the University of Alabama that David Porter Bibb in consequence of profanity, intoxication, riotous conduct, & disrespectful language in presence of the Faculty, be & he is hereby dismissed from this Institution with disgrace—

Resolved that this resolution be read by the Secy to the Students this day, before or after evening prayer, & Be by him communicated to his parents.

Resolved That no student of this Institution be permitted to have more than three recitations per day, but to arrest importunity & silence complaint, each student shall be allowed to make his own selection of studies.

Resolved That the resolution read this morning to the students in relation to the number of their recitations be reconsidered—

Resolved, That the resolution which was read this morning to the students in relation to the number of their studies be so amended as to read in the following manner, viz; Resolved that with the exception already made in favour of the Senior Class, no student be permitted to have more than three daily recitations; unless for very weighty & special reasons the Faculty shall so determine—

Resolved that Thos. M. Mathews, in consequence of insubordination & contempt of lawful authority, be suspended from this Institution for the remainder of the College year, & that the Secretary communicate this resolution to him forthwith, with an injunction to depart immediately; but that the faculty feel themselves at liberty to reconsider this resolution whenever Mr. Mathews satisfies them that he feels properly concerning his offence, & makes suitable acknowledgements—

Resolved that Messrs. Jones, Cameron & Sterrett be permitted to attend three & half recitations a day for the present session.

Resolved that G. F. Manning deserves the disapprobation of the Faculty for having neglected to attend the number of recitations which he agreed to take & for continuing in this neglect after having been admonished by the President in the name of the faculty—& that this resolution be communicated to Mr Manning by the Secretary—

Resolved that Messrs Terryl, Whitfield, Thorington, Townes, Manning, Shortridge, & Warren be permitted to take but two & half recitations per day—

Whereas it is commonly reported that some students of this Institution are in the habit of resorting to town, particularly at night, to the great detriment not only of their own character, but of the reputation of this University, & of the honor of the whole State, therefore

Resolved unanimously, that no student be excused to go to town at night during session terms except by the Faculty, & then only for the most weighty & urgent reasons; & that application be made to the whole faculty for such permission immediately after evening prayers; & that a record of such permissions, with the reasons of them, be kept by the Secretary.

Whereas the major part of the Junior Class have received more instruction in French & less in Mathematics than the by laws require for Juniors, therefore

Resolved that for the remainder of the session, the Profs of Mathematics take the Junior Class at 12 o'clock every other day instead of the professor of Mod-Languages, & that the Prof- of Mod-Lan- continue his least advanced class every other day or oftener if deemed advisable—

Whereas the general conduct of Green W. Wood is such that it does not appear to comport with his own interest nor that of this University to continue him longer in it, therefore resolved unanimously that he be forth-with withdrawn from this Institution—in a private manner & that the Secretary send this preamble & resolution to the individual & to his father—

Whereas Alexander B. Meek has failed in every department to sustain creditably his Senior examinations, therefore resolved unanimously that he is deemed unqualified for graduation—

Whereas the examinations of Thomas A. Walker thus far have not been sustained, & his English scholarship being thought imperfect, therefore resolved unanimously that he be advised to abandon his purpose of applying for partial graduation in this University.

Resolved unanimously that the general conduct of Stephen Marsh has become such as to convince the Faculty that it does not comport with his own interests nor that of this University to continue him in it, & that he be privately dismissed—

Whereas Alex B. Meek failed in his senior examination, & also resorted to most unjustifiable means to sustain himself in that examination but has since made a written apology for said conduct, & also a written apology for much improper language used after his failure in his examination, Therefore unanimously resolved that in consideration of A B Meek's general conduct, & in consideration of his written apologies for his great improprieties in speech & action, he be admitted before Commencement, to another examination; & that the Faculty make such use of the facts connected with this case as they may hereafter judge to be necessary—

Resolved that no translations of college textbooks be loaned hereafter from the Library to the students—

Resolved that in consequence of the sickness of some of the Seniors, T. J. Burke & Thos. M. Peters be appointed to speak at commencement on the following subjects: to wit, The Dignity of Man & the Advantages & Pleasures of Study—

Resolved, that the following members of the Senior Class be appointed to speak at the exhibition on the 23 inst on the subjects attached to their respective names, to wit:

1. J. F. Bailey, The style & moral tendency of Addison's Periodical writings.
2. C. C. Clay.—The unhappy fate of Poland.
3. J. H. Kelly.—The character & writings of B. Franklin.
4. J. H. Mastin.—Europe in the Middle ages.
5. W. Parham.—Europe after the revival of Literature.
6. T. M. Peters.—Character & writings of Henry Brougham.
7. J. B. Read.—The influence of imagination on character.
8. J. M. Smith.—Popular Education, the foundation of popular Liberty.—Minutes in the Library of the University of Alabama. Typescript copy in the Southern Historical Collection, the University of North Carolina.

6. Extracts from address of President Woods of the University of Alabama at its first commencement, 1832

We have been highly interested in perusing in the "Tuscaloosa Inquirer," an address by Dr. Woods, President of the University of Alabama, delivered at its first Commencement, Dec. 19, 1832.

In addressing the students generally, he urges them, 1st, To "aspire to eminence in knowledge;" 2d, "To keep aloof from all the distractions of party politics;" 3d, to form a just estimate of their own attainments and capacities; 4th, To have regard to the moral state of their hearts; and 5th, With all their gettings to "get moral worth."

In laboring to persuade his hearers to aspire to eminence in knowledge, Dr. Woods urges, with much force, the necessity of steady, persevering, untiring efforts, and insists that "labor is the price which our Creator requires us to pay for every earthly good." We do not remember to have seen more cogent reasons adduced for self-instruction, than in the following paragraphs.

"I do not regard any young gentleman as having taken the first step in the road to an honorable eminence who has not ceased to rely upon his friends, and his wealth, and every other factitious aid for success, and, who has not thrown himself entirely upon the energies of his own mind. His whole soul must be imbued with the conviction that his earthly destiny is, under God, in his own hands;—that he is to be what he makes himself, or, be assured, he never will be anything worthy of imitation.

"This, young gentlemen, is the secret of the success of our countryman, Franklin, and of many other men who have not enjoyed the advantages of public education with which you are favored. They soon learned that first lesson of all true greatness, a reliance upon one's own powers and the blessing of God. It was their self-education on which they rose to eminence. And permit me to tell you that every well-educated man, is, in a greater or less degree, a self-educated man. Seminaries of learning are useful, because in them only can the intellectual treasures of past ages and of the present generation, be collected together and spread out before the lovers of knowledge. Seminaries of learning are useful, because in them are gathered youth of noble aspirations; and by their constant intercourse and collision in the same lofty pursuits, their minds become polished, invigorated, and stimulated to higher and still higher attainments.

"Instructors are useful, because they may, by a judicious direction of your studies, prevent a useless expenditure of your time and energies. They may propose subjects for your investigation. They may point you the way to eminence. They may *aid* you in the great work of training and disciplining your mental powers:—but after all, that work must be *yours*. And yours will be the rich reward."—*American Annals of Education and Instruction*, III (1833), 142-43.

7. Henry Barnard comments on the University of Virginia and its students, 1833

The University buildings are situated on a beautiful eminence, a mile and a half from the center of the village about 3 miles from Monticello, the seat of Mr. Jefferson. It consists of a beautiful range of buildings, built on a hollow square—with a splendid Edifice at one end called the Rotunda—the Capitals were bought in Italy and cost a 1000 dollars each—parallel with this upper range, is a lower range of the same style of buildings—The Professors with their families reside in the college buildings. The students board in the college at what is called the Hotel. I took several meals with them—they bolt down their meals as fast as the cadets at Middletown ever did. What should you think of young men bearing the names of our country's distinguished sons, *playing* at marbles—I thought it was something new in a literary way. The students study no text books—hear lectures and are examined on them.

The students do not attend prayers—but the bell rings at 5 in the morning for them to get up and a monitor goes round once a week and if he find them in bed reports them to Board of the Faculty. They are a set of pretty wild fellows generally—principally from Va.—the fact that no religious exercises were introduced into the University here hurt its standing in the community. The students now employ a chaplain to preach to them once every Sunday.—Bernard C. Steiner (ed.), "The South Atlantic States in 1833, as Seen by a New Englander," *Maryland Historical Magazine*, Vol. XIII (September, 1919), 375-76.

8. Henry Barnard visits the University of North Carolina, 1833

I reached this seat of the University of North Carolina in the evening of Friday, a distance of 30 miles. . . . After supper I delivered my letters to Dr. Caldwell, the venerable President of this college, of which he was pleased to take such *kind* notice as to send for my baggage and beg of me to consider his house as my home during my stay in Chapel Hill; . . .

Dr. C. is a very distinguished man—has traveled in Europe, and by his energy and perseverance, built up and sustained this institution for 30 years. There are 3 buildings for students, and recitation rooms etc, and a small chapel and observatory. It numbers about 100 students —800 vols. in all the Library and a very respectable chemical and philo [sophical], apparatus. It was for a long time doubted at the North whether anything like college discipline could be maintained at the South, but I did not observe any difference between the habits of students here and at Yale—except that in this boasted land of refinement their manners are more rough and their dress, even vulgarly plain.—Steiner, *op. cit.*, 324-25.

9. Conditions are reported bad at the College of South Carolina, 1835

Among the various experiments tried in our country, the attempt was made in South Carolina, to establish and maintain a college, from which Christian influence should be in a great measure excluded by the character of its President. The number of students has declined from one hundred and fifty to fifty. The fine college buildings erected at the expense of the state, have fallen, in the language of the Governor, into "a ruinous condition," and the institution, into a "deplorable state of decay and disrepute." He announces to the Legislature from authority derived from every quarter of the State, "that the faculty of the College have become so generally obnoxious to our fellow-citizens on the score of the supposed religious heresies of some of them, and of the relaxation of moral and general discipline, and have so irrevocably lost the public confidence, as suitable persons to guard the morals and mould the opinions of the rising generation, as to render a radical reform, and thorough reorganization of the institution, a measure of indispensable necessity, and the only practicable means of reviving its prosperity, and extending its usefulness." The only "supposed religious heresy," so far as we have been able to learn, was the denial of the truth of Christianity. The officers have been requested to resign; several new professors have been appointed; tutors are to be dispensed with; and a Committee of the Trustees has been chosen to revise the laws, and reorganize the institution, which was to be opened during the last month. It has been intimated that a gentleman distinguished in military and political life will be appointed to the Presidency. We earnestly hope that he will not hazard the reputation he has gained, by attempting a new and delicate task, requiring qualifications so different from those of a statesman or a military officer.—*American Annals of Education and Instruction*, V (February, 1835), 92.

10. J. Marion Sims reports a duel in South Carolina College, 1833

I lived in the age of dueling. I was educated to believe that duels insured the proprieties of society and protected the honor of women. I have hardly a doubt but that, while I was a student in the South Carolina College, if anything had happened to have made it necessary for me to fight a duel, I would have gone out with the utmost coolness and allowed myself to be shot down. But my views on that subject were entirely changed, a long, long time ago.

The boys got up a mock duel one day between Frank Massey and Robert Burns. Frank was in the secret but poor Burns was not. But he behaved bravely. They fired cork bullets at each other. I always thought it a hard and foolish game to play off on a good fellow like Robert Burns.

There was a real duel in South Carolina College, just after I graduated. It was between Roach, of Colleton, and Adams of Richland District. Roach was a young man about six feet high and a physical beauty. Adams was no less so, though not so tall. Both men were of fine families, and Adams was supposed to be a young man of talent and promise. It occurred in this way. They were very intimate friends; they sat opposite to each other in the Stewards' Hall, at table. When the bell rang and the door was opened, the students rushed in, and it was considered a matter of honor, when a man got hold of a dish of butter or bread, or any other dish, it was his. Unfortunately, Roach and Adams sat opposite each other, and both caught hold of a dish of trout at the same moment. Adams did not let go; Roach held on to the dish. Presently Roach let go of the dish and glared fiercely in Adams's face, and said: "Sir, I will see you after supper." They sat there all through the supper, both looking like mad bulls, I presume. Roach left the supper-room first, and Adams immediately followed him. Roach waited outside the door for Adams. There were no hard words and no fisticuffs—all was dignity and solemnity. "Sir," said Roach, "What can I do to insult you?" Adams replied, "This is enough, sir, and you will hear from me." Adams immediately went to his room and sent a challenge to Roach. It was promptly accepted, and each went up town and selected seconds and advisers. And now comes the strange part of this whole affair: No less a person than General Pierce M. Butler, distinguished in the Mexican war as the colonel of the Palmetto regiment, and who became Governor of South Carolina, agreed to act as second to one of these young men. The other man had as his adviser Mr. D. J. McCord, a distinguished lawyer, a most eminent citizen, a man of great talents, whose name lives in the judicial records of the state as being the author of McCord and Nott's reports. Here were two of the most prominent citizens of South Carolina, each of them about forty years of age, aiding and abetting dueling between two young men, neither of them over twenty years of age.

They fought at Lightwood Knot Springs, ten miles from Columbia. They were both men of the coolest courage. My friend Dr. Josiah C. Nott, then of Columbia, and afterward of Mobile, Alabama, who died some eight years ago in Mobile, was the surgeon to one of the parties. They were to fight at ten paces distant. They were to fire at the word "one," raising their pistols. There are two methods of dueling: One is to hold the pistol erect, pointing heavenward, dropping it at right angles with the body at the word "Fire!" and then firing at the word one, two, or three; the other is to hold the muzzle down toward the earth, and then at the word to raise it at arm's length and fire. The latter method was adopted at the Roach-Adams duel. When the word "Fire!" was given, each started to raise his pistol; but each had on a frockcoat, and the flag of Roach's coat caught on his arm, and prevented his pistol from rising. When Adams saw that, he lowered his pistol to the ground. The word was then given a second time: "Are you ready? Fire! One!" They both shot simultaneously; Dr. Nott said it was impossible to tell which was before the other.

Adams was shot through the pelvis, and he lingered a few hours and died in great agony. Roach was shot through the right hip-joint, two or three inches below where his ball entered Adams's body. He lingered for a long time, and came near dying of blood-poisoning; but after weeks and months of suffering, he was able to get up, but was lame for life. I presume he was one of the most unhappy wretches on the face of the earth. He had killed his best friend, became very dissipated, and always, when he was drunk, the murder of Adams was his theme of conversation; doubtless, when he was sober, it troubled his conscience. He studied medicine and went to Philadelphia, to the Jefferson Medical College, and there he gave himself up entirely to dissipation. He had delirium tremens and died in Philadelphia, in an attack of it; I think it was in the month of January, 1836. During the latter part of his illness he was imagining that he was in hell, and begging the author of all torments to pour molten lead down his throat to quench his thirst. This account was given to me by a young man who was an eye-witness of this death-bed scene. . . .—J. Marion Sims, *The Story of My Life* (New York: D. Appleton and Company, 1885), pp. 88-91.*

11. Message of Governor McDuffie on South Carolina, 1835

It gives me very great pleasure to inform you that our College has resumed its labors under the most flattering auspices, and promises to

* For a very interesting account of the distinguished work of the great medical scientist and practitioner, see Seale Harris, M. D., *Woman's Surgeon: The Life Story of J. Marion Sims* (New York: The Macmillan Company, 1950).

be every way worthy of the liberal and enlightened patronage by which it has been heretofore sustained. Under the strong impulse it has received from the zealous exertions of the Board of Trustees, sustained by the patriotism of the whole State, it has already risen from its ruinous condition, and is pressing on, with renovated ardor, in the career of literary and scientific distinction. Under the guidance of a faculty, equally distinguished for high qualifications and devotion to their very important duties, it offers to the rising generation of our State, as many advantages as any similar institution in the United States. I cannot too strongly recommend it to the patronage of an enlightened Legislature, and to the countenance and support of every patriotic citizen. It is scarcely possible to place too high an estimate on its importance. Upon its successful administration will depend, in no small degree, the character and the destiny of the State. The very great and salutary change which it has produced in the character of our community, within the last thirty years, is an evidence of the high purposes to which it can be made subservient. Our experience, however, but too conclusively proves, that a munificent endowment by the Legislature, and a faithful performance of their respective trusts, by the Trustees and Faculty, are not of themselves sufficient to insure the success of this institution. The community at large must give it their countenance and support and in some sort, their superintendence. From all parts of the State, there should be a general attendance of our prominent and educated citizens at the annual commencements, who, with all the public functionaries, should be present to witness the performances of the youthful competitors for literary fame. Nothing could have a more salutory influence, in stimulating the exertions of the young men during the whole course of their college studies, than the prospect of this annual contest for distinction before the assembled intelligence of the State. The parents also, who place their sons in the institution, must give the Trustees their cordial co-operation, in effecting a reform in the extravagant habits of expenditure, which have heretofore prevailed, but too generally, amongst the students. Nothing is more unbecoming the character of a student, or more adverse to his proficiency in literary and scientific attainments, than these habits of extravagance. Every citizen is under obligations of patriotism, not less than of parental duty, to discountenance and repress such pernicious habits by withholding from his son the means of indulging them. Citizens of great wealth, in particular, owe it to the State, to set a public spirited example, in regulating the expenses of their sons, by reducing them to such a standard of economy, that the sons of citizens of moderate fortunes may not be tempted to go beyond their means to avoid disparaging imputations and invidious comparisons. With a view to this important reform, the trustees propose to adopt certain regulations, fixing a uniform dress which every student will be required to wear while under the authority of the College government, and a uniform limitation, upon the different branches of expenditure, which no student will be permitted to exceed.

I confidently hope that no parent will give the least countenance to any attempt on the part of his son to evade these salutary regulations. Small and unimportant as they may seem, the prosperity and usefulness of the College, as a public institution, will materially depend upon their rigid enforcement.

The appropriation made at your last Session for repairing the College edifices, has been applied with judgment and economy by the Committee of the Board of Trustees to whom that duty was confided. The College edifices are now in a complete state of repair, and the fund appropriated will be sufficient to enclose the College Campus, and all the buildings pertaining to the institution, with a substantial brick wall, which is now in progress and will soon be completed.

The number of students now in the College is eighty-five, of whom fifty-two have entered since the 1st of October last, and it is believed that by the 1st of January, the number will be not less than one hundred and ten; exceeding the most sanguine expectations indulged by the friends of the institution...

Before I dismiss the interesting subject of public instruction, I must call your attention to the consideration of a change, which I regard as highly expedient, in the regulations of our College. Though this is appropriately a classical institution, I am nevertheless of the opinion, that a knowledge of the dead languages should not be made an indispensable condition of obtaining all its privileges, its advantages, and its honors. I can perceive no adequate reason why ignorance of these languages should be an insuperable bar to the literary honors of the institution, however highly the candidate might be distinguished in all the other departments of literature and science.

The education of every citizen should be adapted to the pursuits of his future life. To those who are designed for the learned professions, or for employment strictly literary, or scientific, a knowledge of the classical languages of antiquity is highly appropriate, if not absolutely necessary. But those who are destined to follow mercantile or mechanical pursuits can employ the years devoted to education much more profitably than in acquiring a knowledge of the dead languages.

The principal consideration which recommends the proposed change to your favourable notice, will be found in the fact, that under the existing regulations, parents who design their sons for mercantile or mechanical pursuits will not give them a college education. However anxious to give them a liberal education in all other respects, they are unwilling to expend three or four years in what they regard as unprofitable studies to prepare them for obtaining such an education. The consequence is, that these highly important classes of the community usually receive no other education, than what they obtain in the primary schools.—*Journal of the General Assembly of South Carolina, 1835*, pp. 10-13.

12. The Trustees of the University of North Carolina pass resolutions on the death of President Joseph Caldwell, 1835

We have just received for publication the subjoined Resolution, adopted by the Executive Committee of the University, and can not but express our gratification, that the duty of preparing a Memoir of the Life of the late venerated head of the College, has been so appropriately assigned.

Whereas, The Executive Committee, with the deepest emotions of sorrow, have received intelligence of the death of the Reverend Joseph Caldwell, D. D. President of the University,

Resolved Unanimously, That by the eminent purity of his life, his patriotism, and zeal in the cause of learning, and his long, faithful and disinterested public services at the head of the University, Doctor Caldwell has approved himself one of the noblest benefactors of the State, and deserved the lasting gratitude and reverence of his countrymen.

Resolved, That, Professor Anderson be requested to prepare a Memoir, or Oration on the Life and Character of our deceased President, and to deliver the same in the College Chapel, on Wednesday afternoon, preceeding the next annual Commencement, in the presence of the Trustees, Faculty and Students of the Institution, who on that occasion, will wear the usual badge of mourning on the left arm.

Resolved, That his Excellency the Governor, President of the

Board of Trustees Communicate to Mrs. Caldwell, the widow of the deceased, a copy of these Resolutions, with an assurance of our deep sympathy and sincere condolence with her in afflicting bereavement which has fallen to her lot; and that a copy be also transmitted to the Faculty of the University.

Resolved, That these Resolutions be published in the several Gazettes printed in Raleigh.

Dun. Cameron, Ch'n.

By order.
Ch. Manly, Sec'y

Dr. Caldwell—As soon as the intelligence of the death of this estimable man reached Raleigh, Mr. A. S. Waugh, Artist, hastened to Chapel Hill, for the purpose of taking a cast of his countenance. We understand that he succeeded in his object and a bust of this good and great man will be the result.—*Randolph Recorder*, March 13, 1835.

13. Laws for the Government of the University of North Carolina, 1838

Of the Faculty.

The Faculty of the University of North-Carolina shall be composed of the President, Professors, and Tutors; a majority of whom being assembled, after due notice given by the President, or presiding Professor, to all the members, shall be competent to the transaction of business.

2. Every matter brought before the Faculty, shall be decided by votes, and it shall be the additional privilege of the President, or presiding Professor, to give a casting vote, when otherwise there would be a tie.

3. The Professors shall take rank according to the dates of their appointment.

4. The President may convoke the Faculty at his discretion, and the Faculty may also meet by adjournment.

5. The opinion or vote of any member of the Faculty, shall not be made known directly or indirectly to any one who is not a member of the body, except when express order shall be given to that effect by a unanimous decision of the Faculty.

6. A member of the Faculty shall not be a sitting member of any Society of Students.

7. It shall be the duty of every member of the Faculty individu-

ally, to be vigilant in carrying into effect every law of the College: and to report to the President or to the Faculty, such transgressions as ought to be punished by that body.

8. The Faculty shall keep a record of their proceedings; the senior Tutor shall be their Clerk, and make a fair and regular entry of their transactions in a book kept for that purpose. This record shall be laid before the Board of Trustees, when required by them.

9. No act of the Faculty, which is not recorded by their order, shall be considered valid.

10. It shall be the duty of the Tutors to reside in the buildings of the University, to maintain order and decorum among the students, and to assist under the direction of the President and Professors, in the instruction of the classes.

11. The Professors and Tutors shall, in succession, examine the rooms of the College, at least once a week, and see that cleanliness and neatness be preserved. In these visitations, they shall take an account of the locks, doors, windows and furniture, with the names of the inhabitants in each room. When damage of any description in the College buildings is at any time observed by a member of the Faculty, it shall be his duty to report it as soon afterwards as possible to the Bursar, that it may be immediately repaired.

12. It shall be the duty of each member of the Faculty, when he is to hear a class recite, to go to the Recitation Room, and take possession of it a reasonable time before the hour for the bell to ring, to prevent assemblages of Students before the proper time, and to see that the Recitation Room is in a proper condition for the reception of the class. The recitation of the class shall continue through the hour, or at least until the bell shall give notice of its expiration.

13. Every Professor shall have a room appropriated to him in the College. It is expected of the Professors, as pertinent to their office, to pass as much of their time every day in these rooms, as they conveniently can, to aid in the order and instruction of the College. The Board of Trustees will also look to the Professors to visit in succession the rooms of the Students at night, as often as convenient.

14. The Faculty of the University, that is the President and Professors, by and with the consent of the Trustees, shall have the power of conferring all such degrees or marks of literary distinction as are usually conferred in Colleges or Universities.

15. Immediately after every annual Commencement, the Faculty shall cause to be transmitted to the Secretary of the Board of Trustees,

a certificate signed by the Clerk of the Faculty, containing a specification of the persons graduated, and of the degrees respectively conferred upon them.

Of Admission into the University.

1. To take regular standing as a Student in the University, a candidate must sustain an approved examination before the Faculty, on such parts of the plan of education as have been already prosecuted by the class into which he would enter.

2. To become a Student on partial or irregular standing the candidate, if he be not twenty-one years of age, must exhibit a certificate from his parent or guardian, that he is permitted to enter on such terms. If he would prosecute any branch of science, into which a class is already advanced, he must be examined with approbation on such parts of the science as the class has already completed.

3. Every Student, at his admission, shall obtain a copy of the Laws from the Bursar, and a certificate with the name of the President or presiding Professor, signed by himself, of the Student's regular admission into the University; and these shall be at all times, a necessary testimony of his being a Student, to be shown when called for, to any member of the Faculty.

4. Every person, on admission into the University, shall pay the College dues for the session in advance.

5. If a Student shall enter before the session shall be half elapsed, he shall pay for the whole session; if he shall arrive at the middle of the session, or after it, he shall pay for half the session only; but room rent shall always be paid for the whole session.

6. If any person whose object it is to become a Student, shall fail to report himself to the President, on the first day after his arrival, he shall be excluded, if his reasons for delay be deemed valid by the Faculty.

7. Any native of the State, desirous of prosecuting his studies in the University, who shall furnish satisfactory evidence of good talents, studious habits and exemplary morals, and who shall be unable to defray the expense of tuition, may at the discretion of the Faculty, be admitted to all the recitations of the Classes, free from any demand for tuition. Such beneficiaries may occupy the rooms of the College, free of rent, when the rooms are not necessary for the accommodation of such Students as pay tuition and room rent.

8. The Faculty shall be authorised, in all cases, when, from ex-

amination, reasonable hopes can be entertained that deficiencies can be made up, to admit applicants for a single session, to whom regular standing shall be awarded at the end of that time, if the individual shall, upon examination, be found entitled to it.

9. An applicant shall not ordinarily be admitted into the University under the age of sixteen; but any applicant exhibiting in the opinion of the Faculty, the requisite strength and maturity of physical and mental constitution, and ample acquirements, and producing satisfactory testimonials of established moral character and steady habits, may be admitted, in the sound discretion of the Faculty, though he may not have attained this age.

Of the Bursarship.

One of the Professors shall be appointed Bursar of the University. It shall be his duty to receive from the Students the money or drafts for money they may bring with them, and disburse the same in paying the Board, Tuition fees, College dues, and other necessary expenses of the Students. He shall keep an account of the money received of, or for, and disbursed, for each Student, and at the close of each session, he shall render a copy of such account to the Parent or Guardian of each Student, and pay the balance (if any there be) to such Parent or Guardian, or to his or her written order.

2. Each Student, on his arrival at the University, shall pay over to the Bursar all money, or drafts for money, which may be committed to him for the payment of College expenses; and for his so doing, shall be considered as acting under a pledge of honor.

3. The Bursar shall be allowed five dollars for receiving and disbursing the money of each Student, which shall be paid at the close of each session, by the Treasurer of the University.

4. No Student of the University shall, during the session of College, under any pretence, contract any debt whatsoever; and if any Student violate this Ordinance, or if the Parent or Guardian of any such Student, or any other person in his or her behalf, shall pay or satisfy any debt so contracted by any such Student, such Student shall be forthwith dismissed from the University.

Collegiate Duties and Restrictions.

1. The business of the University shall commence without delay, on the first day of the session.

2. From the 1st of November to the 15th of February, morning

prayers shall be at a quarter before 7 o'clock; the rest of the year, morning prayers shall be at sunrise. From the first of September to the first of May, the hours of study in the forenoon shall be from 9 till 12, and from 2 till 5 in the afternoon; and the bell shall be rung for summoning the Students to their rooms at 8 o'clock in the evening. Through the other part of the year, the hours of study in the forenoon shall be from half past 8 till 12, and from 3 till 6 in the afternoon; and the bell shall be rung in the evening at 9 o'clock.

3. Every student shall regularly and punctually attend the recitation of his class at the place appointed by his instructer, and at the ringing of the bell to give him notice. He is not to be at the door of the recitation room, nor within it, nor loitering about the doors or passages of the buildings, before such notice is given. His Professor or Tutor shall call him to account for absence or delay, or neglect of preparation on the subjects assigned, and shall be the judge of his excuse. If a good reason be not shown for the delinquency, he may be cited before the Faculty to answer for it.

4. In the computation of absences from prayers and recitations, two tardinesses will be considered and marked as one absence, and retiring from the Recitation room during the progress of recitation will also be considered equivalent to an absence, and reported accordingly.

5. Whenever the absences of a student other than those occasioned by sickness or consequent upon permission either from prayers or recitation, shall exceed in any one month one fourth the whole number which such student was bound to attend, the fact shall be reported to his parent or guardian, with a request that he be forthwith withdrawn from the Institution, or he shall be dismissed, at the discretion of the Faculty.

6. Every student shall observe a strict propriety of conduct at recitation or lecture; refraining from every thing which shall interrupt business, or divert the attention of others; he shall not recline or lounge upon the benches, nor be employed in reading newspapers, nor any book or paper whatever, except such as the Professor or Tutor at the time shall direct. It is the duty of the student to attend exclusively to the subjects of lecture or recitation, as they proceed with a view to his own improvement and to that of the class. For gross or persevering violations of these rules of decorum, he may be forthwith dismissed from the room, when his instructor shall deem it necessary.

7. For the improvement of the students in public speaking, two or

more of them shall each deliver an oration, every evening immediately after prayers, on the stage in the public hall: and to this duty they shall be called in alphabetical rotation; nor shall any student be exempted from it, except for natural impediments, or other disqualifications, of which the Faculty may judge. The members of the Senior Class shall be excused from these exercises, and instead of them, shall pronounce at stated times, during each session, two orations of their own composition, one of which shall be at the commencement.

8. Should any student be absent from examination, he may be summoned before the Faculty to show the reasons of such absence, and he shall be examined publicly by the Faculty, before he shall be permitted to join his class.

9. No student shall absent himself from the University during the session, without permission first obtained from the President,[1] or in his absence from the presiding Professor. But leave of absence from recitation may be granted to a student by his Professor or Tutor.

10. If any student shall be habitually indolent or inattentive to business, or absent from prayers, recitation or public worship, or at any other time when it shall be his duty to attend, he shall be subject to penalty according to the aggravation of his delinquency.

11. If a student at an examination be found deficient, he may be publicly mentioned as a bad scholar by the Faculty or Trustees, admonished to greater diligence, or put into such class as shall suit his standing.

12. On the day of commencement, the candidates for degrees, shall perform such exercises as shall be appointed them, and no candidate shall decline the exercise assigned him, under penalty of being refused his diploma.

13. Every person obtaining a diploma, shall pay to the President of the University, for the degree of Bachelor of Arts four dollars, and for the degree of Master of Arts, five.

14. Nothing indecent, profane or immoral, shall at any time be delivered on the public stage, under such penalty as the Faculty or Trustees shall think necessary. And with a view to preserve all public exercises of the students from impropriety of any kind, every student, during the whole of his senior year, and previously to his commencement performances, especially, shall show to the President or presiding Professor, or to some officer designated by him, the whole of what

1. Most of the colleges and universities had such a law and many of them retained it in the catalogues until very recent years.

he proposes to speak, and shall not fail to observe such corrections as shall be made, and if any student pronounce any thing in public of a censurable nature, in contradiction to the directions or corrections of the officer to whom he has shown his piece, the President or presiding Professor may stop him on the public stage, and he shall be otherwise censured as the Trustees or Faculty shall determine.

15. If any student shall cut, or injure the buildings or furniture of the College, or in any manner disfigure or deface them, especially with obscenity, profaneness or vulgarity, he shall beside making good the damage, be subject to such other punishment as may be judged necessary.

16. The degree of Bachelor of Arts shall not be conferred on any member of the College, until he shall have been a student at least one year; but the honorary degree of Bachelor of Arts, may be conferred agreeably to former custom.

17. When a student occupies a room at the beginning of a session, he shall continue in it until the end of the session, unless a change be permitted or directed by the Faculty.

18. A student shall not be permitted to make any alterations in the studies which he has undertaken to prosecute in any session, until the session shall expire.

19. There shall be no ball playing [2] in or among the College buildings or against the walls. All athletic exercises must be kept at a distance, so as to prevent damage to the buildings and interruption to study.—*Acts of the General Assembly and Ordinances of the Trustees for the Government of the University of North Carolina* (Raleigh: Office of the Raleigh Register, 1838), pp. 8-14.

14. Rules on the Moral and Religious Conduct of Students in the University of North Carolina, 1838

1. If any student shall deny the being of a God, or the divine authority of the Holy Scriptures, or shall assert, and endeavor to propagate among the students any principle subversive of the Christian religion, he shall be dismissed.

2. Every student, whether he live in College or in the village, shall

2. Play was looked upon as evil generally. At Princeton playing "with balls and sticks" was considered "low and unbecoming gentlemen and students." Besides it was "attended with great danger to the health by sudden and alternate heats and colds," the faculty said. (Thomas Jefferson Wertenbaker, *Princeton, 1746-1896*, p. 138.) There he also says: "One suspects that life at Nassau Hall would have been more orderly had a part of each afternoon been devoted to some form of athletics."

attend public prayers morning and evening in the Chapel, and while attending shall refrain from all noise, conducting himself with such reverence and decorum as are suited to these sacred services. On Sunday it shall be the duty of every student to be present at the reading or delivery of a sermon in the Chapel, at the hour appointed by the Faculty for that purpose. No whispering, talking, reading, laughing or indecent behaviour of any kind shall be allowed on such occasions.

3. The students shall attend such instructions in morals or religion, as their Professors and Tutors, or the Faculty jointly shall appoint on Sunday. And if any student absent himself, or evade such instructions, he shall be punished by his instructor, or by the Faculty, according to his offence.

4. At all times the students shall deport and express themselves respectfully towards the Faculty, and every member of it. Any deficiency in this duty shall be considered as peculiarly in conflict with the laws and principles essential to a College, and shall be punished accordingly.

5. If a student making application for a privilege or immunity to one member of the Faculty, be refused, he shall not go to another member with the same request without informing him of the fact. His application however, may be renewed, if he shall think proper, to the Faculty as a body.

6. A Student shall not possess nor expose to another any book or picture that is impious or obscene.

7. No insulting language or treatment shall be offered by a Student or any number of students, to the people of the village, the country around the University, or of any other place.

8. If any Student or Students shall destroy or trespass on the property in the village or elsewhere, the authority of the College shall inflict an exemplary punishment on him or them, and any combination to prevent the execution of the civil law shall be severely punished.

9. A Student shall not go into the village on any account in the hours of study, without leave from some member of the Faculty.

10. No Student shall absent himself from the University, nor shall he attend any election without leave, unless it be to exercise the right of suffrage.

11. No Student shall make or attend horse races, nor bet upon them. They shall not keep fowls, nor in any manner participate in sporting with them.

12. A Student shall not engage in a game of hazard, nor shall he make any bet.

13. No Student shall keep a dog, or fire arms, or gunpowder. He shall not carry, keep, or own at the College, a sword, dirk, sword-cane, or any deadly weapon; nor shall he use fire arms without permission from the President.

14. No Student shall have spirituous or fermented liquors in his room, or even make use of them without permission from a Professor or Tutor.

15. A Student who shall be guilty of intoxication, shall be admonished, suspended, or dismissed, according to the nature and aggravation of his conduct.

16. No Student shall go to a tavern, beer house, or any such place, for the purposes of entertainment or amusement, without permission from some officer of the College; nor shall he on any occasion, keep company with persons of publicly bad character, under penalty of admonition, and if the practice be continued, of suspension or dismission.

17. If any clubs or combinations [3] of the Students shall at any time take place, either for resisting the authority of the College, interfering in its government, showing disrespect to the Faculty, or to any of its members, or for concealing or executing any evil design, the Faculty are empowered and directed to break up all such combinations as soon as discovered, and to inflict a severer punishment on each individual than if the offence intended had been committed in his individual capacity, whatever be the number concerned, or whatever be the consequence to the College.

18. Written petitions for the removal of grievances, shall not be signed by more than three Students.

19. All profane and indecent language shall be utterly excluded from the University. The Student who is guilty of using such language and on being warned, still perseveres, shall be admonished, suspended or dismissed, according to his offence.

20. Every Student who shall send to any person a challenge or message, either in writing or otherwise, purporting to be a challenge to fight a duel, shall be expelled.

21. Every Student who shall be the bearer of any challenge or message, in writing or otherwise, purporting to be a challenge, or in any wise relating thereto; or who shall, either directly or indirectly,

3. Such a law was often found in most of the colleges, seeming to reflect among governing authorities a fear of uprisings among the students.

have any agency therein, or in the duel that may be the consequence thereof, shall be expelled.

22. Any Student who shall accept a challenge to fight a duel, shall be expelled.

23. When a Student shall be expelled in consequence of the provisions of these Ordinances, he shall be delivered over to the civil authority, to be prosecuted as the law directs.

24. The Faculty of the University shall have full cognizance and jurisdiction of all offences under these laws against the atrocious act of duelling, and are hereby authorised and required to carry the same into full effect.

25. No Student shall associate or keep company with any person expelled from the University, on pain of such punishment as the Faculty shall think proper to inflict, consistently with laws of the Institution; provided that such punishment shall not extend to expulsion.

26. On Sunday the Students shall refrain from their ordinary diversions and exercises. They shall not fish, hunt or swim, nor shall they walk far abroad, but shall observe a quiet and orderly behaviour.

27. If any Student shall use any indecent gesture or language to any other Student or person, he shall be liable to be admonished.

28. If any Student shall be convicted of lying, he shall be admonished, suspended or dismissed, according to the degree of the offence.

29. If any Student, on being requested by any member of the Faculty to open the door of the chamber where he is, shall refuse or delay to comply, the door may be forced open and the Student compelled to make good the damage, and be otherwise punished as the Faculty shall judge proper.

30. If any Student shall be sent for by any member of the Faculty, and shall fail to come, he shall be held guilty of contempt of authority, and be punished accordingly.

31. The Students shall keep their rooms clean, and shall not put or procure to be introduced into the College, filth of any kind. Nor shall they throw on the outside of the College, against the walls, or around the buildings, any sort of dirt or rubbish, under such penalty as the offence may deserve.

32. No shouting, whistling, dancing, or any boisterous noise shall be permitted in the passages or rooms of the College at any time, upon such penalty as the nature of the offence may, in the judgment of the Faculty, properly incur. The Students shall not station themselves

either singly, or in groups in the doors or passages, or any where among the buildings, especially in the hours of study; and at any time when it shall appear necessary to the order of the College, such assemblies may be broken up and dispersed by any member of the Faculty.

33. If a Student shall strike another Student in anger, or in any manner to be guilty of a breach of the peace, it is a high offence, and shall be punished as such.

34. The absence of a Student from prayers, or from his room after the ringing of the bell, without leave in the evening, shall be registered by the Clerk of the Faculty. Once a week the absentees shall be regularly called to show their reasons of absence, and when the absences of a Student from prayers, from recitation, or from his room, especially in the evening, become frequent or numerous, he may be cited to answer for habitual delinquency, and such penalty be adopted as shall be judged necessary by the Faculty.

35. A Student who shall reside within two miles of the University in the vacation, shall be subject to the laws of the Institution in regard to moral conduct, so as to be responsible for violations of them, when he shall apply for admission in the ensuing session.

Punishments.

The punishments authorized for enforcing the laws shall be,

1. Private admonition by a member of the Faculty.

2. Admonition before the Faculty, by the President, or in his absence, by any one of their members whom the Faculty shall appoint.

3. Admonition before the class to which the Student belongs, by the President, or in his absence, by one of the members of the Faculty.

4. Public admonition before all the Students. This may be accompanied with a public confession of the fault, and a promise of reformation.

5. Suspension for a fixed time, not exceeding six months. This may be attended with admonition before the Trustees.

6. Dismission by order.

7. Expulsion; which punishment, except in cases of duelling, shall not be inflicted but with the sanction of five Trustees assembled.

8. When any Student shall be suspended, dismissed, or expelled, the President or presiding Professor shall address a letter to the parent or guardian of such Student, informing him of the event and its cause.

9. Any student who may be suspended or dismissed by the Faculty,

shall not during his suspension, or during the remainder of the session in which he is dismissed, reside within two miles of the University, upon pain of a change of sentence by the Trustees into that of expulsion. To this, exception is admissible, when the parents of the Student live within the assigned limits.

10. When a Student shall so persist in habits of indolence and neglect of collegiate duties, or in disorderly behaviour, that there is no hope of reclaiming him to habits of industry and order, it shall be the duty of the President to address a letter to the parent or guardian of each Student, stating the circumstances and advising him to withdraw him from the Institution; provided nevertheless, that nothing herein contained shall be so construed as to prevent the Faculty from suspending any Student when the same shall appear necessary.

Miscellaneous Regulations.

1. At the beginning of every session, the Students shall pay in advance one dollar each as room rent, and at the same time deposit with the Bursar three dollars each, to repair any damage they may commit; which sum, as far as unexpended, shall be returned at the end of the session; but if the damage shall exceed the sum deposited, the author shall pay the excess.

2. A Student shall not live in the College buildings in the vacation, without permission expressly obtained from the Bursar, or in his absence, from some member of the Faculty. The officer is expected to register the name of the Student thus permitted to reside, who is considered as pledging himself to make good all damages which he may commit. For all damages done in the room which he occupies, he is responsible, whether he cause them personally or not; and he may be directed to relinquish his residence in the buildings at any time in the vacation.

3. The Students on leaving their rooms at the end of the session, or at any other time during the vacation, shall put the keys of their rooms into the hands of the Bursar.

4. It shall be the duty of the Bursar, at the beginning of every vacation, to have the doors and windows of the public buildings carefully fastened, where they are not inhabited. And if damages be done which he could not prevent, and of which the authors are unknown, he shall repair them at the expense of the Board.

5. It is recommended to the Students to be plain in their dress, but it is required of them always to appear neat and cleanly. If any Student

be negligent in this respect, it shall be the duty of the College officers to admonish him for it, and if he persevere, to report him to the Faculty.

6. If a Student be present at the beginning of a session, he may claim the room occupied by him at the end of the preceding session; but if not, it may be inhabited by the first occupant. More than two persons may not live in one room at any time, without permission specially obtained.

7. No Student, without permission from the President or presiding Professor, shall go beyond the prescribed limits in study hours, or at any other time when the bell may call him to his duty.

8. A Student shall not receive visitors into his room, nor shall he visit others in the hours of study, without leave from a member of the Faculty.

9. No Student shall disturb or attempt any imposition on any of his fellow Students in any manner whatever; and every Student shall preserve order and decorum in his own room, and shall be responsible for all disorder committed in it, unless he give information, when in his power, of the person or persons from whom it proceeded.

10. The Faculty may interdict any house in the village as improper for the reception of Students as boarders, on account of the irregularities in which they are permitted or tempted to live, or the disorderly and pernicious examples set before them.

11. A Student may not occupy a room for residence out of College, till each of the rooms shall have two inmates. But Professors may receive Students to reside in their houses, and the Faculty may permit a Student to live in the village, when they shall judge his situation requires such indulgence.

12. At the ringing of the bell the first time in the morning, the Students shall rise to prepare for business. As soon as the bell shall ring a second time, they shall repair to the hall without delay, and attend prayers.—*Ibid.*, pp. 14-20.

15. Rules about the Librarian and the Library of the University of North Carolina, 1838

Of the Librarian and Library.

1. No person but a Trustee or Member of the Faculty shall at any time have access to the Library, without the presence of the Librarian or some officer of the College.

2. The Senior Tutor shall be the Librarian, and at the end of every session, shall present to the Faculty a written report on the state of the Library.

3. Such books as, by a determination of the Faculty, ought not to be taken out by the Students, may be consulted by them in the Library, on such days, and within such hours, as shall be appointed by the Faculty.

4. A Student may not, at any time, take down a book from the shelves of the Library. The Librarian alone is to deliver it to him, and return it to its place.

5. When a Student shall take a book out of the Library, he shall sign a receipt, in which the book shall be specified by the Librarian.

6. A volume shall not be kept out of the Library more than one week, without being returned to the Librarian, and the receipt for it renewed. If any other person shall want the volume at the end of that time, the one who has already had it shall not then take it out anew.

7. When a book shall be given out or returned, the Librarian shall examine it, to see if it be damaged or defaced; and if a Student shall deface or damage a book belonging to the Library, he shall pay according to the damage done, as estimated by the Faculty, even to the re-placing of the set. If he shall lose it, he shall pay to the Librarian its value, as estimated by the Faculty, or else he shall replace it as above. If he shall fail to return it in two weeks after taking it out of the library, he may be judged to have lost it, and the Faculty may proceed accordingly. If a Student shall refuse to comply with the decisions of the Faculty on these subjects, he may be admonished, suspended or dismissed, as the nature of the case may require.

8. The Librarian shall keep a catalogue of all the books of the Library. If any book shall be presented to the University, the name and residence of the donor shall be recorded.

9. The Librarian shall appoint a day and hour for delivering and receiving books, and shall attend once a week for these purposes.

10. While the Students are attending at the Library, they shall observe an orderly deportment.

11. A Student shall not lend a book which he has taken out of the Library, without permission from the Librarian.

12. It shall be the duty of each Professor and Tutor in the University, to keep a regular account of the scholarship of each Student during his course, noting his regularity and moral conduct, and at the end of each session, to furnish the parent or guardian of the Student

with an abstract or account of the same, and cause this account to be laid before the Board of Trustees at the Public Anniversary Examinations.

The Literary Societies.

1. The two Literary Societies having by former compact, agreed to apportion between them the College Buildings, and to make good the damages and dilapidations they may sustain, the following partition shall be recognized and respected, viz: the South ends of the East and West Buildings shall be occupied by the members of the Dialectic Society, and the North ends by those of the Philanthropic; the division of the South Building, as heretofore made by the Societies, shall be still maintained.—*Ibid.*, pp. 8-21.

16. Extracts from the minutes of the faculty of East Tennessee University, 1840-1847

E. T. University
Nov. 13, 1840

The faculty met.

The proceedings of the last meetings of the Faculty were read. The reports of the College classes were made, & entered in file with the records of the Faculty

Res: That hereafter no student that leaves any of the regular College studies shall be enrolled with the regular Classes.

Res: That no student shall have more than four studies at any one time.

Campbell was appointed Monitor for the Senior Class—Moore for the Junior—Martin for the Sophomore—Allen for the Freshman and Zimmerman for the Preparatory Department.

The Faculty reported that rooms of College had been regularly visited during the week, & that the order of College had been good.

Adjourned to meet Friday evening next at early-Candle lighting.

E. T. University
Nov. 20, 1840

The Faculty met.

The proceedings of the last meeting of the Faculty were read.

The Reports of the College Classes were made and entered on file with the records of the Faculty.

The Faculty reported that the rooms of College had been regularly visited during the week, and that the order of College had been good.

Adjourned to meet Friday evening next at early Candle-lighting.

E. T. University
Nov. 27, 1840

The Faculty met.

The proceedings of the last meeting of the Faculty were read.

The reports of the College Classes were made and entered on file with the records of the Faculty.

The Faculty reported that the rooms of College had been regularly visited and that the order of College was good.

Res. That hereafter students be not allowed the recitation rooms, for the purpose of writing &c for the reason that thereby the safety of the property is endangered.

Res. That the Sophomore Class be required hereafter to recite a lesson on each Monday in the year in the Greek Testament, in the place of the usual Greek lesson.

Winter Session
E. T. University
Oct. 21, 1842

The Faculty met, for the first time this session, Members present, Joseph Estabrook, President, Profrs. Garvin, Maynard, & Keith

The following arrangement was made, in the Rhetorical & Belles Lettres department, for the present session—

I. The Freshman Class shall declaim & write compositions once a week, alternately, as heretofore.

II. The Sophomore Class shall [have] a resitation in E. Grammar & Punctuation, Newmans Rhetoric once a week, and also present written compositions, once a fortnight.

III. The Junior Class shall have a recitation once a week in Hedges Logic & write compositions.

IV. The Senior Class, besides publicly speaking their own compositions, shall debate or have some other Rhetorical exercise, as often as may be convenient, before the President, further,

Res. That two from each Class shall publicly declaim in the Chapel once a week, the Seniors speaking their own compositions & that each Profr. shall drill the speakers privately before they appear in public.

Res. That Profr. Maynard visit E. Hall twice a week during the day, & the same of an evening, that Profr. Garvin visit W. Hall in the same manner & Profr. Keith the Dormitories the same.

Res. That every Profr. visiting rooms or at any other time, finding a student absent, or seeing any other deficiency, it is made his duty, to note the crime, on paper, together with the name of the offender, and left in the Presidents room, & that he hand it to the Profr. [incomplete]

Adjourned

June 20/46 The regular meeting of the Faculty was held, the weekly reports made and recorded.

In accordance with a resolution of the Faculty passed at their last meeting Prof. Lea reported the following regulations in relation to the Uniform dress which were adopted;—

The Trustees have enacted that: All students connected with the University are required to wear the following uniform dress viz. For winter, a frock coat with standing collar of Cadet [illegible] or cloth not exceeding $2.50 per square yard; and pantaloons of the same. For summer, the coat & pantaloons may be of lighter material of the same color & must not exceed in cost that prescribed for winter.

For the purpose of carrying into effect the design of the Board of Trustees in the enactment of the foregoing regulations, the Faculty prescribe the following specifications and regulations;—

The coat shall be single breasted, with one row of buttons in front, seven in number ¾ inch in diameter, flat surface, extending down to the waist and not below; collar not exceeding 2¼ inches high & padded so as to stand up; two hooks & eyes in front, both sides of same material; sleeves cut to the shape of the arm, with three small buttons at each wrist, and without other trimmings; shirts lined with plain black stuffs, not exceeding 50 cts per square yard in cost, fold in each behind with button at top and bottom; pockets in folds of shirts & none else where. Shirts to terminate at six inches above knee.

The Pantaloons shall be made plain, with whole falls and without stripes or braid down the seams.

The vest shall be made plain of any color, the cost and pattern and trimmings not to exceed $2—

The Hat shall not exceed $5 in cost for the winter Hat, and $1 for summer Hat including trimmings.

Shoes shall [not] exceed $2 and Boots $4 per pair—

The Over Coat, when purchased hereafter, shall be of same material as the coat for winter, with the same limitations as to cost, made in same manner & with same trimmings except that the collar will be turned down, the buttons 1½ inches in diameter & the skirts to extend six inches below the knee.

The clothing herein prescribed will be worn by every student at all times when engaged in any public duty at the University, or when absent for any purpose from the inclosure around the the University buildings, unless specially excused by some member of the Faculty.

Voted that the disorders of each student be added up, that those having 12 disorder marks be admonished by the President and that those who have been previously admonished by him, be brought before the Faculty and reprimanded. Also that Lenoir & Welch be brought before the Faculty for special disorder.

...At a subsequent meeting S. W. Beckham was reported by Mr. Lyman & Mr. Kirkpatrick, for harboring a profligate woman in his room during a portion of the night, and also for having exhibited a bowie knife. Beckham being called before the Faculty, acknowledged the woman was in his room, said she came on the Hill without his knowledge, said Mr. D. G. Campbell was in the room with him; and that the bowie knife was Mr. Campbell's. After deliberation the Fac. Resolved that S. W. Beckham be dismissed from the Institution. (It was the understanding of the Faculty however, that it was possible for him to be restored next term.) Resolved that the withdrawal of D. G. Campbell, ordered at a previous meeting, be changed into a dismission from the Institution.

Adjourned

E. T. University
August 4, 1847

The Exercises of the Annual Commencement were this day held and the degree of A.B. conferred on the seven young gentlemen, recommended to the Board of Trustees by the Faculty on the 14th Ultimo.

The degree of A.M. was also conferred on

Justin P. Garvin
Albert G. Welcker
Barry C. Hunt
Robert H. Armstrong
John Beauchamp

The result of the Examination of all the classes was made known, whereupon the following orders were passed by the Faculty;

1. That D. B. Branchitt, deficient in French, be required to make up such deficiency in vacation.
2. That J. M. Varner, deficient also in French be required to make up deficiency in vacation.
3. That F. A. Brown, deficient in Greek, be required to make up deficiency by reading Demosthenes 2nd oration during vacation, deficiency also in Composition to be made up by his writing a composition of not less than three pages, and to prepare declamation for the beginning of the next term. Gamble, deficient in Composition, to make up deficiency by writing a composition in vacation. F. A. McClung, being deficient in Greek Mathematics and Composition, was not advanced but required to go over the Sophomore year again. Hu White, deficient in Mathematics and Composition, was prohibited from [grad]uating with his class until such deficiencies are made up. H. L. Moore, deficient in Mathematics, to take Sophomore standing or study during vacation and be examined at the beginning of the next term. Girard Cook deficient in Composition and Declamation. Ingles deficient in Mathematics, Composition and declamation; his father to be informed of the facts, and use his discretion about sending him back another term. Crumpton, deficient in Latin, Greek, Mathematics, Declamation and Composition; not examined in Greek;—to study in vacation and be examined. Snoddy deficient in Latin, Declamation and Composition—deficiencies to be made up in vacation. Moses White, deficient in Mathematics deficiency to be made up in vacation by reviewing Geometry. C. L. Warner deficient in Mathematics—to review Geometry in vacation. That Walthale take Freshman studies next term.

The following are the result of the examination of candidates for admission to the Freshman class—

1 M. W. Baker Admitted.
2 M. M. Armstrong deficient in orthography English Grammar and Greek.
3 M. J. Beardin deficient in orthography History U.S.A. Composition and Latin.
4 G. M. Boyd deficient in Arithmetic and Greek.
5 R. M. McClung deficient in Eng. Grammar.
6 Wm. Dailey Admitted.
7 M. M. McClung deficient in Geography, Composition and Greek.
8 C. D. Moore Deficient in Composition, Latin and Greek.
9 D. H. Parker deficient in Orthography and Greek.

10 G. H. Parker deficient in orthography & writing.
11 P. A. Philpot deficient in Latin.
12 Rathbon deficient in Composition and Greek.
13 J. G. Deaderick, not examined.

–Minutes in the University of Tennessee. Photocopy in the Southern Historical Collection, the University of North Carolina.

SCHEME OF THE EXCERCISES

AT THE

COMMENCEMENT

OF THE

UNIVERSITY OF NORTH CAROLINA,

JUNE 2ND, 1842.

FORENOON.

1. Prayer.
2. Salutatory Oration. FRANCIS T. BRYAN, *Raleigh.*
3. Oration. "Obligations of Educated men." JOSEPH J. SUMMERELL, *Northampton.*
4. Oration. "Principles of the Old Federal Party." RUFUS BARRINGER, *Cabarrus.*
5. Oration. "Spirit of Reform." WILLIAM H. HAIGH, *Fayetteville.*
6. Oration. "Reciprocal influence of Science and Religion." WILLIAM F. LEWIS, *Edgecombe.*

AFTERNOON.

1. Éloge de Louis-Philippe. WILLIAM A. BELL, *Greene Co:, Ala.*
2. Oration. "Reverence for the Past." WILLIAM S. MULLINS, *Fayetteville.*
3. Oration. "The Middle Ages." WILLIAM F. MARTIN, *Elizabeth City.*
4. Degrees conferred.
5. Report of the Faculty.
6. Valedictory. THOMAS J. MORISEY, *Sampson.*
7. Prayer.

Illustrissimo JOHANNI M. MOREHEAD,

Carolinæ Septentrionalis Reipublicæ

GUBERNATORI;

Honorando DAVIDI L. SWAIN,

FACULTATIS PRÆSIDI;

Omnibusque Senatus Academici Sociis;

Universis denique Humanitatis Cultoribus;

Exercitationes hasce Juvenes hodie primi gradus in artibus honorem petentes.

Ricardus-Jacobus Ashe
Rufus Barringer
Gulielmus-Alexander Bell
Franciscus-Theodorus Bryan
Jacobus-Augustus Caldwell
Jacobus-Williamson Campbell
Robertus-McGregor Campbell
David Coleman
Jacobus-Lawrence Dusenbery
Stephanus-Sneed Green
Gulielmus-Hooper Haigh
Gulielmus-White Harriss
Carolus-Paulus Heartwell
Gulielmus-Jacobus Hayes
Petrus-Jacobus Holmes
Joannes-Findley Jack
Gulielmus-Figures Lewis
Gulielmus-Franciscus Martin
Gulielmus-Pinckney McBee
Thomas-Junius Morisey
Gulielmus-Sydney Mullins
Israel-Leonidas Pickens
Nathaniel Hill Quince
Georgius-Washington Ruffin
Joannes-Baptist Smith
Ashley-Wood Spaight
Josephus-Joannes Summerell
Ruffin-Wirt Tomlinson
Ricardus-Don Wilson.

Reverenter dedicant.

Die Junii secundo, Anno Salutis,

MDCCCXLII.

VI

1841–1850

1. John C. Calhoun selects the University of Virginia for his son, John, 1841

I have in a great measure made up my mind to send John to the Virginia University, where he can select his studies. I do not think he has any taste for the classicks. I wish him to cease their study, and direct his studies to arithmetick, Geometry, English Grammar, if not already familiar with it, writing, including spelling and composition, till I return. If it does not put you to inconvenience, I would be glad you would see Mr. Anderson in reference to his studies and request his particular attention to him; and do urge on John the importance of exerting himself.—John C. Calhoun to Thomas G. Clemson, July 11, 1841. J. Franklin Jameson (ed.), "Correspondence of John C. Calhoun," *Annual Report of the American Historical Association*, 1899, Vol. II, 481.

2. A traveler comments on the University of Georgia, 1842

The board of trustees of the University is formed of twenty-seven of the most eminent men in the State, including the governor, several of the judges, barristers, physicians, and private gentlemen of fortune. The faculty consists of a president, six professors, and two tutors, with a librarian and secretary. The students, at present 127 in number, are divided into the classes of seniors, juniors, sophomores, and freshmen.

The period for entering college in the freshman class, must not be earlier than fourteen years of age; and the students often remain till they are past twenty-one. The whole expenses of a student for a year do not exceed 180 dollars; and the charge is thus apportioned—tuition in every branch, 50 dollars; board 114 dollars; washing 9 dollars; fuel, 7 dollars; so that 36 pounds sterling covers the entire cost of board, lodging, washing, attendance, and instruction! There is an annual public examination at "Commencement," as it is called, which occurs on the first week in August, when degrees are conferred, and prizes are awarded; and on this occasion, the families and friends of the students repair to Athens from all parts of the Country, so that the town is literally full. This lasts for about a week, and is succeeded by a week's vacation. The great vacation is, however, in the winter for ten weeks, from the 1st. of November to the 16th. of January, as this is the period of the year in which it is safest and best for such of the students as live in the low country to visit their families and friends.

The salaries of the professors do not exceed 1,500 dollars, or 300 pounds sterling a year; but this may be deemed equivalent to 500 pounds a year in England, as to its sufficiency for maintaining themselves and families, according to the moderate scale of expenditure with the best classes here.—J. S. Buckingham, *The Slave States of America* (Fisher and Son, 1842), II, 74-75.

3. William D. Williamson of Maine visits and comments on the University of North Carolina, 1843

... Six years after the Peace, the subject of Education was brought up in General Assembly. The preamble of the Bill reported, contains these, excellent sentiments. "In all well regulated governments, it is the indispensable duty of every Legislature to consult the happiness of the rising generation, and to endeavor to fit them for an honorable discharge of the several duties of life, by paying the strictest attention to their education; and an University supported by permanent funds and well endowed, will have the most direct tendency to answer this purpose." Therefore, on the 11th day of December, 1789, "THE UNIVERSITY OF NORTH CAROLINA" was established by the Legislature. The Board of Trustees incorporated, consisted of forty gentlemen, the most learned and influential in the State. They had their first meeting, at Fayetteville, in November of the next year; and when organized, they made it their earliest business to devise the means needful for the support of the Institution, and to determine upon a place for its location.

Immediately after the University was chartered, the Legislature granted to the Trustees, all escheated property, and all arrearages due to the State, from receiving officers of the late and present governments up to January 1, 1783. Soon afterwards, Benjamin Smith gave the Board 20,000 acres of land; and the Legislature, in December, 1791, magnanimously loaned them $10,000, which was subsequently converted into a gift. Thus encouraged, the Trustees proceeded to establish the University on a commanding site at Chapel Hill. Shortly afterwards, generous individuals in the vicinity gave them 1,392 acres of land, embracing the area of the site itself; also Charles Gerard conveyed to them other 13,000 acres of valuable land; and in April 1796, General Thomas Pason, of Granville, made them a present of $1,025 in cash. In farther evidence of the inspiring interest generally taken in behalf on the Institution throughout the community, the ladies of Raleigh, for instance, presented it, in 1802, with an elegant pair of globes and a compass; and afterwards, the ladies of Newbern in like manner gave a quadrant, pledging themselves "never to be indifferent to the promotion of science, which so much strengthens the principles of virtue, imparts civility to manners, and embellishes the refinements of life." In additional aid to the University, $5,080 were drawn into its treasury in 1803—the fruits of two lotteries granted by law; in 1809, the Legislative Assembly, granted to the Trustees, all confiscated estates—all monies in executors' and administrators' hands, unclaimed by legatees or heirs; and all debts due to the State up to December 1799. Munificent gentlemen have replenished the Library by donations of valuable books; so that the property owned by the Corporation, and the sums received into their treasury, considerably exceed half a million of dollars; about a third part of which yields an annual income principally appropriated, with the tuition-money, to remunerate the University Instructors. . . .

In 1821 the Board of Trustees was enlarged to sixty-five; the Governor being *ex officio* their president, and all vacancies occurring, the two houses of Assembly filled by a joint ballot. To replenish the library, and form cabinets, Dr. Caldwell, under the patronage of the Trustees, visited Europe, in 1824, and procured a very valuable Philosophical Apparatus, wrought under his own inspection, and obtained a considerable addition to the Library. There has since been added a cabinet of Minerals, which was purchased at Vienna. Dr. Caldwell has been called "the father of the University;" his connexion with it was nearly forty years; his sepulchre is in the vicinity of the college; and his praises are in all the region.

The *Classic Course* is fully prescribed and annually published. To be admitted into the *Freshman Class*, the applicant must in general be sixteen years of age, and sustain an approved examination in the English, Latin and Greek languages, and Latin prosody; in Mair's Introduction on Andrew's Exercises; in 5 books of Caesar's Commentaries; in Gould's edition of extracts from the first six books of Ovid's Metamorphoses; in Virgil's Bucolics, and six first books of the Æneid; in Sallust, in Greca Minora, or the Greek Reader; in Arithmetic, and in ancient and modern Geography.

The studies of the *Freshmen* are Livy, Virgil, Greca Majora, Algebra, Cicero, Geometry, and Exercises in writing Latin.

The Classics of the *Sophomores*, are Greca Majora, Homer's Illiad, Horace, Trigonometry, Logarithms, Mensuration, Geometry, Juvenal, Demosthenes, Surveying and Navigation, Differential and Integral Calculus, a review of Geography, and Exercises in writing Latin.

Those of the *Juniors* are Tacitus, Exercises in Latin Construction, Differential and Integral Calculus, Natural Philosophy, Rhetoric, French, Greek Tragedy, Astronomy, Logic, Elements of History and Chronology.

The *Seniors* study Chemistry, and Mineralogy, Political Economy, Moral Philosophy, Tragedians in Greca Majora, Technology, Exercises in Latin Construction, Astronomy, French, Mental Philosophy, National and Constitutional Law, Chemistry and Geology and Horace's Art of Poetry.

There are other exercises interspersed through the whole course. The three lower classes are required to declaim in private before the Professor of Rhetoric, and afterwards periodically in presence of the Faculty. The Senior Class deliver orations of their composition, on the public stage, twice at least in each term or session. A regular course of Lectures on Chemistry, Mineralogy and Geology, illustrated by experiments and the exhibition of specimens, is delivered to the Senior Class by the Professor of Chemistry; and he also gives lectures in other departments of Natural History. There are likewise lectures and experiments in Natural Philosophy and Mathematics.

The *Text-books* besides those in the Languages, are, the treatises of Professor *Pierce* on Algebra, Geometry, Trigonometry, Logarithms, Mensuration, Navigation, Surveying, Differential and Integral Calculus; *Dr. Blair's* Rhetoric; *Olmstead's* Natural Philosophy and Astronomy; *Hedge's* Logic; *Dr. Mitchell*, a professor of the University, on Chemistry, Mineralogy, and Geology; *Dr. Wayland* on Political Economy, and Moral Philosophy; *Bigelow* on Technology; *Abercrombie* on Mental Philosophy; and *Chancellor Kent* on National and Constitutional Law.

The instruction is committed to *nine* Teachers who devote their whole time to the University and constitute THE FACULTY.

1. Hon. David L. Swain, LL.D. is *President, and Professor of National and Constitutional Law.* He also gives instruction in Mental and Moral Philosophy and in Political Economy. He is a native of Buncome County, N. Carolina, now probably some years past middle aged. He was for a period a student in the University; he then read

law at Raleigh, in that State, where he was admitted to the Bar. He commenced his professional practice in his own county, in which he was permitted however to pursue it a few years only, before he was commissioned to a seat on the Supreme Bench, from which he was elected by the people, the Governor of the State. Next he was chosen to the Presidency of the University; for which his strength of intellect, his acquaintance with human nature, and his weight of character were qualifications everywhere acknowledged. Few men have his capacity to make giant acquisitions from books, and fewer his faculty of success in an easy and judicious management of the students. By well-timed pains-taking and a constant regard for their highest good, he persuades them, as they are the sons of family and privilege, always to be emulous of character and scholarship. In return, they cheerfully render him the meed of true and exalted respect, so much his due. Of the sciences in his department of instruction, he is a learned master; and though he makes no profession, as a church-member, his supreme regard for religion, and his orthodox lectures to the students on Bible history, present a surer test of the excellent principles which he makes the standard of his faith and the rule of his life.

2. Rev. Elisha Mitchell, D.D. is *Professor of Chemistry, Mineralogy, and Geology*. His native place was Litchfield, Connecticut; and he was a graduate in 1813, at Yale College. Most of the next year he was a student in theology at Andover, Ms. Two years his *Alma Mater* employed him as a tutor; and being licensed to preach the gospel, he was elected in 1816, to the professorship of Mathematics in this University. Thorough as he truly is in all the College branches of study, he is esteemed most highly for his superior learning in those of the department he now fills. He has published a short system of Geology, which is used by the students as a Classic. He is a sound evangelical divine of the Presbyterian faith, and an excellent preacher. His doctorate in divinity, he received from the University of Alabama. He is a gentleman of New England manners, accessible, cordial, sedate; and his learned acquaintances assign to him high rank in all the sciences.

3. Rev. James Phillips, A.M., is *Professor of Mathematics and Natural Philosophy*. This gentleman was born and educated in England; A Dissenter there and a Presbyterian here. The reputation he acquired as a teacher in New York, and his character as a man of science, prominently served to advance him to a professorship in the University. He is a true lover of literature and shines in its several

spheres. Of his excellent family—two sons, now resident graduates, are preparing for the Christian ministry, in the study of their pious father.

4. John D. Hooper, A.M., is *Professor of the Latin Language and Literature, and of French.*—He was born in Wilmington, N.C.; graduated at this University in 1831; and in 1836, advanced to his present professorship. He is of Episcopalian profession—a gentleman eminent for his abilities and scholarship; always at home in the Roman tongue, and a remarkably good French linguist.

5. Manual Fetter, A.M., *Professor of Greek Language and Literature,*—is from New York—a graduate and master of arts at Columbia College. He is thoroughly skilled in the idiomatic dialects and attic literature of the ancient Grecians, and has been Professor six or seven years. His high standing as a critical instructor deservedly receives special consideration.

6. Rev. William M. Green is *Professor of Rhetoric and Logic:*—a native of Wilmington, N.C., and in 1814 a graduate at this University. He is an Episcopal clergyman, urbane in his manners, and said to be a very chaste and correct writer and accomplished speaker. He fills his professional chair much to the credit of himself and of the institution.

7. Rev. Charles M. F. Deems, A.M., a graduate, in 1840, of Dickinson College, Carlisle, is *adjunct Professor of Rhetoric and Logic.* This additional establishment evinces what ample provision is made, and emulation manifested in favor of composition and oratory. Mr. Deems is a young minister of the Methodist persuasion, of flowing mind and free utterance. Blessed with fine intellectual powers, a brilliant imagination and a benign temperament, he is calculated to be both a popular preacher and professor.

8. William H. Owen, A.M., is *a Tutor of Ancient Languages.* He was born in Henry County, Virginia; was a graduate of this University, in the class of 1833; and two years afterwards, the Trustees elected him to a Tutorship. To qualify him for his sphere of trust, he possesses a retentive memory, and a discriminating mind,—he is thoroughly read in the science of grammar, and always manifests a very anxious desire that those whose pupilage passes under his tuition, may excel in their studies, and be real scholars. Were his health equal to his mind and his learning, he need thank no one for encomiums. He was been offered a tutorship in the College of William and Mary,—an offer, however, he declined to accept, though tempted by the promise of a larger salary.

9. Ralph H. Graves, A.M., is *a Tutor of Mathematics.* His birthplace was in Granville County, N.C. His fame as a Mathematician, he acquired while a sophister in College; and in 1837, the Trustees elected him a tutor in that department.

These are the members of the Faculty—always accessible to the students, always frank and courteous to strangers. The former are treated as young gentlemen; none of them, not even the Freshmen are accounted underlings to those in higher classes, according to usages in ancient times at our oldest Colleges. All the Faculty receive competent salaries; the President and three or four of the Professors are furnished by the Trustees with dwelling-houses. The Tutors have their rooms in the College-buildings.

The religious character of the University is evangelical or orthodox —not sectarian. Morning and evening prayers are strictly attended daily by professors and students; and special regard is paid to the Sabbath and Divine worship; to the morals of the students and their deportment. There is a Legislative statute, which makes it penal for any person at Chapel Hill, or within two miles of it, either to retail spirituous liquors, to sell any goods, wares or merchandize to a student of the University; or to exhibit any theatrical, sleight of hand or equestrian performances, or rope-dancing, without license in writing from the Faculty; and all games of chance are strictly forbidden by law. So faithfully are these provisions carried into effect, that no spirituous liquors nor wines can be purchased there by a student, or even a stranger, without a Physician's certificate. Every student is likewise strictly forbidden by College-laws to have any spirituous or fermented liquors in his rooms, to keep fire-arms or any dangerous weapon, or to engage in any game of hazard. On the contrary, all encouragement is given to promote learning, and practice the moral virtues. Young men, natives of the State, able to produce evidence of talents, studious habits, and exemplary morals, have their tuition and room-rent free, if they cannot pay for them; and usually ten or twelve students, every year, avail themselves of this privilege. The students are engaged in their studies and recitations from eight to ten hours daily, recite sixteen times in every week; and actually pass nine months in the year at the University. Two or more of them declaim, on the stage in the public Hall, every evening immediately after prayers: often in private before the Professor of Rhetoric, and daily before their class, after recitations.

Appurtenant to the University are two Literary Societies, the DIA-

LECTIC and PHILANTHROPIC, instituted in 1795; and to one or the other belong all the College students. There are two classes of members, *regular* and *honorary*. They have their exhibitions, and alternately choose an older member to deliver an address in the Chapel before the Societies, on the day preceding the annual Commencement. Theirs and the College Libraries contain about 12,000 volumes, besides unbound pamphlets.

The sessions, or terms, the vacations, and the public examinations every year, are severally two. The anniversary Commencement is on the first Thursday of June: appointed so early, that the students may have afterwards their six weeks' vacation, before the return of the sultry season; as this is sometimes unhealthy in more southern latitudes, where many of the students reside. The other vacation is of the same length from the 4th Friday in November. A week or more, before the close of each term, is occupied in the public examination of the classes—witnessed by a select Committee, and strangers, if they wish to attend. These examinations, which are wholly conducted by the Professors and Tutors, are particular and sufficiently extended. The members of each class are examined in all the authors they had previously studied. To myself, present during the last spring examination, there appeared plenary evidence, that the instruction had been able and thorough; and that a little more close and persevering application of the students, would render them equal to the best. At all times during my extended visit there, even in the last days of the session, the deportment of the students was remarkably good and exemplary.

The Commencement anniversary is an occasion of exciting and public interest. The last one was the 45th; and it brought together the most learned and influential in the State. A band of music was procured from Richmond, Virginia, to exhilarate and grace the scene. In the afternoons and evenings preceding, there were rhetorical exercises; such as declamations by selected students from the lower classes; an oration before the two Societies; and a sermon to the Seniors. Of the 33 in the graduating Class, ten only had parts, and these were all orations. The subjects, after the Salutatory in Latin, were, "Moral Influence of Science;"—"Rage for Novelty;"—"Resources of North Carolina;" —"Gradual Improvement of Man;"—"Considerations sur l'Influence intellectuelle de la France"—in French;—"Virtue and Intelligence, the Safeguard of Liberty;"—"Decline of Morals in our Country;"—"Connexion between Intellectual and Moral Cultivation;"—"The Bonds of

Society"—with the *Valedictory* Addresses. The compositions exhibited undoubted marks of genius and maturity of style; and the speaking was energetic and graceful. The whole number of students, the last year, (1843) was 174, namely, resident graduates, 3; Seniors, 33; Juniors, 44; Sophomores, 44; Freshmen, 39; Irregulars, 11; the whole number of those who have gone through a classic course and received a Bachelor's degree are 736; and it is stated that as many others have, since the collegiate instruction first commenced, been *matriculates*, and for longer or shorter periods, been taught in different branches of science. The annual expenses of a student at the University will not exceed two hundred dollars, though the tuition be $50, and the board of 40 weeks, $100 of the amount. In fact, board may be had at the Steward's hall, at eight dollars by the month, equal to that "furnished at the tables of the most respectable boarding houses in any of the neighboring villages."

Such is the University of North Carolina, which has been a seat of science and literature nearly half a century. In the rise and progress of this institution, posterity may perceive what is due to men of letters and public spirit. Through their efforts and bounty, in the legislature and in the community, 736 young gentlemen, three fourths of whom were probably North Carolinians, have received a classical education, and as many more been refreshed by the waters of the same public fountain. If a due proportion of graduates has not gone into the learned professions, and if comparatively few are burning lights at the altars of religion, they have added fresh wreaths to the rising glory of literature. Not only have legislatures, supreme courts of judicature and other places of official trust been ornamented by them and benefitted by their services; numbers have vied for the palm in the halls of the national government. They have trimmed the lamps their fathers lighted; and given strength and vigor to the enterprize their predecessors so perserveringly espoused.

A system of Common Schools has likewise been established under the auspices of their excellent Constitution. To give it efficiency commensurate with its provisions, has been found to require length of time as well as untiring effort. A community cannot be effectually moved in a day. Habits which have prevailed thro' generations, are stubborn. Common Education, to be successful, must be fashionable and popular, as well as seen to be useful. To accomplish an object so great and important, districts must be formed, school-houses erected, individual families make sacrifices, and the private pocket contribute.

The free and common-schools of New England claim an antiquity of nearly two centuries. Their interests have long been deeply ingrained into the law, the heart and the life of the people. If they will recollect the merits of their forefathers in respect to education, they will not look with obloquy upon others who have the whole work to accomplish in a single age. For what State, in like circumstances, has in fact, done more in behalf of learning since the Revolution, than North Carolina? It has been her allotment to begin, as well as to achieve; and good success has been her warrant of future encouragement. To sixty-five men, the Trustees of the University, is to some extent given in charge of the interests of education. They are resident in different parts of the State, and would in general adorn any community. Were Northern men of letters more fully conversant with them, their literary institutions and teachers; had they more personal acquaintance and familiar intercourse with each other, and were there more reciprocity felt in the same exalted cause; would not the effect give to members of the American family more fraternal mutuality of sentiment and feeling? Yes, if Northern students of slender constitutions were to pass their winters at the University of N. Carolina, they could pursue the same classic course, and would lose no time though they return; while they enlarge their acquaintances and local knowledge, try the climate, and probably improve their healths. For like reasons Southern young men might pass summers advantageously at the Northern Colleges; and thus a foundation be laid in early life to dissolve prejudices and inspire a spirit of fraternity among citizens of this Great Republic, whether they fade under a Northern, or burn under a Southern sun. W.D.W.–William D. Williamson, *Boston Recorder*, December 14, 1843. Williamson was graduated from Brown University in 1804, studied law and was admitted to the bar, was a member of the Massachusetts State Senate until the separation of Maine from Massachusetts and then served in the State Senate of Maine. He served in Congress from 1821 to 1825. Visiting the University of North Carolina in 1843 he witnessed the examination of the students and also attended the exercises at commencement. The first part of Williamson's article, photocopy of which is in the Southern Historical Collection, the University of North Carolina, is omitted here.

4. Charter of the University of Mississippi, 1844

Section 1. *Be it enacted by the Legislature of the State of Mississippi*, That J. Alexander Ventress, John A. Quitman, William L.

Sharkey, Alexander M. Clayton, William Y. Gholson, Jacob Thompson, Pryor Lea, Edward C. Wilkinson, James M. Howry, John J. McCaughan, Rev. Francis Hawkes, J. N. Waddel, A. H. Pegues, are hereby appointed Trustees of the University of Mississippi, in Lafayette county, and their successors in office are hereby declared and constituted a body politic and corporate, by the name and style of the "University of Mississippi," a majority of whom shall form a quorum to do business, but a committee of less number may be appointed to transact necessary business, in the interim of a regular session of said Trustees.

Sec. 2. *Be it further enacted,* That said corporation shall be possessed of all the general powers, privileges and emoluments now secured to similar corporations by the constitution and laws of this state, and to adopt such by-laws and rules as they may deem expedient for the accomplishment of the trust reposed in them, not repugnant to the constitution and laws of this State.

Sec. 3. *Be it further enacted,* That the said Board of Trustees shall have full power and entire control over the funds belonging to the "University of Mississippi," or the "Seminary Fund," after it shall have been collected, to be by them applied only towards the consummation of the plan of the "University of Mississippi;" and said Trustees shall have power to devise and adopt such a system of learning as in their judgment they may deem most advisable to be pursued in the course of education in the University; to employ a competent person to draft a plan of the same, and appoint commissioners to contract for the erection of the University building, so soon as they may think advisable.

Sec. 4. *Be it further enacted,* That said Board of Trustees shall have power to fill all vacancies that may occur in their body.

Sec. 5. *And be it further enacted,* That this act shall be repealed at the will of the Legislature, and shall be in force from and after its passage.

Approved, February 24, 1844.—*Laws of the State of Mississippi,* 1844, pp. 227-28.

5. Extracts from the Minutes of the Trustees of the University of Mississippi, 1845-1856

At a meeting of the Board, convened at the Capital of the State, on the 15th day of January 1845, present John A. Quitman, William L. Sharkey, Alexander M. Clayton, James M. Howry, Edward C. Wilkinson, A. H. Pegues, and Pryor Lea—John A. Quitman was appointed Chairman, and Pryor Lea Secretary *pro tempore.*

On motion of Mr. Clayton,

Ordered, that a committee of three be appointed by the Chair to report, as early as practicable, a System of Bye-Laws, for the Government of the Board.

Messrs. Clayton, Howry, and Lea were appointed to be of said committee—to which, on motion of Mr. Sharkey, the Chairman was added.

The Board then adjourned until Friday morning 9 o'clock.

Friday, January 17th 1845.

The Board met pursuant to adjournment—present as before.

Mr. Clayton, from the Committee on Bye-Laws reported the following—

Bye-Laws for the Organization and Government of the Trustees of the University of Mississippi.

1. The Officers of the Corporation shall consist of a President, Secretary, and Treasurer, and an Executive Committee of three trustees.

2. All the Officers shall be elected by ballot annually at the Meetings of the Board in January, and shall hold their respective offices until their successors shall be elected.

3. In case of a failure of any regular meeting in January, the Officers shall be elected at the next meeting thereafter.

4. The President shall preside at all the meetings of the Board, and shall have power at any time, with the consent of two trustees to call a meeting of the Board—but an extraordinary meeting of the Board may be held at Oxford at any time, on the call of any five members.

5. In case of a vacancy in the office of President, or in his absence, the Board may appoint any one of their number President *pro-tem.*

6. The Offices of Secretary and Treasurer may be vested in one person.

7. The Secretary shall record in a well bound book all the proceedings of the Board, preserve files of all papers belonging to the Corporation, and deliver the same to his successor. In case of a vacancy in the Office, or in the absence of the Secretary, the Board may appoint one of their number Secretary *pro tem.*

8. The Treasurer shall take charge of and keep, under the direction of the Board, such moneys, funds, or evidences of debts and

claims, as may from time to time be committed to his charge by resolution of the Board. He shall keep regular accounts of all his receipts and disbursements, and lay before the Board at each stated meeting a full report of his proceedings and accounts.

9. Before entering upon the duties of his Office, the Treasurer shall enter into bond, with sureties to be approved of by the President, in the sum of Five thousand dollars, conditioned that he will faithfully perform the duties of his office, and will account for all moneys, which may come to his hands—which bond shall be payable to the Corporation, and be kept by the President.

10. The Secretary and Treasurer shall semiannually, and immediately after each stated meeting of the Board, transmit to the Office of the Secretary of State, certified transcripts of the proceedings of the Board, and of the accounts of the Treasurer, to be there filed.

11. The person acting as Secretary and Treasurer, as a compensation for his services, shall receive an annual salary of two hundred and fifty dollars, payable semi-annually, and to commence at such time as the Board shall hereafter direct.

12. The Executive Committee shall have such powers, and perform such duties, as may from time to time be prescribed by the Board of Trustees. In case of a vacancy in their number, the President shall have power to appoint a trustee to fill such vacancy until the next election, and in all cases a majority of said committee may act. Said Committee shall keep a journal of their proceedings, & report the same to the Board of trustees at every meeting.

13. No portion of the moneys or funds of the University of Mississippi, or of the Seminary fund, which now is or may hereafter be placed in the State Treasury, shall be withdrawn therefrom, except in pursuance of a resolution adopted by a majority of the whole number of the trustees—and the vote on the passage of such resolution shall always be taken by yeas and nays, and entered on the Journal—and all moneys so drawn from the State Treasury shall be placed in the hands of the Treasurer of the University before disbursement.

14. No money shall be paid by the Treasurer of the University, except on the warrant or written order of a majority of the Executive Committee, or

Every such warrant or order shall be issued in pursuance of a resolution of the Board, and shall specify the particular expenditure for which it is drawn.

15. The Seal of the Corporation shall be procured and kept by the

President, and shall have the words, "University of Mississippi," engraved around the margin, with an Eye in the centre.

16. No contract for the erection of the University buildings shall be valid, unless the Seal of the Corporation be affixed thereto.

17. The stated meetings of the Board shall be held at Oxford on the second Mondays in July & January, except that, when the stated meeting in January occurs during the Regular Session of the Legislature, such meeting shall be held at Jackson.

18. As soon as the buildings shall be in a sufficient state of preparation, the Board of trustees shall prescribe a plan of education, employ teachers, and provide all rules and regulations necessary and proper for the Institution.

19. Additional Bye-Laws, not inconsistent with these, may be adopted at any meeting of the Board—but these shall not be altered without the concurrence of a majority of the whole number of trustees—and on any such alteration the yeas and nays shall be taken and recorded.

Schedule.

To meet contingent expenses for the present, the President shall be authorised to receive from the State Treasurer, an account of interest due on the Seminary fund, the sum of Two hundred and fifty dollars, which sum, or the balance that may remain unexpended, shall be paid to the Treasurer of the University when he shall have given bond.

Which report was received, read, and adopted by a unanimous vote of the Board.

On motion of Mr. Howry.

The Board proceeded to the election of a president—and on counting out the ballots it appeared, that Mr. Clayton was duly elected—who thereupon took the Chair.

Mr. Howry presented the resignation of William Y. Gholson, as a trustee of the University, which was accepted—and thereupon Thomas H. Williams, of Pontotoc, was elected to fill the vacancy.

The Board then proceeded to the election of a Secretary & Treasurer, and an Executive Committee—Whereupon Mr. Williams was elected Secretary and Treasurer—and Messrs. Howry, Pegues, and Quitman the Executive Committee.

Mr. Williams being absent, Mr. Lea was appointed Secretary *pro tem.*

On motion of Mr. Quitman,

1. Resolved, that the President be requested to procure from the State Treasurer a statement of the funds in his hands belonging to the University of Mississippi, and of the amount of interest due thereon to the 1st of January instant—and to procure and lay before the Board such information in relation thereto as he may think advisable.

2. Resolved, that the Secretary & Treasurer be authorised and required to procure a safe or iron chest for the safe-keeping of the moneys and effects, which may be committed to his charge—and that the Executive Committee be authorised, on the certificate of the Treasurer, to draw an order on the Treasurer for the expense of the same.

3. Resolved, that the President be authorised to contract for the printing in pamphlet form of One Hundred copies of the Bye-Laws—One copy of which shall be transmitted to each Trustee—ten copies be forwarded to the Governor—and the remainder be deposited with the Secretary of the University....

Tuesday July 15th 1845

The Board met pursuant to adjournment. Present the same members as on yesterday. Mr. Quitman offered the following resolution. Resolved that a committee of three be appointed by the chair to report to the present meeting of the Board, what amount they will now set apart to commence operations in buildings &c. and what portion of the said fund it will be advisable to invest permanently on interest, and also to report a plan for such investment when the fund shall be collected and placed under the control of the Board, in the event that the State should decline to retain any portion of said fund on interest. Which was adopted, and Messrs. Howry, Davis & Quitman were appointed said committee.

On motion of Mr. Vestress, Mr. Sharkey was added to the committee appointed on yesterday, to examine and report to the next meeting the amount and present state of the University fund.

Wednesday Morning July 16th 1845

The Board met pursuant to adjournment.

Present as on yesterday.

Mr. Quitman made the following report.

The committee to whom it was refered to report what amount of the University fund it is advisable now to set apart to commence operation on the buildings &c. and what portion of the fund should be permanently invested on interest in the event that the State should decline to retain said fund on interest. Report that from the best information they can now obtain it is believed that the amount of about $90,000 of the University fund has been collected and is now in the State Treasury. They are further informed by the report of the Commissioner that in all probability the collections which will be made by him will swell the amount of the fund to the sum of about $150,000. The committee have therefore estimated the latter sum as near the probable amount of the funds, the control and management of which is submitted to the Board of Trustees by their act of incorporation.

Assuming this sum as the probable amount of the fund, your committee are of opinion that at least $100,000 of the fund should be permanently invested, as the basis of an annual and regular revenue to the University, and the remainder so that the amount reserved for expenditure does not in all exceed $50,000 should be set apart for the construction of buildings, outfits, Library apparatus &c. &c. Should by any accident or failure to make collections of the residue, the fund not exceed $100,000, your committee recommend that not more than $25,000 be set apart for buildings &c. and at least $75,000 be permanently invested. It is not proposed that the whole of either of these sums should at once be set apart for the building operations but merely reserved from permanent investment for that purpose. The committee believe that at the present time, the sum of $15,000 may with safety be placed in the hands of the Treasurer of the University, subject to be drawn out according to the provisions of the bye laws for building purposes &c.

In relation to the permanent investment of a sufficient amount of the University funds, your committee beg leave to report that they deem it most advisable that the fund with the exception of such portions thereof as may from time to time be withdrawn for building and other expenses, should remain in the State Treasury so long as the Legislature shall be willing to allow interest thereon, but in the event the Legislature should decline an allowance of reasonable interest upon the fund which may remain from time to time in the State Treasury, your committee know of no investment which can now be made to realise a permanent income to the University, more safe or less exceptionable than to loan under the direction of an efficient committee, the funds to private individuals upon ample personal and real security—Which report was received and on motion of Mr. Thompson unanimously agreed to....

February 25, 1848

Mr. Williams from a committee appointed at a former meeting of this Board to correspond with various Colleges on the subject of rules, regulations, Plan of Education &c. made a report which was recd. and read.

On motion of Mr. Sharkey it was resolved that the Faculty of the University of Mi shall consist of a President, who shall discharge the duties of Professor of Mental & Moral Philosophy, Rhetoric, Evidences of Christianity, Logic and Political Economy.

2. A Professor of Ancient & Modern Languages.
3. A Professor of Mathematics pure & mixed.
4. A Professor of Natural Phillosophy, and Astronomy.
5. A Professor of Chemistry, Geology & Mineralogy.

That the President shall receive an anual sallary of Two thousand dollars, and each of the other Professors one thousand five hundred, with the perquisites arising from tuition fees.

Mr. Sharkey submitted the following resolution. Resolved that the President shall cause notice to be given by publication in the public papers, that five Professors will be elected by the Trustees of the University of Mi (one of whom shall be President) at their next meeting on the 2nd Monday in July next, and that their services will be required about the 1st Octr. next.

July 12, 1848

Mr. Wilkinson from the committee appointed on yesterday to prepare a plan of education in detail submitted the following report—

Resolved that the sessions of the University shall comprise ten months, that each Professor shall instruct two classes, a Junior and a Senior class, That the President shall embrace in his Junior department instruction in the following branches, Mental and moral Phillosophy, Logic and Belles lettres, and in his senior department the following, Political Economy & International law.

2nd. Resolved there shall be a professor of *Mathematicks* and Astronomy, who shall as the President instruct two classes, and who shall be at liberty to assign the different branches of their studies to his classes as shall appear proper to him.

3rd. Resolved there shall be a professor chosen to take charge of the Department of Natural Science, which department shall consist of Chemistry, Geology, Mineralogy, Botany and Natural Phillosophy.

4th. There shall be chosen a Professor of Ancient Languages who shall be required to teach the Latin, Greek and Hebrew Languages.

5th. There shall be a Professor of the Modern Languages of French, Spanish and German, which was received and adopted.

Mr. Davis offered the following resolution. Resolved that the evidences of Christianity be taught in the University.

Mr. Wilkinson moved to amend the resolution of Mr. Davis by striking out all after the word resolved and insert. That a Chaplain shall be chosen by the Faculty and students at the commencement of every Session, to act as such during the session, who shall not be re-eligible for four sessions thereafter, nor shall a chaplain of the same denomination to which he may have belonged, be eligible until after such lapse of time. It shall be the duty of the chaplain to deliver or read morning and evening prayers daily at the University, every student shall be required to attend, and shall pay the chaplain one dollar upon his entrance into College. Upon the adoption of which amendment the yeas and nays were demanded, those who voted in the affirmative were Mrssrs. Pegeus and Wilkinson in the negative Mr. President Smith, Brown Howry Davis Sharkey Williams and Young.

The question recurring on the original resolution offered by Mr. Davis. The yeas and nays were demanded those who voted in the affirmative were Mr. Prest. Smith, Mrssrs. Brown Davis Howry Sharkey Williams and Young. In the negative Mrssrs. Pegeus & Wilkinson. The resolution was therefore adopted.

The Board then proceeded to the election of a Faculty and George Frederick Holmes was declared duly appointed President.

On motion of Mr. Davis the Board adjourned until tomorrow morning 8 oclock....

July 15, 1848

Mr. Young from the committee appointed to prepare and report a plan of education submitted the following report. Mr. President the committee appointed to prepare and report a plan of Education for the University of this State have had the subject under very brief consideration and beg leave to report, That the time allowed them is insufficient for the examination and preparation of so important a work, and believing that the board will be again in session before the opening of the institution, have agreed to submit the following resolutions as embracing all that is essential and proper for the action of the Board now near the close of its present sitting.

Resolved that the Students of the University shall be arranged into four classes, viz. a Freshman a Sophomore, Junior and Senior Class, embracing and running through the usual graduating space of four collegiate years.

Resolved, That to the President shall be assigned instruction in Mental and Moral Phillosophy, Logic Belles Lettres, Political Economy and International law.

Resolved that to the Professor of Mathematicks be assigned instruction in that department and in the Science of Astronomy.

Resolved, That the Professor of Natural Science shall give instruction in Chemistry, Botany, Geology, Mineralogy and Natural Phillosophy

Resolved, That the Professor of Languages shall give instruction in Latin, Greek, Hebrew, French, Spanish & German Languages

Resolved that the President of this Board is authorised and hereby required to give notice in six of the public Gazettes of this State, that the University of this State will go into opperation and be ready for the admission of Students on the first Monday in November next, that the foregoing departments have been organised, and George Frederick Holmes chosen President of the Faculty, Albert Taylor Bledsoe Professor of Mathematicks and Astronomy John Millington Professor of Natural Science and John N. Wadle Professor of Languages. That the qualifications for admission into the several classes will be substantially such as are required in the best regulated universities in the United States and that a full and more perfect plan of instruction as pursued throughout the several classes, with the requisites for admission into each will be prescribed and published for the information of parents and Guardians, prior to or upon the opening of the University, and stating further that the dormitories for lodging the students will be severally furnished with plain and suitable furniture, and board at a Stewards Hall at seven dollars per month.

Mr. Davis moved to amend the report by as follows, resolved That Students may be admitted as irregulars under such regulations as may be hereafter prescribed which was adopted, and the yeas and nays being called upon the adoption of the report was amended. Those who voted in the affirmative were Mrssrs Brown Davis Howry Williams & Young in the Negative Mrssrs. Smith Pegeus Sharkey & Wilkinson the resolutions were therefore adopted.

Mr. Howry offered the following resolutions.

Resolved that the Board retain the right to remove any officer connected with the University at any time upon sufficient cause.

Resolved that the Board retain the right to alter or change the mode of instruction and division of the different branches prescribed among the professors if they may think proper to do so. And that the Secretary be required to furnish each Professor with a copy of these resolutions with the notice of his appointment, which were adopted....

July 9, 1849

This being the day of the commencement of the first annual examination of the Students at the University, the board took a recess at nine o'clock A.M. and attended the examination of the Freshman class on the Latin and Greek Languages, and at 3 o'clock P.M. the board again took a recess and attended the examination of the Freshman class on Mathematics, which close the exercises of the day....

Thursday July 12th 1849—

The Board met pursuant to adjournment. Present the same as on yesterday.

The report of the Faculty was received which shews the whole number of Students matriculated during the first session to be eighty, the number expelled five suspended 8, withdrawn 12, absent on leave 8, whole number in attendance forty seven, which was received.

July 12, 1849

Mr. Young offered the following resolution which was adopted.

Resolved that the Secretary of this Board notify forthwith, the Revd. A. B. Longstreet of his unanimous election to the Presidency of this University and urge upon him the acceptance of the same....

July 12, 1849

Mr. Clayton submitted the following

Whereas the examination of the students of the University just had in our presence, and the whole exercises of the occasion, have given great satisfaction and convinced us that the Professors have faithfully discharged their duty, and that the students exhibited very gratifying evidences of their proficiency we do therefore direct this expression of our opinion to be placed upon the records of our Board. Which was unanimously agreed to.

July 8, 1850

The following statistical report of the University for the session ending 11th July 1850 was received. Number of students at the close of last session 47, whole number of matriculations, in 1849-50 76, expelled during present session none number suspended 3, privately dismissed 2, called home by parents 13, number of deaths 3 only one on the University grounds, number now in Junior class 17, in Sophomore class 8, in Freshman class, 30, irregulars 10, regulars 45, number now in actual attendance 55. Excess at the close of present over last session 8.

July 10, 1850

Mr. Clayton offered the following resolution. Resolved that the sum of $1700 be appropriated to the purchase of books and a pair of globes for the University, and that the Faculty be requested to make out a catalogue of the works most needed by the Institution at present. Also that said sum be placed under the control of W. L. Sharkey to make the purchase of said Books, & that he reserve enough of said sum, to pay insurance and charges thereon to Memphis—
Which was adopted....

Resolved that the Faculty be requested to draw up a Diploma in the Latin Language to be delivered to those students, who may obtain degrees at commencements, and to get a sufficient number printed on Parchment and that each graduate, on receiving a diploma shall pay the Proctor the sum of five dollars for the same, which was adopted.

Mr. Clayton offered the following resolution.

Resolved, that from the fact, that the salaries of the Professors, of the University are paid in consideration of their services to the Institution, it is the opinion of the board, that the payment, made to the late Presdt. G. F. Holmes, is as much as was justly due to him: and that no farther allowance can be made with justice to the institution.

Resolved, that in dissolving the connection between the sd. President and the institution, the board did not design to cast any reflection upon his character, as a man, or his reputation as a scholar....

July 13th 1852
The Board met pursuant to adjournment.

Present, Messrs Clayton President, Brown Davis Earle Thompson & Howry.

The President submitted the following resolutions.

Resolved,

That the Faculty be requested to inform the board of Trustees, whether any & if any, what action was taken by the faculty in relation to the malicious mischief perpetrated on the horse of Col Brown in the month of April last.

Resolved, That the secretary be requested to furnish the President with a copy of this resolution,

The resolutions were unamimously adopted.

The following answer to the foregoing resolution was submitted by President Longstreet.

University 13 July 1852

In answer to the resolution of the Board of Trustees inquiring of me "whether any & if any what action was taken by the Faculty in relation to the malicious mischief perpetrated on the horse of Col Brown in the month of April last" I answer that no judicial action was taken in the matter because though my best exertion was used to get a clew to the offenders, I entirely failed. All that I could do therefore was to deliver a general lecture to the students upon the offence, which I did in severe terms of reprobation.

A. B. Longstreet

July 14 1852
The Board met pursuant to adjournment,
Present, Messrs Clayton Prest, Davis, Earle, Brown, Thompson & Howry

The following communication was received and ordered to spread upon the minutes.

To the Trustees of the University,
Gentlemen,

At a meeting of the students of the University on the evening of the 13th inst the following resolution was unanimously adopted.

Resolved,

That we the students of the University of Mississippi disclaim & disavow the indignity offered to Col. Brown in April last.

Wm P Griffin Chn
G. A. Lester sec'y

July 12, 1853
On motion of Mr Pegues Resolved,
That in consequence of the failure of the annual commencement exercises of the University at the regular time occasioned by the students prematurely leaving College the exercises shall take place after the opening of the next session commencing on the 15th Sept next on Thursday....

January 11, 1854
Mr Howry offered the following resolution.
Resolved,
That the sum of $3,000.00 be appropriated for the purchase of Books Maps &c. and Chemical & philosophical apparatus and such apparatus as may be needed for the Geological Department, and that the Faculty be requested to furnish the Treasurer with an inventory of the same, and that he be authorized to purchase & pay for the same out of the special fund appropriated for this purpose.
Said resolution was unanimously adopted....
The following resolution was adopted by the Board.
Resolved that, if any member of the Faculty shall absent himself from the duties of his chair in the University, unless from actual sickness, it shall be the duty of the Treasurer to deduct from their Salary ten dollars pr diem for such absence; and that such member so absenting himself shall report the number of days he may have been absent, to the Treasurer before their accounts are paid. Provided: this regulation does not take effect until the first day of March next.

January 12, 1854
Mr. Wilkinson from the Committee appointed to prepare a report to the Legislature now in session, made the following report, which was received and agreed to and ordered to be signed by the President and transmitted to the Legislature.

Gentlemen:—
As Trustees of the University of Mississippi we think it our duty to address the Legislature of the State. It appears to us that there is propriety in so doing; for although the Institution has been endowed by the whole nation, this bounty was conferred for the benefit of the people of the state, has been increased somewhat by the state Legislature which has also conferred corporate Faculties upon the University and has encouraged and fostered it from time to time by

favorable Legislation. Whether therefore your honorable body has, or has not strictly speaking material power over the University, it is emphatically the institution of the people. You Gentlemen, are the representatives of the people and are supposed to speak their will, and we have thought it appropriate, through you, to communicate to the people the progress and present condition of the University—to enquire into its adaption—to effectuate the designs of its foundation—and in what it is deficient to this respect, and to make an exhibition of its wants and the extent of its requirements, in order to supply those wants.

The public spirit that originally endowed the University was sufficiently munificient to answer all the ends of such an establishment. The public domain which was given to the State by the Nation for this purpose, was large enough & valuable enough to have afforded opportunity for instruction in most if not all of the branches of education.

But, your honorable body is aware of the unfortunate—we might say perhaps disastrous manner in which the fund was managed, long before it ever passed into the control of the Trustees of the University, and how in consequence, the institution instead of beginning its career as its founders had a right to expect—a bountiful dispenser of knowledge in all its various departments—struggled into existence, crippled and imperfect, and has never been enabled even yet, to assume the proportions corresponding with its name, and belonging to an University of learning.

Nevertheless, under great disadvantages, its progress has been encouraging & steady. The number of its students has been slowly but steadily increasing. It is now 140. They have been generally orderly in their deportment and persevering in their application to their studies, and some who have already been graduated at the school—unless they disappoint the expectation which their youthful promise has excited—will hereafter reflect upon their Alma Mater a renown more than commensurate with the benefits they receive from her.

The Professional chairs from four, now number Eight—the monetary affairs of the University, from a state of inadequacy extremely discouraging when the school began its operations is now sufficient to meet the yearly expenditures of the Board.

The Library is increased to 3,000 volumes. Additional buildings now adorn the grounds, and serve to carry out the beautiful design of the Architect.

A Cabinet of minerals is in the course of Collection and arrangement, and a philosophical Apparatus—Simple, but of extraordinary beauty—has been placed before the chair of the Professor of Physics since the last communication of the board with the Legislature.

Every thing indicates the steady progress and the ultimate prosperity of the University of Mississippi. But there is one great want which the University seriously feels. The circle of the moral sciences, so far from being complete there, is scarcely begun. Rhetoric, Metaphysics, Political Economy, Moral Philosophy, Logic—the last of doubtful utility perhaps—may all be thoroughly taught and well understood but they do not prepare a man to begin the great business of life.

Our graduated young men often aspire to act in the counsels of their country; and history and observation both teach them to look to the Bar as the place of preparation and of trial, to vindicate their fitness for the Halls of legislation. It is well known that for a period of a thousand years the Bar has been the great road to the dignities, the titles, the places and the power of the politician, wheresoever the common law of England has been enforced. The University greatly needs a professorship of Law. But not of Law alone, in the opinion of the undersigned. The Philosophy of Government should be taught together with it, and history, which is philosophy teaching by example.

Instruction in the science of government, we think of high importance to southern youth—to youth everywhere in a Republic, but especially to the youth of our country. We live in a Confederacy of States. The political relations of the states to each other are looked at in somewhat different lights, according to the geographical points of view. Government is taught as a science in some of the states, but in few of the Southern states if in any of them. Our ambitious youth go to the East for instruction in this department, for it is to be found there alone. Such a school may or may not be, antagonistic in its principles to Southern views of the right philosophy of government, but we feel assured that a Southern University of learning could never disseminate views of society and government, which would prove prejudiced to Southern interests. Besides political ethics, a right understanding and a full appreciation of political morality is of the last importance in every Republic.

A youth coming from the walls of the University with enlarged and fixed principles of political justice—with elevated notions of the use, the scope and the design of government—would not be apt to sink into a factionist, or to merge the philosophic statesman in the turbulent damagogue.

To instruction in Law & government, we would superadd (as we have said) instruction in History and international law; and we think a single professor would be adequate to discharge the combined duties that are here indicated. But it would require no ordinary man. Such a man as would fully suit the place would be of more difficult selection, than any other professor in the University. His character—his acquirements, even his place of residence and of education would have to be considered. But it is in the power of compensation to procure such a man, we suppose, and we respectfully ask the Legislature to aid us in raising this compensation. The annual excess of our revenue over our current expenditures is barely sufficient to keep the University in fitting repair, even if there was *then* any excess, it would be proper to apply it to the erection of additional buildings.

It is apparent from the report of the Commissioner of the Seminary fund, now before you, that but little is in future to be expected from that source.

If all the lands now belonging to this fund were sold even at present prices, and its dues were all collected, the annual interest from the whole of it would amount to about fifteen hundred dollars.

With such tuition fees as a Law professor, well known to be qualified for his duties, might command, and a payment annually of two thousand dollars as a fixed salary, we think it probable that the scheme we have developed might be carried into effect.

Having therefore, stated the matter for the consideration of your honorable body, we pray the grant of an appropriation in conformity with the views set forth.

J. Thompson President of the
Board of Trustees of the University of Missi.

July 11, 1855
Mr. Clapp submitted the following report.

The undersigned to whom was referred that portion of the report of President Longstreet which refers to the relative powers & duties of the Board of Trustees & the Faculty & recommends the repeal of the Law which requires the Faculty to report their absences from College have had the subject under consideration and recommend for the adoption of the Board the following minutes & resolution.

The Board of Trustees do not feel it obligatory upon them to make any response to that portion of President Longstreets report in which he discusses the relative powers and duties of this Board and of the Faculty, but they desire to treat the author of this report with entire respect and are not unwilling to give expression to their views upon the subject presented.

The Board deny that they have ever supposed the relation between themselves & the Faculty to be of the character suggested by President Longstreet, or that they have ever by their official acts subjected themselves to such an imputation; on the contrary their earnest desire has ever been to treat the Faculty as a body & its members individually with respect, courtesy & kindness and to promote the harmony of views and concert of action between the two bodies so essential to the success & prosperity of the Institution to whose interests both parties are & should be devoted. But whilst the Board make this avowal of their feelings & wishes, they cannot concede that the Legislature incorporating the University & designating the Trustees as the official guardians of its welfare intended to make them the mere automats supposed by President Longstreet– Were this so, the Board can conceive of no sufficient reason for the creation or continuance of their office since they have at the most but concurrent powers with the Faculty.

The relation between the Board & the Legislature is certainly very different from that subsisting between the Board and the Faculty: The former are the agents or officers selected by the Legislature for the general management of the University and clothed by that body with all the authority necessary for that purpose, receiving no compensation for their services, they can subject themselves to no penalty, but having accepted the trust conferred upon them by the Legislature, they are bound in good faith to discharge with fidelity the duties pertaining to their office or to resign: The Faculty on the other hand are employed by the Trustees as the representatives of the Legislature for a specific purpose and for stipulated wages.

The power conferred upon the Trustees to select the Faculty, necessarily carries along with it the right of general supervision & control, so that the contract entered into between the Board and the members of the Faculty respectively may be executed & enforced; and were the Board to fail to exercise this right, it would on their part be a manifest neglect of duty. Beyond the exercise of this right and the discharge of this duty they have never gone, nor have they any wish or intention to transcend this limit in future.

The law referred to in the report of President Longstreet and which is represented in so odious a light was by the Board deemed necessary at the time of its passage & their power to adopt it they did not question. They disclaim all intention of having designed by the law to irritate or offend the Faculty or any member of that body or to detract from the respect due to their several offices, nor do they think that the law as it now stands, exacts of them ought derogatory to their position as officers of the College, or that can be regarded as disrespectful or offensive. But as it is the sincere wish of the Board to remove every possible ground of complaint & source of conflict or disagreement between the Faculty & themselves & to cultivate relations of cordiality & harmony, they are willing that the law referred to be repealed....

July 14, 1856.

Resolved

That a committee of three be appointed to wait on Dr. Longstreet and acquaint him with the wishes of the Board and ask his compliance with the same Mr. Thompson Mr. Young and Mr. Davis were appointed said Committee....

Mr. Thompson offered the following:

Resolved:

That the Faculty of the University be requested to report to the Board at their next annual meeting, their views of the expediency of establishing in the University two distinct courses of instruction, not parallel but consecutive, the first being planned and arranged exclusively with the object of most effectually developing and training the intellectual faculties and to be distinguished at its close by the degree of Bachelor of Arts, and the second accessible only to graduates, being designed to encourage and facilitate the pursuit of Knowledge for its own sake and to be followed by the Degree of Master of Arts.

Resolved further

That the Faculty, in case the proposed remodelling of the existing system should meet their approval, be desired to state, whether, in their opinion any change should be made in the duration of the present A.B. course, and if so, what the change should be....—Florence E.

Campbell (comp.), Journal of the Minutes of the Board of Trustees of the University of Mississippi, 1845-1860 (Master's Thesis, University of Mississippi, 1939) *passim.* Copy of extracts in the Southern Historical Collection, the University of North Carolina.

6. A student in the University of North Carolina writes of the gaieties in Chapel Hill, 1845

University of N. C. October 3d 1845.

Dear Richard

I have determined to keep you waiting no longer for an answer to your last, (to me) very acceptable letter; lest you may conclude, that my doses of opium are more frequent, than good reasons will justify. But I assure you old Fellow that a letter from none of my correspondents is received with more real pleasure than one from you. I know that many of mine must necessarily prove unentertaining to you from the staleness of their contents, and I have frequently been inclined to destroy them after they are written and to wait the flood-tide of impulse for a second trial. But knowing that you take pleasure in receiving a letter from a friend though it contain nothing more than the usual salutations and assurances, I forget their imperfections, and derive pleasure from the fact that they are directed to a friend who will appreciate them as a whole, without condensing them in part. Although I am opposed to filling a letter with apologies for neglect and such things, yet I am confident you will excuse my present delay, when you learn, that my time has been occupied in preparing a Senior speech for my debut on the stage. I have just finished it; my subject is "The Shade of the Past." It opens a wide field for the imagination as well as for historical illustration. There are thirty one Seniors and some very good declaimers and writers. We expect a very large audience; the ladies both of Hillsborough and Pittsborough, (the one 12, the other 18 miles distant) have engaged rooms in the village for the occasion. We have besides 13 young ladies on the (campus) but some of them the worst I ever saw in my life. I suppose that there will be about 30 or 40 young ladies, and as many matrons. We have engaged a band of musicians, and got up a party for the benefit of the few visitors who may honor us with their presence. We have also succeeded in getting the Faculty: content to allow us to speak at candle light; so that it will occupy three evenings in the week; and such gallavanting as there will be. O! hush! I will venture to say that for the last two weeks, Chapel Hill has been the gayest place this side of the Potomac. We have had a delegation of the Pittsborough girls here on a visit and taking them altogether they are almost ahead of any thing I ever saw. The prettiest, loveliest, liveliest, and most heartbreaking, bone-cracking and study-killing images of Female sweetness, that ever *bustled* in a crowd.

There were three parties as a token of their welcome on the part of the Villagers, and their visit was interspersed with walks, rides, et cetera. For four evenings the five young ladies had 17 visitors each evening. Now a stranger would suppose that common humanity would have groaned under such a weight, but "by Gum" they were primed, charged and as ready for another 17 the fifth evening as they were the first. They left here yesterday and seven of the students accompanied them up to Pitts'. As such sprees occur but rarely, it is not surprising that the fellows make the most of them. I had a very pleasant trip to Raleigh three weeks ago. My sister and two of her friends from Fayetteville were on a visit at Raleigh; one of the young ladies was recently from Alabama with her brother. They all agreed to ride up here and spend one evening and return the next day, as the Young lady from Alabama also had a brother in College. It was a very agreeable surprise; Campbele (the young lady's brother's name) and myself returned with them in the carriages to Raleigh; we got there on Thursday evening and staid till Tuesday morning. On Friday we carried the girls to a Pic Nic about 7 miles from Raleigh, where we had lots of fun. Monday evening there was a large party in Raleigh and as there are very few *Gallants* there, "Chapel Hill grit" beat even "Nova Scotia". Next morning the girls started down to Fayetteville, we hired buggies and rode with them about 10 miles when we parted. We gathered about a pint of the kissing essence in the parting, and filled the jug, after we got to Raleigh with the best old double-distilled Rye in the city. I have kept the best secret for the last; *Ella Marion* was one of the three! and I reckon you can guess who I rode with and talked to all the time "most hardly". It was as much as Campbele could do, to get me back to college, But I will turn over a leaf and change the subject. Our regular Sessional Spree came off last Friday week, about 20 or 30 fellows disguised with calico coats and pants, and paper hats plumed with chicken feathers sallied out in the campus about 11 o'clock at night. They commenced ringing the bell, blowing horns, shooting pistols, and then forming a line, would charge against the trees, and piles of Rocks with a savage vengeance. The Faculty came on the ground, and one attempted to enter one of the passages; the fellows ducked him with two buckets of water, pelted him with apples and finally threw a wash basin at him which made him desist. The Spors in the campus marched round to each of the Tutor's rooms and rocked their windows; after which they dispersed. But the Faculty had concealed themselves near the entrance of the passages, and recognized the fellows as they would go in their rooms. They had up about 20, but only 5 were dismissed; the others were too slipery tongued to be caught. While there are occasional sprees here, generally very good order prevails. The institution is without doubt the best in the country.

I cannot concieve the reason of Luther's not answering my letter written more than two months ago; have you heard from him lately? I saw Sid in Raleigh, and got some wholesome talks from the old fellow on various subjects. And Miss Pad told Lomap that the reason she did not consent to marry him before, was that she loved another better! I wonder if that wasn't you Toby? But she is married thank God, and now if I can stop one other soft-pated petticoat there, I will be satisfied.

Brother Thomas left Fayetteville on Monday last for Texas! I have almost concluded to get married as soon as I graduate and follow suit. Remember me to your brother and each of the Family, to John Howard and all my old acquaintances. Tell me in your next Miss Anna Boothe's post office. Don't be frightened as I am only going to send her an "address". This letter I have been compelled to write between recitation and dinner which must be its apology.

Write soon to yours as ever,

William K. Blake.

—Letter to Richard Irby, Blacks & Whites P.O., Nottoway County, Virginia. In possession of Mrs. F. H. Jordan, Blackstone, Virginia. Used by permission. Typescript copy is in the Southern Historical Collection, the University of North Carolina.

7. The University of Louisiana should be set in operation, 1847

We have permission to publish the following letter received by us in relation to the contemplated University. The plan which it proposes we are disposed to regard very highly, and we believe that it will meet with the consideration which it deserves. Dr. Albert W.

Ely, of this city, has favored us also with a plan which we will gladly give publication to in our next number. It is high time that some efficient steps were taken to organize and set in operation the Institution.

New Orleans, February 10, 1847.

J. D. B. De Bow, Esq.—

You will recollect that in course of conversation with me some time ago the subject of the University of Louisiana was introduced, when you took occasion to express your deep interest in its success, and sympathies with those who were moving to promote it. Though not susceptible of the same enthusiasm, I could not but heartily agree with you in views, and promised then what God forbid I should hesitate to perform, to co-operate in my humble way to the fullest extent of my means and abilities, in any movement which might be made to secure for our citizens what they deemed so important as to ordain in convention.

The fact is, we of a generation which is fast passing away, who were contemporary with the earliest days of Louisiana, who have shared the fortunes of the State in all the stages of its progress, may be allowed to feel some interest in what is to come after us here, particularly in the fortunes of that rising class of our citizens who are to preserve and extend the character of the State, and perfect what we their sires have scarcely more than instituted. The advantages of this generation are far greater than the last. The school master was *at home* and not "abroad" then. We were called upon to struggle with untoward difficulties, content, indeed, if so much could be obtained with the mere rudiments of education. Hence the surprise should not be, that Louisiana has produced, of her own growth, so few men of commanding abilities and information, but that she has produced any at all. We would, however, amend this evil, and let no one henceforward be heard pleading the past in extenuation of his deficiencies, who will not come forward with the means he has acquired here, and by a liberal appropriation of them, preserve his children, or the children of his countrymen, from a similar misfortune.

With such views and impressions I could not be entirely indifferent to the educational movements now in progress among us. Of common schools, those nurseries of early youth where character for life is formed, and well formed when efficiently organized, no one can have a higher estimate. But what after all are common schools, if the system of education must be arrested there. Is it not cruelty to implant a love of knowledge and deny its consummation? The mere elementary provisions of such schools are not sufficient to qualify men for *all* the relations of life. There is that which they can never give, —the power which influences the councils of a people; which directs and executes high national movements; which extends the domain of letters and science, and is felt in the destinies of a country and an age. Will we have this power? The popular voice of the State has wisely determined that we will.

"*A University shall be established in the city of New Orleans, of four Faculties, to wit: One of Law, one of Medicine, one of the Natural Sciences, and one of Belles Lettres.—Art. 137 Constitution.*"

I know that there are many views current in relation to this University, and conflicting schemes. Some altogether too elaborate, complex, and expensive for our present condition and resources, and others little likely to be efficient. The legislature has, I think, wisely obviated the difficulty of determining between these, by adopting and passing the bill introduced by Col. Farrar, of the House, which establishes the institution generally, and confers upon an administration selected by the Governor and Senate, all the details of the system.

The Act says nothing of the number or pay of the Professors, the maximum or minimum rates of tuition, the period of appointing administrators, or of entering upon their duties, nor has there been a dollar appropriated or a provision made for buildings, apparatus, etc.

Although I have the utmost confidence that gentlemen will be appointed to the administration eminently qualified by their knowledge or practical experience, to carry out an organization suited to our condition, wants and resources, I cannot but fear that in aiming too high, or in the disposition to do too much, we shall retard the work, and find ourselves longer than is generally imagined in no better a condition in this particular than at present "resolving and resolving, and resolving," to "die the same," at last.

I shall be pardoned if in my anxiety upon this subject, the anxiety of one who feels that he has lived a long time to have done so little, I should venture to propose to you, who I doubt not have regarded the subject with the same care and interest, a plan plain, practical, ready and economical for an institution of the kind referred to. It is based upon a communication elicited by me from a gentleman of high scholarship residing at Baton Rouge, Professor Burke, with whom I have agreed upon material points. If I am not over confident, it is the most available plan yet suggested. I speak chiefly of the fiscal character, for upon this only do I pretend to pronounce any decided opinion. If I am wrong, the mischief will not be serious, farther than an hour's trespass upon your time, a thing that must always be submitted to patiently in this world.

But to the point: the first and cardinal consideration is, how much money do we want, and how shall we get it? This is the hinge upon which every thing turns. A University without means is a chimera of questionable shape. "Without money and without price" who shall buy and transact, who shall serve and be served, except in heaven?

Let the University partake of the nature of a joint stock incorporation, with a capital of $300,000, in shares or presentations of $1,500 each,—say two hundred presentations. How shall these be taken up?

Let the State subscribe for forty, say	$ 60,000
City of New Orleans, forty, ...	60,000
Private individuals, one hundred and twenty, ...	180,000
	$300,000

And first of the subscription of the State; this is a small sum to be required for so great a cause, and shall a wealthy commonwealth like ours hesitate in the matter? It will be seen directly, however, that an ample equivalent will be held out to the State for her liberality here, independently of having performed a high act of public duty. The State might be even allowed to appropriate her subscription to the *construction of buildings, purchase of apparatus, etc.*

In relation to the city of New Orleans she is deeply interested in the success of this movement. The institution will be located in her midst. It will operate most immediately upon her population and increase her rising influence. She will not find it difficult to obtain the means to appropriate, and the act will be sustained by a unanimous approval of our citizens.

The co-operation of private individuals in all public movements is always demanded, and not often refused. They will come forward with their purses to relieve their country in the hour of peril, they will subscribe liberally when the cause has been demonstrated a good and a great one. We invoke them in this instance in every part of the State to raise for the University the sum of $180,000. How many wealthy and patriot citizens have we? How many single individuals in other States have appropriated as much as we demand from all?

Can there not without difficulty be found five men in the State who will take each four shares—

Twenty shares at $1,500,	$ 30,000
Twenty to take two shares each,	60,000
Sixty to take one share each,	90,000
	$180,000

If considerations of public spirit be supposed insufficient to move the State, city, and individual citizens, to the extent required, others will be alleged in a few moments, which will hardly be regarded as other than the most influential every where. We will see first, however, supposing the $300,000 raised, what is to be done with it?

Sixty thousand dollars will be sufficient for the erection of proper buildings, and a sufficient apparatus for a beginning. This will leave two hundred and forty thousand dollars, which properly invested would yield an interest of nineteen thousand dollars.

Professors must be paid a fixed compensation and sufficient to render the office, as it should be, one the highest dignity and importance. Mere economical notions in these matters are ever misplaced, and defeat the best aims we have in view. The best talent of the country should if possible be commanded, and such talent must be proportionably rewarded.

Let there be then seven professorships.

President and Professor of Moral, Intellectual, and Political Philosophy,	$ 5,000
Professor of Natural Sciences,	3,500
Professor of Commercial and Statistical Information,	3,500
Professor of Rhetoric and Belles Lettres,	3,500
Professor of Mathematics,	3,500
Professor of Ancient Languages,	3,500
Professor of Modern Languages,	3,500
	$26,000
Interest as above,	19,000
Deficit,	7,000

We shall see directly how this and more shall be obtained.

Fixing the rate of instruction at the very low price, so as to attract even citizens of most limited means, of $50 per year (private schools charge now in the city $100) for each student instructed in one or all of the departments, the number of students could not possibly fall short of 140, the Medical College has as large a number, we have at once the sum of $7,000, the amount desired.

In addition to the 140 students, the University shall be required to instruct free of any expense or charge, a certain number of students to be presented as follows.

The State to be allowed to have always in the University twice as many students, selected from the public schools, as she has taken shares or presentations, say 120 students.

The city to have the same privilege from her public schools.

Private individuals to be in the same position, and this is a noble one, if they have no children of their own, to be *in perpetuo* a benefactor to those in humble life, eager for knowledge, but unable to obtain it. What a proud satisfaction for so small an expenditure. This right of presentation would be inheritable, alienable, not liable to taxation, seizure upon execution, &c.

Here, then, is the rough draft of a system which calls upon the State only to erect buildings; which calls upon the 150,000 citizens of New Orleans for 40 cents each; upon our men of large fortunes for a small fraction at the highest interest, and we have educated in Louisiana, in the highest branches of knowledge, 140 students paying the paltry sum of $50 each per annum, and 480 paying nothing at all.

And here, in conclusion, let me observe.

1. The capital of $300,000 is a mere arbitrary one, assured as a minimum; but let it be $1,000,000, if we please, if so much can be raised.

2. The number of professors may be increased or diminished to suit the means of the institution; the same of the rates of tuition.

The law and medical department will stand upon different and independent ground, as made to do by the late act of incorporation.

3. Academical education, with slight modification, could be made a part of the plan.

5. Additional means for apparatus, library, &c., could be obtained by collection throughout the state, from those who, being unable to give $1500, would freely furnish 5, 10, 20, or 50 dollars.

This you will perceive throws much labor upon the administrators to perform, in which, however, they will be moved by high considerations. I think the institution could succeed now upon such a basis. I am very much afraid that it will not succeed for a very long time upon any other. But I see I have written you a long letter, in the dry details of which you are doubtless fatigued. However, forgive the intrusion from the motive,

And believe me to be with high regard

Your friend,

Maunsel White.

–*De Bow's Review*, III (1847), 260-65.

8. An act to establish in the City of New Orleans the University of Louisiana, 1847

Section 1. Be it enacted by the Senate and House of Representatives of the State of Louisiana in General Assembly convened, That in pursuance of title seventh and articles one hundred and thirty-seven, one hundred and thirty-eight, and one hundred and thirty-nine, of the constitution of the State, a State University is hereby instituted and established in the city of New-Orleans, to be called and known by the name and style of the University of Louisiana; and that said University shall be under the immediate control, management and supervision of thirteen persons, to be called the Administrators of the University of Louisiana; of which said body of Administrators, the Governor of the State for the time being, the Chief Justice of the Supreme Court, and the Mayor of the city of New-Orleans shall be, ex-officio, of that number; and the remaining members of said board shall be appointed every four years by the Governor, by and with the advice and consent of the Senate, and commissioned by the Governor, but shall receive no compensation for their services: Provided, that at the first meeting of the Administrators after their appointment, those appointed shall divide themselves by lot into two classes (as equally as can be), and the seats of the first class shall be vacated at the end of two years, and those of the second class at the expiration of four years, to date from the first of April, 1846.

Sec. 2. Be it further enacted, &c.; That said Administrators and their successors, shall be and remain forever a body politic and corporate, in fact and name, by the style of the Administrators of the University of Louisiana, and by that name shall and may have perpetual succession hereafter, and shall be able in law to sue and be sued, implead and be impleaded, answer and be answered unto, defend and be defended in all courts and places whatsoever, and may have a common seal, and may change and alter the same at their pleasure, and shall also be able in law to take by purchase, gift, grant, devise and donations, *inter vivos et mortis causa,* made by individuals or corporations, within this State or elsewhere, and in any manner to hold any real or personal estate whatever; and also, that they and their successors shall have power to grant, bargain, sell, lease, demise or otherwise dispose of (except by mortgage), all or any part of the said real or personal estate, as to them shall seem best for the interest of said University excepting the buildings of the University, the library, apparatus and scientific collections, which shall only be conveyed after the consent of the Legislature to do the same is first had and obtained; and no mortgage shall ever be given on any of the property of said University without first getting the permission of the Legislature on the specific purpose.

Sec. 3. Be it further enacted, &c.; That said University shall be composed of the following departments or faculties, to wit: one of law, one of medicine, one of the natural sciences, and one of letters, and a college proper or academical department; all of which said faculties, as the resources of the University increase, shall be completed by the said administrators, excepting the medical department, which shall be composed of and formed by the Medical College of Louisiana, as it is at present organized and established by law, which said department, as is hereinafter provided for, shall be engrafted on said University and be conducted in manner as will hereinafter be directed.

Sec. 4. Be it further enacted, &c.; That said Administrators and their successors shall forever hereafter have full power to direct and prescribe the course of study and the discipline to be observed in said University; and also to select and appoint by ballot or otherwise, the president of the said University, who shall hold his office at the pleasure of the board and perform the duties of a Professor; and shall also name and appoint such other professor or professors, tutor or tutors, usher or ushers, to assist in the government and instruction of the students, and all other officers that said Administrators shall deem meet, they being removable at the pleasure of the said board of Administrators. And said Administrators shall fix the salaries of the president, professors and tutors in the academical department and fill all vacancies in the Professorship; Provided, that the vacancies in the law or medical department shall be filled from persons first recommended to the Administrators by the respective faculties of those departments in which a vacancy may happen. And provided, also, that no such professor, tutor or other assistant officer shall be Administrator of said University.

Sec. 5. Be it further enacted, &c.; That five of said Administrators lawfully convened, as hereinafter directed, shall be a quorum for the transaction of all business, except for the disposal of real estate, and for the choice or removal of a president, professor or tutor; for either of which purposes there shall be a meeting of at least nine Administrators.

Sec. 6. Be it further enacted, &c.; That said Administrators shall elect one of their number as Chairman of the Board of Administrators, once in every two years, or oftener if they deem necessary, which said chairman shall preside over all of their deliberations.

Sec. 7. Be it further enacted, &c.; That said Administrators shall have power to fill all vacancies in their own board, up to the meeting of the Legislature first after the happening of any vacancy; and also, a majority of the whole board concurring, to declare vacant the seat of any Administrator who shall absent himself from five successive meetings of the Board of Administrators; that they shall meet on their own adjournment, and as often as they shall be summoned by the chairman; or, in his absence, by the senior Administrator, whose seniority shall be accounted according to the order to be made out by said Administrators at the first meeting after their nomination; Provided, that they cause notice of the time and place of said meeting to be advertised in one or more of the newspapers published at New-Orleans and Baton Rouge; and those residing in New-Orleans shall be notified, in writing, of the time and place of every meeting.

Sec. 8. Be it further enacted, &c.; That said Administrators and their successors shall have ample power and authority to make and order all ordinances and by-laws which to them shall seem expedient for carrying into effect the design contemplated by the establishment of this University; Provided, that such ordinances or by-laws shall not make the religious tenet of any person a condition of admission to any privilege or office in said University; nor shall any course of religious instruction be taught or allowed of a sectarian character and tendency; and said ordinances and by-laws shall not be inconsistent with the Constitution and laws of the United States, nor of this State, nor of the provisions of this charter.

Sec. 9. Be it further enacted, &c.; That said Board of Administrators shall have the right of conferring, by diploma, under their common seal, on any person or persons whom they may think worthy thereof, all such literary honors and degrees as are known and usually granted by any University or College in the United States or elsewhere; and the degree of Bachelor at Law and Doctor of Medicine, granted by said Administrators shall authorise the person or persons on whom it is conferred to practise law, or physic and surgery, in this State, anything in any law to the contrary notwithstanding.

Sec. 10. Be it further enacted, &c.; That all diplomas granted by said Board of Administrators shall be signed by the president of the University, the chairman of the Board of Administrators and the professors of the department in which the students may have graduated, and by such other officers of the University as may be provided for by the by-laws of the University.

Sec. 11. Be it further enacted, &c.; That the Board of Administrators shall have ample powers for the government of said University, under such restrictions only as are herein specified; and shall provide for the number of professors and tutors and their appointment; and as they shall, for each department, deem necessary, to afford a full course of instructions in said University, as is contemplated by the constitution; and may from time to time increase or diminish the number of professors or tutors, as the condition and prosperity of the University may require and suggest; Provided, that in the medical department, there shall never be less than seven professors, which number shall be increased only at the suggestion and recommendation of the faculty of that department.

Sec. 12. Be it further enacted, &c.; That said Administrators may, if deemed necessary, establish a preparatory or grammar school to be attached to the University, and shall procure suitable buildings for the same, appoint tutors and ordain by-laws for the discipline and government of said primary department; and may also attach to the University such other institutions, literary or scientific societies, schools and professorships, as to them may seem advisable, all of which so far as relates to instruction, shall be under the control of the Board of Administrators.

Sec. 13. Be it further enacted, &c.; That there shall be but one session within the space of a year, of eight months duration, commencing the first day of November and ending on the thirtieth of June, and students regularly matriculated in the college proper and candidates for degrees shall be required to devote at least one session to each of the classes, Freshmen, Sophomore, Junior and Senior, before graduating, unless their proficiency may, after a satisfactory examination before the Administrators, entitle them to enter a higher class; Provided, however, that every candidate for the degree of Bachelor of Arts be required to devote a full session to the senior course.

Sec. 14. Be it further enacted, &c.; That any student not desiring to pursue all the studies taught in the academical department, shall be entitled to an examination, on any branch of learning pursued in the regular course, and if found proficient, shall receive a certificate under the seal of the University.

Sec. 15. Be it further enacted, &c.; That there shall be provided, by the Administrators of the University, an ordinance fixing a day for an annual public examination of the students in the academical department of the University, and a commencement day for the conferring publicly, degrees on the graduates of that department, and of the law and medical departments.

Sec. 16. Be it further enacted, &c.; That said Board of Administrators shall appoint a treasurer and secretary, to continue in office for four years; that the treasurer shall keep a true and fair account of all moneys by him received and paid out, and that the Secretary shall attend the Board of Administrators, and shall keep a fair journal of the meetings and proceedings of the Board of Administrators, in which the yeas and nays, on all questions, shall be entered, if required by any one of the Administrators present; and to all books and papers of the corporation, every administrator shall always have access, and be permitted to have copies of them.

Sec. 17. Be it further enacted, &c.; That the Legislature shall forever have the power of visiting and inspecting said University by a committee of their own body, to be appointed for that purpose and also of controling by law said corporation, and to repeal this charter; and may require of the Administrators to make a full report to said committee of the situation of the affairs of said University at any time.

Sec. 18. Be it further enacted, &c.; That no person who shall accept the office of Administrator of this University shall act as trustee, president, principal or tutor, or other office in any other school, academy or college in this State.

Sec. 19. Be it further enacted, &c.; That all of the real and personal estate whatsoever, or in any wise belonging to the Medical College of Louisiana be, and the same is hereby transferred to and vested in the University of Louisiana: Provided, the Administrators of said University appropriate the sum which the real and personal estate of said Medical College cost, to the purchase of philosophical and chemical apparatus for the use of said college, and that said Medical School, as it now is organised, is herein and hereby incorporated with and made a part of the said University of Louisiana; and that said Medical college, as it is now established by law, shall constitute the only medical department of said University; and the professors now filling the chairs in that school, shall constitute the medical faculty of the department of medicine of the University and fill the same chairs in the University now filled by them in the Medical School of Louisiana; and hereafter be under the government of the Board of Administrators of the University; Provided, that in the requisites for admission, the examining the candidates for their degrees in said Medical Department and the Law Department, the management of pecuniary concerns, the salaries of the professors, and the price of tuition and terms of admission shall be under the exclusive control of the faculty of said department respectively.

Sec. 20. Be it further enacted, &c.; That the department of law shall consist of three or more professors, to be appointed by the Administrators, who shall be required to give a full course of lectures on international, constitutional, maritime, commercial and municipal or civil law, and instruction in the practice thereof, to be regulated among themselves, by the designating the chairs or professorships, and prescribing the course to be taught by each; and whose salaries shall be paid by the money received for admission to their lectures; and said department to be regulated by the faculty of law, in the same manner and to the same extent as is provided in the foregoing section for the Medical Department of the University.

Sec. 21. Be it further enacted, &c.; That the faculties of the University, the situation of the institution permitting, may admit, free of charge, such number of indigent young men of the State, of good abilities and correct moral deportment as they may deem expedient.

Sec. 22. Be it further enacted, &c.; That the Medical Department of the University shall at all times have free access to the Charity Hospital of New-Orleans, for the purpose of affording their students practical illustrations of the subject they teach.

Sec. 23. Be it further enacted, etc.; That when any scholar who shall have prepared himself at any other school or academy within this State, and is desirous of being admitted to the academical departments of the University, he shall be permitted so to do, if, on due examination by the academical faculty, he shall be found competent, and may enter, according to his progress in sciences, such class as his knowledge and examination may justify, and the provisions of the thirteenth section of this act.

Sec. 24. Be it further enacted, etc.; That the students attending the University, the president, professors, tutors and under officers of the same, for and during their connection with the institution, shall be exempt from militia duties and serving on juries.—*Acts Passed at the Second Session of the First Legislature of the State of Louisiana*, pp. 39-44. See William L. Fleming, *Louisiana State University, 1860-1896* (Baton Rouge: Louisiana State University Press, 1936), p. 19. Fleming says, "The [constitutional] convention [of 1845] was not heartily in favor of state support of higher education. The Constitution authorized a 'University of Louisiana' at New Orleans and directed that the legislature should provide for its further organization and government but shall be under no obligation to contribute to the establishment or support of said university by appropriations." See also William L. Fleming's *General W. T. Sherman as College President* (Cleveland, Ohio: The Arthur H. Clarke Company, 1912).

9. Rules on discipline of students at the University of Mississippi, 1848

Discipline

1. The following penalties for the violation of the Laws & Regulations of the University will be imposed, viz: reproof, reprimand, forfieture of certificate, suspension for the session & fines for injury to the College property.

2. Every student on his admission pledges his honor to abstain from wilfully or deliberately violating the laws & regulations of the University, & the discipline of the college will be directed to the student's sentiments of honor.

3. No student shall be expelled but for giving, receiving or bearing a challenge; acting as second or friend in any matter connected with a duel; for using or threatening to use any weapon in a quarrel; for gambling or for the commission of some flagetious offence.

4. No student shall be suspended or expelled without due notice of the offense with which he stands charged, or without the opportunity of explaining his conduct.

5. No reprimand shall be given but by a resolution of the Faculty.

6. Instead of suspension for the first offence the Faculty, in their

discretion, may permit the student to remain in the University on his good behavior in which case any further violation of the Laws & regulations subjects him to the penalty of suspension.

7. When a student is suspected of having committed any offence, one of the Faculty shall be appointed to confer with him. If he admits it, or refuses to deny it the due penalty shall be enforced by resolution of the Faculty. If he denies it on his honor, he shall be acquitted, unless the evidence of its commission be so strong as to produce a unanimous conviction of his guilt in the minds of the Faculty.

8. Any student who gets drunk, or who wantonly defaces the college buildings or property by writing, cutting or other injury shall be suspended.

9. Any dishonorable conduct shall be visited with suspension.

10. Any violation of gentlemanly propriety of deportment shall be punished in the discretion of the Faculty.

11. Any disrespectful language or conduct to a Professor or other Officer of the University shall be punished with suspension.

12. When a student commits an offence under the eye of a Professor, he shall not be questioned on his honor, but proceeded against.

13. Any student who may be reported five times absent from any class without permission or sufficient excuse or five times unprepared, or eight times in the aggregate of both, shall forfeit his certificate in that class, and any student so forfeiting all his certificates for the season, shall be suspended.

14. A student suspended or expelled from the University shall not remain on the College grounds more than twenty four hours after the notification thereof; nor shall he be permitted to enter them thereafter without express permission from the president.

15. Whenever a student may be suspended or expelled it shall be the duty of the Secretary of the Faculty at once to notify himself and his parent or guardian by letter, of such suspension or expulsion, and of the cause thereof.

16. A student behaving improperly in the lecture room may be sent from it and forbidden to return until he promises amendment.

17. For defacing or injuring College property, besides any other property penalty, the student shall be fined in the discretion of the Faculty, and shall pay for the reparation of such damages.

18. When the student doing such injury is not known, the expense of reparation, if in the students' rooms, shall be divided between

the occupants; in any other part of the dormitories it shall be assessed on the inhabitants of the tenement; in any other buildings, or in the grounds, it shall be assessed upon all.

19. Students are not permitted to have fire-arms or other weapons in their possession; nor to play cards or other gambling games; nor to keep dogs within the college precincts; nor to play on any musical instrument during college hours; or to the disturbance of their fellow-pupils; nor to tear down notices posted up by order of the Faculty, nor otherwise to deface them; nor are they at any time to make any disturbance within the limits of the University.

20. No student shall bring or cause to be brought into the College grounds or on any occasion keep wine or spirits without the written permission of the president.

21. No student shall go to Oxford or absent himself from the University without permission from some member of the Faculty.

22. The student is subject to the laws & regulations of the University during the whole term of his connection with the University, in whatever place he may be, except during the summer vacations.

23. No reproof shall be given by any Prof. in public, except whēre the good order of the class requires it, and in all cases the feelings of the students shall be respected.

24. No lights will be allowed in the dormitorics after 11 o'clock P.M.

25. Many cases may occur which are not provided for expressly by law, and in all such cases the Faculty may punish any student offending according to the nature & circumstances of the case.

26. No society shall be formed without the permission from the Faculty, and no more than two societies shall be in existence at the same time; and it shall always be within the power of the Faculty to suppress any society for sufficient cause.

Redress of Grievances

1. When any individual student has any ground of complaint, he will report it in writing signed with his name to the President, by whom, if necessary, it shall be referred to the Faculty at their next meeting, & considered by them.

2. When any general grievance is complained of, a respectful written address to the Faculty, signed by the complainants, will always meet with attentive consideration.

Free Students

1. Students preparing for the ministry of any denomination will be admitted into each class without tuition fee, on application to the Professors—but whenever the student shall abandon such intention, or shall act in a manner inconsistent therewith, the fees so dispensed with, shall be due.

2. Any young man desirous of entering the University but unable to afford to pay for tuition, will be admitted by the Professors without fee into each of their classes, on standing the regular examination & producing certificates of good moral character, & of his inability to pay; such certificates to be signed by some resident minister, or the principal of some academy in the neighborhood from which he comes. In this case the matriculation fee will not be required nor will the student be required to reside in the dormitories.

3. In both cases strict secrecy will be observed, and there will be no difference in the treatment of different classes of students.

4. A student from each senatorial district in the State, will be admitted upon the recommendation of the Boards of police, tuition free. This admission shall be termed a scholarship, and shall be the reward of merit.

5. This examination will be conducted in the presence of the Boards of Police of each district, by three competent examiners, being good classical scholars, appointed by them.

6. No such student shall be admitted into any other than the Freshman Class and not until after the due examination by the Faculty.

7. When the student selected in such manner as may be prescribed, shall decline to accept the scholarship within one month after his nomination, or any time prior to the opening of the session, the candidate who may have stood the next best examination, shall be entitled to the scholarship, upon the like recommendation of the Board of Police.—Campbell, *op. cit.*, pp. 84-99.

10. Offences and punishments at South Carolina College, 1848

If any student shall keep in his room, or within the College, or in the town of Columbia, or in its vicinity, any pistol, dirk, sword-cane, bowie knife, or other deadly weapon, he shall be forthwith suspended and reported for expulsion.

No student shall bring or use within the precincts of the College, or bring within the same, any spiritous liquors, dogs or arms or ammunition, nor shall any one keep or hire any horse or mule, servant or servants, without permission of the President; and any student who shall violate this rule shall be liable to admonition, suspension or expulsion.

No student shall be permitted to entertain company in his room, and if any student shall refuse to open the door of his room, when required by any one of the Faculty or a Tutor, he shall be liable to admonition, suspension or expulsion.

No student, or students, shall be permitted to make any ball or festive entertainment, except a ball at Commencement; nor shall any student attend or take part in any thing of the kind without the special permission of the President.

No student shall leave the town of Columbia, without the permission of the President.

No student, or students, shall make any bonfire, or other like fire, within or near the College enclosure, nor shall they throw or use any fire-ball or lighted torch in the same, on pain of admonition, suspension or expulsion, at the discretion of the Faculty.

If any student shall be convicted of having or blowing any horn or trumpet, or beating any drum, or of disturbing the quiet of the institution by riding any horse or mule within or near the College enclosure, or of making any loud or unusual noise by any other means, within or about the same, he shall be punished by admonition or suspension, at the discretion of the Faculty.

If any student shall, knowingly, receive, harbor or entertain in his room, any other student who has been suspended and ordered to leave the College by the Faculty, he shall be liable to admonition or suspension, at the discretion of the Faculty.—Edwin L. Green, *A History of the University of South Carolina*, pp. 222-23.

11. Virginia Senators and Representatives in Congress may be members of the Board of Visitors of the University of Virginia, 1848

Whereas doubts have arisen whether the act, entitled "an act to reduce into one act the acts to disable officers of the continental government from holding offices under the authority of this common wealth," passed January sixteenth, eighteen hundred and nineteen, does or does not disable the senators and representatives of Virginia in the congress of the United States from holding or accepting the appointment of visitors of the University of Virginia:

Resolved therefore by the senate and house of delegates of Virginia,

That the above recited act shall not be construed to prevent, or in any manner disqualify any such senator or representative from accepting or holding the place of visitor of the university aforesaid.—*Acts of the General Assembly of Virginia*, 1847-48, p. 356.

12. Commercial College in the University of Louisiana, 1849

This department of the University of Louisiana is now organized and prepared to conduct the education of students, in mercantile and other business matters. *Classes will be formed from November until May.*

There will be two courses of instruction:

1st. *A Course of Lectures* upon—The rise and progress of the science of political economy; productive powers of labor; nature, accumulation, etc., of stock; progress of opulence in different nations; mercantile systems; revenue; sources of public wealth; growth and progress of the United States; ancient commerce; commerce in dark ages; in middle ages; growth of modern commerce; present commercial world; navigation; treaties; tariffs; banks; internal improvements; agriculture; manufactures; population; statistics, etc.

This course will consist of about twenty-five or thirty lectures, during the winter, at such hours, and on such days, as may be most agreeable to the majority of the class.

Tickets for the course—which will be as interesting to all classes of citizens as to those engaged in or preparing for mercantile life—TEN DOLLARS.

2d *Course.*—This is intended for regular matriculated students. Instructions will cover the whole field of commercial education, given daily, in three or four recitations, etc.: Writing, book-keeping, commercial correspondence, accounts, account sales, invoices, general principles of commercial law, banking, insurance, exchange, partnership, factorage, guarantee, brokerage, bankruptcy, wrecks, salvage, freights, privateering, marque and reprisal, quarantine, custom house regulations, etc., sketches of eminent merchants. A course of reading in history and commercial geography and navigation, will be embraced.

Length of term occupied in this course will be five months, and the charge for each student $50. The services of an accomplished tutor, in this department, will be obtained, and no pains spared in making the pupils proficient. Public examinations will also be had. Deductions will be made where students enter after the beginning of term.

In a country like ours, nothing can be more important than such a course of education. The student is at once fitted for the active, busy life, in which he must engage to reach success and fortune. Commercial colleges are growing up in various parts of the Union, and can be more important no where than in New Orleans.

Planters in LOUISIANA and the neighboring States, would do well to consider the advantages of this institution to their sons.

The advantages of public and private libraries, reading rooms, and business experience enjoyed in New Orleans, are unrivaled.

Students admitted at any time. See advertisement in this Review. Address: J. D. B. De Bow, Professor of Political Economy, Commerce and Statistics, University of Louisiana.–*De Bow's Review*, I, No. 1, New Series, 1849, p. 188.

13. A DESCRIPTION OF THE UNIVERSITY OF GEORGIA, 1849

This institution is located in Athens, in Clarke county. As early as 1788-9, the Legislature of Georgia made liberal endowments for the establishment of the University; but it did not go into operation until 1801. Its first President was Mr. Josiah Meigs, Professor of Natural Philosophy and Astronomy in Yale College, a gentleman of high reputation as a scholar, but owing to circumstances which reflect no blame upon him, the University did not realize the expectations of its friends. Mr. Meigs resigned the presidency in 1811, and the Rev. Dr. Kollock, well known as a polished scholar, and great orator, was elected to fill the vacancy. This gentleman, however, declined the appointment, and Dr. Brown, Professor of Moral Philosophy, Columbia College, South Carolina, was then chosen to the office, who continued to preside over the University until 1816, when he resigned. Dr. Finley, of New-Jersey, was appointed his successor. This great and good man applied himself with indefatigable zeal to the advancement of the College, and confidence was felt through the State, that it would soon occupy a prominent stand among the literary institutions of the United States; but the sudden and lamented death of Dr. Finley for a time obscured the cheering prospect. The Rev. N. S. S. Beman was selected to fill the vacancy occasioned by the demise of Dr. Finley; but this gentleman declined serving. In 1819, the celebrated Dr. Moses Waddel, whose name will long be remembered by the citizens of South Carolina and Georgia, was elected President; and under whose administration the University succeeded, to an extent beyond the most sanguine hopes of its friends. Dr. Waddel resigned in 1829, when the present incumbent, Dr. Alonzo Church, of Brattleborough, Vermont, and a graduate of Middlebury College, Vermont, was appointed to this distinguished station. The character of Dr. Church is so favourably known to the people of Georgia, that it is almost superfluous to say any thing in relation to him. With a mind richly furnished with the stores of learning–with manners proverbially captivating–with uncommon kindness of disposition, and with the prudence and firmness requisite to be possessed by those to whom the people of Georgia commit the education of their sons, at a period the most critical in the life of youth, Dr. Church has every qualification for the exalted position which he has so long filled.

Associated with him are seven Professors, viz.

James Jackson, A.M., Professor of Natural History and Modern Languages; appointed in 1823.

James P. Waddel, A.M., Professor of Ancient Languages, a son of Dr. Moses Waddel; appointed in 1836.

Charles F. McCay, A.M., Professor of Mathematics, Astronomy, and Civil Engineering; appointed in 1837.

John Le Conte, M.D., Professor of Natural Philosophy and Chemistry; appointed in 1846.

Hon. Joseph Henry Lumpkin, Professor of Law; appointed in 1847.

N. H. Wood, A. M., Adjunct Professor of Mathematics; appointed in 1848.

The Rev. William T. Brantley, A.M., Professor of Belles Lettres, Oratory, and History; appointed in 1848.

M. C. Fulton, A.M., Tutor in Ancient Languages; appointed in 1847.

The University is now in a state of great prosperity. The number of students, according to the last catalogue, was one hundred and forty.

The resources of the University are 100,000 dollars in stock of the Bank of the State of Georgia, and about 1500 dollars in other stocks, together with the proceeds of the tuition of students, and a small amount of town lots. The buildings are: Two three-story, 120 by 45 feet, for lodging rooms for students; a philosophical hall and chemical laboratory, a chapel, a library and cabinet, president's house, and three houses for the professors. The library contains between eight and nine thousand volumes. The philosophical apparatus is one of the most extensive and complete in the country; the chemical laboratory is ample; the cabinet of minerals large, and the botanic garden in good order.

The College has forty-four acres of ground on which the buildings are erected, and which is set apart by the Legislature of the State for that purpose, and can never be diminished.

Connected with the College are two societies. Each has a very neat and convenient hall, erected at the expense of the society, and costing about 4000 dollars each. The library of each of these associations contains between two and three thousand volumes.—George White, *Statistics of the State of Georgia* (Savannah: W. Thorne Williams, 1849), pp. 74-76.

14. Proposed endowment of the University of Louisiana, 1849

At the last session of Congress, a grant of the unreclaimed and swamp lands, within the State, was made to Louisiana, through the exertions of one of her citizens. It is thought that these lands will repay all the expense of drainage and reclamation and leave a net surplus of at least *one million* or *one million and a half* acres of land, valuable for the culture of sugar and other agricultural purposes. The Legislature of Louisiana will now have an opportunity of endowing, in a becoming manner, the noble institution which was in contemplation by the convention that framed our last constitution. It can make the UNIVERSITY OF LOUISIANA one of the proudest and most distinguished seats of learning in America, and attract to it students from half the Confederacy, from the neighboring islands, from Mexico and portions of South America, and that WITHOUT ONE CENT OF EXPENSE TO THE PEOPLE. We propose that a portion of these reclaimed lands, say two or three hundred thousand acres, be reserved and appropriated as a *University Fund*, to be controlled by a Board of Administrators from the State at large. The grant from government is a pure gratuity, and it becomes a liberal State like Louisiana to apply a portion of it in the manner indicated. We have already a land fund for *school* purposes. The "University Fund," should realize an annual revenue of *forty thousand dollars*, the least sum at which an institution worthy of our position can be sustained. With this, fifteen professorships may be endowed, apparatus, library, cabinets, etc, provided, observatories and additional halls built, needy students educated free, etc. Without such endowment the University must degenerate into a mere grammar school, which its literary and scientific department is now in eminent danger of doing, despite of all the handsome structures erected or in progress.

The University should be required to *educate free* a certain number of students from the public schools of the whole State, and conduct *agricultural, geological, botanical, etc., surveys, of the State and analysis of its crops*, without expense.

It is worthy of remark, that Michigan, a new State, and with little advantage of position, has established a *University Land Fund*, capable of maintaining *twenty-six professorships*, furnishing magnificent buildings, apparatus, etc., and forming one of the most magnificent institutions in America! Alabama has a University Fund of $250,000.

In the same connection we remark, that in the proposed donation to Florida of the unreclaimed Ever Glades, the act reserves the lands for educational purposes for ever.—*De Bow's Review*, I, No. 1, New Series, 1849, pp. 188-89.

15. Annual legislative appropriations to South Carolina College (the University of South Carolina), 1850-1860

V. FOR THE SOUTH CAROLINA COLLEGE. For the salary of the President of the College, three thousand dollars; for the salaries of seven Professors of the College, two thousand five hundred dollars each; for the salary of the Treasurer of the College, five hundred dollars; for the salary of the Librarian of the College, six hundred dollars; for the salary of the Secretary of the Board of Trustees, two hundred dollars; for the salary of the Marshal, four hundred dollars; the salaries of the President, Professors, Treasurer and Librarian, to be paid by the Treasurer of the Upper Division, quarterly, in advance, their draft being countersigned by the Treasurer of the College; for the purchase of books for the College Library, two thousand dollars, to be paid to the draft of the President of the College, countersigned by the Treasurer of the same. (1850)

V. FOR THE SOUTH CAROLINA COLLEGE. For the salary of the President of the College, three thousand dollars; for the salaries of seven Professors of the College, two thousand five hundred dollars each; for the salary of the Treasurer of the College; five hundred dollars; for the salary of the Librarian of the College, six hundred dollars; for the salary of the Secretary of the Board of Trustees, two hundred dollars; for the salary of the Marshal, four hundred dollars; the salaries of the President, Professors, Treasurer and Librarian, to be paid by the Treasurer of the Upper Division, quarterly, in advance, their draft being countersigned by the Treasurer of the College; for the purchase of books for the College Library, two thousand dollars, to be paid to the draft of the President of the College, countersigned by the Treasurer of the same. (1851)

V. FOR THE SOUTH CAROLINA COLLEGE. For the salary of the President of the College, three thousand dollars; for the salaries of seven Professors of the College, two thousand five hundred dollars each; for the salary of the Treasurer of the College, five hundred dollars; for the salary of the Librarian of the College, six hundred dollars; for the salary of the Secretary of the Board of Trustees, two hundred dollars; for the salary of the Marshal, four hundred dollars; the salaries of the President, Professors, Treasurer and Librarian, to be paid by the Treasurer of the Upper Division, quarterly, in advance, their draft being countersigned by the Treasurer of the College; for the purchase of books for the College Library, two thousand dollars, to be paid to the draft of the President of the College, countersigned by the Treasurer of the same; for the expenses of one student at the South Carolina College, sent by the Orphan House in Charleston, four hundred dollars, to be paid to the order of the Chairman of the Board of Commissioners of the Orphan House; for building a new Chapel for said College, fifteen thousand dollars, to be expended by the Trustees of the said College. (1852)

V. FOR THE SOUTH CAROLINA COLLEGE. For the salary of the President of the College, three thousand dollars; for the salaries of seven Professors of the College, two thousand five hundred dollars each; for the salary of the Treasurer of the College, five hundred dollars; for the salary of the Librarian of the College, six hundred dollars; for the salary of the Secretary of the Board of Trustees, two hundred dollars; for the salary of the Marshal, four hundred dollars; the salaries of the President, Professors, Treasurer and Librarian, to be paid by the Treasurer of the Upper Division, quarterly, in advance, their draft being countersigned by the Treasurer of the College; for the purchase of books for the College Library, two thousand dollars, to be paid to the draft of the President of the College, countersigned by the Treasurer of the same; for the expenses of one student at the South Carolina College, sent by the Orphan House in Charleston, four hundred dollars, to be paid to the order of the Chairman of the Board of Commissioners of the Orphan House. (1853)

V. FOR THE SOUTH CAROLINA COLLEGE. For the salary of the President of the College, three thousand dollars; for the salaries of seven Professors of the College, two thousand five hundred dollars each; for the salary of the Treasurer of the College, five hundred dollars; for the salary of the Librarian of the College, six hundred dollars; for the salary of the Secretary of the Board of Trustees, two hundred dollars; for the salary of the Marshal, four hundred dollars; the salaries of the President, Professors, Treasurer and Librarian, to be paid by the Treasurer of the Upper Division, quarterly, in advance, their draft being countersigned by the Treasurer of the College; for the purchase of books for the College Library, two thousand dollars, to be paid to the draft of the President of the College, countersigned by the Treasurer of the same; for the expenses of one student at the South Carolina College, sent by the Orphan House in Charleston, four hundred dollars, to be paid to the order of the Chairman of the Board of Commissioners of the Orphan House. (1854)

V. FOR THE SOUTH CAROLINA COLLEGE. For the salary of the President of the College, three thousand dollars; for the salaries of seven Professors of the College, two thousand five hundred dollars each; for an Assistant for the present year to the Professor of Chemistry, Mineralogy and Geology, six hundred dollars; for the salary of the Treasurer of the College, five hundred dollars; for the salary of the Librarian of the College, six hundred dollars; for the salary of the Secretary of the Board of Trustees, two hundred dollars; for the salary of the Marshal, four hundred dollars; the salaries of the President, Professors, Assistant to the Professor of Chemistry, Mineralogy and Geology, Treasurer and Librarian, to be paid by the Treasurer of the Upper Division, quarterly, in advance, their draft being countersigned by the Treasurer of the College; for the purchase of books for the College Library, two thousand dollars, to be paid to the draft of the President of the College, countersigned by the Treasurer of the same; for the expenses of two students at the South Carolina College, sent by the Orphan House in Charleston, eight hundred dollars, to be paid to the order of the Chairman of the Board of Commissioners of the Orphan House. (1855)

V. FOR THE SOUTH CAROLINA COLLEGE. For the salary of the President of the College, three thousand dollars; for the salaries of seven Professors of the College, two thousand five hundred dollars each; for the salary of the Treasurer of the College, five hundred dollars; for the salary of the Librarian of the College, six hundred dollars; for the salary of the Secretary of the Board of Trustees, two hundred dollars; for the salary of the Marshal, four hundred dollars; the salaries of the President, Professors, Treasurer, and Librarian, to be paid by the Treasurer of the Upper Division, quarterly, in advance, their draft being countersigned by the Treasurer of the College; and for the purchase of books for the College Library, two thousand dollars, to be paid to the draft of the President of the College, countersigned by the Treasurer of the same; for the expenses of one student at the South Carolina College, sent by the Orphan House in Charleston, four hundred dollars, to be paid to the order of the Chairman of the Board of Commissioners of the Orphan House. (1856)

V. FOR THE SOUTH CAROLINA COLLEGE. For the salary of the President of the College, three thousand dollars; for the salaries of seven Professors of the College, two thousand five hundred dollars each; for the salary of the Treasurer of the College, five hundred dollars; for the salary of the Librarian of the College, six hundred dollars; for the salary of the Secretary of the Board of Trustees, two hundred dollars; for the salary of the Marshal, four hundred dollars; the salaries of the President, Professors, Treasurer, and Librarian, to be paid by the Treasurer of the Upper Division, quarterly, in advance, their draft being countersigned by the Treasurer of the College; and for the purchase of books for the College Library, two thousand dollars, to be paid to the draft of the President of the College, countersigned by the Treasurer of the same; for the expenses of one student at the South Carolina College, sent by the Orphan House in Charleston, four hundred dollars, to be paid to the order of the Chairman of the Board of Commissioners of the Orphan House. (1857)

V. FOR THE SOUTH CAROLINA COLLEGE. For the salary of the President of the College, three thousand dollars; for the salaries of seven Professors of the College, two thousand five hundred dollars each; for the salary of the Treasurer of the College, five hundred dollars; for the salary of the Librarian of the College, six hundred dollars; for the salary of the Secretary of the Board of Trustees, two hundred dollars; for the salary of the Marshal, four hundred dollars;

the salaries of the President, Professors, Treasurer, and Librarian, to be paid by the Treasurer of the Upper Division, quarterly, in advance, their draft being countersigned by the Treasurer of the College; and for the purchase of books for the College Library, two thousand dollars, to be paid to the draft of the President of the College, countersigned by the Treasurer of the same; for the expenses of one student at the South Carolina College, sent by the Orphan House in Charleston, four hundred dollars, to be paid to the order of the Chairman of the Board of Commissioners of the Orphan House. (1858)

V. FOR THE SOUTH CAROLINA COLLEGE. For the salary of the President of the College, three thousand dollars; for the salaries of seven Professors of the College, two thousand five hundred dollars each; for the salary of the Treasurer of the College, five hundred dollars; for the salary of the Librarian of the College, six hundred dollars; for the salary of the Secretary of the Board of Trustees, two hundred dollars; for the salary of the Marshal, five hundred dollars, and, also, one hundred dollars for error in the appropriation of last year; the salaries of the President, Professors, Treasurer and Librarian, to be paid by the Treasurer of the Upper Division, quarterly, in advance, their draft being countersigned by the Treasurer of the College; and for the purchase of books for the College Library, two thousand dollars, to be paid to the draft of the President of the College, countersigned by the Treasurer of the same; for the expenses of one student at the South Carolina College, sent by the Orphan House in Charleston, four hundred dollars, to be paid to the order of the Chairman of the Board of Commissioners of the Orphan House. (1859)

V. FOR THE SOUTH CAROLINA COLLEGE. For the salary of the President of the College, three thousand dollars; for the salaries of seven Professors of the College, two thousand five hundred dollars each; for the salary of the Treasurer of the College, five hundred dollars; for the salary of the Librarian of the College, six hundred dollars; for the salary of the Secretary of the Board of Trustees, two hundred dollars; for the salary of the Marshal, four hundred dollars, the salaries of the President, Professors, Treasurer and Librarian, to be paid by the Treasurer of the Upper Division, quarterly, in advance, their draft being countersigned by the Treasurer of the College; for the expense of one student at the South Carolina College, sent by the Orphan House in Charleston, four hundred dollars to be paid to the order of the Chairman of the Board of Commissioners of the Orphan House.—*The Statutes at Large of South Carolina*, XII, 6, (1850); 70-71, (1851); 130, (1852); 200-01, (1853); 274, (1854); 347-48, (1855); 418-19, (1856); 513, (1857); 585-86, (1858); 639-40, (1859); 722, (1860).

VII

1851–1860

1. Extracts from President Basil Manly's report on collegiate education to the Trustees of the University of Alabama, 1852

The following pages claim only to be a compilation of such facts and views on the subject of college organization as came within the reach of the writer, and of his colleague, Prof. L. C. Garland, during a very hurried journey in August and September, 1851. As the report was written singly for the use of the Trustees of the University of Alabama, and with no view to publication,—care was taken only to secure accuracy in the statement of facts; and no reference to the sources of information has been preserved. The writer drew freely from all sources,—conversations, discussions, catalogues and pamphlets; and put down what he deemed pertinent to the specific object before him, with no care of composition, and no claim of having exhausted the subject. Since the Trustees have ordered its publication for their own use, no time is enjoyed for its re-construction:—Such as it is, it must go before the public.

B. M.

University of Alabama,
July 20, 1852.

At the last annual session of the Trustees of the University of Alabama, the Board directed enquiry to be made whether any changes in the system of education pursued in the University are necessary and proper, in order to extend the benefits of the Institution to a greater number of the citizens of the State. To meet the purposes of this enquiry is the aim of the following pages.

The University of Alabama was opened, for instruction, April 17, A. D. 1831. It aimed to establish the four regular college classes, and the general features of the ordinary college system; yet it freely admitted students to the partial course;—and, among those who were candidates for a diploma, it allowed of their reciting with different classes according to their stage of advancement.

The written memorials preserved of the first two years do not distinguish students of the partial and of the regular course; nor without much labor can we certainly distinguish, out of the aggregate numbers in each of the first seven years of its existence, those which were new students in each year. A preparatory school was begun in 1835, and continued through that year and the next.

The following table exhibits statistics of the years from 1831 to 1837, inclusive.

Year.	No. students.	Par. course	New students.	Graduates.	Prep. sch.
1831	94	0	0	0	0
1832	111	0	0	0	1
1833	93	30	0	6	0
1834	101	37	0	11	0
1835	105	21	0	8	11
1836	157	52	0	10	27
1837	101	39	0	0	0

During the period from 1838 to 1852, inclusive, there was no preparatory school connected with the University; the classes were kept distinct; students were not admitted to the partial course, at will,—nor without a special reason calling for such indulgence; and it was the steady aim of the Faculty to attain an elevated standard of scholarship. During the last 10 years about 34 per cent. of all who had gained admittance into each class, including partial course students, have been graduated; and, in the same period about 22 per cent. of the students registered have annually withdrawn, on different accounts; —varying from 07 to 33 per cent. Failures to sustain themselves in study have rarely occurred in the mathematical or scientific departments, unless there was also a very low standing, if not a failure, in the classical. Of applicants for admission, since 1842, many have failed to attain the class to which they had aspired, comparatively few applicants have wholly withdrawn, without joining some class.

After the experience of twenty years, the Trustees have seen fit to pause and take a deliberate survey of all questions affecting the prospect of greater and more extended usefulness of the Institution; and it would be wholly unbecoming the age, as well as their own high trusts, to do this with prejudice, or in the spirit of party.

It has been charged on colleges that, while everything else is progressive, they are immoveable; conservative, indeed, but of knowledge, elsewhere forgotten or useless, opposed to what is intelligible, practical and popular. This is a serious charge, if true. It is admitted, that they do not consider every change an improvement; that they do not reject or abandon methods because they are old; and that they are more disposed to repair, than to overturn.

If the college system of this country, maintaining a remarkable similarity notwithstanding varieties and changes, were originally the result of intelligent consideration, as is fair to be presumed, this is a becoming spirit. In any well-considered scheme, changes must *grow; and gradually incorporate themselves into the original structure;*—nor should the conceit of superior, or exclusive, wisdom in succeeding generations of managers be suffered to obliterate the labors of predecessors. Every thing we enjoy is, in some degree, inherited....

If the present collegiate system has preserved its main features without radical modifications, for centuries, is it from a stolid aversion to change? or because the inventive generations have found nothing substantially better?

The main features of the collegiate system appear to be, a substratum, required alike of all, formed by the contemporaneous study of the ancient classics, (the latin and the greek languages and their literature) and of mathematics; to which a provision is made for adding, with some variety according to circumstances, a knowledge of the sciences successively developed, and of their applications to the useful purposes of life.

Of the importance of mathematics, not only as a means of cultivating a capacity for profound consecutive investigation, for close conclusive reasoning, but also as fundamental to much of our most important knowledge and business, less doubt seems to be entertained, than with respect to the ancient classics—on which the severest assault has been made.

As no satisfactory attainment can be made in this branch of knowledge without much and long-continued labor, the time for the acquisition of dead languages, which are the exclusive repositories of no science, is regarded by some as thrown away,—for all purposes of practical utility.

To this it is replied, that these languages are the most finished and refined ever spoken or written; that they are fountains of eloquence never surpassed, seldom equalled; that, if it be one of the highest attainments of a man of action and thought, to reason, instruct, convince and persuade, the knowledge of such an instrument as these afford cannot be dispensed with, but gives him a double advantage—that of the mastery of language, and of sharpening his own powers by intercourse with the master-minds of the world. These languages have been deemed indispensable to a thorough education for the last thousand years, in every clime, under all governments, and by every fraternity of learned men. If *we* should agree to call men learned without them, would the rest of the world think so? Among colleges, there is a republic, a sort of fellowship, of letters; the maintenance of which is of greater importance and wider scope than the temporary advantages gained, in numbers or popularity, by trimming or abridging their course to suit individual circumstances. The diplomas of colleges must mean and certify, substantially, the same thing, or they will certify nothing definite and intelligible; and he, that would ascertain the literary qualifications of another, for any purpose, must examine him for himself. And this consideration is specially important for us, as Americans—a people isolated and peculiar, who must hold an elevated rank as scholars among the nations of the earth.

So large a part of our own language, especially in the terminology of the learned professions and of the sciences, is derived from the ancient classics, that we cannot be masters of our own language without them. These, too, are the basis of the living tongue, the languages of commerce and of modern science; in so much that the full mastery of these will be even most economically made through the intervention of the classics.

As mathematics are more difficult, and require a greater vigor and maturity of mind, these languages furnish a needful preparation for them, filling up, with varied practice in the most useful description of training, the sort of intercalary period between elementary studies and the exact sciences. Below a certain period, difficult to fix, because varying with different individuals, the too early prosecution of mathematics and other studies demanding the vigorous and continued exertion of the reasoning powers may operate injuriously, even on those whose ready memory and ardent ambition may bear them successfully through. Precocity is usually followed by a stunted growth; —and the importance of the classics, as an intermediate exercise, has been considered so great that a finished instructor in mathematics has been wont to say that he would inscribe over the door of his recitation room—"Let no one ignorant of the classics enter here."

It is obvious that mathematics, also, are open to objections of this class. The unwilling student, with great force *to his own mind*, raises the question, "Of what possible use, in the business of life, can these mathematical abstractions be?" In reply, it might be asked,—how can any man, claiming to be *liberally educated*, imagine a position in life appropriate to *such a character*, in which he may not need them?

Through this branch of knowledge, in its various applications, it is that all the powers of nature have been brought under man's control. All knowledge, like the bays and inlets of the ocean, is connected and dependent; and the stress of an occasion may, at any time, require us to lean on points of support, and to draw on resources, wholly unforeseen. Facts of this kind are of daily occurrence among the elevated walks and stirring scenes of life. A thorough college training, other things being equal, will enable its possessor, placed in such contingencies, to outstrip his competitors, who have not that training; he will have confidence in his own resources, and feel the consciousness of power:—furnished generally for self-mastery, with elevated tastes and aspirations,—he appears *a man*, and difficulties and men give way before him. All subjects in Education are *instruments*, not *ends;* and their value is to be estimated by their bearing, first and mainly, *on education;* and through that chiefly on practical life. It might be difficult, in some cases, to say what particular portions of college studies have remained to be of direct use in the business of life: but there is *something* left, the fruit of them, which *is* of direct use,—viz., the ability and habit of applying the mind vigorously and successfully in any direction to which the business of life may call,—acuteness and energy on the one hand, refinement and grace on the other. Could any result be more practical, more directly useful?

The general voice, if consulted, would not be more diverse and inconsistent on any subject, perhaps,—than with respect to the object of education. Some would have every thing of *direct* utility;—others would *train the mind*. It would seem but rational to conclude that the first thing is to *subdue and train the faculties*—first, in the order of time, as well as in importance. The study of languages and mathematics affords an equable culture of the various powers—attention, memory, comparison, abstraction, association, analysis, and the methods of reasoning by induction and analogy. For this purpose, no substitute has been found for them. The exact sciences are but the application of mathematics to a few data derived from the universal experience of mankind; and, therefore, cannot be thought of as substitutes for those studies upon which they so exclusively depend. The natural sciences have been proposed, but are clearly inadequate; many of them are not of a nature to offer such training; a large part of the residue, great and glorious as they are, cannot be understood, as sciences, by a mind that has not learned to enquire, discriminate, reflect, and apply itself severely to other subjects;—while some absolutely demand both previous knowledge and training to be studied at all. Even in logic and intellectual philosophy, all is mist and fog, without. . . .

The proper object of collegiate education is the knowledge of principles and causes, rather than of facts, which belongs to a specific or professional education. The one is fundamental to the other. If the foundation be broad, deep and substantial, the superstructure, whatever its specific designation, is secure. Professional education, commencing its adventurous career at the point where the college curriculum has completed its functions, can be rendered as specific and definite as we wish, and efficient to some purpose. And here is the true point of divergence. The college suits all alike, affording the substratum which all intellectual pursuits require. To limit its usefulness to what are called learned professions, those of law, medicine, and theology, is but tacitly confessing that other professions are not intellectual, and require no high exercise of mind. So weak and shallow an imputation this busy age will not even stop to refute or consider; and even its haste and enterprize, so eager for tangible and immediate results, cannot wholly overlook the genial and productive influence of superior preparation in all the active departments of life.

The relative position, to which the sons of Southern planters seem, by their very birth-right, devoted, combines within itself the high and varied functions of law-giver, physician, moralist and judge; and, if the benefit of a liberal culture is peculiarly suitable to any class of men under heaven, it must be to those whose leisure, otherwise a curse, admits, while their responsibilities demand, it. The question is portentous, what will Southern youth become, if not highly educated?

And even if the theory of education did not prescribe a common training for all those who aspire to a position above that of the mere laborer, other considerations, conjointly would.

A college is a miniature world; and the commingling of all classes within it, on terms of equality, preparatory to entrance on the actual world, forms the character best. Engaged in the same studies, with equal facilities and burdens, conceit finds a cure, and diffidence encouragement; friendships are formed, relations are fixed, and the habit of self-command established;—indispensable attainments all,—which no other situation can so well impart.—The organization of a college, involving great expense in officers and complicated arrangements, is not susceptible of accommodating itself to an extended variety of cases.

If pupils of unequal attainments are thrown together in the same classes, the instructor will be under an invariable tendency to adapt his instruction to the weaker portion; and, if his compensation is made to depend on the numbers attracted and retained under his instruction, the effect will be inevitable. Thus the grade of attainment will be insensibly lowered, to the injury of the better prepared portion, and the detriment of the general interests of learning, without such adaptation or depression in the style and quality of instruction, the association in the same tasks of parties materially unequal, either retards the advance of the better qualified portion, or inflicts the evil of superficial, confused and unsatisfactory attainments on the less qualified.

If an attempt is made to accommodate the varying attainments and wants of all, by the multiplication of classes or sections, beyond a certain limit this soon runs into an expense and complication which no establishment can bear;—while classes broken into shreds, lose the stimulus of numbers, the excitement of competition—of mind whetting against mind.

To provide for the accommodation of the greatest number of promising subjects, within the means to which each institution is limited is both a duty and privilege of public educators. But a specific accommodation to each would require as many colleges, with all their costly equipments, as there are students; or in a proportion corresponding to the degree in which the accommodation is made specific. It then becomes a question to be settled by expediency and the nature of the case,—shall the college adapt itself to the varieties of students? or shall they adapt themselves to the college? To us, it seems to meet the responsibilities of a college, if they can comprehend within their plan the peculiarities of the *greater part* of those who come into their sphere,—while they afford to all equal opportunity of access to means of instruction *requisite for all*, and *sufficient for all*. The college having gone so far toward a compromise, it devolves on the minority of the individuals concerned to accomplish the remainder....—*Report on Collegiate Education, Made to the Trustees of the University of Alabama*, July, 1852 (Tuskaloosa: Printed by M. D. J. Slade, 1852).

CATALOGUS

SENATUS ACADEMICI

ET EORUM

Qui Munera et Officia Academica Gesserunt,

QUIQUE ALIQUOVIS GRADU EXORNATI SUNT,

IN

UNIVERSITATE CAROLINÆ-BOREALIS.

RALEGÆ:
GULIELMUS-DEWEY COOKE, TYPOGRAPHO.

M DCCC LII.

2. President James H. Thornwell of South Carolina College on the elective system in collegiate instruction, 1853

The South Carolina College.

...The first in the order of establishment, as well as the first in the order of importance, is the college. Devoted to the interests of general, in contradistinction from professional education, its design is to cultivate the mind without reference to any ulterior pursuits.... The culture of the mind, however, for itself, contributes to its perfection as an instrument, so that general education, while it directly prepares and qualifies for no special destination, indirectly trains for every vocation in which success is dependent upon intellectual exertion. It has taught the mind the use of its powers, and imparted those habits without which its powers would be useless; it makes men, and consequently promotes every enterprise in which men are to act. General education being the design of the college, the fundamental principles of its organization are easily deduced. The selection of studies must be made, not with reference to the comparative importance of their matter, or the practical value of the knowledge, but with reference to their influence in unfolding and strengthening the powers of the mind; as the end is to improve mind, the fitness for the end is the prime consideration....For speculative knowledge, of whatever kind, is only profitable to the student in his liberal cultivation, inasmuch as it supplies him with the object and occasion of exerting his faculties; since powers are only developed in proportion as they are exercised, that is put forth into energy. The mere possession of scientific truth is, for its own sake, valueless; and education is only education, inasmuch as it at once determines and enables the student to educate himself. Hence, the introduction of studies upon the ground of their practical utility is pro tanto, subversive of the college. It is not its office to make planters, mechanics, lawyers, physicians, or divines. It has nothing directly to do with the uses of knowledge. Its business is with minds, and it employs science only as an instrument for the improvement and perfection of mind. With it the habit of sound thinking is more than a thousand thoughts. When, therefore, the question is asked, as it often is asked by ignorance and empiricism, what is the use of certain departments of the college curriculum, the answer should turn, not upon the benefits which in after life may be reaped from these pursuits, but upon their immediate subjective influence upon the cultivation of the human faculties. They are selected in preference to others, because they better train the mind.

The End of College Instruction.

It can not be too earnestly inculcated that knowledge is not the principal end of college instruction, but habits. The acquisition of knowledge is the necessary result of those exercises which terminate in habits, and the maturity of the habit is measured by the degree and accuracy of the knowledge, but still the habits are the main thing. In the next place it is equally important that the whole course of studies be rigidly exacted of every student. Their value as a discipline depends altogether upôn their being studied, and every college is defective in its arrangments which fails to secure, as far as legislation can secure it, this indispensable condition of success. Whatever may be the case in Europe, it is found from experience in this country that nothing will avail but the authority of law. The curriculum must be compulsory or the majority of the students will neglect it. All must be subjected to catechetical examination in the lecture room, and all must undergo the regular examination of their class as the condition of their residence in college. The moment they are exempted from the stringency of this rule all other means lose their power upon the mass of pupils. Much may be accomplished by rewards and by stimulating the spirit of competition, and great reliance should be placed upon them to secure a high standard of attainment; but in most men the love of ease is stronger than ambition, and indolence is a greater luxury than thought. For whilst mental effort is the one condition of all mental improvement, yet this effort is at first and for a time painful—positively painful in proportion as it is intense, and comparatively painful as it abstracts from other and positively pleasurable activities. It is painful because its energy is imperfect, difficult, forced. But as the effort is gradually perfected, gradually facilitated, it becomes gradually pleasing; and when finally perfected—that is, when the power is fully developed and the effort changed into a spontaneity, becomes an exertion absolutely easy. It remains purely, intensely, and alone insatiably pleasureable. For pleasure is nothing but the concomitant or reflex of the enforced and unimpeded energy of a natural faculty or acquired habit, the degree or permanence of pleasure being also in proportion to the intensity and purity of the mental energy.

The great postulate in education is, therefore, to induce the pupil to enter and persevere in such a course of effort, good in its result and delectable, but primarily and in itself irksome. The argument of necessity helps to reconcile him to the weariness of study; what he feels that he must do he will endeavor to do with grace, and as there is no alternative, he will be more open to the generous and manly influence which the rewards and distinctions of the college are suited to exert. There are always causes at work apart from the repulsiveness of intellectual labor to seduce the student from his books; and, before his habits are yet formed and the love of study grounded into his nature, it is of the utmost consequence to keep these causes in check. No other motive will be sufficient without compulsion of law co-operating with this. There are many others which, if they do not positively sweeten his toil, may help to mitigate the agony of thought. I have insisted upon this point because it is the point in regard to which the most dangerous innovations are to be apprehended.

The Elective Plan.

Two changes have at different times been proposed, one of which would be absolutely fatal and the other seriously detrimental to the interest of the college as a place of liberal education. The first is to convert it into a collection of independent schools, each of which shall be complete in itself, it being left to the choice of the student what schools he shall enter. The other is to remit the obligation of the whole course in reference to a certain class of students, and allow them to pursue such parts of it as they may choose. In relation to the first, young men are incompetent to pronounce beforehand what studies are subjectively the most beneficial. It requires those who have experienced the disciplinary power of different studies to determine their relative value. Only a scholar can say what will make a scholar. The experiences of the world has settled down upon a certain class and order of studies, and the verdict of ages and generations is not to be set aside by the caprices, whims, and prejudices of those who are not even able to comprehend the main end of education. In the next place, if our undergraduates were competent to form a judgment, their natural love of indolence and ease would, in the majority of cases, lead them to exclude those very studies which are the most improving, precisely they are so—that is, because in themselves and in the method of teaching them, they involve a degree, an intensity, of mental exercise which is positively painful. Self-denial is not natural to man, and he manifests but little experience and acquaintance with human nature who presumes, as a matter of course, that they will choose what the judgment commends.... Permit them to select their own studies and the majority will select those that are thought to be the easiest. The principle of choice will be the very opposite of that upon which the efficiency of a study depends. Experience is decisive on this point. What creates more trouble in the interior management of our colleges than the constant desire of pupils to evade recitations? And is it not universally found that the departments which are the most popular are those which least task the energies of the student? I do not say that the professors who fill these departments are themselves most respected. That will depend upon their merit; and in matters of this sort the judgments of the young are generally right. But easy exercises are preferred, simply because they do not tax the mind. The practical problem with the mass of students is the least work and easiest done. Is it easy? Is it short? These are the questions which are first asked about a lesson. I must therefore consider any attempt to relax the compulsory features of the college course as an infallible expedient for degrading education. The college will cease to train. It may be a place for literary trifles, but a place for students it can not be.

College and University.

There is much in a name and the change here condemned is delusively sought to be insinuated under the pretext of converting the college into a university. The latter title sounds more imposing, and carried the appearance of greater dignity. But the truth is, there is hardly a more equivocal word in the language.... In its ordinary acceptation in this country it is either synonymous with college as an institution of higher education, and in this sense we are already a university; or it denotes a college with professional schools attached. It is clear, however, that the introduction of the faculties of law, medicine, and theology necessitates no change in the faculty of philosophy and arts. It is not necessary to make general education voluntary in order to provide for professional instruction. There is, consequently, nothing in the name or the nature of the case which demands a fundamental change in the system in order that the South Carolina College may become the South Carolina University. For myself I am content with our present title, and if it promises less I am sure it will accomplish more than the new title for the corresponding change. As to the expediency of adding the faculties of law and medicine—theology is out of the question to the present organization—I have only to say that it will multiply and complicate the difficulties of the internal management of the institution without securing an increased proficiency in these departments of knowledge—that is, if there is to be any real connection between the faculty of arts and those of law and medicine. I dread the experiment. I think it better that the professions should be left to provide for themselves than that a multitude of inexperienced young men should be brought together, many of whom are comparatively free from the restraints of discipline, and yet have an easy and ready access to those who are more under law. The very liberty of the resident would be a temptation to undergraduates. I have no objection, however, to the founding of professional schools by the State. All that I am anxious for is that they should not be so connected with the college as that the members of all the schools should reside together. To be under a common government is impossible; to be under a different government would breed interminable confusion and disorder. That sort of nominal connection which requires that all medical and law degrees should be conferred by the authorities of the college, and which is perfectly consistent with the law and medical schools, being established in a different place, would, of course, be harmless. But this difficulty might arise: The college would be unwilling to confer any degree without a liberal education—it could not, without abjuring the very principles of its existence, grant its honors upon mere professional attainment. With respect to the other change, that of allowing students, under certain circumstances, to pursue a partial course, it is evidently contradictory to the fundamental end of the college. These students are not seeking knowledge for the sake of discipline, but with reference to ulterior uses. They come not to be trained to think, but to learn to act in definite departments of exertion. It is professional, not liberal, education which they want. The want, I acknowledge, ought to be gratified—it is a want which should be supplied—but the college is not the place to do it. That was founded for other purposes and it is simply preposterous to abrogate its constitution out of concessions to a necessity, because the necessity happens to be real. What, therefore, ought to be done is not to change the nature of the college, but, leaving it untouched to do its own work, to organize schools with special reference to this class of wants. We have the elements of such an organization in the arsenal and citadel academies.

The Intermediate Schools.

Let these be converted into seminaries of special education, which will be only an extension of their present plan, and they will form that intermediate class of schools between the elementary and the college, which the circumstances of every civilized community, in proportion to the complication of its interests, demand. These changes in the college have been favored on the ground that they will increase its numbers; but the success of the college is not to be estimated by the numbers in attendance, but by the numbers educated. It should never include more than those who are seeking for a liberal education; and if it includes all these, whether they be 50 or 200, it is doing the whole of its appropriate work. No doubt, by the changes in question, our catalogue might be increased two or three fold, but we should not educate a single individual more than we educate now. Numbers in themselves are nothing unless they represent those who are really devoted to the business of the place. What real advantage would it be to have four or five hundred pupils matriculated here if some remained only a few months, others remained longer in idleness, and out of the whole number only four or five applied for a degree. That four or five would be the true criterion of success. The real question, I insist, is, How many graduate? This is the decisive point. As long as we receive the whole number of young men in the State who are to be liberally educated, whether that number be greater or smaller, we are doing all that we were appointed to do, or that we can be legitimately expected to do; and a decline in numbers is not a necessary proof of the declension of the college—it may be only a proof that the demand is ceasing for higher education. The work, however, to be done loses none of its importance in consequence of the failure to appreciate its value, and the remedy is not to give up and yield to empirical innovations, but to persevere in faith and patience, relying upon time as the great teacher of wisdom.

Independence of Teachers.

Another cardinal principle in the organization of the college is the independence of its teachers. They should be raised above all temptation of catering for popularity, of degrading the standard of education for the sake of the loaves and fishes. They should be prepared to officiate as priests in the temple of learning, with pure vestments, and with hands unstained with a bribe. It has been suggested that if the stipends of the professors were made dependent upon the number of pupils, the strong motive of personal interest, added to the higher incentives which they are expected to feel, would increase their efficiency by stimulating their zeal and activity. They would be anxious to achieve a reputation for the college which would enable it to command students. This argument proceeds upon a hypothesis which, I am ashamed to say, my own experience pronounces to be false. In the state of things in this country there is a constant conflict between the government of the college and the candidates for its privileges, the one attempting to raise and the other to lower the standard of admission, and every effort of the faculty in the right direction is met with a determined resistance. It is not to be presumed that young men, at the age of our undergraduates generally, should have any steady and precise notions of the nature of education. A college is a college, and when they are debating the question, whither shall they go, the most important items in the calculation are not the efficiency, but the cheapness of the place and the shortness of the time within which a degree may be obtained. The consequence is that no college can resist the current unless its teachers are independent. In that case they may stand their ground, and, though they can never hope to equal feebler institutions in numbers, they will still accomplish a great work and confer a lasting benefit on society. The South Carolina College has raised her standard. She has proclaimed her purpose to be to educate well, and I should deplore any measure that might remotely tend to drive her from this position. The true security for the ability of the professional corps is not to be sought in starving them, or in making them scramble for a livelihood, but in the competency, zeal, and integrity of the body that appoints them, and in the strict responsibility to which they are held. An impartial board of overseers to elect faithful and turn out incompetent men, a board that has the nerve to do its duty, will be a stronger check upon indolence and inefficiency than an empty larder. The motive of necessity may lead them to degrade instruction to increase their fees; the motive of responsibility to a board that can appreciate their labors will always operate in the right direction. . . . So far as the undergraduates are concerned, I think that all these conditions of success are measurably filled in the present arrangement of the college, as much so as the general state of education will allow. No changes in this respect are desirable. But the interests of higher education demand something more than that culture "in passage", as Bacon expresses it, which is all that is contemplated in provisions for undergraduates....[1]—From Thornwell's famous letter to Governor Manning on education in South Carolina, one of the most important educational statements in the South before 1860. The General Assembly of South Carolina ordered the publication of 5,000 copies of the letter, which in 1885 was reprinted in *The News and Courier* by the Charleston City Council, as the best answer to opponents of public education in that state. For the letter in full see *Report*, United States Commissioner of Education, 1899-1900, I, 403-26.

3. Order of procession at commencement at the University of South Carolina, 1853

On Commencement day a procession shall, at 9½ o'clock A.M., be formed in the College campus, under the direction of the Professor of Mathematics, consisting of the Professors of the College, Librarian, Resident Graduates, graduating class and under-graduates in the order of their classes. It shall march with music to the Governor's quarters, where it shall join the general procession organized under the resolutions of the Legislature.

If any member of the graduating class shall fail to join the procession and continue in it until it reaches the Hall, he shall, without a good excuse, to be approved by the President of the College, be deprived of his Diploma and reported to the Board. If any other student of the College shall so fail to join and continue in the Procession, he shall, without a good excuse, be suspended at the discretion of the Faculty.—College Laws of 1853. Given in Edwin L. Green, *A History of the University of South Carolina*, 207-8.

1. Thornwell proceeded to present arguments for the better support of the South Carolina College which, like many colleges in this country in the middle of the nineteenth century, was subjected to many criticisms: higher education was designed only for the benefit of the few who could bear its heavy expense; it was aristocratic and haughty; and it belonged primarily to religious organizations and private enterprise and was not a function of the state. Thornwell said that the only question which South Carolina College asked of applicants concerned their academic fitness for admission. "All who are prepared to comply with its requisitions are welcomed to its halls, whether rich or poor. Poverty may, indeed, be a remote and accidental cause of exclusion, as it incapacitates for acquiring the fitness which the college exacts, and which is absolutely indispensable to the end it has in view. But in these cases it is not the poverty which the college considers, but the ignorance and wants of preparatory training.... It shuts its doors upon none but those who shut them upon themselves or against whom Providence has closed them. A free college means a college absolutely without expense.... But if an institution is not *ipso facto* aristocratic, because the members of it have to pay for their vituals and clothes, then the South Carolina College is not an aristocratic or class institution...."

4. The "honor principle" at the College of South Carolina, 1853

As the end of the University is to train a body of gentlemen in knowledge, virtue, religion and refinement, whatever has a tendency to defeat this end, or is inconsistent with it, shall be treated and punished as an offense, whether expressly mentioned in the laws or not....

The Board (of Trustees) expects and requires the students to maintain the character of refined and elevated Christian gentlemen. It would be ashamed of any man who would excuse breaches of morality, propriety and decorum, on the plea that the acts in question are not specifically condemned in the University code. It earnestly desires that the students may be influenced to good conduct and diligence in study by higher motives than the coercion of law; and it mainly relies for the success of the institution, as a place of liberal education, on moral and religious principles, on a sense of duty, and on the generous feelings which belong to young men engaged in honorable pursuits. ...–By-laws of the Board of South Carolina College, 1853. Given in the catalogue of the University of South Carolina, 1946-47, p. 8.

5. Rules on crimes and punishments at the University of Georgia, 1853

1. Every absence of a student from any College duty shall be reported by his instructor, and he may be punished in such manner as the Faculty shall think proper.

2. If a student shall be habitually inattentive to the exercises of the chapel, or to recitations, or shall be otherwise negligent or disorderly in his conduct, or should his example be thought injurious, the Faculty may send him privately from the Institution.

3. Any student found in possession of any deadly weapon or weapons calculated to produce death, or who shall be guilty of blasphemy, robbery, theft, forgery, fornication, or of any crimes for which an infamous punishment may be inflicted by law, shall be expelled.

4. Any student convicted of sending or accepting a challenge to fight a duel, or who shall carry such challenge, or be second in a duel, or in any wise aid or abet it, shall immediately be expelled by the Faculty.

5. No student shall possess or exhibit any indecent picture, nor purchase or read in College any lascivious, impious or irreligious

books; and if any student shall be convicted thereof, or of lying, profaneness, obscenity, theft, uncleanliness, playing at unlawful games, (such as cards, dice, back-gammon,) or other gross immoralities or impieties, he shall be punished according to the nature or heinousness of the offence, by fine, admonition, public reprehension, dismission, or expulsion from College.

6. If any student quarrel with, abuse, or insult a fellow student, or any person whatever, he shall upon conviction, be punished according to the nature of the fault, and as the Faculty may determine.

7. No student shall bring or cause to be brought into College, or on any occasion keep in his room any spirituous or fermented liquors, without an express permission from the President.

8. No student shall go to a tavern, eating house, beer house, or any place of such kind, for the purpose of entertainment or amusement, without permission from the President; nor shall he on any occasion keep company with persons of publicly bad character, under the penalty of admonition; and, if the practice be continued, of dismission or expulsion.

9. Whenever any student is found buying or drinking any spirits in any of the stores, shops or taverns, in Athens, or found intoxicated therein or elsewhere, he shall for the first offence be punished by admonition, suspension, or dismission, at the discretion of the Faculty, and for the second be dismissed or expelled from the College, without the right of restoration but by the consent of the Board of Trustees.

10. No hallooing, loud talking, jumping, dancing, or any other boisterous noise, shall be permitted in the entries or rooms of the College at any time, under such penalty as the nature of the offence shall be judged by the Faculty to deserve.

11. No student shall be allowed to disturb, or attempt any imposition on his fellow students, in any manner whatever; and every student shall be required to preserve order and decorum in his own room, and shall be responsible for all disorder therein, unless he give information, when in his power, of the person or persons from whom it proceeded.

12. If any combination or agreement be formed by the students to do any unlawful act, or to forbear a compliance with any injunction from lawful authority, or if any enormity, disorder, or act of disobedience shall be perpetrated agreeably to, or in consequence of such combinations, so many of the offenders shall be punished by

degradation, suspension, dismission, or expulsion, according to the circumstances of the offence, as may be by the Faculty judged necessary for the preservation of good order in the Institution.

13. No students suspended, dismissed or expelled from College, shall be permitted to enter the edifice, or come on the College grounds, without express permission from the President, and in case of his persisting to intrude, it shall be the duty of the President to have an action of trespass commenced against said intruder.

14. No woman shall be permitted, on any pretence, to go into the College, except strangers who wish to see the buildings, or citizens of the neighbourhood, accompanied by an officer of the Institution, or some person appointed by him.

15. No student shall keep for his use or pleasure, any riding animal or dog.

16. In all cases where the walls of the entries or rooms of College, or of the chapel, shall be defaced by the drawing of grossly indecent figures, outraging alike religion and morality, the perpetrator of the same, if discovered, shall be punished by suspension, dismission, or expulsion, according to the aggravation of the act, at the discretion of the Faculty.

17. Every student when required, shall give evidence respecting the violation of any laws; and if he refuse such evidence when called on, or wilfully falsify therein, he may be punished by the Faculty, even to dismission.

18. No student shall be questioned for any testimony he may give in regard to violation of any law of this College; and in case any student shall so question his fellow, to ascertain whether such testimony have been given, with intention to bring him into contempt, the student so acting shall be deemed to have committed an offence, and shall be punished by the Faculty according to the aggravation of the offence, even to dismission.

19. Every student against whom the sentence of expulsion has been pronounced, may by letter, addressed to the President within ten days after the said sentence, appeal to the Board of Trustees, who at the next session thereafter shall make a final decision thereon.

20. Whereas cases may occur, which are not expressly provided for by law, in all such cases, the President, Professors and Tutors, shall provide according to their best discretion, and may punish any student offending, by fine, admonition, suspension, dismission, or expulsion, according to the nature and circumstances of the crime.

21. The Faculty of College shall have power to make such regulations relative to the police of the College, and the behaviour of the students, either as respects the decency of their deportment, or the regularity of their habits and practices, as to them shall seem expedient: *Provided,* That the same be not inconsistent with this code, and are submitted to the Trustees at their next regular meeting for their confirmation or rejection.

22. No student of College shall engage in any dramatic performances whatever, in the Town of Athens, whether in term time or vacation, under the penalty of being expelled from College.

23. No student shall hereafter be regularly discharged from the College, without the consent or request of his parent or guardian, made to the Faculty in writing, and then the discharge shall be couched in such terms as the conduct of the applicant while a student may warrant.

24. The Trustees shall have power to make such other and further regulations, touching the general affairs of the University, and the better government of the College, as they in their discretion may think proper: *Provided,* That they are not repugnant to the laws of the State, and that they operate only until the next regular meeting of the Senatus Academicus, by whom they shall be either confirmed or rejected.—*A Code of Laws for the Government of Franklin College (University of Georgia), Made, Enacted and Ordained by the Senatus Academicus, at their Session in Milledgeville, in November, 1853* (Athens, Ga.: Franklin Job Office Print, 1854), pp. 10-14.

6. Some tourists describe a visit to the University of Virginia, 1853

. . . Their equipage was accommodated precisely as it had been after the accident near Lynchburg; and, notwithstanding its somewhat cumbersome appearance, made their way to Charlottesville, thirteen miles distant, with comparative ease and rapidity.

The girls, who never were able to attain that stoical contempt for appearances so frequently enlarged upon by their philosophic companion, could not but congratulate themselves that they passed the University during the lecture hours, and, in consequence, escaped the observation of some five hundred quizzing students.

After dinner they set off on foot to visit the University, which is about one mile distant from the town of Charlottesville. On the way Crayon indulged in some sage observations on the subject of giggling;

general propriety of deportment, especially among strangers—more especially if the strangers happen to be young persons—students, for example. Not, indeed, that he intended these remarks to be understood as suggestions upon this occasion; hoped the ladies would not think so for a moment; too much confidence etc. But seeing students always reminded him of dignity, "As Caesar's triumph shorn of Pompey's bust," etc.

Having at length arrived at the College, they felt at a loss for a chaperon. Dora intimated that her cousin, Ned Twiggs, was then at the University—that he was an amiable, well-mannered youth—but she felt a delicacy in interrupting his studies, as she had understood from his letters home that he was in the habit of studying nineteen hours a day. Fanny thought it was a great shame only to allow himself five hours for sleep and recreation, and that his health must give way under it. Crayon heard these remarks with a contemptuous shrug, and went directly to the proctor's office to ascertain the number of Ned's room.

Now that young gentleman did look as if he hadn't slept his wholesome allowance for some time; but Crayon took pains to insinuate afterward that young men at colleges sometimes lost their rest from other causes than mere devotion to their legitimate studies. Ned was vastly delighted to see his fair relatives, and undertook the office of chaperon with an alacrity and good-humor that fully justified Dora's good opinion of his manners.

"Indeed," says Crayon, "it gives me great pleasure to say that, although the vivacity of these blooded colts at our Virginia colleges frequently leads them into all sorts of deviltries and excesses, they have almost invariably the manners of gentlemen."

The University was established by an act of Assembly dated January 25, 1819, upon the site of the Central College of Albemarle. It was planned, built, and organized under the immediate supervision of Mr. Jefferson.

The students' dormitories, professors' houses, and classrooms, are built upon three sides of a quadrangle, and are connected by a continuous colonnade. Outside of these, at some distance, are second lines of dormitories and offices, the space between the ranges being occupied by well cultivated gardens. The whole has a very pleasing and pretty effect, but the buildings are too low, and the architecture wants finish.

Although this institution was an especial pet of its distinguished founder, and bequeathed by him to the fostering care of our venerable Commonwealth, it was not eminently successful in its early years. Latterly, however, it seems to be taking the position that it should have attained long ago, and its present catalogue shows over five hundred students.

The ladies were so much delighted with every thing they saw, and had so much to say about the students, that Crayon began to grow morose and cynical.

"Women," said he, "always make the most fuss about matters of which they know the least. They are prodigious admirers of learning, or more strictly speaking, the name of learning; for any owlish fellow who gets a reputation for profundity, or malapert who has written verses for a magazine, is, in their estimation, a Newton or a Milton. While they pretend to be in love with scholarship, they are sworn foes of every means of acquiring it. So jealous and exacting of the time and attention of their unlucky admirers, that an interesting book is as bad as a rival beauty; the solution of an abstruse problem is equivalent to a quarrel; the study of a science amounts to prolonged absence and consequent oblivion. As for themselves, they will read nothing but novels, and listen to nothing but nonsense. Improving conversation is ever drowned in untimely giggling, and a useful lecture is looked upon as an inadmissible bore."

"I think," interrupted Fanny, "that lectures may be bores without even the pretense of being useful."

"If I had Cousin Porte's talents," said Minnie, "I would write a novel to demonstrate the impropriety of novel reading, and deliver a public lecture on the frivolity of frivolousness."

Dora yawned, and, with an air of unaffected simplicity, avowed that, for her part, she thought more of the scholars than she did of scholarship.

"To be sure," said Minnie, with enthusiasm, "we do not so much admire the laborious, pains-taking student, the mere bookworm; but the brilliant, dashing genius, whose productions seem the results of intuition rather than of labor, whose eloquence is unstudied, whose verses are impromptu—"

Minnie stopped suddenly, and turned away her suffused cheek under the pretense of arranging her sewing. Crayon bit his lip, and began whistling like a fifer, when, fortunately, the servant ushered in Mr. Twiggs and several of his friends.

While the Freshmen are paying their compliments to the ladies, we can not forbear indulging in a few moral reflections.

While every body's mouth and every body's book are filled with laudations of Nature, her skill in adapting her gifts to the necessities of every age and clime, the unerring truth of her teachings, the infallibility of her intuitions, the eternal fitness of things, why has not some bold philosopher overthrown this host of slang, and battered this castle of paper walls with the artillery of every-day facts and experiences? Why do babies cry after the moon? Why does all the world want what it can't get? Why have boys of sixteen or thereabout such an inordinate desire for beards? And why, when the gift would be most acceptable, does the hard-hearted dame insult them with a sprinkling of peach fuzz instead? And why, when years have matured the hirsute harvest, does the desire for it disappear, and the man become involved in expenditure of time and money to get rid of that appendage which, as a youth, he would have gloried in?

During the journey our hero's beard had grown broad and long, until he resembled a *sapeur* of the French Guard. In looking on the downy lips of the students, a most unphilosophic sense of superiority took possession of him. He was annoyed, at the same time, to perceive the interest which the ladies appeared to take in their beardless conversation.

Crayon assumed a magisterial air. "Ned, my boy, how are you getting on with the classics?"

Ned replied, modestly, that he had passed his last examination very creditably.

"Are you of opinion that Dido was really in love with the pious Aeneas?"

"Virgil says so," replied Ned.

"But does not Virgil frequently say, '*Dido et Dux,*' and, worse than all, '*Dux Trojanorum*' (which species was probably larger than our fowl—a sort of aquatic Shanghai), and how do you reconcile this with his previous statement?"

"If she *eat* ducks," said Dora, "she certainly couldn't have been much in love."

"Certainly not. Dido was a humbug."

"Cousin Crayon," said Ned, beginning to show a little pluck, "who was first found guilty of a breach of the peace?"

"According to Holy Writ," said Porte, "it must have been *the first Cain.*"

"Not so," said Ned; "for before his time, and even before the creation, it is said '*Nihil fit!*'"

"So he did, indeed," said Crayon.

Although the girls did not entirely understand this sally, they laughed all the more, while Crayon looked quite vexed.

"Very well, youngster, very well; you'll get along. With twenty years of study and patience you may become a ripe scholar, and grow a beard like mine, probably. For the present, Ned, let me counsel you to cream your face and submit to the cat; and for the rest, be content with the distinctions that appertain to your age and condition."—Porte Crayon (David Hunter Strother), *Virginia Illustrated: Containing a Visit to the Virginian Canaan, and the Adventures of Porte Crayon and His Cousins* (New York: Harper and Brothers, 1871), pp. 240-45.

7. Schedule of classes, South Carolina College, 1854

	FRESHMAN	SOPHOMORE	JUNIOR	SENIOR
Monday:				
7 a.m.	Hist.	Math.	Mor. Phil.	Butler's Ana.
11 a.m.	Math.	Greek.	Logic.	Pol. Ec., Pol.
4 p.m.	Math.	Latin.	Greek.	Geol., Agr. Ch.
Tuesday:				
7 a.m.	Rhet.	Math.	Mor. Phil.	Phil. of Mind.
11 a.m.	Greek.	Chem.	Rhet.	Latin.
4 p.m.	Greek.	Latin.	Rhet.	Astro., Civ. Eng.
Wednesday:				
7 a.m.	Hist.	Math.	Latin.	Butler's Ana.
11 a.m.	Latin.	Rhet. Eloc.	Chem., Min.	Greek.
4 p.m.	Math.	Hist.	Greek.	Geol., Agr. Ch.
Thursday:				
7 a.m.	Latin.	Physiol.	Mech. Phil.	Pol. Ec., Pol. Eth.
11 a.m.	Greek.	Rhet. Eloc.	Logic.	Geol., Agr. Chem.
4 p.m.	Math.	Greek.	Hist., Pol. Phil.	Crit. Eloc.
Friday:				
7 a.m.	Latin.	Physiol.	Hist., Pol. Phil.	Astro., Civ. Eng.
11 a.m.	Greek.	Latin.	Chem., Min.	Crit. Eloc.
4 p.m.	Rhet.	Greek.	Mech. Phil.	Phil. of Mind.
Saturday:				
7 a.m.	Latin.	Physiol.	Mor. Phil.	Pol. Ec., Pol. Phil.

—Green, *op. cit.*, 202.

8. Henry Harrisse of the University of North Carolina on collegiate education, 1854

The main object of education [2] consists in disciplining the mind, giving to it habits of activity, spontaneous and continued attention, ready recollection, analysis, generalization; in fine, to teach men to think. It requires no high-wrought arguments to demonstrate this truth, nor elaborate vindications to exonerate it from the attacks of prejudice. It is obvious. And whether we consider the student as "an end unto himself," or his academical career as "an instrument towards some ultimate end," the principle it involves loses none of its authority. This truth, however, is not exclusive; and further, we hold it reconcilable with the well-known dictum of Aristotle, that men, in their youth, "ought to be instructed in things subservient to the purpose of external accommodation, in proportion to their utility or necessity."

To others, better qualified to elucidate and harmonize metaphysical abstractions, we leave the task of showing the impossibility of conceiving how the mind can receive impressions, either true or fallacious, abstract or concrete, without retaining indelible traces of the instrument which produced them; and the absolute necessity, therefore, of selecting these instruments, not only as regards their specific worth

2. The second quarter of the nineteenth century was marked by increasing discussions of collegiate studies. In 1825 George Ticknor, eminent professor at Harvard, published *Remarks on Changes Lately Proposed or Adopted in Harvard College*, giving arguments for reform and in favor of electives. In 1829 the faculty of Yale College published in *American Journal of Science and Arts*, XV (January, 1829), 297-351, "Original Papers in Relation to a Course of Liberal Education," which defended mental discipline and the prescribed collegiate course. Josiah Quincy, prominent president of Harvard, in 1841 published *Remarks on the Nature and Probable Effects of Introducing the Voluntary System in the Studies of Greek and Latin*, in which he urged the elective system. President Francis Wayland of Brown University in 1842 published his *Thoughts on the Present Collegiate System in the United States* and in 1850 his *Report to the Corporation of Brown University, on Changes in the System of Collegiate Education*, which made vigorous attacks on Brown's prescribed curriculum. President Henry Tappan of the University of Michigan in 1851 published *University Education*, which showed high admiration for the German system of higher education.

Two able discussions of the issue appeared in the South, one by Henry Harrisse of the University of North Carolina in 1854, but only recently discovered, and the other in the same year from the University of Alabama, written largely by F. A. P. Barnard, who was for many years professor of mathematics and natural history in that institution. He was professor of mathematics and natural philosophy in the University of Mississippi from 1854 to 1856, president of the institution from 1856 to 1858 and chancellor from 1858 to 1861, and later he became president of Columbia College in New York. His change from a vigorous defender of the prescribed classical course to a defender of the elective system at Columbia shows "the compromises that conservative educators were forced to make in the face of influences demanding greater as training mediums for the time being, but also as channels of knowledge and means to "instruct the student in things subservient to the purpose of external accommodation." Practical questions, when considered too abstractly,—often with the intention of placing them beyond the reach of plain and unassuming thinkers,— or discussed in the abstruse form and wording of philosophical argumentation,— induce distrust, check sincere investigations, and fail to convince. Clothed in logical subtilties, these questions, thus garbled and obscured, may please, perhaps, idle lawyers and presumptuous rhetoricians, but they can never interest the worthy citizen who yields sooner to the dictates of common sense than to the cavils of sophistry.

We will then condense and simplify, as much as we can, whatever recondite notions may occasionally and necessarily spring from the very nature of our subject.

Knowledge is necessary to man at all times. How can we realize the idea of reason without assimilating to it the idea of knowledge? You may easily represent to yourself mind without knowledge, as you sometimes think of a steam-engine unsupplied with steam, or the circulatory organs deprived of blood; but from the moment you speak of locomotion, of circulation, of reason, you must add the idea of vapor, of fluid, of knowledge. . . .

---

use of the elective system." See R. Freeman Butts, *The College Charts Its Course* (New York: McGraw-Hill Book Company, 1939), p. 189.

Henry Harrisse is perhaps best and most favorably known for his services to American scholarship. He was born in Paris in 1830, came to this country as a child, taught in Mt. Zion Academy at Winnsboro in South Carolina and received an honorary master's degree from the South Carolina College. From the little that has been written about this man and his life of "tumultuous scholarship" and from some of his own writings he appears as a very individualistic and somewhat erratic character. But he was a keen student, a bibliophile and devoted book-collector, a distinguished bibliographer, the author of the "monumental volume," *Bibliotheca Americana Vetustissima,* and remarkable works on Columbus. Harrisse is also known for his unhappy experiences at Chapel Hill with students, colleagues, the administration, and the trustees, while an instructor in French and a student in the law school in the University of North Carolina in the middle 1850's. In that institution he "raised the devil generally on the board of trustees and faculty of her University by my strenuous efforts to improve the curriculum and pedagogical methods according to a system of my own."

Harrisse's essay "On the Organization, Regulation and Management of a Literary Institution Best Adapted to the Wants and Interests of North Carolina," extracts from which are here given, was written in competition for a prize of $200 offered by Normal College, which grew into Trinity College around which Duke University was organized and developed. The contest for the prize was called off, to the keen disappointment and irritation of Harrisse who involved many important people in the controversy. The original essay now is the property of the New York Public Library. Microcopy is in the Southern Historical Collection, the University of North Carolina. See Edgar W. Knight (ed.), *Henry Harrisse on Collegiate Education* (Chapel Hill: The University of North Carolina Press, 1947). There the essay appears in full.

Knowledge is a compound of multifarious materials; and each one of these materials, say, "fact," has a value—not the only value—enhanced or lessened, proportionally as it promotes the intellectual progress of the student. It often happens that of two of these "facts" being equal in point of immediate utility, one possesses inherent qualities denied to the other. As, for instance, a fact, the acquisition of which is an exercise well fitted for sharpening the mental faculties of the student, and at the same time for increasing his individual sum of useful knowledge; whilst the other fact only trains the faculties, and leaves besides nothing but useless knowledge. In this case, is it not self-evident that the former ought not to be preferred to the latter? We should then, in the process of education, so select and employ those facts, as to unfold the mental powers of the student, and simultaneously increase the sum of his useful knowledge.

Have our collegiate and academical systems been framed in accordance with the above principles? In no instance can it be said with truth that the training of the mind and the acquisition of necessary information, have been so blended as to promote both. One is, with us, always rendered subservient to the other; and if the course adopted in one institution aims at promoting the training, the other keeps only in view the advancement of the student's scientific attainments. The studies selected in the former result in no ulterior utility whatever, and for the present, (chiefly on account of the mode of teaching) are no better training, perhaps, than other studies, which if properly taught, would certainly both invigorate his mental powers, and increase his acquaintance with facts. In the latter, science, and the application of science to the arts, are the sole objects of their attention; although the instructor does not seem to be aware that his pupils' mind is not yet ready even for the comprehension of such specific facts; which, in consequence, only clog their memory with crude elements; and, if the understanding is not naturally very vigorous, forever impair at least their originality of thought and acuteness of perception.

The range of collegiate studies is far from extensive, nor is it so perfect as not to admit of a change. It would be well then to enquire whether some new studies might not be introduced; others, left out so as to obtain a greater allowance of time, or elevated in point of importance, and taught in a way better calculated to leave a permanent impression upon the pupil's mind. What are the studies that must be abandoned; which ones should be introduced in their stead; what improvements might be successfully applied in the mode of teaching; what is the system of education best calculated to improve the mind of the students, and at the same time leave a residue of knowledge both applicable and useful; in fine, what is the character of the literary institution best adapted to the wants and interests of North Carolina"? Such are the questions which we propose to solve, and, we trust, to the satisfaction of impartial and practical thinkers.

All our colleges, universities and classical academies, seem to have adopted a stereotyped course of studies and mode of instruction....

We would not insist, if it had not been promised by very able advocates of the study of the Latin and Greek languages in this country, as superior means of promoting mental habits, that the maturity of these habits is to be measured "by the degree and accuracy of the knowledge."

In point of natural abilities, it is incontestable that the Americans are certainly not inferior to the Europeans. The comfort which our people enjoy; the extensive diffusion of elementary knowledge among all classes; and the freedom of our political institutions, cannot but promote the further acquisition of learning. In proportion to their population, the United States possess, perhaps a greater number of Universities and Colleges, than any one trans-atlantic state, except Prussia; our students commence their education at a more advanced age, and with a maturity of mind far beyond the Germans or French: —How is it, then, that notwithstanding such great advantages and the number of young men we have already educated in the last fifty years, and who have devoted themselves to teaching or Literature, America has not yet produced a single classical scholar, whose philological labors ever drew or merited the approbation of competent and impartial judges,—whilst she can justly boast of astronomers, engineers, and mathematicians equal in many respects to any in Europe? ...

How many of our graduates can read the ancient authors of Rome and Athens in the original, with sufficient ease to enjoy and appreciate them? Alas! but few; and these owe their rare proficiency to subsequent studies and congenial pursuits. If then, we do not initiate the American scholar into these only repositories of undoubted literary excellence, are we more successful in training their minds through the medium of these very classical studies? ...

When we say that the study of Latin and Greek exercises and invigorates the mind in a greater degree than some other branches of learning, we attach, we fear, to the word "study," a meaning somewhat different from that generally understood by American instructors. A mere verbal translation, often in impure or disconnected English, with grammatical answers, now and then, is NOT the kind of study calculated to improve greatly the pupil's mental powers. The mind, to derive any profit from a classical course, requires constant appeals to other means of far greater efficacy. Frequent transpositions from Latin into Greek, and from English into Latin; daily written exercises and compositions of verses in these languages; immediate translations into Latin from an English text read aloud; extempore and exegetical readings; turning different dialects into each other, and English verse in Iambic Trimeters &c &c—such are among the multifarious means to which the teacher must resort, if he has truly in view the training of his pupil. It is the method pursued at Leipzig, Paris and Oxford.

Can we, in America, where our children from their very infancy, contract obdurate habits of physical and mental independence, where any kind of restraint is considered a tyranny, and the age of fourteen entirely too early for collegiate instruction, can we ever think of introducing such a system and its necessary train of restrictions and innovations? For, how could we pretend to teach the languages in this way, unless a change of diet, studies in common and under the watchful eyes of rigid tutors, a confinement and catalogue of severe penalties, such as no American youth would ever submit to, were also introduced? Yet, we candidly believe that one is subservient to the other; and in this, lies the secret of the strict discipline so uniformly enforced in all the gymnasia and colleges of Europe. . . .

We have neither the time nor the space to discuss at length whether the mind of the student should be especially and wholly trained in view of the particular pursuit he intends to follow in after life; or whether there ought to be only one training for all students, without regard to the profession he may ultimately adopt. It seems to us, however, that although a physician requires a mental discipline altogether different from a lawyer, a merchant from a farmer, and an engineer from a politician, the training preparatory to the acquisition of the specific facts required for the successful prosecution of a profession, should be general. It is necessary to all, and such as no man, whatever be the nature of his ulterior aim, can dispense with.

But, how far, and how long, must the students be subjected to this general training? Is it necessary that the totality of the four years spent in college, should be devoted to it? If so, where and when is he to acquire the knowledge, the bare knowledge, so indispensable to his success in life? We deem it dangerous to leave it to the student to acquire it by himself where and when he pleases; and to postpone it indefinitely is to run too great a risk of his not acquiring it at all. Students should be considered not as they *ought* to be, but as *they are* and ever will be! As soon as they get rid of collegiate shackles,– and often before– they launch at once into the study of a profession. The intended lawyer enters an attorney's office, studies the theory and practice of the Law, hastens to obtain his county court license, and without any further preparation, assumes all the duties and functions of active life. The medical student follows a similar course; and the engineer, whether mentally and bodily prepared or not, immediately enrols himself for a surveying expedition.

On the other hand, has it been fairly tested whether "the instruction in things subservient to the purpose of external accommodation," might not be rendered an excellent mental exercise? And, if so, why not prefer such "utilitarian" studies, since they may simultaneously train the mind and impart the necessary knowledge, which the student "is not expected" to acquire at college, and cannot obtain afterwards,– the functions of active life being too exclusive? . . .

Though referring so often to pertinent authorities, and expressing ourselves rather frankly, we do not mean to cast blame upon this or that particular college, either in North Carolina or out of it. Upon the whole, the institutions in the Old North State, are perhaps superior to any in the country. Her University has educated many men who afterwards became eminent; and its alumni do not fall below the standard of American scholarship; but we must confess that neither North Carolina nor any other state in the Union, professes that kind of institution which, having in view both the mental training and the acquisition of useful knowledge, can, through a particular system of instruction, so train its pupils as to enable them to study afterwards any profession whatever with better success; impart the indispensable knowledge which they have not the opportunity of studying when out of college; and, at the same time, give to all those who expect to lead the life of independent farmers, merchants, and citizens, an education that may become from the moment they graduate, an inexhaustible source of literary enjoyment and of materials for thought.

We are well aware that there is hardly a college in the United States which does not lay claim to such a system; but experience has shown, and we hope to have demonstrated, that such is not the case;— however strenuous the effort and meritorious the intention....

Our Institution resembles neither a College, an Academy, nor a High School; but as we should avoid introducing foreign words or coining new terms, we adopt the word "College" as the nearest we can find in the English language. Johnson and Bailey define it "a number of persons acting or living under the same laws and the same rules; applied especially to those who devote themselves to learning or religion." Learning "consists in the knowledge of facts imparted through instruction and study," says Webster. It is self-evident that the object of our Institution is to collect a number of persons willing to live under the same rules, in order to devote themselves to learning;— which we purpose to impart to them through instruction. We may then, in all propriety, employ the word "College," though we should reject certain branches of learning usually taught in collegiate institutions.

Being convinced that the study of the Latin and Greek languages—(as now taught and as they will ever be taught in this country—) does not enable the student to read the classical authors with sufficient ease in the original to appreciate their literary excellence, and use them as models of taste and style, or vehicles of information; and that considered specially as a means of mutual training, this study when partially taught does not discipline the mind in a higher degree than other studies which, besides professing this quality, may also impart a great deal of useful and necessary knowledge, the Greek and Latin languages form no part of our curriculum.

That which we substitute instead, is neither new nor obsolete. It consists merely in extending several of the very studies pursued in all the literary institutions of this country, adding a few others, and adopting a method of instruction which exacts more from both student and instructor. Through this method, the whole sum of physical and mental application which can be expected from an American youth in educational pursuits, will be obtained.

The vast amount of time hitherto devoted to an imperfect acquisition of the dead languages, we transfer to a profound study of our own language and literature, a foreign tongue universally spoken, that can be acquired in a few years, and which at the same time trains the mental powers in a satisfactory degree; a comprehensive study of History, both ancient and modern; Drawing and Penmanship, Mental Philosophy, Logic, Constitutional Law, Political Economy, Mathematics, Natural Philosophy, Chemistry, Geology and Gymnastics, complete the course.

The Faculty to whom are committed the government and instruction of the students, consists of seven members, viz: a Professor of Mental Philosophy, Political Economy and Constitutional Law. This chair is filled by the President:— a Professor of French Language and Drawing; a Professor of History, Antiquities and Geography; a Professor of Mathematics and Natural Philosophy; a Professor of Chemistry, Geology and Minerology; an adjunct Professor of English Literature; and an Instructor in Gymnastics who also fills the office of Marshall. The youngest member of the Faculty is ex-officio, Secretary of the body.

As soon as the endowment will allow it, assistant professors will be added to all the departments, except the English.

The qualifications of the teacher are naturally to be sought in his proficiency to teach the branch of science or learning entrusted to him. And to repeat here, that he must be a thorough master of his Department; accustomed both to teach and study, — "for the one exclusive sign of a thorough knowledge is the power of teaching" — a strong friend of the institution; a man who is ever above the petty selfishness and jealousy which so often prevail among the members of academical senates and looks upon the profession of teacher, more as the discharge of a noble, *life time* and solemn duty, than a make-shift or means of temporary support, would perhaps appear trite or idle. There are, no doubt, some specific requisites which we must expect from our Instructors; these, however, will be defined under the head of "Method of Instruction." . . .

As for the duties of the teachers, there is hardly a digest of collegiate by-laws, which does not clearly define them. These rules constitute the whole amount of experience ever gathered on the subject of education; and they have so often been revised, corrected and improved, that we deem the digest of any college whatever as good a compendium as can be desired. In fact, the instructor's duties, from the humble assistant of an "old field" teacher to the dignified professor in a State University, are similar in the main; and differ only in those unimportant particulars, which arise from the peculiar locality, or importance, of the Institution.

They all declare that it is his duty to inspect the conduct of the students within the college walls; to see that the hours of study and retirement are faithfully observed, the students not out of their rooms at improper times; that the quiet of the campus is not disturbed by noises, shouts, or boisterous calls; to suppress all disorderly conduct; examine in turn the rooms of the college at least once a week, and see that cleanliness and neatness are preserved. In fine, he must be vigilant in carrying into effect any law of the institution and report to the Faculty, such transgressions as ought to be punished by that body.

He is not permitted to engage in pursuits for emolument unconnected with the service of the College; and, if a clergyman, cannot take charge permanently of any church, in or out of the village where the Institution is located.

A Trustee is generally a retired public officer, a gentleman of leisure or an influential lawyer who knows but little and cares still less about the management of a literary institution. His title was conferred as a mere compliment, or on account of his well known abilities in other pursuits. Often, however, it is simply by reason of his high-sounding name. We know of such trustees who have been figuring in college catalogues for twenty years, without ever attending a single monthly or annual meeting.

Our trustees are men of experience and activity. We do not wish a numerous board, but a few diligent members who are required and never fail to attend, all the regular examinations; thus adding by their presence, importance to a ceremony which in some colleges is rapidly degenerating into a solemn mockery.

The number of trustees is limited to ten. The President of the college is ex-officio a member, has a vote, but is ineligible to the office of chairman of the Board. He, however, with four of the trustees, can call occasional meetings whenever it appears necessary. Six members and the President of the college are the number to constitute a quorum, and to fill up, by ballot, any vacancies that may occur either in the Board or in the Faculty.

The trustees elect, and may remove from office, the President and all the officers connected with the Institution.

They prescribe and amend the course of studies to be pursued by the students. They meet regularly at the end of each term, and individually visit the college by turns at least four times in the year.

They have the exclusive right of expelling a student; and may reverse all sentences of suspension pronounced by the Faculty. All other penalties, their degree and mode of infliction, are wholly left to the Faculty. We need not add that corporeal punishments of any sort are strictly prohibited.

The Trustees confer degrees; and if anyone fails to attend the board during four stated meetings in succession, it is deemed a refusal to act, and the board proceeds to appoint a successor; except of course in case of sickness or temporary absence from the State at the time.

Here again . . . we must refer to the digest of any collegiate by-laws; leaving to the teachers themselves, whatever local alterations may prove necessary. As for sundry regulations which we wish to introduce, they will be found at length in the chapter treating of the method of instruction, and others. These new regulations are not so numerous as to require a separate chapter; and if we ventured to sum them up under one head before exhibiting an outline of the system, they would appear totally disconnected, and perhaps, unintelligible or trifling.

One, however, we beg leave to expatiate upon. It is the extreme facility with which a student is so often permitted to pass from one class to another, without professing even the amount of knowledge strictly necessary to understand the studies of his own class. In American colleges, we frequently see students who scarcely ever study during the session. They get one of their classmates to read over the lesson to them whenever there is a probability of being "called up." If they fear that on account of their constantly bad recitations they run the risk of being brought before the Faculty,— which rarely proves of any avail—; marked "bad" on the report, or "disapproved"—which is seldom the case, though often apprehending it— they devote themselves during a day or more, perhaps, to an earnest and unwholesome study of their text books. Thus cramming and "reviewing" that which they never before learned; and by dint of close application during a short time, abundance of literal translations and the friendly assistance of learned class-mates, they save themselves from a mere though apparently serious, threat of rustication or dismissal.

We use the words "mere threat" because it has become of late a prevailing opinion in some institutions, that a great number of students is the only evidence of the prosperity of a college, — thus forgetting "that the intrinsic excellence of a school is not to be confounded with its external prosperity, estimated by the multitude of those who flock to it for education." To be better able to issue yearly a crowded catalogue, they leniently admit candidates who are deficient in some studies under the pretence that they may afterwards "make up" — as if the college course and every day's task were not already sufficiently difficult and absorbing, to engross all their time; —

add the names of those who have left the Institution, or been expelled, or deceased for some time; and often slide over offences which would be punished severely, if thereby their singular scale of collegiate prosperity were not to show a decrease by the omission of a few names.

Whether it is possible for any student to require in two days what is deemed necessary by sensible persons to study during five months is one of those questions which may be solved in a satisfactory manner when we consider how many ignorant students do graduate, and how few are turned out of college as deficient in scholarship, though deserving it. Now, there is not perhaps a single evil in the whole catalogue of collegiate nuisances which, so loudly calls for immediate censure and extirpation. . . .

There is only one session, which commences on the first Friday in September, and continues forty-five weeks, including public speaking, examinations and Commencement.

The session is divided into three terms of fifteen weeks, at the end of which terms all the classes are examined by divisions in presence of the Trustees and Faculty. In this way, a frequent opportunity is offered to the students who have been successful in the prosecution of their studies, to pass into a higher section; and an annual vacation of seven weeks is secured. This is more than sufficient. In the Royal Colleges of France, where a greater amount of study and confinement is required of the collegians, they have only one month,– but we must make allowances for the nature of our pupils, their habits, and the bad condition of our Southern roads.

Let no smile of incredulity play on the lips of our readers; an imperious necessity demands that collegiate vacations should be shortened in duration, and less frequent. In themselves, these vacations are productive of good,– the bow keeps on the stretch better from being occasionally unstrung,–but when recurring often, the perturbation they occasion in the studies is too great. The very anticipation of them makes itself felt; and it takes at least two weeks to settle the mind of the student after his return. We have introduced then, only two holidays, viz–. Christmas, which lasts ten days, appointed by the Faculty, and the 1st day of April.

The public speaking of the graduating class takes place the very week preceding Commencement. No member of the other classes, declaim publicly on the occasion. The number of students is limited to two hundred. It can never be increased; even with the addition of professors and buildings. The students are divided into four classes called Freshmen, Sophomores, Juniors and Seniors. Each one of these classes is subdivided into two divisions. The first division consists of the more advanced scholars; and at the end of each term, those of the second division who have stood a satisfactory examination join the first division; those who have not, remain where they are; or after one more unsuccessful trial in the same division are dismissed. This system we are told works well at West Point; and we do not see why it should not meet with a like success in our college. By these means, the more attentive students proceed rapidly and are not thwarted in their career by the "gentlemen of leisure" whom President Barnwell [3] is reported to have said, we must expect to admit and retain, and endure, and graduate, in all the institutions throughout the length and breadth of this blessed country.

The classes recite and hear the lectures by divisions. They study by sections of one fourth of the whole class, when it numbers 50; of one third when less than forty.

All the students, *Seniors not excepted*, have three recitations a day [4] during five days in the week; on Saturday they recite twice, and Sunday only once. Monday and Saturday mornings are set apart for Drawing; the former on account of the Sabbath evening, and the latter of the Debating Societies, which prevent the preparation of a recitation for the following morning.

As in all other colleges, they have prayer every day at Sun rise and at Sun down; and service in the Chapel on Sundays. . . .

But very few colleges in America can support themselves without the help of private donations or appropriations from the Legislature. The University of Virginia, Brown, Alabama and many others, if not all, were liberally endowed even before they went into operation; and the South Carolina College has cost the State nearly a million of dollars within the last 45 years. Hence it is that these Institutions can afford so to lower their price of tuition as to render it accessible to all. At the University of Michigan, they make no charges whatever; at Bowdoin, they amount only to $24, at Hamilton, $26, Dartmouth, $27;

3. Robert W. Barnwell (1801-1882) became president of the College of South Carolina in 1835, succeeding Thomas Cooper, whose theological liberalism or radicalism had greatly reduced or had threatened to reduce the prestige of that institution.

4. Harrisse then gives a schedule of classes and outlines the work of the various collegiate departments: English literature, rhetoric and logic; mathematics, natural philosophy and astronomy; antiquities, history and geography; French language and literature; constitutional law, political economy, and mental philosophy; drawing, painting and penmanship; gymnastics.

but these colleges have resources of their own; and as our Institution is supposed to rely solely upon itself for support, we adopt the average price for tuition, room rent, &c, &c, viz $60 per annum.

The number of students is limited to 200, which yields an income (on paper) of $12,000. This sum we deem sufficient to cover the actual expenses of the Institution.

For the present, and with the understanding, that they will be doubled as soon as the endowment will allow it, we fix the President's

salary at	$1,500
the Professor's at	1,200
the adjunct Professors' at	1,000
the Marshal's at	500

We think it impossible to get and keep men of abilities for less than 2 or $3,000 a year, inasmuch as their labors are great and confinement still greater. Nor must we lose sight of the fact that we require from our instructors accomplishments and talents not often to be found in the generality of American Professors. It is a misconceived economy or near-sighted policy, to curtail the teacher's compensation. It tends to render him anxious to leave the college as soon as he can obtain a more profitable situation elsewhere; and thereby hinders him from bringing to the discharge of his duty, the predilection, nay, the enthusiasm, so necessary to the prosperity of any literary Institution....

It is the collegian's nature to be prone to idleness; to consider study as a severe infliction and the college discipline as a tyranny, which he constantly and ingeniously strives to elude. Even those who are urged to application by the laudable ambition of acquiring knowledge, college honors or the commendations of their fond parents, often look upon the day's recitation as a task which they endeavor to alleviate. Hence their frequent use of translations, readiness to avail themselves of the Professor's occasional mistakes in giving out the lesson; and those little associations when the preparation of the lesson is carried out in concert, each member contributing his share of lexical researches to the mass; or the best scholar in the company translating the text aloud for the accommodation of his artful classmates.

This natural tendency to self-indulgence is greatly abetted by the excessive liberty granted to our students. Provided they are in their rooms at a stated time, nothing more seems to be required of them. They may occupy the study hours in reading newspapers, dozing in a rocking chair or whittling soft pine sticks, no one will or can compel them to study. If they do not know their lesson, they get a bad mark, and in the opinion of the Faculty, stand low in the scale of scholarship. A very unenviable estimation, no doubt, but which has no influence whatever upon their ulterior conduct. They are too well aware that a student is hardly ever dismissed from college on account of deficiency; or refused to be re-instated after an easy trial, when perchance he has been "disapproved." In some institutions it may even be said that the greatest danger he runs of losing his diploma is to be short of the money required to pay the college fees.

Such an unlimited freedom of action is altogether out of place within the walls of a college. Both the curriculum and the study must be compulsory and attended to. No door should be left open to shifting or evasions of any kind. Every expedient should be adopted to obtain the utmost degree of perseverance and continued attention; in fine, all inducements, all temptations towards inaction and idleness must by all means be removed. Close application, prolonged mental efforts should be enforced on students, whatever be their age, wealth, intellectual superiority or family connections. Is there anything more unjustifiable, more revolting, than to see a student placed above the rules of college, and setting at defiance both teachers and citizens, because he is the son of an influential man? . . .

We confess to be altogether unable to find a single plausible reason in behalf of denominational colleges; on the other hand, we deem it obvious that any institution purporting the education of Christian youths, should be free from sectarian influence.

Religion must be imparted to collegians, not, indeed, to promote the interest or progress of any particular creed, but to supply the most imperious of human wants; purify and direct all the aspirations and passions of man, and fit him for the discharge of those solemn duties which he owes to himself, to God and the Commonwealth.

Let the Bible then be taught and expounded within the walls of our college; let its truths and sublime precepts in all their lofty simplicity be inculcated on the youthful mind of our pupils; let them even exalt in hymns of praise and gratitude for the precious gifts which the Supreme Ruler has so bountifully bestowed on them; but let us beware of dogmatic teachings, lest we should entail a continuance of religious intolerance, and weaken the cause of Protestantism in perpetuating the strife of sects.

Our institution, therefore, is not denominational. Clergymen of different demonimations, taken from among the Faculty and Ministers in the neighborhood, are invited to preach by turns to the students.

All the classes are required to attend Divine Worship in the College Chapel on Sunday forenoon; and in the afternoon the Freshmen and Sophomores recite in the Historical parts of the Old and New Testaments.

The Juniors, in Wayland's Moral Science and the Seniors in Butler's Analogy. . . .

The hope of a palpable reward, however slight in point of pecuniary worth, is at times a powerful incentive to students. The sets of finely bound books or the simple wreath of ivy awarded at the Sorbonne are often more highly valued than the most pompous newspaper accounts of these literary contests. It is a natural ambition which urges the student to untiring efforts, and it frequently achieves what all other means failed to accomplish. We feel confident that in many instances the "Deturs" of the Hopkins' Foundation,[5] have been more productive of good than the well-deserved commendations which the Professors rarely fail to lavish on their favorite pupils.

We therefore add to the diplomas of the First and Second Honor men, a set of not less than twelve books, finely bound; and to those who received the distinctions, six handsome volumes, all selected from standard authors. The distinction man in Drawing gets a box of Mathematical instruments; the best gymnastician receives a pair of silver spurs.

We also award for the best English Composition—the competitors to be Freshmen,—a gold medal. For the best historical dissertation—the competitors to be Sophomores—a gold medal. For the best French composition—the competitors to be Juniors,—a gold medal. For the best essay on Moral or Intellectual Philosophy—the competitors to be Seniors,—a gold medal.

The roll is not called in the Chapel; the monitors report the members of their sections who are absent. Each section has a separate pew. Calling the roll aloud, will do for a barrack, but it is not becoming in a place of public worship.

5. Edward Hopkins was a London merchant who came to this country in 1637, was several times governor of Connecticut, and made some important educational gifts to New England for the purpose of providing "some encouragement in those foreign plantations, for the breeding of hopeful youths, both at the grammar school and college, for the public service of the country at future times." Part of the income of one of his gifts is still used at Harvard College for the purchase of books called "Deturs" for meritorious students. Detur is the Latin for "Let there be given."

The use of tobacco, in any way, is strictly prohibited. The faculty may remove from the institution any student who has thrice infringed this rule.

Our college confers no honorary degrees of any kind; nor are the graduates of three years standing, or more, entitled to the "Mastership." [6]

No student can be admitted to a partial course;—all the studies being obligatory.

9. A Committee of the Faculty of the University of Alabama Opposes the Elective System of the University of Virginia, 1854

At a meeting of the Faculty of the University of Alabama, held on Friday, the 14th day of July, 1854, the following paper was read by the President:—

The President of the Board, and the Trustees now present, are unanimously in favor of modifying the present system of instruction in the University of Alabama, and respectfully request the Faculty of the University to report to an adjourned meeting of the Board, on Monday, the 25th of September next, the plan and details for the initiation and continuance of a system, conforming, as near as our circumstances will allow, to the arrangements in the University of Virginia.

John A. Winston.
Wm. H. Forney.
John N. Malone.
Ed. Baptist.
H. W. Collier.

University of Ala., July 12, 1854.

This paper was referred to a committee appointed by the President, consisting of Professors F. A. P. Barnard, John W. Pratt, and George Benagh; which committee was instructed to report to the Faculty at an adjourned meeting, to be held on Monday, the 18th of September.

6. Before 1860, and perhaps later, the master's degree was often conferred on graduates of three years beyond the A.B. degree, upon the payment of a fee, no additional work or attendance being required. Professor Samuel Eliot Morison says (*Three Centuries of Harvard,* p. 35) that "in the nineteenth century it was a saying that all a Harvard man had to do for his Master's degree was to pay five dollars and stay out of jail." For a good account of the practice of awarding honorary degrees in the United States see Stephen E. Epler, *Honorary Degrees: A Survey of Their Use and Abuse* (Washington, D. C.: American Council on Public Affairs, 1943).

On that day the Faculty accordingly re-assembled; but adjourned without transacting business, in consequence of the absence of the President. At a called meeting, on Thursday, the 21st, the committee reported in explicit compliance with the terms of the request of the Board of Trustees; and the report which follows, was subsequently presented by Professor Barnard, on behalf of himself and Professor Pratt, of the majority. It was ordered by the Faculty, at a subsequent meeting, that this document should be communicated to the Board of Trustees. The report was accordingly read before that body, on Tuesday and Wednesday, the 26th and 27th of September. The deliberations of the Board resulted, however, in the adoption neither of the plan originally suggested in the paper above given, nor of that recommended in this report; but of one which may perhaps be regarded as an experiment substantially new; conservative, in the main, of the features of the existing college system, but providing opportunity for such departures from it, in particular cases, as the judgment of the Faculty shall approve. The nature of this plan may be more particularly gathered from the following ordinance:—

1. That the studies now pursued in the University, the extent to which they are carried, and the number of recitations heard by each officer, shall remain as at present established, as near as may be.

2. That twelve recitations shall be heard upon each day of the week, except Sunday. The Faculty may, in their discretion, reduce the number of recitations upon Saturday, so that there be not less than four upon that day.

3. That the recitations of each day shall be assigned by the Faculty to the different hours in such a manner that a student, by taking three recitations per day, may accomplish all the studies taught in the University in four years. In doing this, the recitations of the Professor of Ancient Languages, the Tutor of Ancient Languages, and the Professor of Modern Languages, may be assigned to the same hours; so, also, those of the Professors of Mixed Mathematics and Pure Mathematics; also, those of the Professors of Chemistry and Geology. All other recitations must be assigned to hours at which no others are held.

4. Each student under the age of twenty-one years, desiring to select a particular study, shall be required to produce from his parent or guardian, if he has one, a written declaration of the special object of the applicant in coming to the University; and the Faculty shall then prescribe for him the course of study which will accomplish his object

in the shortest time and in the best manner, having regard to the next two provisions.

5. Every student must have three recitations a day, as near as may be.

6. A student shall not enter upon the study he may select, until he has passed such an examination as will satisfy the faculty that he may, by proper application, prosecute it successfully.

7. Upon a student's completing, and standing an approved examination upon, all the studies in any department, he shall receive the degree of graduate in that department, and a certificate bearing the seal of the University, and delivered at commencement, in the usual mode.

8. The degree of Bachelor of Arts shall be conferred upon a student only after he shall have passed approved examinations upon *all* the studies taught in the University.

9. Honorary degrees shall not be conferred by this University, except by a unanimous vote of the Board of Trustees.

10. All laws or ordinances, or parts of the same, now existing, which conflict with the foregoing ordinance, are hereby repealed.

Report.

The undersigned, a majority of the Committee appointed by the Faculty of the University of Alabama, to consider and report on a request emanating from certain members of the Board of Trustees, in regard to a re-organization of the plan of instruction in the University, having consented to unite with the minority in a literal compliance with the request alluded to, and having discharged that duty, beg leave respectfully to present certain distinct views of their own, having a bearing on the general question raised by the proposition referred to them, and also on the considerations out of which, as they have reason to believe, this proposition has grown.

Change, it is hardly necessary to say, will never be sought for its own sake. Whenever and wherever there arises a steady and earnest demand for a new order of things in regard to matters which deeply concern mankind, whether they be affairs of state or systems of education, it is obvious, from the very nature of the interests involved, that the degree to which this demand is real and sincere, must be matter of easy ascertainment. And when, to a majority of the community, the existence of a general feeling of dissatisfaction with the actual state of things is entirely unsuspected and imperceptible, it may well be questioned whether the impressions of a few, however decided, can be wisely accepted as of more weight in evidence than the tranquil contentment of nearly all beside.

It is by no means the belief of the undersigned, that those members of the Board whose names are appended to the request, which has led to the appointment of this Committee, are all of them, by previous conviction, in favor of the introduction into this University of the system of which they ask for the details. It is quite sufficient to suppose that the request was dictated by a desire, on the one hand, to know explicitly and definitely what it is which it is proposed to substitute here, in place of a system that, if not the best, has, nevertheless, the sanction of some centuries of experiment, and the present support of the general suffrage; and an equal desire, on the other, to satisfy the outside advocates of change, that the Board are always willing to examine any project for the improvement of the University, which, in the view of any friend of the cause of education, may deserve their deliberate attention. Those members of the Board to whom this inquiry is owing, are therefore regarded by the undersigned as occupying, equally with their colleagues, the attitude of judges, whose opinions are yet to be expressed, and not that of partizans, who are waiting only to act upon a judgment already formed.

The friends of the University, whose suggestions to the members of the Board have probably occasioned the present inquiry, appear to have been laboring under some impressions which a candid examination of facts cannot fail to dispel. These are—

1st. That the actual state of the University is not prosperous;

2d. That the number of students is smaller than is usual in colleges of equal standing in years;

3d. That there really exists an outside demand for a radical reorganization of the University, powerful enough, if resisted, to sweep down opposition before it;

4th. That neither the Trustees nor the Faculty have heretofore given thought to the possibility of introducing improvement into the institution; but that both bodies have manifested indifference to the spirit of progress which characterizes the age.

In speaking of the prosperity of an institution of learning, the general public seem to regard but a single criterion—that of the number of students it attracts, or succeeds in retaining. But this is a test which serves very ill to enable us to judge either of the value of the institution as a part of the educational machinery of the State, or of the esteem in which it is held by the surrounding people. It is perfectly well known to the undersigned, that many who would be students of the University are prevented from being so now, not because of any objection to the course of study here prescribed, but because of what they please to consider the too great severity of the tests imposed to secure a certain respectable degree of scholarship and attainment. Could the Faculty be induced to think it wise to permit a material degradation of the standard of scholarship insisted on in this University, there can be no doubt that, without any other change whatever, an immediate and large increase of numbers might be realized. It is often charged that this Faculty is more severe in its exactions than that of any other college in the Southwestern States. Upon such an assertion it is not for the undersigned to express any opinion. The Faculty of the University of Alabama have acted without reference to what may or may not be demanded elsewhere. They have aimed but at the single object of making this institution one in which scholars may be formed worthy to be compared with those who issue from the celebrated and time-honored Universities of the older States. Whether in this they have succeeded or not, there can be no doubt, since it is matter of pretty frequent complaint, that they have set up here what is generally regarded as a high standard of scholarship. They have secured to the University of Alabama the respect of the surrounding community, and that of sister institutions throughout the country. To say that, in regard to the great ultimate ends for which colleges are instituted, there has been any failure here, or that there exists a want of a prosperity of the noblest kind, is at once unreasonable and absurd.

But in regard to the point of numbers. There is not, we must admit, a large number of students in this University, if we compare catalogues with Harvard or Yale, or even with the State institutions of North and South Carolina. But Harvard and Yale have several thousand living alumni; and the two last-mentioned colleges have several hundred—perhaps not less than a thousand—each. All of these old institutions are, or have been, the direct beneficiaries of the States to which they belong, or of many of their wealthy citizens; and they thus secure that interest and those sympathies from the surrounding communities, which all men bestow upon the objects they have befriended and cherished. The adult population of Alabama is yet mainly immigrant; the affections of the fathers of our youth still cling around the homes of their childhood, and their spirits still do homage at those shrines of learning, where they themselves, perhaps, were first imbued with the love of letters. In addition to this, there are growing up in this State, as in every other, institutions endowed and patronized by particular religious denominations; which cannot fail, even though they should offer advantages for mere intellectual culture much inferior to those which the University presents, to draw around them many who would otherwise swell our numbers. Nor has this institution yet a hold on the feeling of State pride, such as so powerfully sustains the State Universities of the two Carolinas and of Virginia. The population itself is too heterogeneous, and too newly thrown together, to have learned even to recognize the feeling; and this feeling, so far as it is represented at all, is at present but humbly represented by a sort of sentiment of common interest. All these considerations are unfavorable to the growth of an institution erected in the midst of a people like this, by funds not contributed by themselves, interesting them by no associations connected with the past, and allying itself with no sympathies of theirs which may be linked with the present, or may extend to the future.

Under circumstances like these, ought it not to be a great thing, if the University is able to command from Alabama an attendance as large, in proportion to population, as the University of Virginia commands from the people of Virginia? The name of the Sage of Monticello ought itself alone to be a sufficient guaranty for a host of youthful devotees at the altar which he reared to learning. The tone of exultant pride, in which every Virginian alludes to this enduring monument of the wisdom of Jefferson, would seem to indicate that no other institution could have a charm like this, to fill the imagination of a native of the Old Dominion. And, to leave speculation aside, it is in fact universally admitted, that the University of Virginia is a flourishing and prosperous institution. Now, in comparing that University with ours, in regard to numbers, we must manifestly reject from both catalogues all students from beyond the limits of the respective States. We must remember how many of the sons of Virginia have emigrated South and West; we must remember what attractive associations cluster around the name of the patriot founder; we must bear in mind how easily, by means of the immense railway system of the Atlantic States, students even from our own borders may reach the Virginia University, more quickly and more agreeably than they can our own. Of this species of advantages we have not one. Hence we confine the comparison strictly to the numbers furnished by the respective States in which the Universities are situated, alone....

That there can be no popular demand for the introduction of the Virginia system here, is further evident from the fact, that not one in twenty of the people knows what the Virginia system is. It certainly is not what it is apparently believed by some to be; and that is, a system which permits any student to pursue any study selected by himself or his guardians, at any time, to any extent, and with any rapidity he pleases. And the prevalent misapprehension on this subject, amounts really to a serious evil; since the expectations which have been held out regarding the plan are sure, should it be adopted here, to be sadly disappointed. But on this point the undersigned propose to speak more fully in its proper place.

The absence of any popular demand for this species of change is still further evidenced by the tone of the public press, both before and after the request of the members of the Board, who were present in July, was laid before the public. Nothing can be more certain than that, throughout the collegiate year of 1853-'54, down to the month of May, when some slight troubles entirely connected with *discipline* elicited some discontented remarks, not one word appeared in any public print in Alabama, in relation to the University (and the notices were many), which was not congratulatory and almost exultant, in view of the steady improvement of the Institution in prosperity, and in view of its well-established reputation for thorough and judicious methods of instruction, and for the sound and substantial attainments of its students. And in the expressions of discontent just alluded to, and which were directed entirely toward police and other regulations and measures for the government and not for the instruction of the undergraduates, it is worthy of remark how generally, and in fact how almost universally, the conductors of the press mingled with their words of dissatisfaction the regret that these events should have befallen at a moment when the University, having lived down its disasters, had become so proudly prosperous, and had succeeded in raising itself so deservedly high in the confidence of the people of Alabama. Whoever has had access to the public prints of the State generally for the past twelve months cannot but be forcibly struck with the truth of these reminiscences. The undersigned therefore assert, without fear of contradiction, that, if the tone of the public press can be regarded as in any degree an index of that of public sentiment among a people, then it is so far from being true, that there is a popular demand for the subversion here of our time-honored course of instruction for the sake of introducing one not even known to a majority of the people, that the feeling of the masses has been entirely the other way,—entirely one of satisfaction and content....

Let it be understood in the outset, that it is in no spirit of unfriendliness or opposition to institutions for professional, technical, special, or partial education, that the undersigned are disposed to remonstrate against the transformation to which it is proposed to subject this University. If there is a demand for such institutions, let them be created; if it is true, as is so frequently asserted, that hundreds of young men are absolutely cut off from any opportunity to acquire the education they need, because the University will not (it would be more just to say, cannot) give it to them, then there should be no delay in providing the facilities which their case requires. It cannot be that means are wanting, or ever will be so, if the alleged demand be real, to endow and furnish schools fashioned in the strictest conformity to the popular dictation; for schools to which hundreds are waiting to resort so soon as their doors shall be opened, can never fail to prove eminently lucrative, considered merely as pecuniary investments. If, then, this demand be real, there exists not the slightest reason for insisting that the University shall provide for it; and if it be not, the argument in favor of change crumbles away into nothing....

But perhaps it will be said that the University of Virginia, from which it is proposed to draw the plan of our remodeled system of instruction, has not a numerous body of instructors—has not, in fact, a larger number of officers in its Faculty of Arts than we have in ours. This fact is certainly undeniable; but this very fact proves that the arguments which are most confidently relied on in favor of change, are entirely baseless. It is said that we must introduce here the system of the University of Virginia, in order that every student may have the opportunity, in the words of Dr. Wayland, to study "what he chooses, all that he chooses, and nothing but what he chooses." Yet this the undersigned have, as they believe, shown to be impossible, without that large number of teachers which confessedly the University of Virginia has not. And if we refer to the statement contained in the catalogue of that institution for the last collegiate year, we shall find that the Faculty, instead of making any pretence to provide for the varying wants of young men who wish to study "what they choose, and nothing but what they choose," merely arrange their students in classes—not the usual college classes, which are the same with every officer—but in classes which may be different in different departments, while in the same department they are constant throughout the course. It appears, from this authority, that the number of classes receiving instruction in each department is only in a few cases greater, but is quite as often less, in the University of Virginia, than in the University of Alabama. In illustration of this statement the following comparison may be made. It exhibits the number of classes simultaneously reciting similar subjects, in the two institutions.

	Univ. of Ala.	Univ. of Va.
Latin and its Literature,	Four	Two.
Greek " " "	Four	Two.
French,	Three	Three.
Mathematics, pure,	Two	Three.*
" mixed,	Two	Three.
Geology, &c.,	One	One.
Chemistry,	One	One.
Ethics, &c.	Four	Three.
Total,	Twenty-one.	Eighteen.

The Virginia University appears to offer no advantage over our own, as it regards the freedom of the student within a given department to select his own studies, if we except a slight one in the departments which embrace the exact sciences. Supposing, therefore, that the ordinance of the Board of Trustees of this University, which was enacted in 1831, opening the institution to what was called "partial-course students," should be now again revived; it would require but very slight alterations in regard to the hours of lecture and recitation, and in regard to the number of classes in each department, to give to this college the plan of the University of Virginia complete. The language of the law referred to is the following, as printed by order of the Board in 1837. "The University shall be open to persons who do not desire to take the full course and to be graduated as Bachelors of Arts, but who desire to take a partial course and be graduated in particular departments only; provided they are found qualified for the studies of the department which they wish to join; and provided they take not less than the usual number of departments," &c., &c.

* The department of pure mathematics in the University of Virginia has nominally four classes; but one of these is a class in mixed mathematics. The department of mixed mathematics proper has but two classes.

But it is certainly not this plan which we are told that the people demand. The promise held out, has been that the University, as reorganized, should give instruction to all who come here to demand it, should give them precisely what they demand, and should give it precisely when they demand it. Such, at least, is undoubtedly the popular understanding of the proposition made and widely published in regard to our University. If the call for change has assumed the definite shape of a demand for the system of the University of Virginia, it is not because that system, as it exists there, is known to the people of Alabama in general, and by them approved; but because that name has been used to stand for the thing desired, and which, by the proposed reorganization, it is hoped to obtain. Expressly on this ground would the undersigned, under any circumstances, resist the alteration; for since the system called by this—for the moment perhaps popular—name is certainly not the thing which the people who are said to ask for change expect, it is folly to suppose that they will be satisfied with it after they come to see what it actually is. The thing which the people do really desire, if they desire any thing, is that which the undersigned have shown to be what it does not belong to this University to attempt to supply, on the ground that it either will not pay and is therefore impracticable and cannot but be ruinous, or that if it will pay, it has no need of the University....

To those, therefore, who cry out for the omission of mathematical studies from the college curriculum, or for a system so conveniently open that they may be able to omit them for themselves, the undersigned would reply that the omission destroys one of the most important of the guaranties hitherto regarded as indispensable, that the course of study shall produce the result, which the University, by its diploma, is to certify to have been produced—symmetrical mental training and sound scholarship.

But if the mathematics, and especially the higher mathematics of the college course, have been subjects of attack, the ancient classics have been no less so. "It is often asked," says President Sparks, in his inaugural address, "Why waste so much time in studying the dead languages, in acquiring Greek and Latin, which are seldom used afterwards? Why not fill up this long period with studies of *more immediate utility*, which, at the same time that they help to train the mind and form the character, communicate a knowledge of men and things, *which may be turned to account in the common affairs of life?*" In the same spirit, an anonymous English writer, in a vigorous onslaught upon classical learning, published in 1850, and considered of importance enough to be made the subject of an article in one of the leading British reviews, inquires, "Is the mere classical scholar as well fitted as persons trained in other ways, for doing the things which need be done in such times as those in which we are living? Do we find that this is the best training, in an active and jostling and stirring age like the present, for the senate, the bar, the platform, or the press? Can the mere scholar *sway the minds of the men of Manchester or of Birmingham?*" Without stopping to remark that the men who leave the universities of Oxford and Cambridge, and who are here signalized as "mere scholars," have, for the most part, swayed the minds of the men of Manchester and of Birmingham, down to the present day, it is sufficient to observe that in these extracts and many other similar ones which might be quoted, we have still the idea standing prominently out, that the college curriculum *ought* to furnish "knowledge which may be turned to account in the common affairs of life;" and that the course of undergraduate training *ought* to be conducted with the view to turn out youth immediately fit "to sway the minds of the men of Manchester and of Birmingham." The perpetual recurrence of this idea in all the writing of all the modern advocates of new systems of collegiate instruction, is truly disheartening. The apparent absence of any just apprehension of what it is which a college, in its intention, undertakes to do, or of any sort of appreciation of the value of the object at which the college aims, makes it necessary continually to fall back upon first principles, and to fritter away time and waste breath in endless explanations....

Is it possible, then, that the Trustees of this University will deliberately resolve to award the honor of graduation, to confer the diploma which, from the earliest history of colleges, has been recognized only as the certificate of genuine scholarship, upon men who willfully neglect that which always has been, and inevitably always must be, the first essential to the scholar? Is it possible that they will do this ruinous thing, at a time when the University is in the enjoyment of a sound and healthy prosperity, such as it never has experienced before; and such as, to all who have been familiar with the early history of other colleges, is not only satisfactory but highly encouraging? Is it possible that they will do it, with the evidence before them of an entirely tranquil contentment pervading the whole people, in regard to the system of instruction in operation here; and in view of the fact that the proposition for a change, published everywhere throughout the

State, has awakened only an occasional and feeble response; while it has at the same time elicited from the scattered friends of sound education so numerous and elaborate and able vindications of the existing order of things, as to prove beyond all question that the sound sense of the people is satisfied with what we have, and asks for nothing better? Is it possible that they will do this, and in doing so substitute in place of a tried and approved system, one which has not even the guaranty of past success to recommend it; but which is actually, in spite of all impressions heretofore existing to the contrary, unpopular at home, and which has, in point of fact, already broken down in every other institution which has attempted to borrow it? Surely this cannot be....

If, finally, appeal be made to the catalogue of the University of Virginia itself, where the utmost freedom is allowed the student in the selection of his studies, we shall find the weight of evidence still leaning the same way, and tending to demonstrate the fact that the people *will* not abandon the Latin and the Greek. In each of these languages, the course of the University covers two years only; and it is presumed that there, as elsewhere, the two may be pursued simultaneously. Now, if from the total of the catalogue for 1853-54, which is 466, we subtract 199 students entirely professional, there remain 267 students under the Faculty of Arts. Of these, 176 are in the department of ancient languages, and 156 only in that of the modern. In mathematics there are 179, and in chemistry 220, many of the medical students taking this department; while in the remaining departments of natural philosophy and moral philosophy (the latter comprehending also metaphysics, rhetoric, logic, criticism, and political economy), the numbers fall as low as 106 and 112 respectively. It appears, therefore, that in this University, in which students who aim at education remain three or four years, while the classical courses are completed in two, the proportion of the whole number (two-thirds) who, by the latest catalogue appear to be studying the learned languages, is so great as to indicate that nearly all, at one period or another, enroll themselves in that department....

The unreasonableness of expecting our colleges, whose proper business is, and has been from the beginning, to do this work of education proper, to provide also, in the brief space of time allotted to them with their pupils, that professional or technical training which shall prepare them to engage directly in the business of life, has been already sufficiently considered. But to what has been said may very properly be added the important consideration suggested by the question, How much, after all, could the college accomplish, provided it were converted altogether into a school for the study of the professions and the practical arts of life? . . .

In conclusion, the undersigned cannot but believe, that, on questions of this kind, some consideration is due to the weight of authority. The most eminent educators of youth in America, are almost with one voice opposed to a system like that of the University of Virginia, for American colleges. The Faculty of Yale College, at the time of the publication of their ably argued letter to the trustees of that institution, from which repeated quotations have been made in this Report, embraced some of the most distinguished and experienced instructors whom this country has produced; among whom we may especially signalize President Day, and Professors Kingsley, Silliman, Goodrich, and Olmsted.

It is certain that no college in the United States has ever commanded a higher respect, or possessed a more extended popularity, than this. And it is remarkable that though it was among the first—perhaps quite the first—to take a public and decided stand in opposition to the views of those who would break up the existing college system, and especially of those who would discard the learned languages from the curriculum of college study, yet no period of its whole history has been distinguished by a more signal prosperity than that which has since elapsed. At no time have the Faculty of that celebrated institution shown the slightest disposition to descend from the high position which they assumed in 1828; and a recent letter received from Dr. Woolsey, the accomplished scholar who at present presides over it, accords entirely with the views which have been expressed in this Report. "We have ever," writes Dr. Woolsey, "been averse to the system pursued at Charlottesville, on the ground principally that students, at that stage of their education when they are in college, are incompetent to choose what they ought to study; and on the ground that, at that season, there is need of drilling and close examination—of a daily responsibility—habits of study being yet unformed, and immediate motives being needed to put young minds at work. It is surprising how much stronger a motive acts in professional study than in preparatory; the student in the former case feeling that success in life is in a good degree connected with his diligence, and by no means so much in the latter. Hence we are disinclined to an optional and to a lecture system. We would introduce both sparingly, and toward the close of a college life. And indeed a lecture system, without frequent examination, is of small account."

Dr. Woolsey then proceeds to consider the objections which are usually urged against the existing system. He observes, "There are two principal ones, 1st, that students will not study what they do not like; and 2d, that there is an inaptitude in some for certain branches. To which may be added, that the course from the first may be accommodated, on the optional system, to the profession chosen. In reply to the last objection, we say that the discipline of languages and mathematics, and of moral science, is too evidently needed by all to allow us to doubt that it is, in the main, the correct system. The one-sidedness of men educated only (for example) for and in physical science, is quite apparent. . . ."

In regard to our own University, in case a reorganization of the plan of instruction be resolved on, the following, in the opinion of the undersigned, are the principles according to which it should be regulated:—

1. To prescribe a definite curriculum of study, designed as a mental discipline, to extend over the entire four years, and to which all regular candidates for graduation are to be required to conform. In this, however, to include only those branches of study, or certainly very few but those, which, by the consent of the learned of all ages, are entitled to be regarded as the best instruments for evolving and exercising the powers of the mind.

2. To embrace all the remaining studies of the course, which are thus thrown out, in a group, out of which the Faculty may, at the proper time, select such as seem fittest to the intellectual wants of each individual student, as ascertained by the observation of his tastes, mental habits, and actual attainments during the earlier years of study; and to provide for his instruction in these, without exacting from him, as at present, attention to the whole number.

In the application of these principles, it seems to the undersigned advisable that, during the first two years of the course, no study should be introduced which is not obligatory upon all the students. The present arrangement of the hours at which the daily exercises occur, need not therefore of necessity be interfered with. Whether or not that is the best arrangement, the undersigned do not undertake to pronounce; but at present they see no reason to recommend any alteration in this respect, in regard to this part of the course. Should, however, any portion of the studies of the junior and senior year, or of either, be made elective, it will probably be found convenient to assign recitations or lectures for these classes in some branches at other hours, additional to those fixed by the present regulations, and without disturbing the latter. What particular distribution of time may be best adapted to secure all the ends aimed at by this new system of instruction, it will perhaps be best to leave to the more mature deliberation of the Faculty. A table of exercises, or *roster*, herewith submitted, may be regarded as simply in the light of a suggestion for the purpose of inviting amendment, than as a positive recommendation.

Should a reorganization of the plan of instruction on these principles be resolved upon, it becomes important to decide what studies shall be placed in the elective group. To this class, it appears to the undersigned, that there can be no hesitation in referring,—

1st. All such as deal principally in facts of observation;

2nd. Such as require a peculiar natural aptitude for their successful prosecution; and

3d. The study of the languages, ancient or modern, pursued beyond the limit prescribed by the obligatory course.

Under the first head may be included all the branches of natural history, and also geology, mineralogy, physiology, meteorology, and possibly, a second course of chemistry.

Under the second may be embraced all the branches of the mathematics which rest upon the algebraic, or symbolic, method (elementary algebra excepted), and embracing in the existing course, algebra applied to geometry, analytical geometry, and the calculus, differential and integral; to which may be added spherical trigonometry.

The third requires no specifications.

The undersigned design to enter into no argument as to the propriety of the distinctions which they have thus made between the subjects now overloading the curriculum of college study. Since it is an admitted fact that no student can possibly now be thorough in all of them, limited as he is to the very few weeks which can only be given to each, according to present arrangements, it can be no serious objection to the proposed plan to say, that it must necessarily cut off every student from something. That is very true; but it is equally true that the entirely voluntary system permits him to do the same for himself; and what is more, makes it nearly certain that he will do it, while it fails to guaranty to him a systematic intellectual training at all.

The studies which will remain obligatory upon every individual, after those above specified are excluded from the regular course, are such as are universally regarded as furnishing the best discipline of the mind and the most equable exercise of the various faculties; and such as, at the same time, by a consent almost universal, and quite so if we except the learned languages from the list, are esteemed as being in themselves attainments absolutely indispensable to every man of education. Moreover, in regard to the learned languages, it has already been shown, that the dissent just hinted at, is actually more imaginary than real, that it is limited to a very small number of persons, and that in this number we find hardly a single name of any authority either in the great field of education, or in the world of letters. . . .

There remains one other particular, in regard to which a change appears to be desirable. According to the rules at present existing in this University, if a student fails in the performance of any particular exercise, on account of sickness, or other sufficient excuse, he is permitted to prepare and perform this exercise by himself separately, and is entitled to receive credit for the performance, precisely as if it had been accomplished in its due season. Should the principle of estimating scholarship according to the recorded marks of the term exercises be abandoned, then this regulation, as dependent on it, may as well be abandoned likewise. But if otherwise, it is still to be desired that this, as the undersigned believe, worse than useless rule, should be dispensed with by itself. In the first place, the student ought to be habituated in college, to contemplate the stern truth that men's misfortunes will never be accepted in life, as a reason why their competitors should pause and wait for them, or should offer them a second trial, in the race for the world's distinctions. By sickness, or other misfortune, the student loses the benefit of a performance which might have counted in his favor. Be it so—let him accept the loss like a man. Another day it may befall his rival. And it is well to learn, by small mishaps like these, to bear those greater ills which may lie before us in the world's ceaseless struggle, where the race too often *is* to the swift, and the battle to the strong. More than this, it is well to cultivate that energetic spirit which scorns to droop at every trivial pain, or to relax effort at every insignificant discouragement; but which presses steadily onward to its purpose, with a perseverance which never flags while progress is a possibility.

With these suggestions, the undersigned conclude what they have to say in regard to the important subject now pending before the Faculty and the Board of Trustees. At the time of their appointment, they had not contemplated any further action than a simple compliance with the request contained in the communication of the Board, accompanied, perhaps, by a mere programme of such a scheme as they have endeavored to describe in this Report, for comparison with that which had been specifically called for. Any very radical change in a system of instruction so generally approved as that which has long existed here, they had not regarded as a possibility. A growing conviction, however, that the cause of sound education in Alabama is more seriously in danger than they had supposed, has constrained them, under the pressure of a deep sense of duty, to present in full the reasons which lead them to deprecate the introduction here of an educational system which a majority of our wisest men regard with distrust, and which has never been more than doubtfully successful in any college which has tried it in the United States.

F. A. P. Barnard,
Jno. W. Pratt.

University of Alabama, Sept. 18, 1854.

—*Report on a Proposition to Modify the Plan of Instruction in the University of Alabama. Made to the Faculty of the University. Read to the Faculty, Sept. 21, and before the Board of Trustees, Sept. 26, 1854* (New York: D. Appleton and Company, 1855). While at Alabama and Mississippi, Barnard had praised the prescribed curriculum; as president of Columbia University he came to embrace the elective system and to defend some of the arguments, including economic considerations, which he had attacked in 1854.

10. Scale of salaries at the University of Virginia, 1855-1856

PROFESSORS' SALARIES.

1855.			
July 1, To	S. Maupin,	quarter's salary,	250.00
	John B. Minor,	"	250.00
	James P. Holcombe,	"	250.00
	Francis H. Smith,	"	250.00
	M. Schele De Vere,	"	250.00
	James L. Cabell,	"	250.00
	Albert T. Bledsoe,	"	250.00
	H. Howard,	"	250.00

PROFESSORS' SALARIES

1855.				
July 1, To	Gessner Harrison,	quarter's salary,	250.00	
	Wm. H. McGuffey,	"	250.00	
Oct. 1, To	S. Maupin,	"	250.00	
	John B. Minor,	"	250.00	
	James P. Holcombe,	"	250.00	
	Francis H. Smith,	"	250.00	
	M. Schele De Vere,	"	250.00	
	James L. Cabell,	"	250.00	
	A. T. Bledsoe,	"	250.00	
	H. Howard,	"	250.00	
	Gessner Harrison,	"	250.00	
	Wm. H. McGuffey,	"	250.00	
1856.				
Jan'y 1,	S. Maupin,	"	250.00	
	John B. Minor,	"	250.00	
	James P. Holcombe,	"	250.00	
	F. H. Smith,	"	250.00	
	M. Schele De Vere,	"	250.00	
	Jas. L. Cabell,	"	250.00	
	A. T. Bledsoe,	"	250.00	
	H. Howard,	"	250.00	
	Gessner Harrison,	"	250.00	
	Wm. H. McGuffey,	"	250.00	
April 1,	S. Maupin,	"	250.00	
	John B. Minor,	"	250.00	
	F. H. Smith,	"	250.00	
	M. Schele De Vere,	"	250.00	
	Jas. L. Cabell,	"	250.00	
	Jas. P. Holcombe,	"	250.00	
	A. T. Bledsoe,	"	250.00	
	H. Howard,	"	250.00	
	Gessner Harrison,	"	250.00	
	Wm. H. McGuffey,	"	250.00	
May 30,	Jas. P. Holcombe, for rent of house, under special order of board of visitors,		300.00	
	Total professors' salaries,			10,300.00

Assistant Instructors.

1855.					
July 2,	To	S. E. W. Becker,	quarter's salary,	175.00	
Oct. 1,		Wm. Dinwiddie,	"	175.00	
2,		S. E. W. Becker,	"	200.00	
		E. B. Smith,	"	175.00	
5,		E. S. Joynes,	"	200.00	
1856.					
Jan'y 1,		E. S. Joynes,	"	200.00	
		S. E. W. Becker,	"	200.00	
		Wm. Dinwiddie,	"	175.00	
		E. B. Smith,	"	175.00	
April 1,		E. S. Joynes,	"	200.00	
		S. E. W. Becker,	"	200.00	
		Wm. Dinwiddie,	"	175.00	
		E. B. Smith,	"	175.00	
June 14,		E. S. Joynes,	"	200.00	
		Total Assistant instructors,			2,625.00

Officers' Salaries.

1855.				
July 2,	To	S. Maupin, chairman,	quarter's salary	125.00
		Robt. R. Prentis, proctor and patron	"	375.00
		E. Rawls, proctor's clerk,	"	125.00
		Wm. Wertenbaker, librarian, &c.	"	125.00
		R. T. W. Duke, sec'y B. of V.	"	50.00
		N. H. Massie, comm'r.	"	50.00
		John Smith, janitor,	"	43.75
13,		Wm. A. Bibb, bursar, coms. on disbts.	"	248.55
1855.				
Oct. 1,	To	Robt. R. Prentis proctor and patron	quarter's salary,	125.00

Officers' Salaries.

1855.				
Oct. 1,	To S. Maupin, chairman,	quarter's salary,	375.00	
	E. Rawls, proctor's clerk,	"	125.00	
	Wm. Wertenbaker, librarian &c.	"	125.00	
	John Smith, janitor,	"	43.75	
	N. H. Massie, comm'r,	"	50.00	
	R. T. W. Duke, sec'y B. of V.	"	50.00	
22,	E. Rawls, one month's salary as clerk,	"	41.66	
1856.				
Jan'y 1,	S. Maupin, chairman,	"	125.00	
	Robt. R. Prentis, proctor and patron	"	375.00	
	S. M. Hart, 2 months' salary as clerk,	"	83.34	
	Wm. Wertenbaker, librarian, &c.	"	125.00	
	John Smith, janitor,	"	43.75	
	R. T. W. Duke, sec'y B. of V.	"	50.00	
	N. H. Massie, comm'r,	"	50.00	
April 1,	S. Maupin, chairman,	"	125.00	
	Robt. R. Prentis, proctor and patron,	"	375.00	
	S. M. Hart, proctor's clerk,	"	125.00	
	Wm. Wertenbaker, librarian &c.	"	125.00	
	R. T. W. Duke, sec'y B. of V.	"	50.00	
	N. H. Massie, comm'r,	"	50.00	
	John Smith, janitor,	"	43.75	
	Total officers' salaries,			3,823.55

—*Public Documents of Virginia*, 1857, Doc. No. 12, pp. 15-17.

11. Amelia M. Murray comments on the University of Virginia, 1855

At the University, however, I was most kindly welcomed by the Professor and Mrs. Minor; he and Professor Maupin showed me the buildings, and an extensive view from the roof of the dome. This educational establishment was founded by Jefferson. It is ruled by nine trustees, who are newly appointed every four years by the incoming President [7] of the United States; and it has this peculiarity— that the governing head of the institution is changed every two years. There is no professor of Natural History in any of its branches, and no teacher of Chemistry, either agricultural or medical; so that one cannot much wonder that ignorance respecting the soils and the mineral riches of this State should be evident, even to an unpractised eye. January 21, 1855.

—Hon. Amelia M. Murray, *Letters From the United States, Cuba and Canada* (New York: G. P. Putnam and Company, 1856), p. 189.

12. A senator in the Legislature of Texas opposes the bill for a university, 1856

Mr. Armstrong moved to amend the Bill by striking out the word "University" wherever it occurred in the Bill and insert "*Common Schools* in the several counties of the State," and said, I have offered the amendment to decide the question whether the masses of the people or a few shall be the recipients of the benefits of our legislation. Common schools are for the people generally. Universities are for those who are most able to pay for their education....

I am no advocate of the University system. My plan is *first* Common Schools then Seminaries of learning in the counties. The Common Schools above all. Universities are the ovens to heat up and hatch all manner of vice, immorality and crime. Where the youth is removed from the presence of their parents and guardians, they run into every excess and come forth steeped in sin and reckless of all

7. Not by the President of the United States but by the Governor of Virginia. The number of Visitors had been increased from eight to nine by legislative act of 1852. These nine were to be appointed by the governor and they themselves elected the Rector from their own number. At the beginning of 1855 "the Rector and Visitors of the University of Virginia" (the legal title of the corporation) consisted of Joseph C. Cabell, Rector; James L. Carr, Sherrard Clemens, William Lucas, Fleming B. Miller, William J. Robertson, Andrew Stevenson, Harrison B. Tomlin, and Henry A. Wise. Later in the year Wise was replaced by M. R. H. Garnett.

consequences. While the youth reared in the country, mingling manual labor with his studies, where their physical and mental faculties are alike strengthened, cultivated and developed. Among the first class there are some exceptions, but among the last class of students, we must look for the heroes and statesmen who shall govern and defend our beloved country. When war is the word, then you see who does the fighting and suffers the fatigues of marching. They come from the masses of the people, and not from the colleges, with few exceptions. In the country schools we find all the virtues which ennoble our race taught and practiced. I do not say that virtue is wanting in Universities, but I speak comparatively. I say let the system of education be like a pyramid beginning at the foundation. General information first among the people. Then our liberties as a free people, are safe; but let the masses be left in ignorance and superstition and the educated few will soon reduce them to the condition of the down-trodden nations of the Old World, who are mere property in the hands of those for whom they toil. . . .

The diffusion of useful knowledge among the people generally should be our first care—discarding all the useless reading of the age. Of what avail is it that the youth can tell you of lost languages or obsolete sciences, or that they should puzzle their brains with the visionary theories of the ancient schoolmen in trying to discover how they could travel from one place to another without passing the intermediate space? Cannot the youth of the country at the school houses travel from his spelling book to the celestial mechanics of La Place? Is it not as fit a place to learn all things for man to know the school houses as the college. I say more so, for there are too many allurements and attractions around the fashionable and crowded universities for the youth to contemplate upon the knotty questions in philosophy and mathematics; not so at the school houses. The abatement of universities will send the teachers to the schools. Schools in every neighborhood will be filled with intelligent teachers and pupils, and the people will have among them all the means of useful information, but the contrary if the sciences are favored at a few places. It is putting it out of the power of the people generally to send off their children to college. They must remain at home to aid their parents to obtain a support, while the sons and daughters of the wealthy, can enjoy the privilege and receive the benefits of the poor man's money in attending these Universities built by the State. Making the poor man contribute to educate the rich man's child while his own children labor. Making the poor man subservient to the rich, a species of legislation at variance with the principles of a democratic government. I do not speak this to draw distinctions, but I must say it is anything but republican and democratic. It is a tendency, a leaning to the remnants of exclusivism, a longing after the principles of centralism. Our government is the people, then let our institutions of learning and all privileges of free government belong to the people, and leave it to the other governments to teach the few to rule the many, the few to enjoy the blood and toil of the many. I say first common schools, afterwards, and when needed, other institutions of learning might be encouraged, but the time has not yet come for the university system to be established by the State. . . .

The Senator from Brazoria argues that erection of universities in our own State will dispense with the necessity of sending our children to the North to be educated, there to receive their impressions of the North injurious to the rights of the South, to be taught principles at variance with the South. I reply, let them have their children educated in the seminaries and schools of our State, established and to be established in our State without aid. Let them erect such institutions in our own State. Those who are able to pay for university education in the North are able to apply the same means in our State. Their State pride will prompt them without legislative incentives and assistance. As to our youth being denied intercourse with the people of the North, I differ with the Senator. It is our duty to mingle with and associate with our fellow-citizens of the North. We are citizens of one Government, one common country. We can best understand our common wants by associating together, and regarding each other as belonging to one great neighborhood. We ought to encourage by every means the most intimate and friendly relations with our brethren of the North. Let us inform the various sections of the Union of our common and separate rights—our common duty, and interest, and mutual dependence on each other, and we will be the better enabled to understand our relative rights and duties. And in no way can our friendly relations with our brethren be better prompted than by a genial intercourse encouraged by every possible means. Let us not denounce in general terms the whole North, for it is to the conservative power of the national democratic party of the North that we look for the protection of Southern rights and the maintenance of the guarantees of the constitution. We look to that party for our rights, yet we condemn and denounce the whole North. We teach doctrines of non-intercourse with the North. We would discourage all friendly connections and intercourse with the North. Yet we turn to the democratic party in all times of trouble. If we by our acts alienate the feelings of the people of the North, we may expect nothing from them and then will follow in haste the dissolution of the Union with all its disastrous consequences.—H. Y. Benedict, *A Source Book of the University of Texas*, pp. 58-61. Governor Pease in his message to the legislature November 6, 1855, urged the establishment of a university in that state and a bill was introduced in the Senate to create a fund for the purpose. Sharp debate in both the House and the Senate began and continued during that session and the next, with the struggle ending in 1858 when a bill for a University was approved. Some people urged two universities, one in the eastern and one in the western part of the State; some urged only one; and there were those who were opposed to any.

13. The trustees of the University of Mississippi make stirring appeal for its adequate support, 1856

To the Honorable, the Senate and House of Representatives of the State of Mississippi:

The undersigned, the Trustees of the University of Miss. beg leave respectfully to present, that the University has now been in actual operation for a period of more than seven years, and that its success, up to the present time, has been satisfactory beyond the anticipations of its most sanguine friends. That its present condition, in all those particulars in which the prosperity of such an institution is within the control of those, who conduct or superintend its operations, is sound and flourishing, and furnishes equal cause of gratulation, whether we regard the solid benefits which it is immediately dispensing to the people of the State, or the flattering promise which it holds out of growing usefulness in the future. And that abundant evidence of the truth of these statements may be found, by bringing the present condition of the University, and its past brief history, to the test of any criterion by which such questions may be properly decided.

The direct evidence, most palpable to the world, of the value of any institution for the education of youth, is that which is furnished by attainments of the pupils whom it trains. Judged by this test, the University of Mississippi may safely challenge comparison with the colleges and universities longest established and of the highest reputation in the United States. Large, intelligent and annually increasing audiences have thronged the halls of the University every year, on each of its public anniversaries; and the testimony which has been borne by those best qualified to judge of such exercises, to the character of the performances of the graduates on these occasions, has been that it has exhibited an ability as decided as it was unexpected. Persons who have enjoyed abundant opportunities to compare the displays of knowledge and the evidences of intellectual discipline manifested by the youth educated in our University, with those which are presented on similar occasions, in the older colleges of the Atlantic States, have pronounced them in no respect inferior to the best which they have elsewhere witnessed.

If the standing of the University is to be judged by that of its officers of instruction, the undersigned are disposed to claim that the decision must be equally in its favor. It has been their aim, kept constantly in view by them as Trustees, to secure men to fill the chairs of the several professorships, who should combine distinguished ability and large acquirements with those qualities of disposition and temper, which are not less essential to render them successful as governors of youth, and the consequence has been, that they believe they have now a Faculty, which will compare advantageously with any in the South, as for the same numbers, with any in the Union.

If attention be given to the history of the University in regard to internal tranquillity, good order, and attention to duty on the part of the under-graduates the result cannot but be equally gratifying to every friend of education in Mississippi. It is believed that, in no similar institution in the United States has there been more uniformly prevalent spirit of subordination, or a more willing submission to necessary rules of discipline, than in this.

The undersigned would further represent, that, as a natural consequence of the facts, which have just been enumerated, the public confidence in the University as a school of thorough education and as a well ordered community, has been steadily growing, from the beginning up to the present time; and that this confirmed and augmented confidence is made manifest by an increase in the number of students so uniform and steady, as to prove that it is owing to no accidental or transient cause, while it has been, at the same time, so rapid as to have already outrun the means of the undersigned to provide for the comfortable accommodation of the entire body. The catalogue of the present year, will probably show an increase of twenty or twenty five per cent, upon the total of the last, and when it is considered that the reputation of the University is beginning to draw students from the states of our borders, which are at present unprovided with colleges equally well grounded in the popular favor, it is impossible to doubt that something like the present rate of increase will be maintained for many years to come.

While such are the indications of the growing popularity and usefulness of the University, the undersigned are compelled further to represent, that in many respects the institution is deficient in matters indispensable to its complete efficiency as a school of letters and science, and that the resources of the undersigned are inadequate to the supply of these deficiencies. The number of officers of instruction is entirely insufficient to insure to each student the amount of personal attention which is desirable that he should receive, and this evil is necessarily felt more and more seriously as the numbers swell. Not a single department of science is provided with suitable illustrative apparatus; the library is but the beginning of a collection of books, and offers no aid at all for the prosecution of such researches in the different branches of knowledge as are necessary to perfect the instructors themselves, to promote their usefulness to the University, and to enable them to connect their names honorably with the intellectual history of the age, cabinets of natural history in every branch are yet to be wholly created, lecture rooms offering suitable facilities for the experimental illustration of several branches of physical science are to be provided and arranged at considerable expense, and besides all this, the erection of additional buildings for the accommodation of the increasing number of students is imperatively demanded, and must be commenced at once, if we would not be compelled to submit to the mortifying necessity of daily turning applicants for admission away from our doors.

It may not be thought improper for the undersigned in thus briefly setting forth the embarrassments of the University, to observe that had not the University Fund, during the period which intervened between the commencement of its accumulation and the organization of the present Board of Trustees, suffered enormous and lamentable losses, it would have been abundantly adequate, today not merely to supply in a creditable manner the deficiencies just enumerated, but so completely and thoroughly to supply them in all their details, as to place the University of Mississippi in these respects, in the very front rank of American colleges—perhaps in advance of every other.

The undersigned cannot regard without the deepest pain the undeniable fact, that the entire amount of this fund, at present including that part of it, which being invested in buildings for purposes of revenue, does not exceed, if even equals, one fourth part of what, but for the unfortunate losses just alluded to, it would have been. The fact that these losses to the fund befell it while it was directly held in trust by the legislature, for the purposes to which its remains have been since applied, appears to the undersigned to constitute a fair ground of appeal to the justice of your honorable body in praying for relief from the embarrassments under which the University at present labors.

The wants of the University in regard to scientific apparatus are so great, as to reduce it in this respect, at present, far below respectability, and seriously to hazard, unless they are promptly supplied, the permanence of that unexampled prosperity which it has thus far enjoyed. In the state of development to which, in our day, the physical sciences have attained, it is absolutely impossible to illustrate their principles with clearness, or to make intelligible the methods by which their countless astonishing truths have been brought to light, without so large a variety of instruments and special contrivances as to impose upon every institution for higher education a heavy outlay. In some branches of science, necessary instruments are nearly every one of them costly, and in others, where there are separately less expensive, they are exceedingly numerous. The University of the neighboring State of Alabama has expended for instance, about ten thousand dollars in the single department of Astronomy. Harvard University, a few years since, paid twenty thousand dollars for a single instrument, the great refracting Telescope, which has already become so famous. There are many colleges in the country which, in nearly every one of the several departments of Optics, Acoustics, Electricity, Magnetism, Pneumatics, Hydrostatics and Chemistry have expended more money than the University has yet been able to appropriate to all of them together. The undersigned have endeavored to the extent of their means, to supply the deficiencies which seemed most urgently to demand their attention, but burthened, as they have been, by the necessity of building— a necessity now forced upon them anew by the very prosperity of the University itself—and trammeled in their action by the entire inadequacy of their resources to meet the necessities of the case, they have been able, as yet, to make but little progress. In fact, they have no prospect of being able, unassisted, to put the University upon a creditable footing in these respects for many years.

What has been said of apparatus is more or less applicable also to a library. The importance of an extensive library to an institution of learning is by many imperfectly understood. Nothing is more true than that to be a successful teacher, even of the elements of knowledge, a man must himself know much besides those elements.

And the light, which any instructor will be capable of shedding around the simplest facts, will be greater just in proportion as he himself approaches the mastery of the entire subject to which those facts belong.

Every teacher, therefore, who is fit for his position, and who does his duty, will be himself a learner as long as he lives. And it is the truest policy of the supervisory government of any college to spread before the officers of instruction the largest field in letters and science, which their means allow. It is much more in reference to college Faculties than to college students that comprehensive Libraries are desirable. The mental expansion of the student advances through the training which the course of study furnishes, and which is sufficient for the most part to occupy him. But the officer, without unrestrained access to books, is in danger of intellectual stagnation.

Upon this topic it may be further observed, that our colleges and universities are the sources to which people look for authoritative opinions in all those abstruser matters with which the mass of men are unfamiliar. That they may possess the means of pronouncing such opinions, and thus answer the expectations formed of them, it is absolutely indispensable that they should have the command of those records of the world's progress in knowledge, which are to be found in books, so that, whatever question may be presented for solution, they may be able to produce every thing valuable, which has ever been put forth relating to the subject.

The possession of well selected and extensive libraries thus give dignity and character to a seminary of learning which cannot be secured without it, and these advantages, which are certainly desirable for every institution for higher education, are eminently so for one which is understood to represent the learning of a State. Again it is undoubtedly true, that the reputation of colleges is to a great extent dependent upon the personal reputation for talents and learning of the professors who conduct them. So strikingly is this the case, that a single man has often been known to build up an institution of learning all together; and the loss of a single man has no less frequently pulled such an institution down. Now most certainly no man can acquire a high reputation as a man of science or letters without the opportunity to consult what has been already published in his chosen department. Hence a college without a copious library can rarely count on the great advantage of embracing in its faculty a man, whose name is familiar to the learned world. But libraries again are costly, and of the making of many books there is no end. The University of Mississippi, if left to be entirely dependent on its annual income, will long be lamentably deficient in this most important particular.

Upon these circumstances, the undersigned after mature deliberation, have felt it to be their duty to make an appeal at once to the justice and to the liberality of the Legislature of the State, in behalf of the University. It is undoubtedly among the highest duties of a government to provide for the education of the people. And where political institutions, like ours, are founded on the principles of liberty, this duty becomes identified with the truest interest of the commonwealth. To every thoughtful man, therefore, upon whom, to any extent rests the responsibility of directing the legislation of a State, the question in what manner it may present itself and may be practicable most effectually to diffuse intelligence among the masses of the people, and to secure the systematic and thorough training of all in the elements of knowledge, must present itself as one of the most important that can occupy his attention. The prominent place which the subject of elementary education is usually found to hold in the Legislation of every enlightened people, need not therefore be a matter of surprise. But no truth can be more undeniably certain, than this, that where institutions for higher learning do not exist, or existing, do not flourish, an efficient system of popular education cannot reasonably be looked for, or if looked for will very surely not be found. In proof of this position it would be quite a sufficient argument to appeal to history. If we search the world over, not a single spot can be found, where elementary education has ever become general among any people, not without having been preceded, and in fact, introduced by that higher education, which in the nature of things, cannot be entirely general.

So constant has been this succession of events, everywhere, and ever since a record of human affairs began to be preserved for the benefit of posterity, that it may be securely regarded as partaking of the character of a law, so that we are justified in predicting of any people, whatever be their social or political condition, that they never can be generally well informed, or enjoy the benefits of a thorough system of popular education, so long as their colleges and universities are in a languid and unprosperous condition.

If a reason be sought for a truth so abundantly confirmed by the past experience of mankind, we need not go far to find it. There can never arise a popular sense of a want, without a just conception or understanding of the nature of the thing presumed to be wanting, nor can there be a popular demand for any thing, however desirable, without a popular sense of its value or necessity.

The ignorant, so long as they are conversant with the ignorant only, can form no idea whatever, of the advantages, which knowledge bestows. It is only when they come into contact with the better informed, that they begin to perceive their inferiority. Hence it is that no savage races have ever exhibited any tendency to spontaneous civilization; hence no merely civilized people has ever become enlightened in consequence of a general simultaneous movement of the masses. The progress of intellectual, like that of physical light, has been always from certain definite centres, outward. These centres, in the earliest times, were formed in the schools of philosophers, and in the later, they have been the universities, which have trained up the men, by whom the policy of nations has been shaped no less in regard to education, than to civil, political and military affairs. Look where you will, we shall find the apostles of popular education to have been men prepared for their work in the schools of higher learning. It would probably be impossible to point out a single eminent exception. What can be more evident, than that, in so far as the labors of such men have resulted in the creation of admirable systems of popular education, those systems and that education have been the legitimate offspring of the universities from which their authors sprung.

But not only is it true that the schools of higher learning produce naturally the systems of elementary education, by producing the men, who devise them, and awakening in such men the zeal in their support, without which they would be devised in vain, but it is further true that the same higher schools are necessary to produce the teachers by whom the lower are to be conducted. It would be in vain that the wisest scheme of popular education ever conceived should be by law established, if its operations were, of necessity, to be entrusted to incompetent hands. Where there are no schools of higher learning, there will be few competent instructors in those of lower grade. And though it is not to be expected that all, nor perhaps even many of the teachers of the most elementary schools will ever or anywhere be graduates of universities, yet the influence of the university is hardly less felt in their training, than if they were so: for, while the primary schools take their character from the secondary, the secondary are almost invariably in the hands of the university graduates.

The whole southwest is at this moment deficient in any thing like a digested system of primary education. It has become customary to offer various apologies for this defect; and it cannot be denied that the sparseness of our population presents a difficulty in the way of such a system, which is not equally felt in States less exclusively devoted to a peculiar agriculture. But the capital difficulty after all at present, is the want of a sufficient number of permanent and thorough schools of secondary education in our towns and villages, to furnish an adequate supply of competent teachers for the open country.

Were public provisions to be made to day for the payment of teachers in every inhabited township in the State, were schoolhouses to be erected, and the regular attendance of the children to be secured, it is seriously to be doubted, whether the practical results attained would be immediately encouraging, and this simply because, unquestionably, the quality of the instruction given would be, in many cases, exceedingly inferior. There is but one way effectually, to remove this difficulty. It is so to cherish the University, that it may become a grand agency by which to elevate the grade of all the secondary schools, and thus, through them to insure competent teachers of the primary.

In evidence that these remarks are not entirely hypothetical the undersigned would refer to the experience of the neighboring State of Alabama. It is now ten or twelve years since earnest efforts were made by the Legislature of that State, to systematize the common schools of the state, and improve their efficiency. For this purpose, special appropriations were made, for two or three years, to the amount of two hundred thousand dollars per annum, and in aid of the revenue derived from the common school fund (of which the principal exceeded a million and a half of dollars) yet so little satisfactory was the result obtained that the effort was at length abandoned.

During the years which have elapsed since this abortive attempt, many of the alumni of the University of Alabama have devoted themselves to the business of teaching in the principal towns of the States, thus materially elevating the standard of secondary education and others have become not uninfluential actors in public life. One of the latter class, at the last biennial meeting of the Legislature, was the author, and others were the supporters and advocates of a bill to establish a uniform and organized system of public schools throughout the State, under the direction of a single superintendent; and this bill having become a law, is now in operation, with results already salutary, and with a promise of increasing usefulness in the future. The two-fold influence of the University upon popular education is here happily illustrated, first: in the preparation of the way for the introduction of a successful system; and secondly, in the raising up of men capable of planning, expounding and vindicating such a system and of finally securing its adoption. If to these considerations it should be thought necessary to add others in support of the policy of fostering by liberal measures, the University of the State of Mississippi they may be found in the example of other States to which our own is accustomed to look with deference, and from which many of our own citizens are sprung. The University of Virginia, now holding rank, in point of numbers, with the very first upon the American continent, was for many years a very feeble institution, yet, during all the period of its weakness, as well as now in the day of its strength, it received, as it continues to receive, fifteen thousand dollars per annum from the treasury of the State, and Virginians, who look with pride upon what their University, thus wisely cherished by the public munificence has become, esteem the price, they have paid for it, well bestowed. The college of South Carolina is well known likewise to be sustained entirely by the State. The annual appropriations for its support are made with the same regularity and in the same form as those for the payments of the salaries of the public officers. There was never but a single moment, in which the Legislature of that State manifested the slightest hesitation in regard to these appropriations, and in that moment, stood forth George McDuffie, himself a graduate of the college, and then in the opening of a career which became subsequently so splendid, to speak in triumphant defence and enthusiastic eulogy of the institution, to which he owed his own intellectual training. His efforts on that occasion is made memorable by the remark of Judge Huger, uttered as he took his seat, "If the College of South Carolina had done nothing but to produce the author of that speech, she would have well repaid the State for all she ever received from it." The policy which is a wise and sound one in Virginia and South Carolina cannot be unwise or unsound in Mississippi, and if those States have been compensated, as undoubtedly they have been a thousandfold, for all that they have bestowed upon their institutions of learning, how is it possible to doubt that here too, a policy which, at first view, may appear to be only and purely liberal and generous, may in literal fact be the very policy which the most severely calculating self-interest would dictate.

But, further, the undersigned cannot wholly neglect to present a consideration which directly addresses the pride of every Mississippian, it is that the name and credit of the State are inseparably identified with those of the University. Whenever the name of any State institution is pronounced, it is impossible, not to compare it with those of other States, and had we no higher motive for desiring to see our University provided with all the appliances of a school of letters and science of the highest grade, we might find one in the consideration, that we can in no other manner avoid the stamp of an inferiority, which is by so much the more discreditable to us, as it is not the necessity of our poverty, but the evidence of our insensibility to that which constitutes a people's truest greatness. It is a fact that the unprovided condition of the University of Mississippi, in regard to scientific apparatus in every department, to library, collections of minerals and fossils, museums of natural history, and every thing else which is auxiliary to the business of instruction, is such as to reduce it to a position absolutely mean, by the side of the universities of Alabama, North and South Carolina and Virginia. The undersigned have actually had the mortification, in a recent instance of losing the services of a professor elect, distinguished for high reputation and eminent abilities, even after he had taken the trouble to visit the University from a distance of fifteen hundred miles, and that simply, because the inadequacy of the illustrative apparatus in his department was such as to convince him (to use his own words) that he could neither satisfy himself, nor give satisfaction to others. Certainly no true Mississippian can be content, that an institution of learning recognized by law as the State University, and therefore as the representative of the State in the highest department of education, should continue to be so miserably provided in all those particulars on which its respectability depends, that he dare not compare it with any other of its class in the country.—Florence E. Campbell (Comp.), Journal of the Minutes of the Board of Trustees of the University of Mississippi, 1845-1860 (Master's Thesis, University of Mississippi, 1939) pp. 259-75. The date of the memorial is January 21, 1856.

14. The University of North Carolina is highly praised, 1856

The University of North Carolina was never so flourishing as at present. There are between four and five hundred students and the cry is "still they come." The Faculty will compare with the ablest in the Union.

We recently spent a few days in Chapel Hill, one of the prettiest places in the State, and during our short sojourn there we had the good fortune to form the acquaintance of a number of students. We must say that we have never met up with a more orderly, well-behaved and polite set of youths. The idea entertained abroad that the students at this college are "worse" than those at other colleges is an erroneous idea. The boys at Chapel Hill are not half so "bad" as people at a distance think—and we regard the College as ranking with the best in the Union.—*The Greensborough Patriot*, August 20, 1856.

15. Classification of students in the University of Virginia by subjects studied, 1857

Schools	Students in attendance
Latin,	249
Greek,	168
Modern Languages,	241
Mathematics,	251
Natural Philosophy,	172
Chemistry,	248
Medecine,	109
Comparative Anatomy, Physiology and Surgery,	119
Anatomy,	113
Moral Philosophy,	200
Law.	113

—*Public Documents of Virginia*, 1857, Doc. No. 12, p. 118.

16. Residence of students in the University of Virginia, 1857

STATES &c.	Number
Virginia,	333
Alabama,	51
South Carolina,	50
Louisiana,	44
Mississippi,	41
Georgia,	40
Kentucky,	14
Maryland,	11
North Carolina,	11
Tennessee,	10
District of Columbia,	9
Missouri,	8
Florida,	8
Texas,	7
California,	3
Delaware,	1
Pennsylvania,	1
New York,	1
Arkansas,	1
Ohio,	1
Total,	645

–*Ibid.*, p. 118.

17. A member of the House opposes a university for Texas, 1857

I repeat, Sir, that it is undemocratic to educate the few at the expense of the many. I repeat, Sir, that the money of the people should not be so appropriated that all cannot be benefited. And, Sir, I regard the declaration of the gentleman from Smith, that "if either the high schools and colleges, or the common schools had to be given up, he would freely wipe the common schools out of existence," as monstrous.

It is true I have no sympathy with such Democracy.

THE COMMON SCHOOLS ARE THE PEOPLE'S COLLEGES. And, Sir, my Democracy whether palpable or not, would favor the entire appropriation of the fund contemplated for the

University, to the common schools of the State. I advocate the greatest good to the greatest number—the appropriation of money directly to the education of the children of the people, instead of expending hundreds of thousands of dollars in the erection of costly and magnificent buildings alone—"Temples of Futurity," the gentleman from Smith calls them—"Temples of Futurity," indeed; that in the far distant future, could we but lift the veil, we may see the children of my constituents represented by other gentlemen upon this floor—the children of the poor people of the State of Texas—gathering around the massive structure, and upon their bended knees, looking up in wonder, amazement and astonishment at the fluted columns and "lofty domes and towering spires" of the proud "temple of futurity," erected in fatuity by the Legislature of the State, out of the money and the substance of the whole people, for the benefit of the few rich and well-born!

The wildest views seem to prevail in the minds of some of the honorable gentlemen as to what should be the course of study in this great university. It has even been proposed, that in addition to the usual branches taught in our literary institutions, there should be provision made for magnificent Law, Medical and other departments! To such propositions I dissent, *in toto*. Let those who may wish to receive what is called the genteel polish of a "finished professional education," not call upon the people in the humble walks of life, upon whom they may in future show their professional skill, in fleecing or physicing, to pay for educating them. Let us have no Doctors or Lawyers manufactured by a State institution; and I say it with all becoming respect to gentlemen of the learned professions, God knows we have enough of them in the country, with a rising prospect of "more of the same sort!" Were it proposed to establish an Agricultural Bureau, a measure which my friend from Galveston (Mr. Brown) has much at heart, it would not be so much out of place, inasmuch as whatever tends to promote the success of those engaged in the culture of the soil adds to the general prosperity of the State. But there is no such thing thought of by those having the management of this great University; it is to benefit those who *eat bread, and not those who make it. . . .*

How many of this 87,000 of the common school children of the State would be benefited by the establishment of this great University?

By this time next year, there will be 100,000 children attending the common schools—and as each year passes by, there will be more and more—the increase never stops. And it so happens, in the wise providence of God, to whom he grants not riches he grants children in abundance—and for the education of the hundreds of thousands of poor children of our rapidly increasing State, I plead now to you, and before long they will themselves demand their rights. This grand University will confer benefits upon the children of the rich—upon the few only.

I am no enemy to education, collegiate, literary or classical; on the contrary, I am glad to see the young striving to obtain it. But, Sir, the common school system, perfected as it might, and will be in time, will give proper direction to the minds of the rising people of our great and growing State, many of whom will afterwards avail themselves of opportunities offered by Schools of higher order and colleges in their midst. We have already colleges and institutions of learning of a high grade incorporated in the State, and to all such I would be willing to offer encouragement. Willingly would I aid the establishing and endowing of colleges in various parts of the country. And, Sir, by this means we would be placing a liberal education more nearly within the reach of all the children of the State.

Much has been said, during this extended discussion, about the location of the University—whether it should be East or West, at Austin or elsewhere. By the plan I suggest, the "bone of contention" would be removed. The people would foster, and encourage, and patronize their own home institutions. Those who desire to avail themselves of a college course, would find it to their interest to attend the institutions in their own neighborhood, and this they could do without being compelled to expend all their substance and much of their time in traveling hundreds of miles to a State University, which, to locate it where you will, in a State seven times the size of the largest in the Union, would give them generally a distance equivalent to journeying across Louisiana, Mississippi and Alabama! In point of fact, locate it as you will, the expense of going to, and of remaining during sessions, would place it out of the power of the generality of the people of the State to attend it, and, for one, I am not disposed to appropriate such a vast sum for the benefit of the sons of the wealthy cotton and sugar planters, and where the boys of the humble stock-raiser, the small farmer, and the man of moderate means, could not be benefited at all.

No, Sir, I have already said more upon this subject than I had designed doing, as I simply intended submitting a few remarks upon the propriety of postponing the consideration to a future day; but having, by frequent interruptions, been thrown off my guard, and led to remarks I would not otherwise have submitted at this late period, and after such prolonged debate, I will briefly direct the attention of gentlemen to another point, and one not hitherto alluded to in the discussion, and that is, Mr. Speaker, that exclusive State Universities, in this country, have not been able to compete with, or in other words, been as productive of good results, as colleges established and sustained by individual effort, by private association, or denominational or sectarian enterprise. Gentlemen favoring the project, during their remarks, have pointed, with peculiar pride and exultations, to the University of Virginia, as the model institution, and one of the great literary institutions of the day, which should serve as a pattern for our imitation. This, it is claimed, should be in several respects the pattern one; especially has it been mentioned as the object to be established free of all sectarian influence. To this, it may be, and has, on the other hand been replied, that even this institution in its day, failed to meet the expectation of its great founder, Mr. Jefferson. Was it not, let me ask, in part, the design to exclude from its professorships all ministers of the gospel! And is it not the fact, that they have been compelled to abandon this, the favorite measure of many of the advocates of this plan? In the various chairs will be found Rev. Wm. McGuffey, of the Old School Presbyterian faith, and Rev. Albert Bledsoe, of the Episcopal Church, and others!

They forget to tell us, too, how small has been the number of F.F.V's in attendance! And they also seem unmindful of the fact that the sons of the "Old Dominion" have, from time immemorial, been receiving instruction from the time-honored institutions of William and Mary, Hampden and Sidney, Washington College at Lexington, and more recently from Randolph Macon, Pomroy and Henry, and their younger sister of Bethany. And these various colleges, founded and fostered by pious and good men, have contributed more to the diffusion of knowledge than the peculiar favorite at Charlottesville. They seem entirely unmindful of the fact that the first and foremost institutions of America are the result of private associate enterprise, and of sectarian effort. Let me point you to Bowdoin and Waterville colleges, Maine; Brown University, Rhode Island; Yale and Trinity, Connecticut; Harvard and Williams, Massachusetts; Middlebury, Vermont; Princeton and Burlington, New Jersey; Pennsylvania, with her Washington, Jefferson, Alleghany and Dickinson *et als.;* New York, with her Hamilton, Geneva, Union, Columbia, and others; Ohio, with her Kenyon, Miami, Hudson, Wesleyan, *et als.;* Kentucky, with her colleges at Danville, Bardstown, etc.—and so I might proceed enumerating the various colleges and universities of like character in the land, which have been founded as aforesaid, and challenge the scrutiny and investigation of the honorable gentlemen advocating this proposition for one grand State University, to show me, in all the States which I have enumerated—in fact in any and all of the States in the Union, where like efforts have been made, the instances where the special pet, favorite and bantling of the State, with all its superior advantages, has turned out better scholars, or more of them, to reflect credit on their *alma mater*, and the State at large.

I hold it to be an utter impossibility to legislate great learning and abilities into heads to which God Almighty hath given little or no brains. Men make themselves, to a considerable extent, and those of the children of our State who, by dint of a common school education, and attrition with their fellow scholars, acquire the elementary branches, will soon surpass the more favored, by means of higher schools and colleges already in existence in the State. Our statute books are full of acts incorporating institutions of learning in various parts of the State, and many of these the result of private enterprise and munificence, have acquired, at this early day in the State's history, an exalted position. Will the State now adopt a course of policy to break down or maim and cripple these institutions? It will either practically do this, or it will manufacture, at great expense, a great humbug! If the State University should be established, with an appropriation of one hundred leagues of land and four hundred thousand dollars, it must so completely over-tower all other institutions as measurably to withdraw public patronage from them, or it must be inferior to them, and fail of having that full attendance of pupils, which will cause it to be regarded as a complete failure.

Which course shall be pursued by you, gentlemen, that of fostering and encouraging those institutions which we already have, and inducing the organization of others in different parts of our great State, to meet the necessities of the people as they may manifest themselves, or that of concentrating, consolidating, appropriating, a vast amount of the money of the people to benefit a select few only?

Allusions have been made by several of the gentlemen who have preceded me, to the gray-haired and venerable President of Austin College, who is now here, soliciting at our hands aid for an institution already located and at work disseminating sound learning in the country. Shall his petition be heeded, or will we turn a deaf ear to the respectful request therefor. We have already in our State, in my humble opinion, the germs that may produce fruit glorious to look upon, if blessed with *seasonable* relief. Surely those who laud so highly the brave and magnanimous deeds of the pioneers of Texas civilization and liberty, will not be unmindful of the exalted service of Stephen F. Austin, the founder of the infant colony, the father of its distinctive political existence! To all who thirst and long for an opportunity to show their high regard for literary institutions, I commend Austin College, at Huntsville, and also can point to many other worthy objects in successful operation, such as Baylor University, at Independence; Tyler University, in Smith county; Forshey's Monumental Institute, at Rutersville; Marshall University; Aranama College, I believe the Institution in the district in the far South West, represented here by one of the brave survivors of Fannin's Massacre, Dr. Bernard, of Goliad; Bastrop College; Mackenzie Institute, and others of like character, called into being by citizens of the State impelled by a laudable desire for the increase of knowledge and the dissemination of literature, religion and sound morality throughout the land.

Believing that upon the education of the people will depend the perpetuity of our government, and looking entirely to the general diffusion of knowledge for the permanency and prosperity of our Institutions, I will be found ever ready to aid in such legislation as will serve to promote this; and whatever will elevate the standard of common school education or promote the success of colleges and academies already, or that may be hereafter incorporated, in my humble opinion, should receive encouragement at our hands.

Having trespassed upon the patience of the members far beyond my expectation upon taking the floor, I can but hope that the motion to postpone may prevail, and that upon further discussion of this very important subject, we may be enabled to adopt that course of policy which will redound the most to the credit of the State and the benefit of the people.—Benedict, *op. cit.*, 105-10.

18. EXTRACTS FROM LETTERS OF CHARLES WOODWARD HUTSON OF THE CLASS OF 1860, SOUTH CAROLINA COLLEGE, 1857, 1860

2d Feb. 1857
Columbia, So. Ca.

Dear E———

Saturday night I joined the Euphradian Society, and W——M—— the Clariosophic. The subject on debate in our society was one very interesting to me, and as I had something to say on it, I rose to say it; but words were wanting and I hesitated and stammered dreadfully at first, but got through at last. I will not soon again venture extempore speaking.

LeConte called me up for the second time this morning, and McCay just now (midday). I have only been called up to recite three times since I have been here.

Friday night we had a beautiful sight—a blackride in the Campus. There were four or five riders half masked with their faces blacked, dressed in red flannel coats, with flaming torches of camphene in their hands. It was a splendid sight to see them galloping up and down the Campus, waving their flambeaux; and the students, who had crowded out, yelling at the top of their lungs. One of them rode to McCay's house and shook his torch at it. This morning some four or five were called up before the faculty to answer as to the part they took in the blackride, and the serenade (tin pan) of the night before. It is reported that they confessed to the serenade, but refused to answer as to the blackride.

This morning we had a college meeting to appoint a committee to attend the remains of the Hon. Preston S. Brooks home.

Another meeting was called just at second recitation time to determine to support the men, if suspended, or to refuse to answer if the whole College was called up, I don't know for which purpose; but for either one or both. As the object of the meeting was illegal, as well the meeting itself without the authority of the President, I refused to attend, and with my monitor and a few others of the class went to recitation, where McCay wool'd us considerably, as the meeting in the morning had prevented our studying much. A paper was brought around to be signed after the College meeting, being of a rebellious purport. T———, M——— and I refused to sign any paper whatever. The College is now in a pretty fix. If the President does his duty now, there *may* be a rebellion; if he does not, there will certainly be one before long. I am perfectly disgusted at the rowdyism of the few being so permitted and shielded by the many. I have heard a great many express their regret at the present state of things, which they say is worse than it ever was before–say they know how much it tends to break down the College, and yet they yield to custom, attend the College meeting, and then come away when it is half over in disgust. I have seen ten or twelve do this. But enough of these disorders; their issue must come soon.

10th Feb. 1857.
So. Carolina College.

My Dear Mother:

...We had a College Meeting this evening to send a Committee to the President to ask leave, I believe, for the College to attend in procession the remains of Brooks, which will come through Columbia tomorrow. That's the latest news. The Campus is exceedingly quiet now. Nothing happens of any kind. Last night someone lectured up town and the students *of course* got the morning professors to lecture instead of calling up any one at recitation. The supposition was, that we would go to hear the lecture, and have no time to study at night. Do not think this is so schoolboy a love for holiday, as it seems; for the hard students are very glad to get it, so as to have spare time to study for some other recitation.

Wednesday Night. Had another College Meeting this evening, I hardly know what for–some Committee concern about Brooks. We are to accompany his body in procession tomorrow from the depot.

I am very busy now, was wool'd this morning by Barnwell and mean to study to make up. And that wasn't the worst of it, for he called me immediately after recitation to ask me about my composition on "Lyric Poetry," to which he paid a very equivocal compliment. He told me that he wished to find out how original it was, so as to know how to mark me, as he said, "it showed an older hand, and more information, than he thought consistent with my years" (perhaps he means recitations). I did not satisfy him, for I hardly know what true originality is. We walked together from the recitation room to Chapel to Evening prayers, and on the way he asked whose son I was, and when I told him remarked that we were related, to which I assented, and there we stopped. I don't like his suspecting me of copying, for a suspicion it is clearly.

17th Feb. 1857

My Dear Father:

I received your letter of yesterday at about twelve o'clock today. I wish the mails from Pocotaligo came so quickly. I am glad to hear you were well enough to attend Court, as you wished.

I have not acted in the recent difficulties in the College, as rightly, as you supposed; for on the night of the Blackride I could not resist the temptation of going out into the Campus and whooping with the rest. I knew at the time that it was wrong, but could not, or rather did not control myself.

I do not find the studies at all difficult, although to make a good recitation requires rather more study, than I have been doing of late. I am getting gradually to study a little harder than at first. Everything here seems to teach extemporizing, except the Classics. In the Society it is something of an evil, for there seems to be rather more extempore speaking, than preparation of any kind. Personalities and rhetoric occupy a much higher place than sound reasoning. However I am much pleased with it, although I did not expect so much of this sort of thing.

The new professors seem to be quite the favourites here. Barnwell "wools" terribly, but he is making his mark. A lecture which he delivered to the Seniors or Juniors on Chivalry I heard described by some of them as a splendid thing, every point being exquisitely analyzed. They seem to be very much pleased with him. Everyone says that the Faculty, with only one or two exceptions, is a very able one. If the President were only less timid, all would be right. Since those four men were suspended, everything has been very quiet—a little yelling in the Campus and a little firing off of crackers, but that is all. For instance a tremendous volley of crackers carried us to the windows just now, but all is still and quiet now. . . .

Pelham, who goes the rounds of our Tenement, has just called me to see whether we were in, for the first time, since I have been here. This was in consequence of the crackers just fired off.

21st Feb. 1857.
So. Carolina College.

My Dear Mother:

Attended last night a supper given by Doby, a Classmate, and enjoyed myself tolerably. 'Twas an awfully rowdy concern though, and showed most sensibly the want of female society. We did not stay very long however, but slipped off at about eleven to our rooms, and to bed.

The President told us this morning, that as tomorrow is the 22nd, and 'tis customary to celebrate the day after, when it falls on Sunday, the College exercises would be suspended 'till Tuesday morning. So, as Pelham is still absent, and we therefore had no recitation this morning, the Fresh Class has rest today, tomorrow and the day after.

May 2d, 1857
So. Ca. College.

Dear Father:

Received today your 1st, 2d, 3d person letter, and took five minutes to make it out. About my not writing, the fault must lie in the mails, for it seems to me I have written pretty often. As for study, I can study as hard as any one else on an emergency; but it is an extensive bore to be obliged to study steadily, and on an uncertainty too, whether one will be called up or no. I will be almost satisfied, if I come off no worse this term than last. . . .

On Sunday we read the Bible, sit down listlessly or talk idly, besides going to church twice in the day; but we do nothing very wrong, and don't even study, as is the fashion here.

I suppose Charley has told you of all the fusses and confusions we have had here of late. One of these is over, but quieted in no very proper manner. Three men of the Junior Class were suspended; the Juniors threatened to leave, and the Faculty were weak enough to take them back, and revoke their sentence.

The other day, too, the President tried to break through the established custom of letting us off from morning recitation, when a professor spoke the night before, and this without officially informing us of his intention to do so. The consequence was that very few went to recitation the next morning. This may cause some trouble yet. The fact is, the Faculty seem to leap hastily into difficulties without having the slightest idea of the consequences, and are exceedingly irresolute, when those consequences are too big for them.

Both Charley and I have been a little sickish at different times this week with bad colds and as a consequence general bad feelings all over. The weather is very disagreeably half and half at present.

We are to have an abundance of speechification at May Celebration next week, and so will have something to talk about together with the May parties that are to come off soon.

12th May, 1857.
So. Carolina College.

Dear Mother,

...Barnwell stayed here until very late last night talking over all the College matters. He seems to be disgusted with the dollars and cents system, which old Mc [8] has introduced here. He said, he thought we were perfectly right in not going to recitation the other morning, when Reynolds lectured the night before, and based his opinion on the very ground on which I refused to go, namely, that it was not officially announced to us that we would have recitation, when the custom has lately been to the contrary. So, you see, when I rebel, 'tis with some right on my side, as far as professional judgment can make a thing right. The truth is, old Mc is the moving cause of whatever happens wrong in the College. The gas fixtures have been determined on, and we will soon give up our Burning Fluid lamps. The same fuss will be made about the gas charges, as about the wood, speaking, as Barnwell says, "a dollars-and-cents" spirit among the students, to which he is very much opposed.

Wednesday. Have just received your letter. Last night we went up to the Congaree House and serenaded Keitt, who gave us a very fine speech not in the least political, but relating almost entirely to the College, and full of rich classical allusions. I'm inclined to think 'twas not entirely extemporaneous. He spoke a good deal against turning the College into a University. Larey replied, and made one of the prettiest little speeches I ever heard. We then came back, and serenaded old Mc, who told us, that the Trustees had forbidden him to give us extra holidays on such occasions. Upon which we marched in front of his house in a groaning procession, the Music playing a dead march. Afterwards we danced a grand "College reel" in front of the Chapel, and took exercise if we did nothing else.

We serenaded Barnwell, and called for a speech; he came out and told us, as "Homerus aliquando dormitat," 'twas no wonder common mortals should sometimes be caught napping; we would therefore

8. Charles F. McCay, president 1856-1857.

have to record a flash against him. Some of the fellows told him very kindly, that we would take it off.

26th May, 1857
So. Ca. College

Dear Mother:

The College is on the eve of a breakup. Some time ago three men of the Junior Class were suspended on what the Class deemed insufficient evidence. McCay was so anxious to prevent the leaving of the Class, that he misrepresented the opinions of the Committee to the Faculty and withheld a communication of the Faculty to the Class. The Committee then acting upon the statements of some of the Professors investigated the matter thoroughly, showing throughout the affair the greatest moderation. They came to the conclusion that McCay had been guilty of doubledealing. McCay begged them with tears in his eyes to say that they believed him to have acted with good faith. They refused to answer, as they wished to spare his feelings, and the matter then came before the Faculty, being a question of veracity between McCay and several of the Professors. The Committee of the Faculty brought in their report before the Faculty Meeting held this morning, which report one of the Faculty moved be received. McCay refused to submit the report to the Faculty, stating that it was false, upon which the Faculty broke up and the professors turned their backs on him and walked off. I do not know what will be done, as we cannot consistently meet McCay as Professor, when the Faculty refuse to meet him as President. The Professors have begged us to go on just as usual, although, there being no legal Faculty, we can break up just when we choose. I think the students are disposed to be quiet and recite. 'Tis the strangest thing that has happened for a long time, the rebellion being on the part of the Faculty and not the students, and indeed the latter acting in a most exemplary manner throughout. Through the whole affair, which was very complicated, the Junior Class Committee committed no one error and indeed were very lenient to McCay. I suppose, if the Students agree to cooperate with the Faculty, the latter will appoint a President pro. tem., as McCay has refused to act, and matters may go on smoothly. There's no telling though, what will happen, for the men are tired and anxious to get home. Of one thing there can be no doubt. The Trustees may do what they please, but neither Faculty nor students can stay here, if they sustain McCay, for he has been convicted of a downright lie....

28th May, 1857.
So. Car. College.

Dear Mother;

The faculty and College are just waiting now for the action of the Trustees on Mc's case. He has got himself into a bad box and innumerable are the equivocations, evasions and falsehoods, which he has practiced to get out of it. Yesterday he agreed to meet the Faculty, and they drew up their statement on the one side and he is to draw up his on the other, and the Trustees are to meet and decide on it. They will have to choose between the President on the one hand, and the Faculty & College on the other. Today one of his most direct falsehoods has just been discovered. He wrote a note to the Committee of the Junior Class in the beginning trying to effect a compromise. The committee refused peremptorily to agree to his terms and returned him the note. As he intended representing the opinion of the Committee as favourable to his plan (and he afterwards did it) in order that their decided refusal should not be known by the Faculty, he very willingly agreed to say nothing about it. The Faculty by some means heard of it, and one of the professors taxed him with this secret note. His reply was: "See, how they treat me! Upon my word I never wrote a note to that Committee." He has got out of several lies already by pleading the treachery of his memory, but unfortunately for him that plea won't serve him in this case, for the note was such an important thing, that the Committee have had frequent occasions to allude to it during their conferences, and he could not easily have forgotten a thing, which was an awfully false step in his diplomacy. With all his mathematical clearness and foxlike art in debating the affair, his side has been such a bad one that in every interview, which he has had with the Junior Class Committee, they were always able to turn every analogy he presented, to serve his case, against him. The College is going on very regularly now, except of course that very little study is done, as everybody is loafing all day under the trees, talking over affairs in general; and we go to all the recitations, except McCay's. I hope the board of Trustees will meet soon, that we may know what to do.

14th Nov. 1857.
So. Car. College.

Dear—

... Last night we had a fine debate in our Society among some four or five of our honorary members on the advisability of turning the

College into a University. Davison (or Davidson), the author of the article in the last number of Russell's Mag. on Edgar A. Poe, made, I think, much the best speech, though few of his audience would, I suppose, agree with me, as he is a very diffident man and speaks like one, more accustomed to the pen than the stage. His arguments were very much the same, as those, which Father used in his piece on the University idea. A Mr. Goodman, who was in College at the same time with Prof. Barnwell, and is a great friend of his, also made a very good speech, only rather long, and took occasion to pronounce a very high panegyric upon Barnwell. Dr. Gaston spoke very well on the University side, but merely, I believe, for the sake of debate.

Barnwell preached a fine sermon this morning from the same text, which Cousin Bazile took, when he preached up here during the meeting of Presbytery. It was curious to compare them, they handled the subject so differently. Cousin Bazile's bore away the palm in purity of style, simplicity of diction and a straight forward Presbyterian way of getting at the root of the matter. Barnwell's excelled in Ciceronian roundness of periods and exuberance of language, a rather too flowery profusion of ornament and the suggestion of ideas not pursued.

Feb. 1860.

... Ned Fishburne and I called on Miss Longstreet. But she and the Judge's daughter, Mrs. Lamar, who are the young people of the household, were out. However the Judge and the old lady, who is a very pleasant old soul, entreated us to stay and have a talk with them. So, we sat down, and the old Judge got his pipe and fell to smoking, and we all chatted

Sixth of Oct. 1860
College Campus.

Dear Father

I received this morning the very welcome supply contained in your letter, had the order cashed at once, and immediately paid in at the Library the one dollar required. We are relieved by this time on the subject of cigars. By diligent search, we have hit upon a shop, where we can obtain very tolerable Americans, and are now supplied to our hearts' content. I am in hopes, by steady study to get my diploma without any great trouble. The Examination was much more awful in anticipation, than it will be in reality.

From accounts given by students from the upper districts, and from the excitement prevailing in Columbia, political alarmists seem to be somewhat plentiful in the State; but we of the graduating class are fortunately too busy to bother our heads about such things.

Saturday, Oct. 1860
So. Carolina College.

Dear Mother,

We are all so much excited here about the state of political affairs, that many of us are making by no means diligent preparation for the coming examination. Our men—those of my class, I mean—are anxious to be at home, either to join companies already organized, or to aid in organizing new ones.

There ought to be a corps of mounted riflemen in Prince William's for arms ought to be procured and drill commenced as soon as possible. I do not think it by any means certain that we will have either Secession or War immediately; but in the event of the Black Republicans being defeated even, I am inclined to believe that the incipient step towards Disunion will only be shifted from us to the North. That fanatical party has now for the first time felt the full measure of its strength and will not brook defeat. The more moderate men among them will in vain attempt to stem the torrent of their crusading zeal; and the probability is, that before the presidential inauguration takes place, we will have an attempt at a general insurrection and a raid into the border states much more general and much more formidable than that of John Brown. If matters are likely to take such a turn, and our Legislature proves so besotted as to be satisfied with Breckenridge's election, it will be wise for the sound Districts to arm volunteer companies at once and be prepared for the sudden call which the State will then make upon her citizens. In any event, if the State will not act now of her free will, I believe that the day will ultimately come, when she will be driven into—not Secession, but—immediate War by armed hordes upon her frontiers. Nor do the signs of the times bear us out in supposing that the day will be a distant one. I therefore think that we, who are not absolutely blind like those who assume to be our statesmen, ought to be getting ready at once; and I hope somebody will organize a volunteer troop in Prince William's,—not one of these trifling politico-military associations with no definite object and a rascally liberal platform—but a purely military organization.—Green, *op. cit.*, pp. 349-61.

19. Expenses at the University of Virginia are reported high, 1857

Among the expenses of the various colleges, which I can refer to, I find University College, Virginia—the terms of which occupy 44 weeks—is the most expensive. The annual charges for a student are the following:—College expenses, 40 £.; board, 22 £.; washing, fuel, and lights, 4 £.—in all 70 £. It is obvious that no provision is made here for champagne suppers, hunters, tandems, and other "necessaries," of our University students, including a few "auxiliaries," in the shape of I O U's, red coats, top boots, Hudson's regalias, and mysterious jewelery bills for articles that men don't wear. Doubtless some papas would prefer the Virginian bill of fare; but then they must remember that the republican lads go to college to learn something, whereas many papas send their first-born hopes to Oxford and Cambridge to save themselves trouble, . . .—Captain Henry A. Murray, R.N., *Lands of the Slave and the Free* (London: G. Routledge and Company, 1857), p. 427.

20. Students leave Franklin College (University of Georgia), 1858

The University.—A correspondent of the Augusta *Despatch*, writes from Athens on the 27th ult.:

"I understand in the streets to-day, several of the Students of Franklin College are selling of their books, &c., and are going to leave. The cause of their leaving I was not able to learn. It was also whispered to-day there would not be more than 25 students in the College, at the next commencement. I hope this is not true."—*The Times* (Greensboro, N.C.,), March 13, 1858.

21. An act to establish the University of Texas, 1858

Whereas, From the earliest times, it has been the cherished design of the people of the Republic and of the State of Texas, that there shall be established, within her limits, an Institution of learning, for the instruction of the youths of the land in the higher branches of learning, and in the liberal arts and sciences, and to be so endowed, supported and maintained, as to place within the reach of our people, whether rich or poor, the opportunity of conferring upon the sons of the State, a thorough education, and as a means whereby the attachment of the young men of the State to the interest, the institution, the rights of the State, and the liberties of the people, might be encouraged and increased, and to this end, hitherto liberal appropriations of the public domain have been made; and,

Whereas, The increasing population and wealth of the State, and the tendency of events, indicate the fitness of now putting that cherished design in effect, therefore,

Section 1. Be it enacted by the Legislature of the State of Texas, That there is hereby established, within this State, an Institution of learning, to be styled "The University of Texas," to be located at such place and in such manner as may be determined by law.

Sec. 2. The sum of one hundred thousand dollars of the United States bonds in the Treasury not otherwise appropriated, is hereby set apart and appropriated to the establishment and maintenance of the same. The fifty leagues of land, which, by the Act of January 26, 1839, entitled "An Act appropriating certain lands for the establishment of a general system of education," were set apart and appropriated for the establishment and endowment of two Colleges or Universities, are hereby set apart and appropriated to the establishment and maintenance of the University of Texas. There is hereby set apart and appropriated to the same purpose, one section of land out of every ten sections of land which have heretofore been, or may hereafter be surveyed and reserved for the use of the State, under the provisions of the Act of January 30, 1854, entitled "An Act to encourage the construction of railroads in Texas by donations of land," and under the provisions of any general or special law heretofore passed, granting lands to railroad companies, and under the provisions of the Act of February 11, 1854, granting lands to the Galveston and Brazos Navigation Company. The Governor of the State shall select the sections hereby appropriated, so that no sections selected shall adjoin, out of the lands now surveyed, as soon as practicable, and out of the lands hereafter to be surveyed, as soon thereafter as practicable, and shall cause a record to be made, in the Land Office of the State, of the sections so selected; and, thereupon, it shall be the duty of the Commissioner of the General Land Office to designate, upon the maps, the sections so selected as University lands. The sale of these sections shall hereafter be regulated by special law.

Sec. 3. The control, management and supervision, of the University, and the care and preservation of its property, subject always to the control of the legislature, is committed to a Board of ten persons, to be styled "The Administrators of the University of Texas," which shall be composed of the Governor of the State of Texas, the Chief Justice of the Supreme Court of Texas, and eight others, who shall be appointed by the Governor, by and with the consent of the Senate, to hold office for four years, and until their successors are qualified. The Administrators shall receive no compensation for their services.

Sec. 4. The following branches of learning shall be taught at the University, viz: Ancient and Modern Languages, the different branches of Mathematics, pure and physical, Natural Philosophy, Chemistry, Mineralogy, including Geology, the principles of Agriculture, Botany, Anatomy, Surgery and Medicine, Zoology, History, Ethics, Rhetoric and Belles-Letters, Civil Government, Political Economy, the Law of Nature, of Nations, and Municipal Law.

Sec. 5. The religious tenet of any person shall not be made a condition of admission to any privilege or office in the University; nor shall any course of religious instruction be taught or allowed, of a sectarian character and tendency.

Sec. 6. The Administrators shall have the power to appoint the President, Faculty, Instructors, and Officers, of the University, and prescribe the course of instruction and discipline to be observed, in the University. They shall fix the salaries of the President, Faculty, Instructors, and Officers of the University. Five of the Administrators, with the Governor or the Chief Justice, lawfully convened, shall be a quorum for the transaction of business. They shall meet at least once in every year, for the transaction of business, and shall keep a record of their proceedings. They shall have a Secretary, to be elected by them. They shall have power to make all regulations, which, to them, shall seem expedient for carrying into effect the design contemplated by the establishment of this University, not inconsistent with the laws of the State.

Sec. 7. The Administrators shall have the right of conferring, on any person whom they think worthy thereof, all literary honors and degrees known and usually granted by any University or College in the United States or elsewhere.

Sec. 8. The Administrators shall report to the Legislature, at each session, the situation of the affairs of the University.

Sec. 9. Instruction at the University shall be free, and the Administrators shall prescribe what degree of proficiencies shall entitle students to admission.

Sec. 10. A committee, to be appointed by the Legislature at each session, shall attend the annual examinations of the students of the University, and report to the Legislature thereon.

Sec. 11. The reasonable expenses incurred by the Administrators and visiting committee, in the discharge of their duties, shall be paid out of the funds of the University.

Sec. 12. The Treasurer of the State shall be Treasurer of the University funds.

Sec. 13. So soon as the location of the University is determined upon, it shall be the duty of the Administrators to proceed to the construction of the necessary buildings, and for that purpose, shall procure the services of a competent architect, who shall superintend the work; such plan and design for the building shall be adopted, as shall be consistent with the addition of wings or other structures hereafter, without marring the architectural beauty and fitness of the whole. There shall be constructed suitable buildings for the accommodation of the Professors and their families. The contracts for the buildings shall require the performance of the work under ample security for its fitness and faithfulness.

Sec. 14. The expenditure of the University, for the construction of buildings, or otherwise, shall be made under the order of the Administrators; and when money is required for the payment of the same, it shall be drawn upon the warrant of the Governor, countersigned by the Secretary, upon the Treasurer, who shall pay the same out of the University funds. And this Act shall take effect and be in force from and after its passage.

Approved February 11, 1858.

–H. P. N. Gammel (Comp.), *The Laws of Texas*, IV, 1020-23.

22. Basil Manly of the University of Alabama is invited to become president of Howard College, April 25, 1858

Marion Ala. April 25th 1858

Revd. B. Manly D.D.

My Dear Broth

Your favor, in answer to mine, inviting you to become the President of Howard College, was recvd. When I recve. a letter from you, I am forced to let my better half read it. I handed the one in question to her, and have not seen it since. I am not in consequence able to answer it "secundemartem."

I have been trying to make up my mind as to whether I could attent the meeting at Greenville. I have determined, within the last few days, that it will not be in my power to do so. I write to assure you of the regret I feel in being compelled to abandon the hope of seeing you. As *I am* anxious for the success of the enterprise contemplated in the meeting at Greenville I will take the liberty of offering one or two suggestions. Let the course of instruction embrace three years. Let the term of study for each year begin about the first of Novm. and close about the first of July. The students will, under that arrangement, have four months of each year to devote to the active work of the ministry. As evangelists they will do nearly as much for our cause as they can in the pastorate.

If as many as four instructors are appointed, have two distinct courses of study marked out,—one for those who have enjoyed the advantage of only an English education, and one embracing a full and complete course of Theological education. I cannot in the space of a single sheet of paper give my reasons for this but it is the result of my experience and observation.

Do not allow the thought of state lines to enter into the selections of officers of the Inst. If the best men can be found in So. Ca. take them all from that state. If they can be had in Va. let them be taken from thence. If I was in the Con. I would vote for the following; Revd. B. Manly D.D., Revd. Boyce, Rev. Brandus, Revd. B. Manly Jr. If we are compelled to have reference to this miserable state feeling, which has, for so many years crippled us in our action, So. Ca. has a right to two of the four Profs. for she has contributed the money for their support. My idea is to select the best men wherever they can be found. If the Inst. can be established, I will do my best to send to it from one to four students—graduates of college—for the next three years and in future as many as God will give me the means of educating—provided they are truly pious.

We have just closed a meeting of three weeks continuance here. It has been truly profitable to the church. Some fourteen have been recd for baptism. Others will join.

With the above exception there is nothing of special interest in our community. We are getting on quietly in the col. The baptists of the state have contributed near $20,000 to the fund for the endowment since I arrd.

My wife and self unite in love to sister Manly, and the family.

May the good Lord be with you, in the meeting at G–, and give you wisdom to direct all things, as shall be for his glory.

Affectionately & truly yours,
H. Talbird.

–Southern Historical Collection, University of North Carolina.

23. A North Carolina newspaper urges the establishment of agricultural colleges, 1858

It may be that some of our readers have seen notice of a bill introduced into Congress,[9] providing for the establishment of Agricultural Colleges in the several states of the Union, from a percent of the proceeds of the public lands. We say it *may be* that such a notice has been seen, because we think it exceedingly doubtful, from the fact that it has met with little attention from Congress and still less from the public press. Kansas, with its assumed *principles*, has from month to month engrossed the public mind; though the intrinsic merits of the points at issue did not possess a tithe of the importance and value to the government, embraced in the bill for the establishment of Agricultural Colleges. It is to be hoped, however, that the Kansas excitement is near its end, and that the calm to succeed may be devoted to labors for the good of the country, for the development of her resources and the building up of her internal wealth.

In a government of popular sentiment like ours, the press is the main moving power. It both furnishes the material and leads the direction of public thought.–Hence it is important, it is indispensable, to gain the co-operation of the press in prosecuting with success any work of great importance. And in what direction shall we look for a more important work, than the enriching of our farming interest. If he is called a benefactor who, where one blade of grass grew before, can make two, what a grand field is opening for the exercise of beneficence by the general government.

For example, in some of our wheat growing states, fourteen bushels per acre is an averaged crop; while in some of the scientific farming countries of Europe the average crop is forty bushels per acre.–According to the last census report, the annual product of wheat is not less than 110.000.000 bushels. By the increased fertility of the land, it

9. The Morrill Bill which President Buchanan vetoed. President Lincoln signed it in 1862.

would be from the above estimate 300.000.000, being an increase of 190.000.000, which, at 50 cents per bushel, would be equivalent to a donation of $90.000.000 to the farmers of the country; more by $20.000.000 than is required to carry on the entire machinery of our Federal Government. Is there nothing to be gained in the difference between fourteen and forty bushels of wheat to the acre?

And further, the exhaustion and deterioration of the soil by the modes of farming in the United States, has been estimated at ten cents per acre annually. There are about 130.000.000 acres of arable land in the United States. There must be, therefore, a loss of $13.000.000 annually, and mostly for want of practical skill in resuscitation of the land.

From these two items, by no means the most important, some idea may be gained of the good to result from the establishment of these Colleges. But how stands Congress as to the farming interest of the country? The annual expenditures of the government amount to $70.000.000. And nearly this entire sum is consumed in supporting destructive agencies. The Army costs more than $18.000.000, and the Navy more than $12.000.000. While the Patent Office, the only creative and positively producing function of the government, designed to foster and promote inventive genius, to abridge human labor, and to bring comfort to every door, is compelled to support itself by exacting fees from inventors. Out of the $70.000.000, it is true $75.000 per annum have been appropriated for the purchase and distribution of seeds, plants, cuttings, etc. What a pittance! and yet even that must result in comparatively little good, since it lacks a system for experimenting, and each individual farmer must run the risk of the success of his own experiments.

We have merely introduced the subject in this brief article. Our object was to call the attention of the press and the public to the importance of the subject and to prepare for future discussions in which we hope to be able to show the design and benefit of such institutions; and the importance of immediate creative action of Congress.—*The Times* (Greensboro, N.C.), April 17, 1858.

24. Remarks of Jefferson Davis on the agricultural colleges bill, 1859

Mr. President, I think that in the search for precedents some mistake is found. I grant the Senator from New Hampshire, who has cited the case of the deaf and dumb asylum in Kentucky, to have one that is somewhat in point. I think, however, it is a very bad precedent, and should not be followed. It is subject to all the constitutional objections which apply to this bill. But the other cases are those in which land was granted for seminaries of learning; colleges within the Territories, or granted at the time of the compact between the General Government and the State, in which the State surrendered the right to tax the land whilst owned by the General Government, and for five years after the day of sale. This is a contract entered into between the sovereign people of the State and the United States, in relation to the public domain situated within the limits of the State. Anterior to that, the power comes under the general provision, which makes this Government a trustee for the States owning the territory; and the exercise of the power in the Territories constitutes no justification for assuming to exercise a like power within the limits of a State. So much for the precedents, to which I do not indeed attach a great deal of value, even if they were otherwise.

This is a provision, taking the bill generally, to establish schools for the instruction of persons who may be devoted to farming or other pursuits; for it says they are not to exclude scientific and other studies, but they are to direct themselves particularly to that of farming. The argument is made, that the same right exists to instruct farmers as to instruct sailors and soldiers. If I conceded to gentlemen who make this argument, that the Federal Government had established academies to instruct persons hereafter to enter the Army or the Navy, then I would say there was some force in the position which they take; but that is not true. The General Government does not educate persons, that they may hereafter enter the Army and the Navy. It does not establish academies for the instruction of youth, that they may hereafter enter the military service. It does appoint warrant officers, in both the land and naval service, and it does choose to send them to an academy as the best mode of instructing them, and the most economical mode, and perhaps the only mode in which it can give them a thorough elementary education.

The argument, therefore, that you may as well establish an academy for one species of education as another, has no application to what the Government has done and is doing. The cadets are a part of the Army; the midshipmen are a part of the Navy. Instead of sending them to serve with companies, and in a long course of years to get such military knowledge as will enable them to perform their duties on land or sea, you send them to an academy, and there give them instruction; and it is a defect in our organization which probably will not be corrected, unless we should have the misfortune to require a large army, that we have not also a school of application, where, having been taught the elements, they should likewise be taught the application before they were allowed to command men. Such is the perfect system adopted in Governments of a more strictly military character than our own; and it constitutes no argument, no basis of justification, for the proposition which is now pending.

I have seen the growth of this proposition to do something for the agricultural interest, and I believed it was always delusive, not to say fraudulent. It needs no aid. The agricultural interest takes care of itself, and is drained to take care of every other pursuit in the country. I have looked upon it as a mere sham for other pursuits draining and to drain the agriculturist, to come and say, "Let us do something for the agriculturist." From whose pocket is to be drawn the means of conferring this benefit? Mainly from the agriculturists themselves, who are then to receive a share of the whole sum which they are required to pay out. Agriculture needs no teaching by Congress. The wide extent of our country, the great variety of its soil and climate and product, render it impossible that there should be anything else than local teaching in relation to agriculture. The States are sovereign; and there is the care of the education of their youth, and their direction into any pursuits which the public weal may require. This Government was instituted for no such purpose; and when it invades that prerogative of the States, it commits violence on the sovereignty of those by whom it is created. I was pleased to hear the Senator from Minnesota (Mr. Rice) this morning state, with such clearness and force, the unconstitutionality of the measure which is pending, and the abuses which it would work in the new and landholding States.

There is another provision, which, so far as I have heard the debate, has not yet been noticed. It provides for working a forfeiture, attaching a penalty to a State which shall sell some part of the land and not establish a college, requiring it hereafter to refund the money. Did Senators forget that it was that fatal blunder of the old Confederation which utterly destroyed it, rendered it incapable of performing its duties, either in peace or in war; that it was that fatal error committed by the formers of the Confederation which rendered it necessary, subsequently, to revise it, and to form the more perfect Union, which now exists? This Government cannot coerce a State;

this Government cannot require of a State to pay money; and the error being discovered, our system was corrected, and the present mode of gathering taxes from the people adopted, making the laws work upon individuals, where they may operate, instead of upon the States, where they cannot be enforced. But the human mind has been said to be represented by a circle; and if the constant returning to exploded errors as soon as they have been forgotten, prove it, we find in this but another example, that having completed the circle, we get back to the very error from which we originally departed. In the third provision of the fifth section of this bill, one of the provisions of the grant is, that failing to establish an agricultural college, "said State shall be bound to pay the United States the amount received of any lands previously sold, and the title to purchasers under the States shall be valid." How, pray, is that money to be collected? Are Senators willing to commence this controversy with a State? Do they propose by law, to provide for levying upon the property of a State, subjecting it to execution, compelling the State to pay? All the benefits which gentlemen may anticipate from their agricultural colleges, will fall greatly short of an evil to be worked by a single such example.

I have not risen to discuss this bill. Others have done it before me; and but for one or two remarks which remained unanswered, I should have been silent upon the subject. It is, disguise it as you may, the mere adoption of that which is thought to be the largest and most influential class in the country, to cover an attempt to found colleges in the States for the benefit of the education of youth, to found them by the United States instead of by the sovereign people, who are the true guardians of their own youth, and in whose hand I much prefer to leave their custody.

On the Agricultural College Bill.

Feb. 7, 1859.

Mr. President, I concur very fully with the views this morning presented by the honorable Senator from Alabama on the constitutional and moral questions involved in this bill. I shall avoid, therefore, entering upon the same ground, which I think he has covered so ably as to leave nothing more to be said. I merely wish to say, at this time, that all arguments founded upon a reference to the lexicons to find the meaning of the term "dispose of," seem to me rather beneath the dignity of Senators. We should go to the history of the transaction to learn what the word meant in the connection in which it was used.

It is known that, after the close of the revolutionary struggle, when the States were burdened with debts, certain States held very large amounts of territory, and it constituted a ground of complaint on the part of the States holding no such territory; and especially against Virginia the argument was directed that the Northwest Territory, then claimed by Virginia, had been conquered by the joint forces of the States; that it constituted the foundation of a part of the public debt which then existed; and that it should be given for its liquidation. Georgia, holding a very large amount of territory, what was afterwards known as the Southwest Territory, from the same motives and high generosity which actuated Virginia, made, by deed of cession, as in the case of Virginia, this vast territory to become a public fund, common for the States; and it was provided that it should be disposed of, and applied *pro rata* to the States, to relieve them of the burdens of the expenditure of the General Government. If the argument which ingenuity brings in at this day, that the right "to dispose" of gave the power to grant, without compensation, had been applied to the public domain, and it had been given away, what faith would have been kept with the deed of cession? What would there have been to distribute, to relieve the States of the burdens of Government? How would the quotas demanded of the States, for the expenditures of the Government, have been diminished, by giving away the vast domain which these States had ceded to the Federal Union? To present the question, and to state it, is to answer it. Argument cannot refute what is so plain upon the very surface.

If, then, Mr. President, these lands were given, and for such specific objects named in the deed of cession, could it ensue, by using the brief language of the grant in the Constitution, that the terms of the cession could be abrogated, so that one of the contracting parties would lose all the benefit anticipated, and the very purpose for which the grant was made be swept away by a subsequent construction of the grant, expressed in such brief terms as not to imply all that was contained in the contract between the States generally and the particular State making the cession?

The Senator from Tennessee, however, directs his argument to the fact, that grants have been made to particular States; and asks, why should not the other States have grants like them? The difference between Tennessee and Alabama is, that Alabama has received a certain portion of the public land within her limits, and Tennessee the whole. What more would the Senator want for Tennessee than all the land that lay within her borders? The new States have received a part; the old States got all; and yet this constant appeal is made to Congress against the new States as having been the beneficiaries of grants of which the old States are deprived. The case is otherwise.

But again, sir: the grants to which he alluded, if they were made from any sound principle, were to increase the value of the property, and to promote the revenue of the United States. So far as grants of land have been made to construct railroads, merely on the general theory that railroads were a good thing, the Federal Government has violated its trust and exceeded the powers conferred upon it; but where a grant has been made of a certain portion of land, to increase the value of the residue, and bring it into cultivation, and by its product to promote the commerce and wealth of the country, and thus to increase the ability of the Government to bear its burdens, it rests on a principle such as a prudent proprietor would apply to the conduct of his own affairs. Thus far it is defensible; no further. The land grants to the new States for education rests on the same general principle, together with this: that the new States, sovereigns like the old, admitted to be equal, before taking both the eminent and the useful domain, entered into a contract with the other States, that they would relieve from taxation the land within their borders while owned by the General Government, and, since the credit system, for five years after the day of sale. This is the consideration for which land grants have been made to the new States; and a high price they have paid for all that has been granted for educational purposes.

So far as the swamp or overflowed lands were granted, they were granted upon the theory that the land was not only useless to the General Government until it was drained, but that it was injurious to the neighboring population; and that it was a duty on the part of the Federal Government to grant the land away, that it might be drained, and the nuisance which the swamp created upon the neighboring population thus be removed by the application of the overflowed land to that object.

In every case, so far as I am aware, in which grants have been made within the new States, they have come within one of these conditions. If frauds have been perpetrated, if pretenses have been adopted, and grants have been obtained under them, still, I say, they stand excused by the fact that this reason was presented; and it was necessary to practice delusion before the Government could be warped so far from the path it had previously followed.—Dunbar Rowland (ed.), *Jefferson Davis, Constitutionalist* (Jackson, Miss.: Mississippi Department of Archives and History, 1923), pp. 517-22. For President Buchanan's veto message on the Morrill Bill see James D. Richardson, *A Compilation of the Messages and Papers of the Presidents*, V (Washington: Government Printing Office, 1897), 543-50. For wide interest in agricultural education see J. B. Turner's plan for industrial universities, given in E. J. James, *The Origin of the Land Grant College Act of 1862 and Some Account of Its Author, Jonathan B. Turner* (Urbana-Champaign, Illinois: The University of Illinois Press, 1910). James says that it was Turner who first devised and formulated the plan for land grant colleges.

25. The Trustees of the University of Alabama report to the General Assembly of that State, 1859

As required by law, the Trustees of the University of Alabama beg leave to make the following Report. There was in the Treasury of the University at the end of the Collegiate year of 1857 as shown by the last report,

		$6,635.51
The receipts from all sources during the year ending 1st July, 1858, amount to		31,661.16
During the year ending 1st July, 1859,		26,550.00
Making a total to 1st July, 1859,		$64,847.57
During the same years the disbursements were,		
For 1858, : : :	$29, 292 90	
For 1859, : : :	33, 762 55	
Total disbursements,		$63,055.45
The balance in the Treasury 1st July, 1859,		$1,792.12

At the time at which the Treasurer's Report was made up the last quarter of the salary of several of the officers was unpaid, and also one or two small appropriations not drawn. These exceeded the balance shown by the Report; so that in point of fact, for the expenses of the Collegiate year ending 1st July, 1859, there is still due a small balance.

The ordinary annual expenses of the University are as follows:—

For the Faculty,—8 Professors and Tutors	....	$15,000.00
" " Trustees, about	...	450.00
" " Treasurer,	...	200.00
" " Librarian,	...	300.00
" " Bellman, about	...	150.00
" " Secretary of the Trustees,	...	50.00
" " Ordinary repairs, Contingent Expenses & Coal,	...	1,200.00
" " Servants,	...	600.00
" " Library,	...	200.00
" " Laboratory,	...	150.00
" " Philosophical Apparatus,	...	100.00
" " Extra accounts which cannot be provided for beforehand, (about)	....	300.00
		$18,700.00

At the time of the death of the late Prof. Tuomey, his collection of Geological specimens was so intermingled with that belonging to the University that to separate them would have required the services, for some time, of a scientific man, the cost of which, it was ascertained, would equal, if not exceed, the price for which Prof. Tuomey's interest might be purchased. The collection was a valuable one to the University, and the Trustees, therefore, purchased of Mrs. Tuomey the interest of Prof. T. at the sum of $2,000.00 one-fourth of which has already been paid; and the balance is to be paid in three annual installments of $500 each. This added to the sum of $18,700 will make the annual expenses of the University for the next three years, $19,200.00.

The estimated income for the year 1859-'60 is:—

From the State, interest on the fund,	....	$15,000.00
" Tuition Charges,	...	3,500.00
" Interest on money lent,	...	740.00
Making a total income,	...	$19,240.00

Showing a balance of income over the ordinary expenses, of $40.00.

These expenses cannot, it is believed, be reduced consistently with the interests of the institution; indeed, they are now on a scale far too limited for the operation of a University of its grade. The small sums annually appropriated to the Laboratory and Philosophical Apparatus are barely sufficient to supply the necessary materials for experiment and to meet the necessary repairs which are constantly required. The Philosophical apparatus belonging to the University is very incomplete and imperfect, and to supply this want alone, would require several thousand dollars. Since the death of Prof. Tuomey the chair of Geology has remained vacant. Though the Trustees recognize the great importance of this department, they have not felt authorized to fill it. But to say nothing of these wants, and others that might be mentioned, which the means of the University will not permit the Trustees to supply, the most pressing necessity is the repairs demanded by the buildings of the institution. The usual appropriation of $1,200.00 is barely sufficient, upon the most economical expenditure, to keep the buildings in a habitable condition, and to meet the other contingent expenses which are necessarily incurred. The inside repairs have not been attended to since the opening of the University in 1831, except to put in broken glass, and to mend or patch the plastering, &c. Any house will wear out in a term of years, and no house will do so more rapidly than one occupied by students. It is unnecessary to specify the work that is necessary to put the buildings in thorough repair. They have been examined by a competent workman and according to his estimate, $10,000.00 will be required for this purpose: and until the repairs are made, dilapidation will continue to go on, and the dormitories especially soon become untenantable. Unless some addition, therefore, be made to the resources of the University, it is impossible to appropriate anything to this object without such a contraction of its other expenditures as would be greatly detrimental to its usefulness as an institution of a higher grade.

The Trustees have heretofore reported to the General Assembly the erection of one new dormitory and three Professor's houses. The first was rendered necessary by the increased number of students, and the others by the burning of the houses several years since, then occupied by the Professors.—These buildings have been erected on as economical a plan as could be adopted to make them either comfortable or substantial. The total cost up to 1st July, 1859, was $29,620.88

To complete them, the Trustees at their last meeting appropriated, ...	1,245.64
Making their total cost, ...	$30,866.52

The money applied to these buildings was raised by reserving for a series of years a portion of the annual interest accruing on the "University Fund," and lending it out upon interest. To make this saving, the ordinary expenses of the institution were reduced; all repairs, except such as were absolutely necessary, were omitted; the grade of the Faculty was lowered, by substituting tutors at small salaries in lieu of more competent Professors. Nothing but the urgent demand for these buildings could justify such retrenchment, and to have longer continued it would have cost the University the degradation of its character as an institution, and the utter dilapidation of its public buildings. The amount thus reserved was on the 1st of July, 1857, $31,596.00, the receipt and disbursement of which are embraced in the account on the first page of this Report. This sum having been exhausted in the use for which it was reserved, the University is again left to its ordinary income, which, it has been shown, is barely sufficient to meet its most restricted ordinary expenses.

As the Trustees are required by law to accompany their Report "with such suggestions as to them seem advisable," they beg leave in this connection, to present to the General Assembly the claim the University has against the State for a portion of its capital fund which has been withheld from her since the 21st February, 1848.

To a proper understanding of the merits of this claim, a brief review of the history of the "University Fund" is necessary.

The University of Alabama owes its foundation to the bounty of the Government of the United States. By the Act of Congress for the admission of Alabama into the Union the Sixteenth Section of every Township of the Public Lands in the State was reserved for the benefit of public schools; and seventy-two (72) sections, or 46,080 acres "for the use of a Seminary of learning and vested in the Legislature of the State to be appropriated solely for the use of such seminary by the said legislature." This was one of the conditions of the admission of Alabama into the Union, which the people of the State, in Convention, accepted by an ordinance "declared irrevocable without the consent of Congress;" and they embodied in their fundamental law, on this subject, the following just and wise provision, viz:—

The General Assembly shall take like measures (as were to be taken in reference to the 16th Sections) for the improvement of such lands as may have been, or may be hereafter granted by the United States to this State for the support of a Seminary of learning and *the moneys which may be raised from such lands by rent, lease, or sale, or from any other quarter, for the purpose aforesaid, shall be, and remain a fund for the exclusive support of a State University for the promotion of the arts, literature and sciences; and it shall be the duty of the General Assembly, as early as may be, to provide effectual means for the improvement and permanent security of the lands and endowments of such institutions.*

By the acceptance in the condition of the act of admission, the State of Alabama became the Trustee of these lands and assumed the obligation to administer them for the sole benefit of the Seminary to whose use they were granted. The language of the grant is too plain to require either argument or authority to show that the relation of Trustee and *cestui que trust* was established between the State and the Seminary contemplated. The Legislature, by its various enactments in reference to the grant, has repeatedly recognized this and acted upon it. If, however, authority is necessary it is furnished by the Supreme Court of the State by the decision of the case of Long and Long *vs.* Brown,—4th Ala. Rep., 622. That decision was made in reference to the grant of the lands for the use of public schools; but the same language is used in the grant for the use of a Seminary of learning, and both grants are embraced in the same section of the act of Congress. The decision is, therefore, as applicable to one as to the other. In speaking of the title to the school lands the Court (on page 629) says: "Nor can any doubt be entertained that the legal title was intended to be vested by the act of Congress in this State, and did so vest, by the acceptance of the conditions proposed by the act of 2nd of March, 1819, by the Convention of this State, in August of the same year. By the acceptance of *this trust*, the State impliedly stipulated to do those acts which were necessary to give full effect to the grant," &c. "It was intended as a grant to the State, to be held in perpetuity for the use and benefit" of the Seminary of learning.

It was not only a trust, but it was an inalienable and perpetual trust, from which the State could not relieve itself except with the consent of Congress. "When the Legislature converted the lands into money, it still retained its character as Trustee, and was bound to the same duties it was before the sale of the land.—When it deposited the money in the State Bank for safe keeping, and when it again converted it into capital of that institution for the use of the State it remained a Trustee still. The deposite of the fund in Bank, or the conversion of it into Bank capital, worked no mutation in the character, or the duties of that body, but left matters precisely as they were before, except that in the last case the State became liable for the fund converted to its own use."—(Taylor's Address.) . . .

Prior to the conversion of the fund in 1833 into Bank capital, the Trustees of the University were, by an act passed in 1823, required to deposit in the Treasury of the State all the moneys received by them from whatever source. On the moneys thus deposited there had accrued, up to 1833, an amount of interest of $25,963.05 which the State withheld from the University.

Thus, then, the matters between the State and the University stood at the opening of the session of the Legislature in 1847; the State had actually received and converted to its own use $300,000 of the proceeds of the sales of the lands which it held in trust for the University, for which the Trustees held the State's "certificates of debt," with a pledge of the public faith and credit for their security, and upon which the interest had been annually paid to the University, since 1833. *About this there was no controversy.*

But the University claimed as equitably due to her the losses sustained by the relief laws of 1832 and 1834, amounting with interest at 6 per cent. up to that time, to, $255,745.73

And also the amount of interest on her deposits which at the same rate of interest, was about the sum of . . . . $ 47,771.97

Making her total controverted claim $303,517.70

The University at the same time was indebted to the State Bank for money borrowed to erect its buildings, in the sum of $64,500.00, for which the State held the notes of the Trustees. This debt with interest at 6 per cent., in 1847, amounted to about $100,000.00.

The Trustees, being desirous of adjusting these mutual claims between the University and the State, proposed to the General Assembly in 1847, to make a compromise by extinguishing their respective claims in the way of off-sett. In response to this proposition the House of Representatives appointed a Committee to investigate the subject, who in due time reported a bill accompanied by an able and elaborate exposition of its provisions and intendment. As it came from the Committee the Bill fixed the "University fund" at $300,000, and in this shape it passed the House; but the Senate amended it by reducing the fund to $250,000.00, which amendment, the House concurring in it, became a law. The first two sections are as follows, viz:

I. That the sum of $250,000 be and the same is hereby recognized and declared to be the amount of the "University Fund"; for the permanent security of which and the punctual payment of the interest thereon forever, at the rate of 6 per cent. per annum, the faith and credit of the State of Alabama are hereby solemnly pledged....

From these facts it is undeniably clear that the 2d section of the Act of 1848 contains all the terms and stipulations of the compromise made, and intended to be made, between the University and the State. It was a literal compliance with the proposition submitted by the Board of Trustees, and receives consequently its authoritative interpretation from the report of the Trustees submitting the proposition of compromise and the report of the Committee in the House recommending its adoption. Here then was the compromise and the *whole* compromise made between the University and the State on the adoption of the 2d section of the act of 21st February, 1848; *the State cancelled its debt against the University, in consideration of which the University relinquished its claims for interest and losses on the re-sales of the lands under the relief law of 1834.*

Returning now to the 1st section of this act, the claim of the University intended to be set up in this Report will appear to be most undeniably just and legal. This section, as reported from the Committee, recognized $300,000 as the permanent fund of the University. It passed the House without amendment, but, having been amended by the Senate, finally passed as it is now found in the statute-book, *with a reduction of* $50,000.—For this sum thus withheld from the University there was no equivalent given; it was not embraced in the compromise, but was taken from the fund of the University by an act of *legislative spoliation*, or more properly, of *undisguised repudiation.*—Without mooting the question of the power or authority of the Trustees to make *any* compromise by which any of the rights of the University are impaired or prejudiced, or how far the State, whose creatures and agents they are, can treat with them as a party to such compromise, the Trustees make no impeachment of the validity of the act of 1847, but regard it as conclusive as to all matters embraced in it. It is clear, from what has already been said, that the surrender of the $50,000 constituted no part of that compromise; but if it had, being a part of the capital fund of the University, it might well be questioned whether the State could without a violation of the trust created by the act of Congress, thus reduce that fund; and if the validity of the act depended upon the assent of the Trustees, then it is indisputable that it could not, because the Trustees are the mere agents of the State in reference to the University; are appointed by the Legislature, and have no authority or power over the fund of the University save such as the Legislature vests in them. Waiving that objection, however, the question recurs, is the University estopped from claiming that sum by the compromise of 1848? Did the $50,000 form any part of the consideration to the State in this compromise? From what has been said, it appears that for $100,000, the State received $303,517.70, which it would seem was ample consideration without this sum. But it may be said that this sum of $303,517.70 was not a debt recognized by the State, and therefore it was just and proper to appropriate a part of the fund to the extinguishment of the debt from the University; but without looking to the unmistakable language of the act itself, or the report of the Committee interpreting it, it is quite evident that the State recognized the claims which constituted the sum of $303,517.70; for its debt against the University was $100,000, to extinguish which something more than the sum scaled from the fund was necessary. Having recognized and admitted its liability, it was bound to the whole extent of the loss sustained by the University, and though these losses may have been but one half the amount stated, yet the consideration was ample to the State without this sum of $50,000.

Again, it may be said that the Trustees are precluded from this claim by the relinquishment required by the 2d section of the act of 1848, to be filled in the office of the Secretary of State. But it is clear that this relinquishment embraced and could properly embrace, a relinquishment only of the claims which the Trustees had, or pretended to have, against the State for interest, damages or losses sustained by the University fund *prior* to the passage of the act. The scope and legal effect of the relinquishment are thus clearly defined by the express terms of the section itself. The language of the section is "all claims which the Trustees have or pretend to have, against the State for interest, damages or losses sustained of every kind of description whatever, *up to the date of this act*." This claim could not therefore have been embraced in the relinquishment, for as has already been shown, it was no part of the "interest, damages or losses" mentioned in the 2d section; and because it did not exist prior to the *date of the act* but *grew out of*, or was *created by the very act itself*. The State had never denied the right of the University to the whole sum of $300,000, but had annually recognized it by the payment of the interest accruing thereon. The first denial of any part of it was by the act of 1848, and at its passage arose for the first time this claim against the State.

It thus appears, that by the act of 1848, $50,000 was taken by the State from the fund which it held in trust for the University of Alabama, without any consideration to the University therefor, without the assent of the Trustees, if that was requisite to give validity to the act, and in violation of the grant under which it became possessed of the fund. This sum the State, therefore, justly owes to the University of Alabama. It is a debt of equal obligation with any debt the State ever owed; and indeed of a higher moral obligation, as it springs from the bounty of the General Government, intended for the promotion of education among the people of the State, and was confided *solely* to the *honor* and *integrity* of the Legislature. To refuse the payment of it would be an act of repudiation which would forever tarnish the bright escutcheon of Alabama. We cannot persuade ourselves that there are now any characters in Alabama who would consent to have this dishonor brought upon her. Even in the darkest days of their financial history, when the disasters which followed the failure of the banking system, were pouring like a destructive flood upon them, and there was no escape from the ruin which seemed to impend but in repudiation or a submission to taxation of almost overpowering weight, the people of Alabama determined to make whatever sacrifice was necessary to preserve the honor and faith of the State; and their Representatives in General Assembly (in 1845) gave utterance to this noble resolve in a series of joint resolutions....

It is the earnest desire of the Trustees to see the usefulness of the University extended and increased; that the bounty which was generously bestowed upon it by the general government may be enjoyed in the most ample manner by the people of the State. A connection between it and the scheme of public schools now in operation in Alabama would unquestionably be greatly promotive of this end; and that such a union should exist seems both natural and right.—The University and the public schools owe their origin to the same common source; and were doubtless intended to form one general system of education "with one great luminary in the center, and lesser lights kindled up over the whole extent of the State." This relation between the two was recognized by the Legislature in the 9th section of the act of the "school law" already quoted, and the common schools are thereby to some extent made tributary to the University. The Trustees would respectfully suggest one mode of connection which, in their judgment, would be materially beneficial to both and tend to advance the cause of education in the State. They can do no more, however, in this report than simply to state what that mode is with a brief enumeration of some of the reasons in support of it.

It has already been stated that under a By-law of the University two young men from each county, in indigent circumstances are entitled to their education in the University without charge. Those who avail themselves of this provision are selected by the superintendents of the several counties and must be youths of good character and are for the most part young men of talent and ambition who intend to make scholars of themselves. Now if a corresponding provision was made in the common school law whereby this meritorious class of the youth of the state would become entitled to teach with such salaries as are paid in the common schools, the Trustees could so amend their bye-laws as to require of them as a condition of admission under its provisions a promise to teach in the state for two years after their graduation.

This would impose no hardship upon them. For the most part they intend or expect to teach after leaving college and are generally forced to do so for the means of support while making preparation to enter upon some profession, or during the probation which precedes the commencement of the business of life. Here then would be secured to them an honorable position in connection with the great interest of education in the State, and at the same time the present means of support with the opportunity of advancement. Besides, the consciousness that they would in the future repay the State for the benefits which it was conferring by a gratuitous education would relieve them during their college career of that sense of dependence which they necessarily feel. At other Institutions in this country and in England, where education is given gratuitously, a similar requirement is made of the beneficiaries; but the Trustees propose to make such a requirement of the beneficiaries of the University only upon the condition that they are admitted to teach in the common schools of the State. Without such a right young men would be deterred from becoming beneficiaries lest they might thereby incur an obligation which they might not be able to discharge; but the certainty of immediate employment this right would secure, would be an inducement to them to enter the University, and thus the Common Schools would be annually supplied with competent teachers from the most meritorious of the young men of the State who had been especially educated for them.

The first benefit then that the State would derive from a connection like this would be, that it would no longer be necessary to look to other States for the teachers of her youth; they would be supplied from her own sons who are "to the manor born" and deeply imbued with all the sentiments of her people.

2d. Education would be imparted by a system which pervaded every step of its progress from the primary school to the University; and thus thoroughness and accuracy of scholarship would be secured.

3d. The University and the Common Schools would act and re-act upon each other, extending the reputation and expanding the influence of the former, and elevating and improving the latter.

4th. The benefit which the University freely confers upon its beneficiaries would be more widely diffused among the people, and the education conferred upon them would be multiplied by their teachings to the children of the State.

5th. Nor would such a connection operate injuriously upon the other Institutions of learning in the State. It would have a strong tendency to stimulate the cause of education, to increase the number of those who go to College, and to draw to our own institutions those who now go abroad for instruction, thus creating a demand for new institutions of a high grade in the State, adding to the prosperity and usefulness of those already in existence, and conforming them all to one harmonious system.

That there are some objections to this suggestion the Trustees are aware; but they think, upon examination, these will be found less practical than theoretical. Without expanding this report to notice them, the whole subject is submitted to the wisdom of the Legislature.

At the late meeting of the Board of Trustees the system of instruction which heretofore prevailed in the University, was abolished, and a more liberal system adopted in its stead. A circular issued by the Faculty explaining this system, is hereto attached.

The Rev. Edward Babtist, a Trustee for the 1st Judicial Circuit, having been absent during one entire session of the Board, and at the commencement of the last session, his seat was declared vacant by a vote of the Board, and remains for the Legislature to fill.

The Trustees take pleasure in bearing testimony to the able and faithful manner in which the Faculty have discharged their duties during the last two Collegiate years; and in the expression of the opinion that they are entitled to the confidence of the parents of Alabama.

All of which is respectfully submitted by order of the Board of Trustees.

THO'S H. HERNDON, Chairman
JOHN J. ORMOND, } Committee.
JOHN S. STORRS,

–Pamphlet in possession of George Coffin Taylor, Columbia, S. C., and here used with his permission. Microcopy is in the Southern Historical Collection, the University of North Carolina.

26. President James Buchanan Vetoes the Morrill (Land-Grant College) Act, 1859

I return with my objections to the House of Representatives in which it originated, the bill entitled "An act donating public lands to the several States and Territories which may provide Colleges for the benefit of agriculture and mechanic arts. . . ." [9]

I shall now proceed to state my objections to this bill. I deem it to be both inexpedient and unconstitutional.

1. This bill has been passed at a period when we can with great difficulty raise sufficient revenue to sustain the expenses of the Government. Should it become a law the Treasury will be deprived of the whole, or nearly the whole, of our income from the sale of public lands, which for the next fiscal year has been estimated at $5,000,000. . . .

Surely the present is the most unpropitious moment which could have been selected for the passage of this bill.

2. Waiving for the present the question of constitutional power, what effect will this bill have on the relations established between the Federal and State Governments? The Constitution is a grant to Congress of a few enumerated but most important powers, relating chiefly to war, peace, foreign and domestic commerce, negotiation, and other subjects which can be best or alone exercised beneficially by the com-

9. The full text of the message appears in Edgar W. Knight and Clifton L. Hall, *Readings in American Educational History* (New York: Appleton-Century-Crofts, 1951), pp. 282-89.

mon Government. All other powers are reserved to the States and to the people. For the efficient and harmonious working of both, it is necessary that their several spheres of action should be kept distinct from each other. This alone can prevent conflict and mutual injury. Should the time ever arrive when the State governments shall look to the Federal Treasury for the means of supporting themselves and maintaining their systems of education and internal policy, the character of both Governments will be greatly deteriorated...

3. This bill, should it become a law, will operate greatly to the injury of the new States. The progress of settlements and the increase of an industrious population owning an interest in the soil they cultivate are the causes which will build them up into great and flourishing commonwealths. Nothing could be more prejudicial to their interests than for wealthy individuals to acquire large tracts of the public land and hold them for speculative purposes. The low price to which this land scrip will probably be reduced will tempt speculators to buy it in large amounts and locate it on the best lands belonging to the Government. The eventual consequence must be that the men who desire to cultivate the soil will be compelled to purchase these very lands at rates much higher than the price at which they could be obtained from the Government.

4. It is extremely doubtful, to say the least, whether this bill would contribute to the advancement of agriculture and the mechanic arts—objects the dignity and value of which can not be too highly appreciated.

The Federal Government, which makes the donation, has confessedly no constitutional power to follow it into the States and enforce the application of the fund to the intended objects....

5. This bill will injuriously interfere with existing colleges in the different States, in many of which agriculture is taught as a science and in all of which it ought to be so taught. These institutions of learning have grown up with the growth of the country, under the fostering care of the States and the munificence of individuals, to meet the advancing demands for education. They have proved great blessings to the people. Many, indeed most, of them are poor and sustain themselves with difficulty. What the effect will be on these institutions of creating an indefinite number of rival colleges sustained by the endowment of the Federal Government it is not difficult to determine....

6. But does Congress possess the power under the Constitution to

make a donation of public lands to the different States of the Union to provide colleges for the purpose of educating their own people?

I presume the general proposition is undeniable that Congress does not possess the power to appropriate money in the Treasury, raised by taxes on the people of the United States, for the purpose of educating the people of the respective States. It will not be pretended that any such power is to be found among the specific powers granted to Congress nor that "it is necessary and proper for carrying into execution" any one of these powers. Should Congress exercise such a power, this would be to break down the barriers which have been so carefully constructed in the Constitution to separate Federal from State authority....—James D. Richardson, *A Compilation of the Messages and Papers of the Presidents* (Washington: Government Printing Office, 1897), V, 543-50.

27. Governor Sam Houston's message to the Legislature of Texas on the university and on giving aid to other institutions, 1860

The $2,000,000 set apart for the school fund yet remains, but the balance of the $5,000,000, received from the sale of our Santa Fe territory to the United States is exhausted, except the amount set apart for the University fund, amounting to $106,972.26 and the balance mentioned of $411,402.69, belonging to the general fund....

I would also commend to your consideration the importance of extending a reasonable aid to institutions of learning, now in operation in our State, supported by private enterprize, and to encourage by a general law the establishment of others. Our citizens have already displayed much zeal and enterprise in rearing up in our midst institutions which are accomplishing great good, to sustain these is difficult, and as the benefits arising from these are to be felt in the general prosperity of the State, and the intelligence of its entire people, a proper encouragement at the hands of the Legislature should be extended. Surrounded by proper guards a measure of this character would be productive of great good.

The establishment of a University, is, in my opinion, a matter alone for the future. At this time it is neither expedient, nor is it good policy to provide for the sale of those lands set apart for the University fund. If, at some future period it should be deemed expedient, or in keeping with a more enlarged policy, to devote our entire energies to a more general diffusion of knowledge than a University would afford, or even if the voice of the State should demand the establishment of one of these lands will then provide the means of advancing the cause of education. When that period arrives, their value will be greatly increased. If sold now, but little will be realized from them, and before the expiration of twenty years—the time upon which over fifty thousand acres would have been sold—the lands will be worth more than three-fold the amount they would bring now, with accumulated interest.

So far as the one hundred thousand dollars of bonds, and their interest, taken from the general and applied to the University fund, by the last Legislature, are concerned, I believe the condition of the treasury and our immediate necessities demand that the act be repealed, and the money again placed subject to appropriation. We need money for the protection of our frontier, and to save us from taxation, more than for a fund which promises no immediate benefit. Our common school fund already provides for the education contemplated by the Constitution, and if this amount, thus unnecessarily withdrawn from the general fund, will reduce the burthens of taxation, the people will be better able, in the future, to bear taxation to support a University, if one should be necessary.—*House Journal*, Eighth Legislature, Regular Session, pp. 393, 395.

28. Chancellor F. A. P. Barnard is tried and exonerated by the Board of Tustees of the University of Mississippi, 1860

At a called meeting of the Board of Trustees of the University of Mississippi, convoked by order of His Excellency J. J. Pettus, *ex-officio* President of the Board, at the town of Oxford, on the 1st day of March, 1860, there were present, of the Trustees:

Hon. James M. Howry, Secretary of the Board, Hon. J. A. Ventress, Hon. Isaac N. Davis, Hon. A. H. Pegues, Col. James Brown, Col. Geo. H. Young, Wm. F. Dowd, Esq., Hon. J. W. Clapp, Hon. Charles Clark and Hon. Alex. M. Clayton.

His Excellency, Gov. Pettus, not having arrived, on motion, the Hon. Alex. M. Clayton was elected as President *pro tempore*.

The following communication from Dr. F. A. P. Barnard, Chancellor of the University of Mississippi, was laid before the Board, and read:

University of Mississippi, February 29, 1860.

To the Honorable the Board of Trustees of the University of Mississippi:

Gentlemen: In a letter addressed to your President on the 2d instant, requesting him to assemble your honorable body in special session at the present time, I assigned, as a reason for the request, a condition of things, existing in the University, which rendered such a meeting, in my view, indispensable, at the earliest possible day. The object of this communication is to explain that state of things.

Some time during the month of January, I became aware that charges had been repeatedly and publicly made against me, by Dr. Henry R. Branham, a citizen of Oxford, the tendency of which was to undermine me in the confidence of the people of the South, and thus, by injuring me, to affect very seriously the prosperity of the University.

These charges were never made in my presence, and, so long as they seemed not to menace serious harm, I treated them with little attention. Having at length learned what they were, or, at least, what some of them were, I authorized a friend to meet them with a denial. But this only provoked a reiteration of them with angry violence, which reiteration was accompanied by a citation of the names of several of my colleagues in the Faculty, as authorities who would confirm their truth.

In regard to a certain portion of the charges and specifications, other members of the Faculty besides myself were implicated; and by one of these the subject was brought before the body in session. During a discussion which arose upon it, at a meeting held on the 2d instant, there was developed such a state of things as to satisfy me, that, without the interposition of the Board of Trustees, the ordinary business of the University cou'd no longer be harmoniously prosecuted: so that, apart from the great injury likely to accrue from the injurious charges persistently uttered against myself, and to a certain extent, against some of my colleagues, I found an urgent reason for soliciting an immediate convocation of your honorable body, in the imminent danger of a state of complete disorganization.

In order that the charges, above alluded to, might be presented for your investigation in precisely the form in which they have been publicly uttered, I have obtained, from one of the gentlemen to whom they were personally addressed, the following written statement:

(Copied from a note addressed by Col. A. H. Pegues to Prof. Wm. F. Stearns, on the 24th of February, 1860).

"On the 1st day of this month, in Kindel & Rascoe's store, Dr. Branham, in the presence of Dr. Green, Dr. Carter, (M.D., of Oxford,) and others, made the following charges against Dr. Barnard:

"1st. That he (Barnard) was unsound upon the slavery question.

"2d. That he was in favor of, and did advocate, the taking of negro testimony against a student.

"3d. That H. (a student) was arraigned and tried upon negro testimony.

"4th. That upon the question of the expulsion of H., the vote was sectionally divided—Barnard, Boynton and Moore voting in the affirmative, and the Southern men voting in the negative.

"5th. That, pending the discussion upon the case of H., Barnard asked Richardson if he would not believe his negro man, Henry, against a student, and when Richardson said he would not, Barnard said *he would*.

"6th. That all the information in the H. case was furnished by a negro woman; and that it was proposed by the other members of the Faculty, that, if Barnard and Boynton had other sources of information and would assert positively that they *knew* H. was guilty, they (the other members) would vote accordingly.

"7th. That Barnard stated that Jane (the negro woman) afterwards recognized H., and pointed him out as the man who had assailed her.

"8th. That notwithstanding the vote of expulsion failed, Barnard wrote to the guardian of the student to take him away, which he did.

"9th. That if the Board of Trustees persisted in their refusal to arraign and try Barnard for taking negro testimony against a student, he (Branham) would publish the whole thing, in the *Mississippian*, to the people of the State, over his own signature."

Col. Pegues adds: "The above are very nearly literally the charges made on the occasion alluded to, with the exception of that part in which the woman (Jane) is introduced; and even here, although I admit the possibility of not having understood or recollected the *words*, exactly, the impression made upon my mind fully warrants, I think, the report which I have made."

Of these allegations, and of the whole matter or matters to which they relate, I invite the fullest and most searching investigation, on the part of your honorable body. I invite, further, an examination into the tenor of my past life, not only for the period of twenty-two years that I have spent in unwearied devotion to the cause of Southern education, but for that earlier period of youth when I had not yet expected ever to be a resident of a Southern State; but in regard to which I have, providentially, in my possession, testimonials by Southern men, of the most unexceptionable character.

If I entertain sentiments now, or if your investigations shall discover that I have ever entertained sentiments, which shall justify any man however captious, in pronouncing me "unsound upon the slavery question," then, gentlemen, do your duty, and remove me from a position for which I am morally disqualified.

But if, on the contrary, after the severest scrutiny of my acts and my utterances, you find that the injurious allegations by which it has been attempted to strike me down from my post of usefulness, to deprive me of my occupation, and to expose me to public opprobrium, are totally and entirely groundless and false, then I ask of you, in justice to one who has, for nearly six years, honestly, conscientiously, and faithfully consecrated to your service all the energies of his intellectual and physical being, to put the stamp of your emphatic condemnation upon an outrage, in my view without a parallel in the annals of civilization.

I remain, gentlemen, respectfully, your ob't serv't,
F. A. P. BARNARD,
Chancellor of the University of Mississippi.

Henry R. Branham, M.D., of Oxford, who was present, by permission of the Board, when the foregoing communication from Chancellor Barnard was read, submitted the following as the only charges and specifications he now had to make against Dr. Barnard:—

"1st. That Dr. Barnard offered the statement of a negro as evidence against a student of the University of Mississippi, Mr. H.

2nd. That after the Faculty refused to sustain the charge upon the testimony adduced, Dr. Barnard without the authority of the Faculty, wrote to his guardian a letter which resulted in the withdrawal of Mr. H. from the University.

3rd. That Dr. Barnard interposed and objected to Mr. H's re-admission into the University at the opening of the following session, and thus prevented his return.

H. R. BRANHAM."

March 1st, 1860.

Chancellor Barnard, who was present, thereupon drew up and filed the following response to the charges submitted by Dr. Branham:—

"The charges of Dr. Branham are by no means so sweeping as I desire the investigation to be. I rejoin, and undertake to prove:—

1. That I proceeded against H. upon entirely sufficient and satisfactory evidence, before I ever knew what the negro said: the negro being my own servant, and having been cruelly outraged and beaten.

That I never spoke to the servant on the subject of the outrage in my life, neither before nor since the occurrence.

That during the progress of the affair, which lasted about a week, my wife mentioned to me that the servant had told her the story, and repeated it to me without any solicitation of mine.

That at the trial of H., I presented the evidence which had satisfied me, and during the discussion, I mentioned what my wife had said of the negro's story, and did say that I regarded the coincidence as a confirmatory circumstance.

That the Faculty did, by resolution, declare that they were morally convinced of the guilt of H.

That this resolution was publicly read, and elicited from the students no expression of dissent.

That H. *did* commit the act.

2. That H. was a student of bad character before.

That it was perfectly competent to me, as Chancellor of the University, to desire his Guardian to withdraw him, if I thought he was doing ill and exerting a bad influence,—that I *did* think so,—that the resolution of the Faculty, declaring their conviction of his guilt, amply justified my action in desiring him to be withdrawn.

That I often so act in analogous cases, and that it is my right and duty so to do.

3. That I did refuse to re-admit H., because he was undesirable as a student. That such is my prerogative and right.

That, therefore, charges 2 and 3 are totally frivolous.

Further, as to charge 1, if it were in any sense true, I was but doing my duty as a christian master, to protect my servant from outrage; and that I am sustained in this view by the highest authorities, among whom I am permitted to offer the written opinion of the Hon. Jacob Thompson.

That college government is a parental, and not a municipal government:

And, finally, that the question, which concerns the Board and the public, is not, whether, on a particular occasion, I committed an error of judgment or not; but whether I do entertain the principles which it is sought by these charges to fasten upon me; and in regard to this I aver that I am as "sound on the slavery question" as Dr. Branham, or any member of this Board.

F. A. P. BARNARD."

Thereupon, the following resolution was adopted by the Board:—

Resolved, That the extent of our investigation be such as to embrace the charges specifically made by Dr. Branham against Dr. Barnard, upon which an issue has been made up by Dr. Barnard to the Board, relating to charges against him, which, if true, render him an unsuitable person to preside over a Southern University.

That, in conducting the examination, Dr. Branham shall have an opportunity to produce all the evidence, documentary and oral, upon which he relies to support his charges, and to examine witnesses, himself; and Dr. Barnard shall have the like opportunity;—both of the parties having also the right to cross-examine as the investigation progresses; and the Board reserves the right to each member thereof to ask any question pertinent to the matter under investigation, and to examine the parties to the issue—Dr. Branham and Dr. Barnard.

That each witness be put upon his honor as to the truth of his statement, and each one be examined separately from the others.

The Board also think it a proper and important subject of investigation, as to the manner in which the proceedings of the Faculty, in their official sessions, have been divulged, or came to the knowledge of Dr. Branham; and they think it proper that the testimony introduced, upon every material point investigated, shall be reduced to writing by some person designated for that purpose by the President of the Board. . . .

Oxford, Mississippi, March 8, 1860.

I, Wm. F. Stearns, as official reporter in the case, do hereby certify that the foregoing is a full, true and correct transcript of the testimony given in before the Board of Trustees of the University of Mississippi, on the 1st and 2d instants, upon the investigation, at the request of Dr. F. A. P. Barnard, Chancellor of the University, of the charges then and previously preferred against him by Dr. H. R. Branham; all the oral testimony, (except my own, and that of Prof. Geo W. Carter, which was reduced to writing by Mr. Clapp), having been taken down by myself, and mostly read over to and approved by the witnesses in the presence of Dr. Branham.

WM. F. STEARNS,
Reporter.

March 2nd, 1860.

His Excellency, J. J. Pettus, Governor of the State of Mississippi, and *ex officio* President of the Board of Trustees of the University, this day appeared and took his seat with the other members of the Board, who were mentioned as being present yesterday; and the testimony taken before his arrival was submitted to his examination.

The taking of the testimony being concluded after dark, Dr. Branham made a few remarks, but declined to discuss the merits of the case; when Dr. Barnard addressed the Board at some length, but purposely abstained, he said, from making any comments upon the evidence.

Dr. Branham having no desire to say any thing further, he and Dr. Barnard retired and left the Board to its deliberations.

Whereupon, on motion of Mr. Clark, it was moved, as the sense of the Board, that Dr. Barnard be acquitted of all the charges against him; and, the yeas and nays being called for, the said motion was carried by the following vote:

Yeas—Messrs. Pettus, (President) Clayton, Davis, Clark, Ventress, Young, Dowd, Pegues, Brown, Clapp and Howry—11.

Nays—None.

On motion of Mr. Clark it was then moved, as the sense of the Board, that our confidence in Dr. Barnard is increased rather than diminished in consequence of this investigation; and, the yeas and nays being called for, the said motion was carried by the same unanimous vote above stated.

A committee, consisting of Messrs. Clayton, Clapp and Pettus, was then, on motion of Judge Clayton, appointed to draw up resolutions embodying the decisions just made by the Board; and that committee, through Judge Clayton, its chairman, made the following report:—

The committee to draw up resolutions embodying the decisions of the Board upon the charges preferred against Dr. F. A. P. Barnard, the Chancellor of the University, report the following:

Resolved, That the charges are, in their opinion, wholly unsustained by the evidence, and that the said F. A. P. Barnard stands fully and honorably acquitted of every charge brought against him.

Resolved, That after a patient hearing and investigation of all the testimony in the case, we as Trustees and as Southern men, have found our confidence in the ability and integrity of the Chancellor, and his fitness for his position, increased rather than diminished, and declare our full conviction that his labors are doing great service to the cause of education and science, and placing the reputation of the University upon an immovable basis.

The said report having been received and agreed to, the said two resolutions were then unanimously adopted by the Board.

On motion of Judge Clayton, it was

Resolved, That the Secretary inform Prof. W. F. Stearns that he is required, as a part of his duty as reporter in this case, to furnish, at as early a day as practicable, the testimony given in this case, together with the written documents introduced by any of the witnesses, to the Secretary of the Board, to be by him filed and preserved amongst the records of this Board.

I have compared the foregoing with the record in my possession and find it correct.

J. M. HOWRY, *Sec'y of the Board.*

—*Record of the Testimony and Proceedings in the Matter of the Investigation of the Trustees of the University of Mississippi . . . of the Charges Made Against the Chancellor of the University* (Jackson, Miss.: Printed at the Mississippian Office, 1860). The trial was held on March 1 and 2, 1860. The entire testimony in this interesting case runs to thirty closely printed pages, but only the most pertinent extracts are given here. This was one of numerous examples of southern opposition to northern educational influences in the second quarter of the nineteenth century. Criticism of such influences became more numerous and spirited before 1860. Following John Brown's attack on Harper's Ferry in October, 1859, about two hundred southern students left medical schools in Philadelphia and returned home. *Philadelphia Bulletin,* December 20, 1859; *Richmond Enquirer,* December 23, 1859; and *Daily Dispatch* (Richmond, Va.), December 23, 1859; Edgar W. Knight, "Southern Opposition to Northern Education," *The Educational Forum,* XIV (November, 1949); Thomas L. Patrick, Southern Criticism of Northern Educational Influences (Doctoral Dissertation, University of North Carolina, 1950).

29. Governor Joseph E. Brown on the University of Georgia, 1860

The far seeing wisdom of those who framed our State constitution not only grasped but fully comprehended the importance of promoting the Arts and Sciences when they inserted in that instrument the following clause:

"The Arts and Sciences shall be promoted in one or more seminaries of learning; and the Legislature *shall*, as soon as may be, give such *further donations* and privileges to those *already established* (the State University was then established), as may be necessary to secure the objects of their institution."

This is still a portion of the constitution, which I, and each of you, have sworn to "observe, conform to, support, and defend." Have the spirit and intention of this provision of the constitution been carried into effect by the Legislature in the meagre endowment which the State University has received from the State? Have the objects for which the University was instituted been *secured?* If not, is the State not abundantly able to carry the spirit and intention of the constitution into effect without embarrassment to her government or burden to her people? If so, can we consistently, with the oaths which we have taken, refuse to make the necessary appropriation? These are questions well worthy the serious consideration of each and every one of us. But, aside from any obligation which the constitution imposes upon us, can we doubt the wisdom and sound statesmanship of such a course? I cannot think that it is sound policy for Georgia to refuse to endow her University, while her people send out of the State in a few years for the education of their children a sum of money more than sufficient to make the endowment which would be necessary to draw large numbers of the youths of other States to our University to be educated. This would cause Georgia to receive the money of other States, for the education of their children, instead of paying her money to other States for the education of her own.

That State is always the most wealthy, powerful, and respected in which knowledge is most generally diffused and learning in all its branches most liberally encouraged. We cannot doubt that England is indebted in a very great degree to her Universities of Oxford and Cambridge, and to the influences which have gone out from them, for her ability to dictate laws to a large portion of the world and to draw wealth from every quarter of the globe. Nor can we deny that Massachusetts by her liberal course towards her Cambridge, and Connecticut by her liberality to Yale College, have greatly enlarged their wealth at home and increased their influence abroad; and have been able through the instrumentality of their Universities to instil into the youthful minds of the educated of all the other States of the Union many of their own peculiar notions of religion and government, while they have drawn millions of money from other States for the education of their children. Georgia has contributed largely to build up Northern colleges, and has purchased from them, or those educated by them, most of her text and school books and much of her literature. Most of those Northern colleges, which have shared so largely the Southern patronage, are now hostile to Southern institutions. Notwithstanding all this they still get Georgia patronage, because it is believed they can furnish educational advantages superior to those offered by Georgia colleges. This might not now have been the case had the money sent out of Georgia by parents and guardians for education been expended at our own University. Is it not time we had learned wisdom by experience? We claim that ours is the Empire State of the South. Why then should we refuse to endow and build up our University where the sons of the South may enjoy educational advantages equal, if not superior, to those offered by New England colleges; where authors may be reared and literature and school books produced which will enlighten and elevate the minds of our youths without subjecting them to abolition taint or New England fanaticism?

After mature deliberation upon this question, I feel it my duty to recommend the appropriation of five hundred thousand dollars, to be paid in five annual instalments, of one hundred thousand dollars each, for the endowment of our State University. This sum, added to the present endowment, would be sufficient to construct the buildings, purchase the library and apparatus, and endow the professorships, necessary to make it, in a few years, a first class University; and would further enable the trustees to pay such salaries as would command the services of the most distinguished professors in the country. This would at once give the University a commanding position in the Southern States, and relieve us from the necessity of further patronising Northern Colleges. I think the heart of every Georgian should swell with pride at the contemplation. And I do not doubt, when the question shall be fully discussed before our people, that they will be found to be in advance of most of our politicians upon this subject. He who does right will seldom have cause to fear the popular verdict.

The aggregate *taxable* property of this State is supposed to be, this year, about $700,000,000. The seventieth part of *one* per cent. upon this sum, will raise, annually, the $100,000. This will be a fraction less than *one cent* and *a half*, per annum, on each one hundred dollars' worth of taxable property, or a fraction over *seven cents* on each one hundred dollars of taxable property, to be paid in *five annual instalments.*

What Georgian is so destitute of State pride, apart from every consideration of patriotism and sense of duty, that he would refuse to pay this small sum to see our State University fully endowed, for all time to come, and put in a position of equality with any University in the Union? I think I know the great masses of the farmers and mechanics of our State, who are its very bone and sinew, and upon whom every other class of citizens is dependent for its support, well enough to say for them, in advance, that many of our public men underrate their intelligence and liberality; and that not one in every twenty of them, who pays tax on one thousand dollars' worth of property, would hesitate a moment to contribute a *dime and a half a year, for five years,* for the purpose of building up a University which would place Georgia in the very front rank of all her Southern sisters, where the young men of the South who, in future, are to conduct its government, direct its energies and defend its honor, may be educated, without assisting by their patronage, to build up, elsewhere, institutions at war with our dearest rights. But it is not indispensably necessary that even the small additional tax above mentioned, should be collected from the people for this purpose. Each annual payment might be made out of the incomes of the Western & Atlantic Railroad, and the tax at present paid by the people of this State, be *reduced* within the five years; and we would still have money enough to meet promptly, in times of peace and prosperity, all the necessary expenses of the government.

In return for this appropriation, the University should be required to educate and maintain, from year to year, such number of poor young men as the Legislature which makes the appropriation, may direct. I would suggest that the number be one from each county in the State; to be selected in such manner as the Legislature may prescribe. The young men selected as beneficiaries should be such only as have not the means to educate themselves, and whose parents are unable to defray the expenses of a collegiate education for them. Each should be required, when he enters the University, as a consideration for the instruction he is about to receive from the State, to sign a pledge of honor, that he will, if not providentially prevented, teach school, in Georgia, as many years next after he leaves the University as he was instructed in the University, or refund to the State the money expended in his education with lawful interest. The benefits of a collegiate education should not be confined to the sons of the wealthy; but the State should provide, as far as possible, for the education of moral young men who are talented and promising; and who, by reason of their poverty, are unable to educate themselves. From this class would rise up many of our most distinguished and useful citizens. Many of the brightest and most intelligent boys in Georgia are found among the poorest and humblest of her citizens. Inured to labor from their infancy, when the portals of the college are thrown open to them, they are not unfrequently found to outstrip the more favored students; and afterwards, when they come to enter the arena of active life, they are usually more energetic and more likely to become distinguished and useful than those whom necessity has never taught the value of personal exertion. Many of these young men would make teaching a profession for life, which few of the sons of the wealthy after graduating in college are willing to do.

It is generally admitted by the most intelligent and best informed, that the establishment of a State University of a high character would work no detriment to the denominational, or other colleges of the State. The graduates of our other colleges, desirous of pursuing their studies beyond the college course, and of fitting themselves, by still higher attainments in learning, for the duties of authors, professors, etc., would transfer themselves to our own University without being under the necessity of leaving our own State to secure the necessary advantages. The building up of the University, upon the plan proposed, would also do much to advance our common school project, as it would send out in a few years a large number of young men as teachers, truly southern in sentiment and well qualified for the position. This would supply, in a great measure, what is now a lamentable deficiency, and would elevate and give new life and vigor to our whole educational system.—Herbert Fielder, *A Sketch of the Life and Times and Speeches of Joseph E. Brown* (Springfield, Mass.: Press of the Springfield Printing Company, 1883), pp. 152-55.

INDEX